Story & Art by
Chika Shiomi

Yukarism

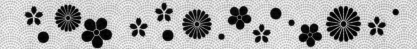

[Volume 1 Contents]

❀ Chapter 1 ... 4

❀ Chapter 2 ... 57

❀ Chapter 3 ... 101

❀ Bonus Manga ... 146

❀ Chapter 4 ... 147

❀ Notes ... 192

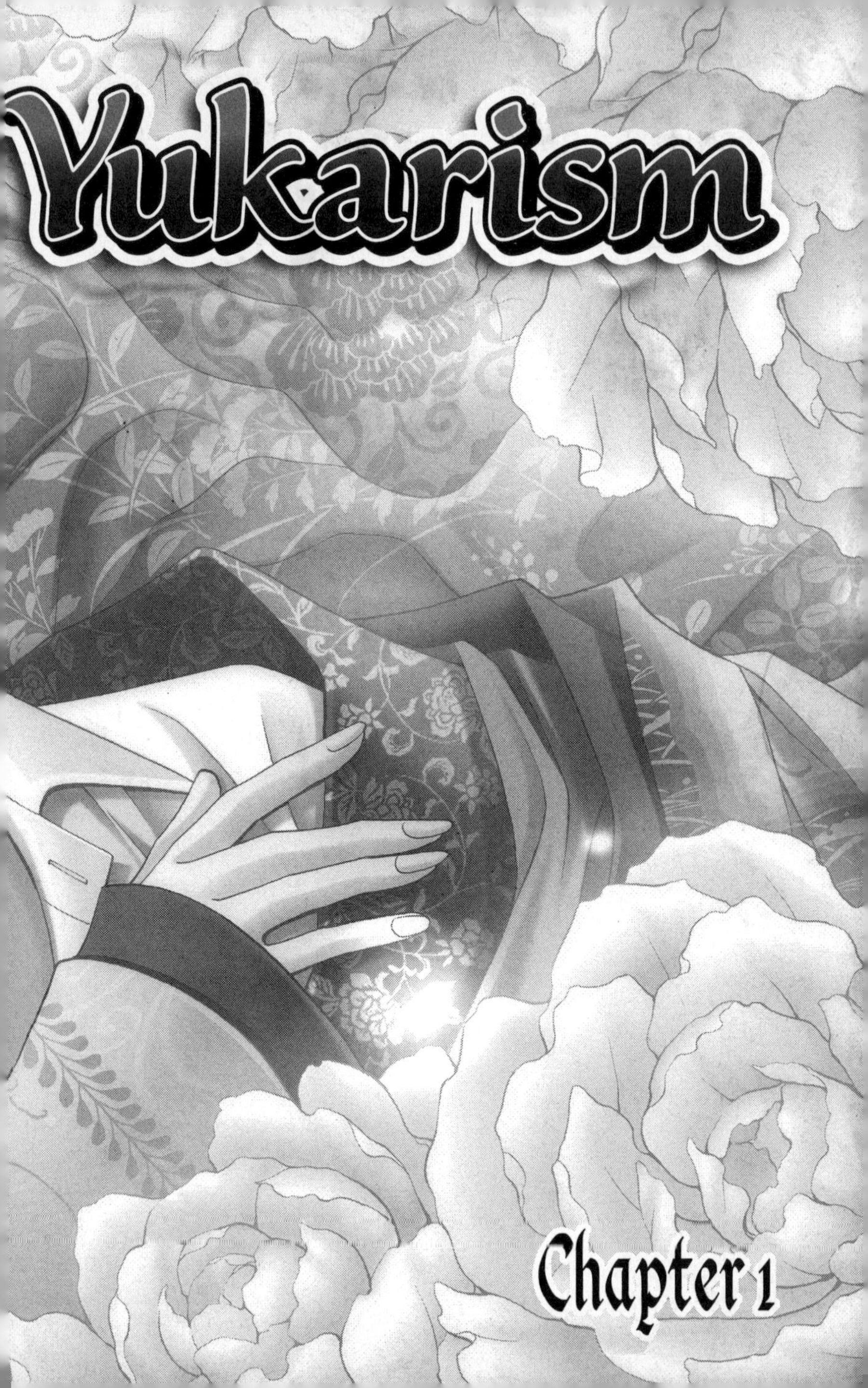
Yukarism
Chapter 1

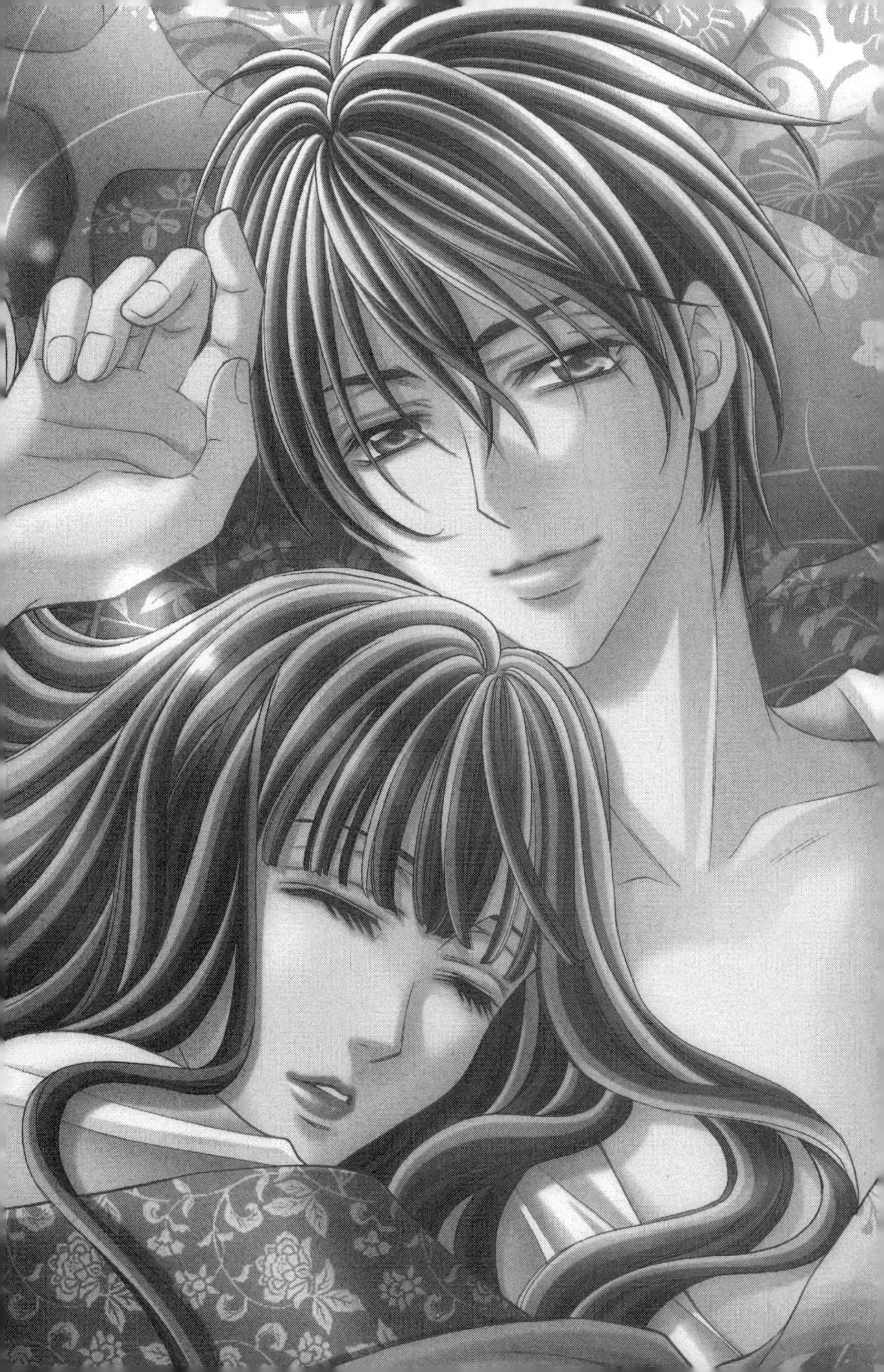

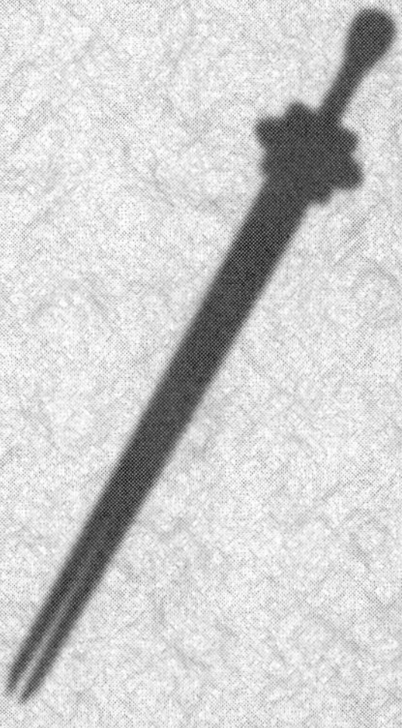

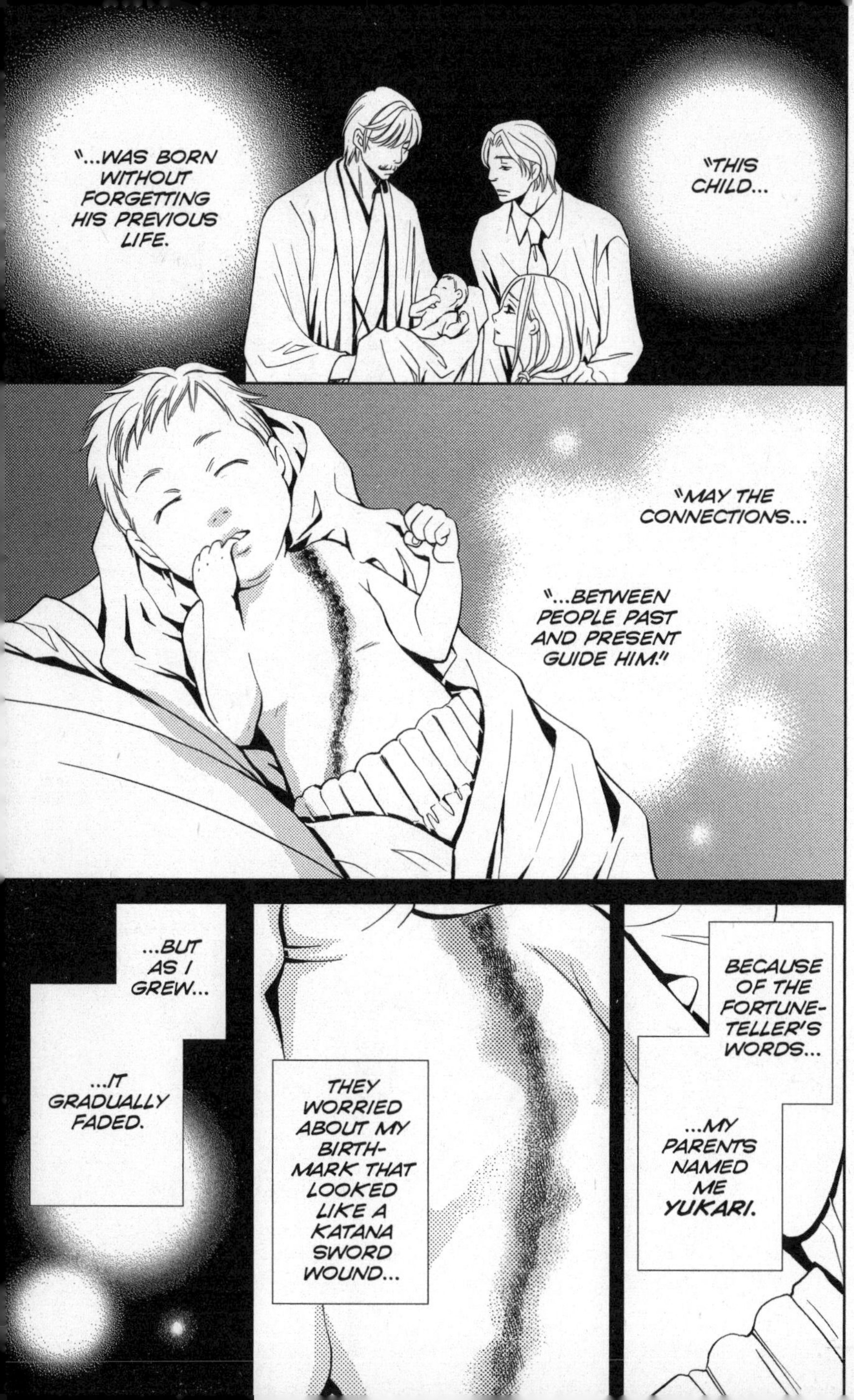
"THIS CHILD...
"...WAS BORN WITHOUT FORGETTING HIS PREVIOUS LIFE.
"MAY THE CONNECTIONS...
"...BETWEEN PEOPLE PAST AND PRESENT GUIDE HIM."
BECAUSE OF THE FORTUNE-TELLER'S WORDS...
...MY PARENTS NAMED ME YUKARI.
THEY WORRIED ABOUT MY BIRTH-MARK THAT LOOKED LIKE A KATANA SWORD WOUND...
...BUT AS I GREW...
...IT GRADUALLY FADED.

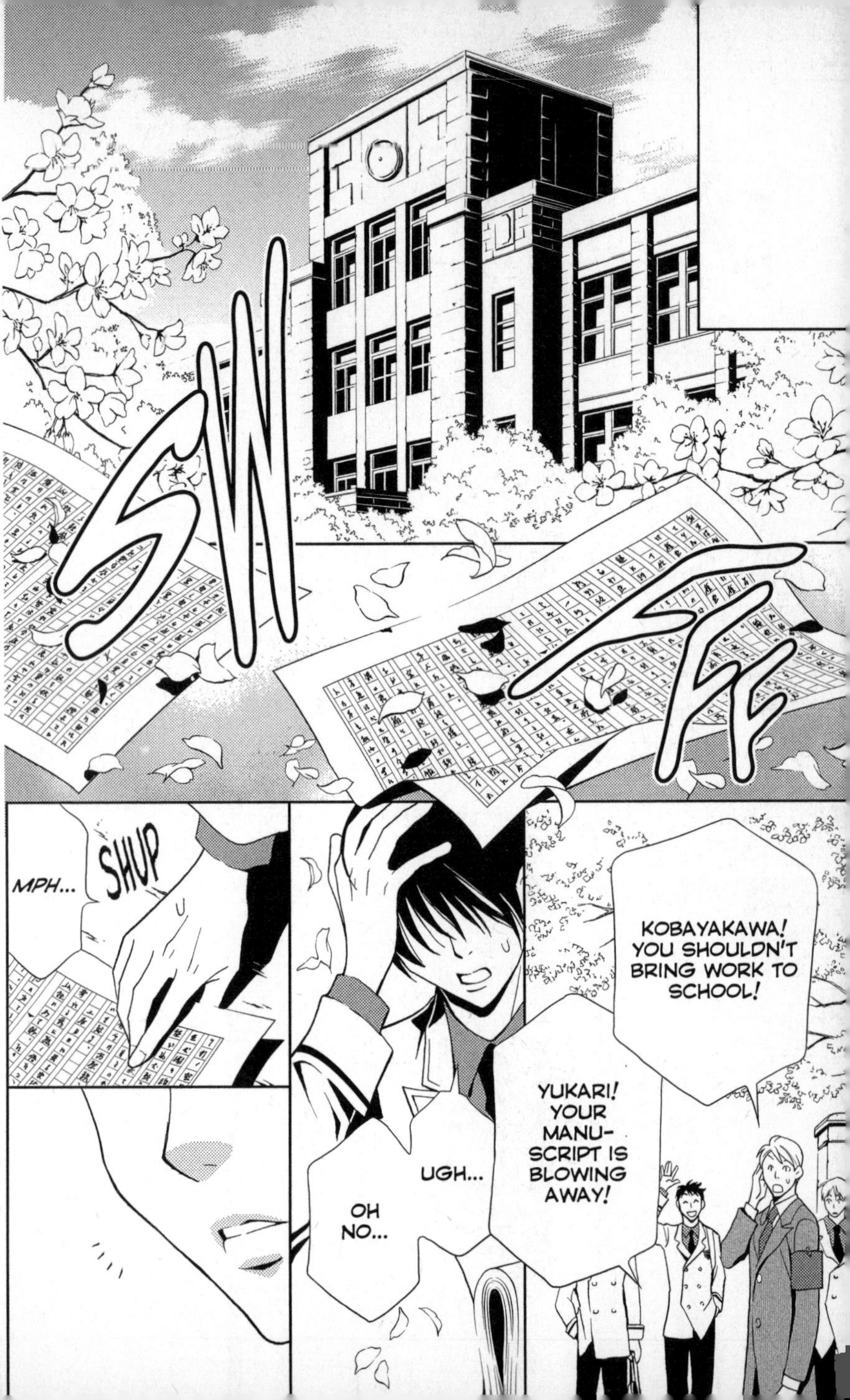
SWFF
KOBAYAKAWA! YOU SHOULDN'T BRING WORK TO SCHOOL!
YUKARI! YOUR MANU-SCRIPT IS BLOWING AWAY!
UGH...
OH NO...
SHUP
MPH...

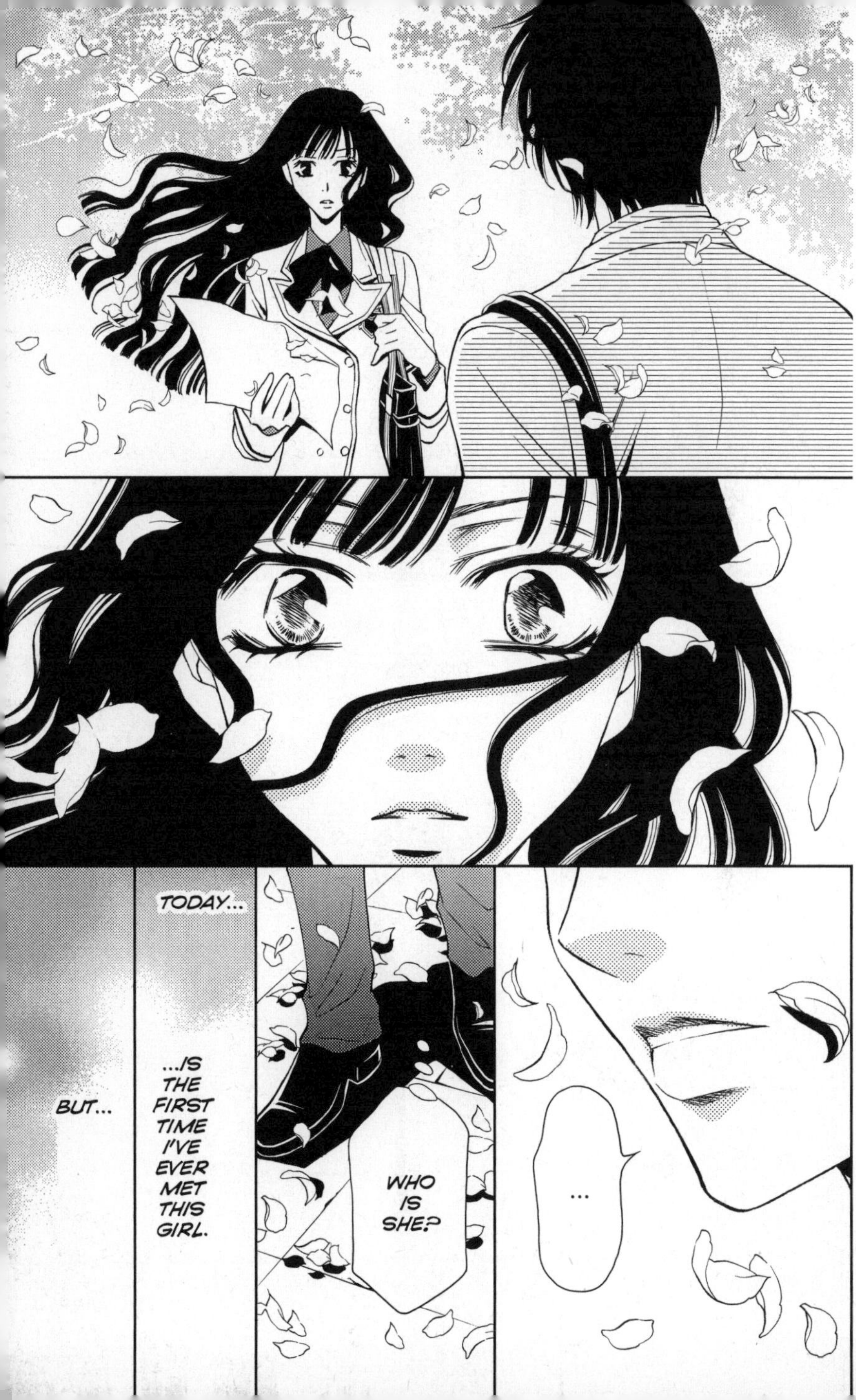
...
WHO IS SHE?
TODAY...
...IS THE FIRST TIME I'VE EVER MET THIS GIRL.
BUT...

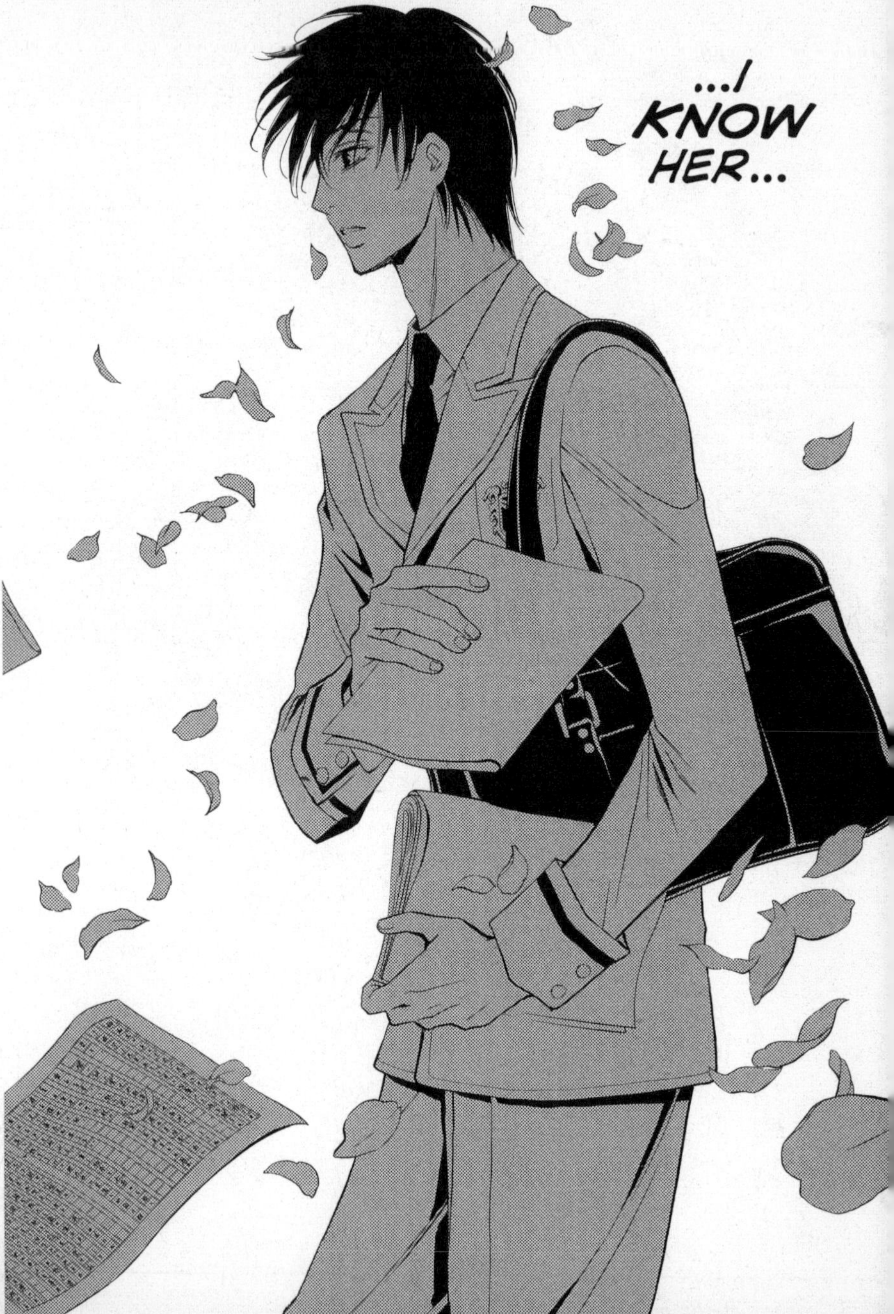
...I KNOW HER...

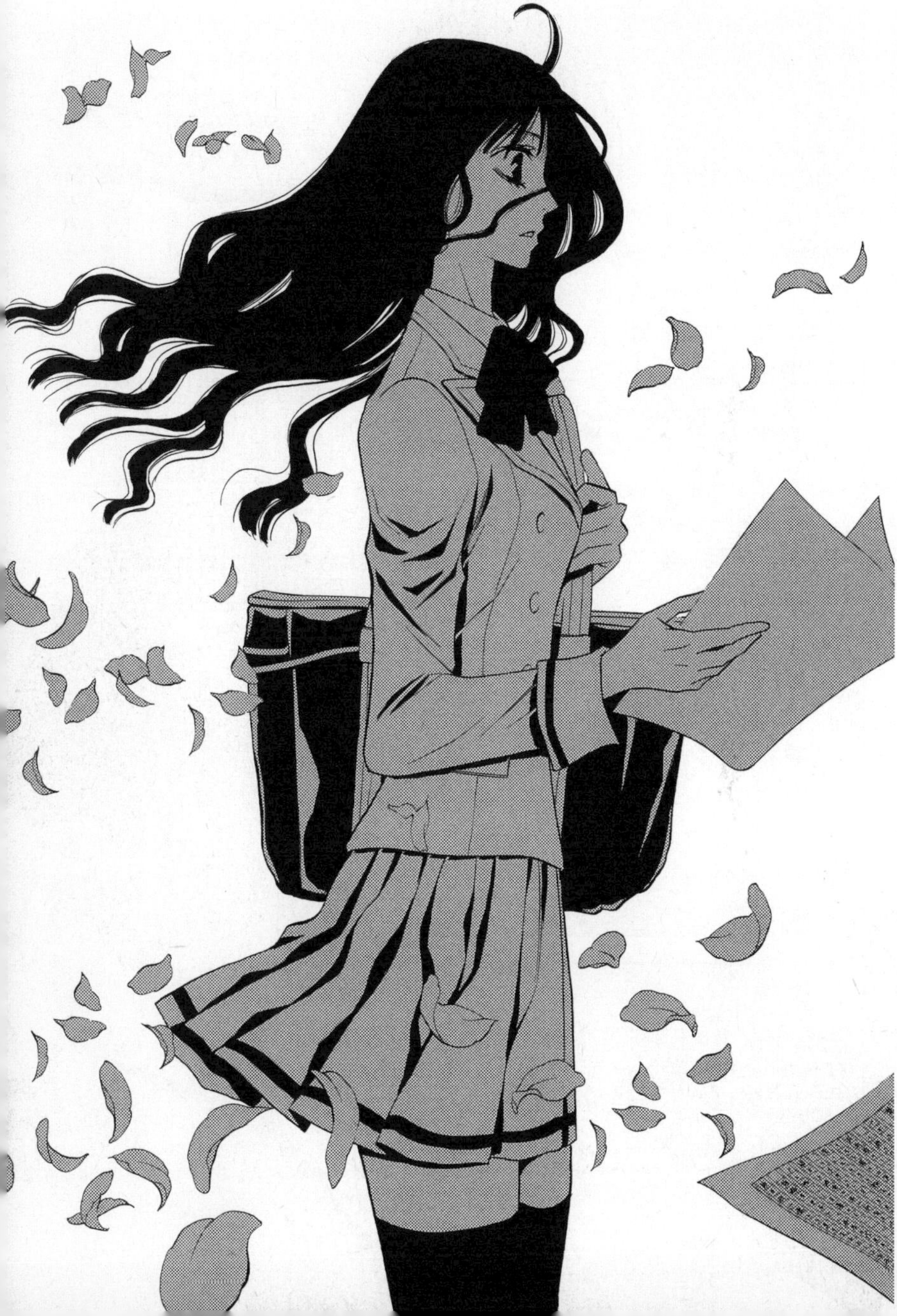

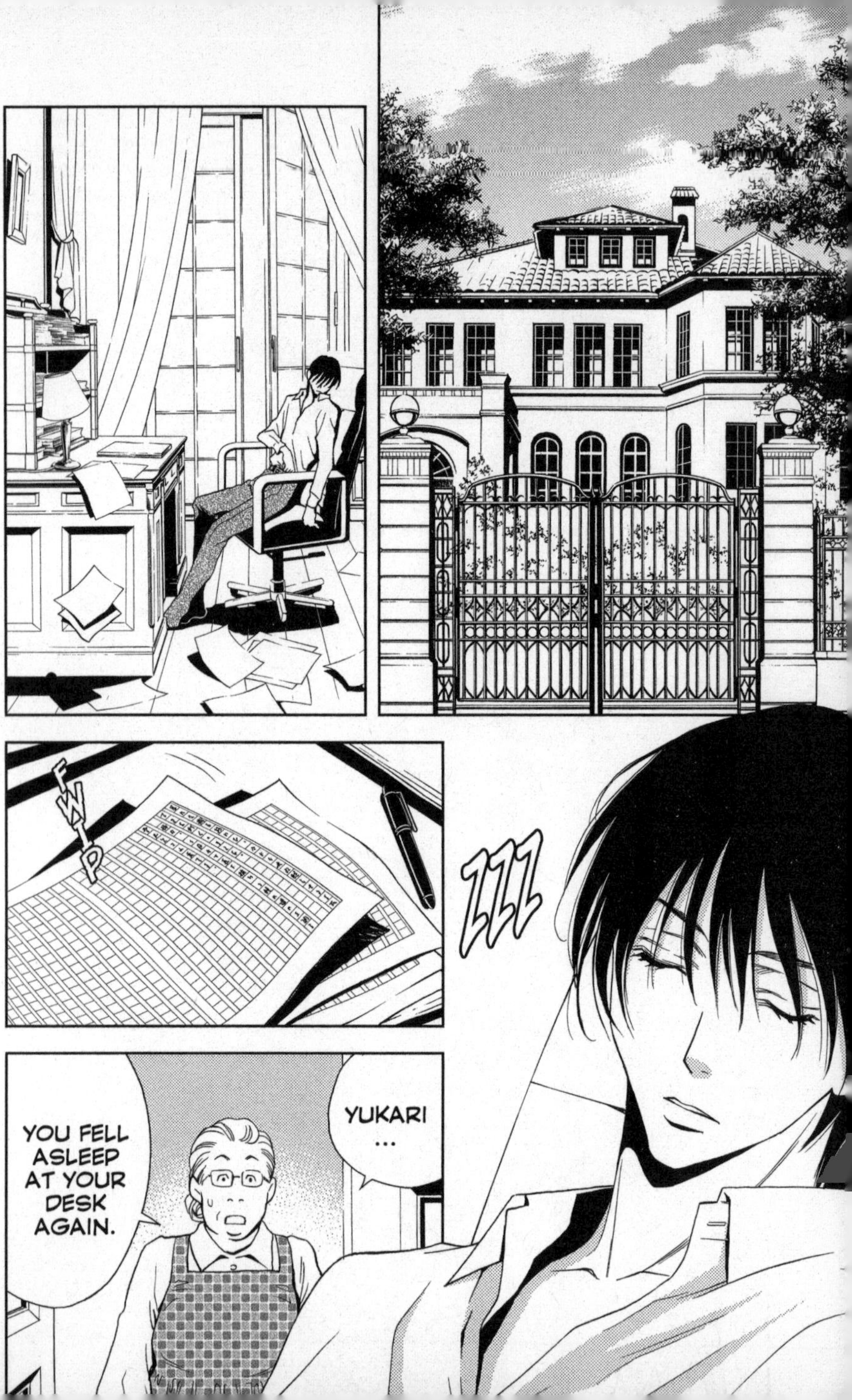
ZZZ
FWIP
YUKARI ...
YOU FELL ASLEEP AT YOUR DESK AGAIN.

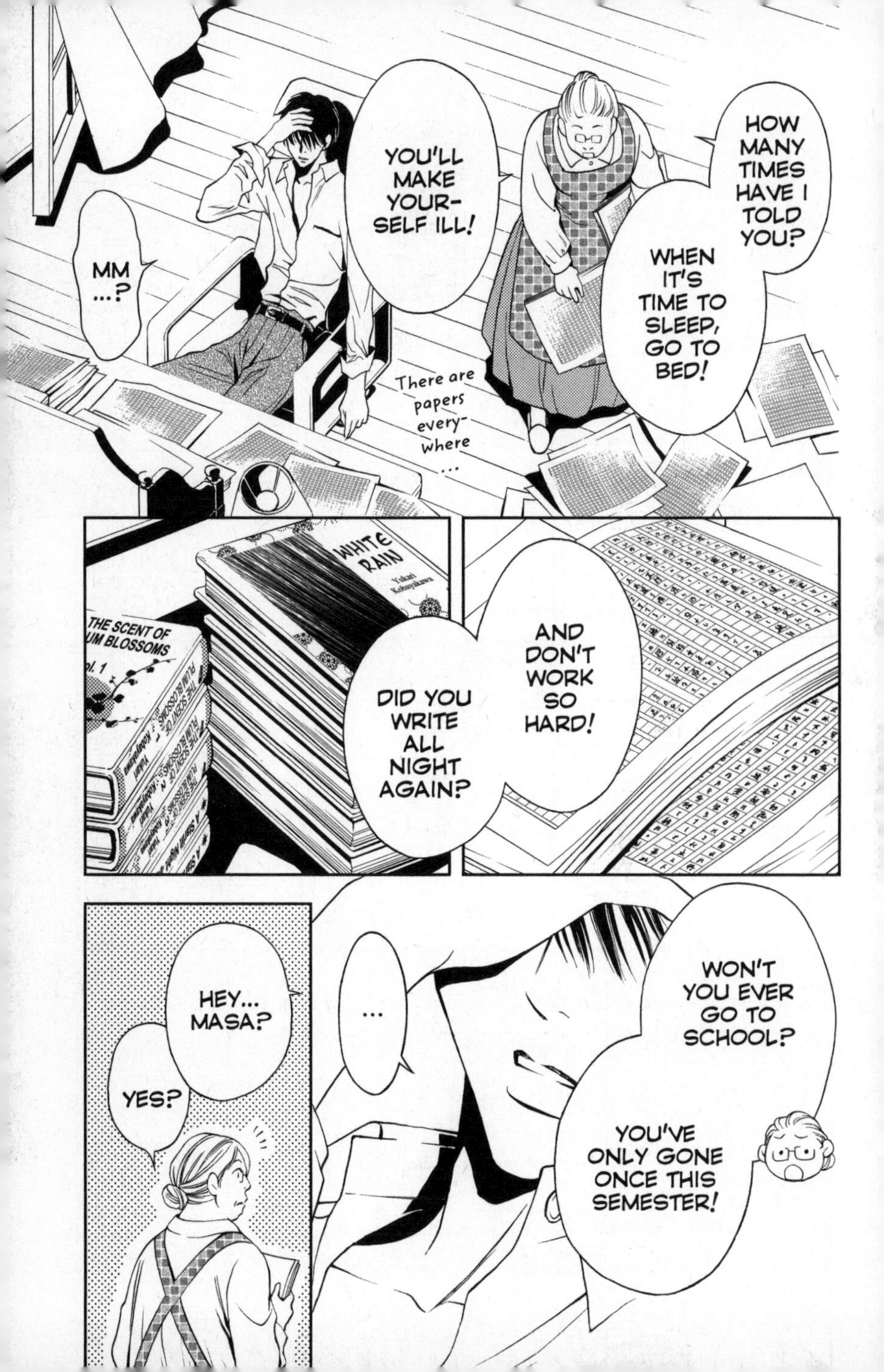
HOW MANY TIMES HAVE I TOLD YOU?
WHEN IT'S TIME TO SLEEP, GO TO BED!
YOU'LL MAKE YOUR-SELF ILL!
MM ...?
There are papers every-where ...
WHITE RAIN
Yukari Kobayakawa
AND DON'T WORK SO HARD!
THE SCENT OF
UM BLOSSOMS
DID YOU WRITE ALL NIGHT AGAIN?
WON'T YOU EVER GO TO SCHOOL?
YOU'VE ONLY GONE ONCE THIS SEMESTER!
...
HEY... MASA?
YES?

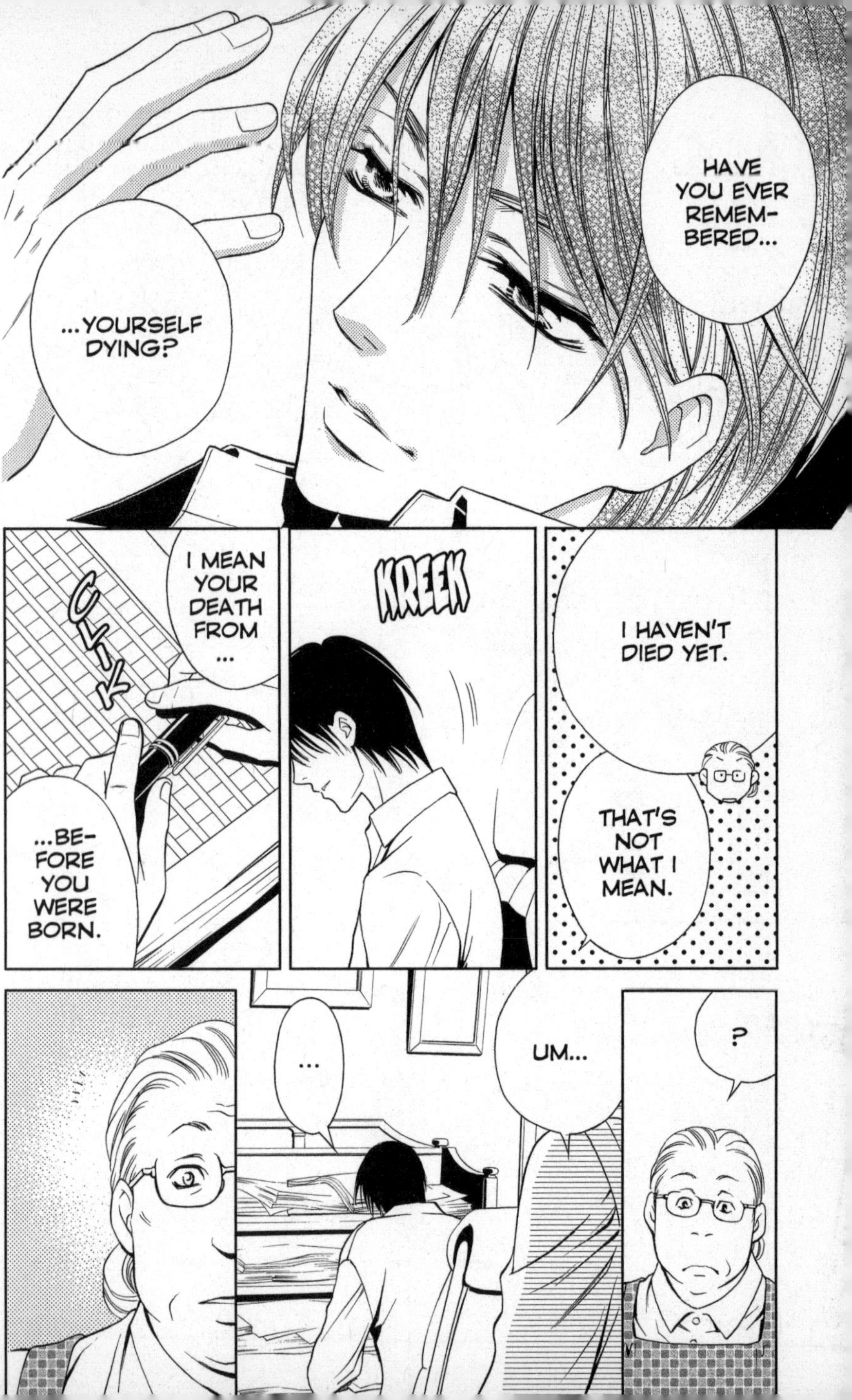
HAVE YOU EVER REMEMBERED...
...YOURSELF DYING?
I HAVEN'T DIED YET.
THAT'S NOT WHAT I MEAN.
KREEK
I MEAN YOUR DEATH FROM ...
CLIK
...BEFORE YOU WERE BORN.
?
UM...
...

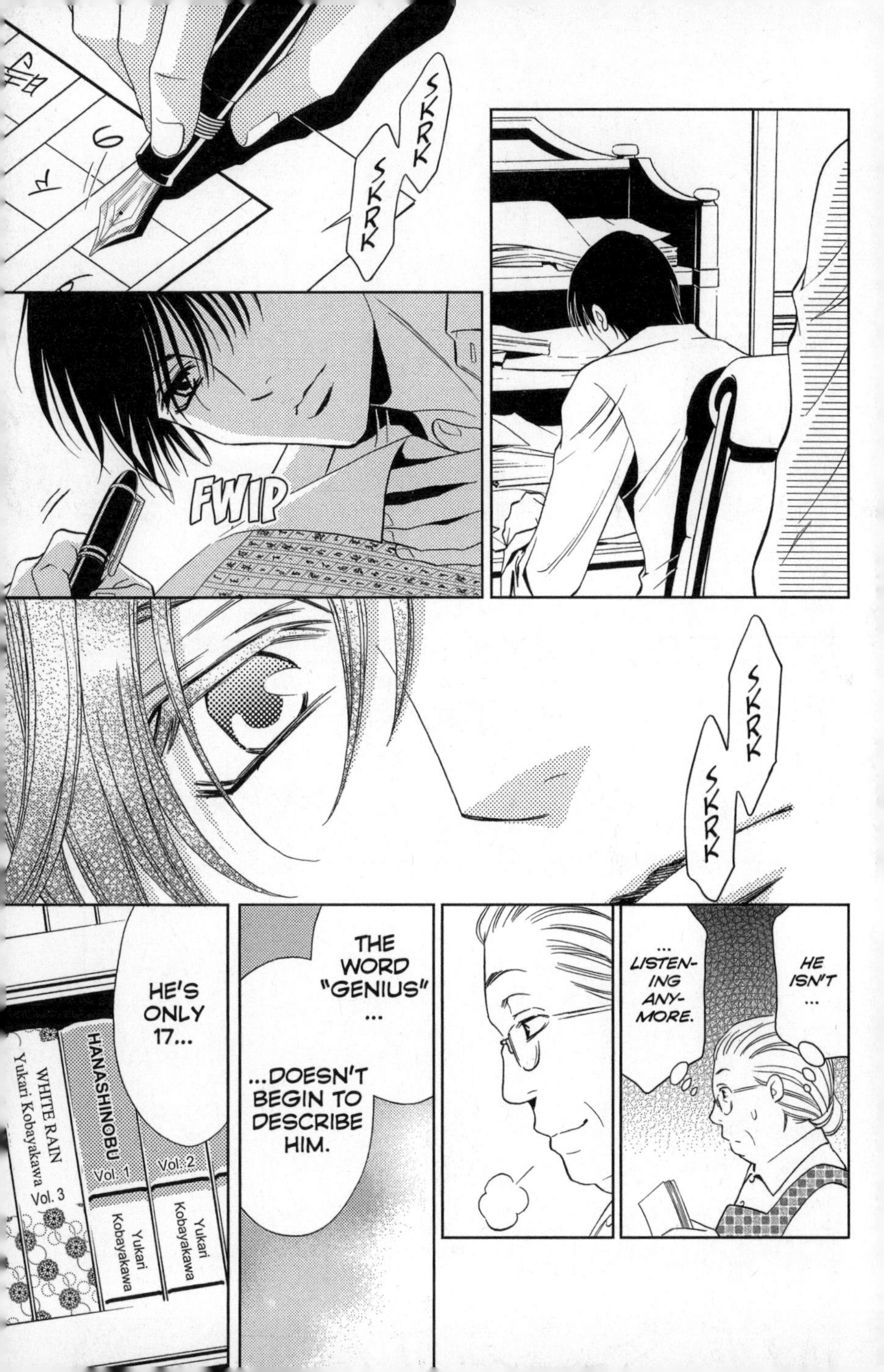
SKRK
SKRK
FWIP
SKRK
SKRK
HE ISN'T ...
... LISTENING ANYMORE.
THE WORD "GENIUS" ...
...DOESN'T BEGIN TO DESCRIBE HIM.
HE'S ONLY 17...
HANASHINOBU Vol. 1 Yukari Kobayakawa
Vol. 2 Yukari Kobayakawa
WHITE RAIN Yukari Kobayakawa Vol. 3

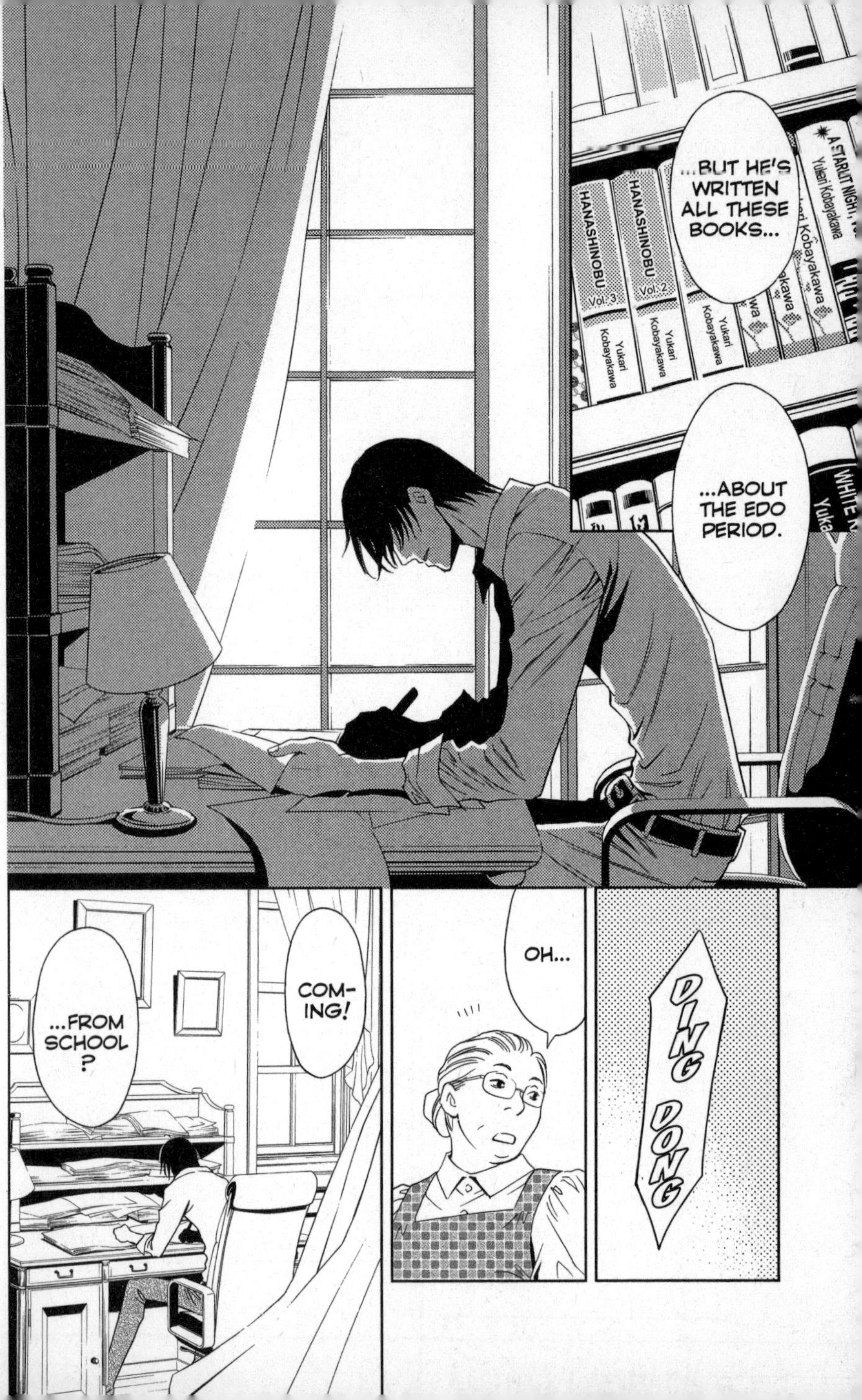
...BUT HE'S WRITTEN ALL THESE BOOKS...
...ABOUT THE EDO PERIOD.
A STARLIT NIGHT
Yukari Kobayakawa
HANASHINOBU Vol. 2 Yukari Kobayakawa
HANASHINOBU Vol. 3 Yukari Kobayakawa
DING DONG
OH...
COMING!
...FROM SCHOOL?

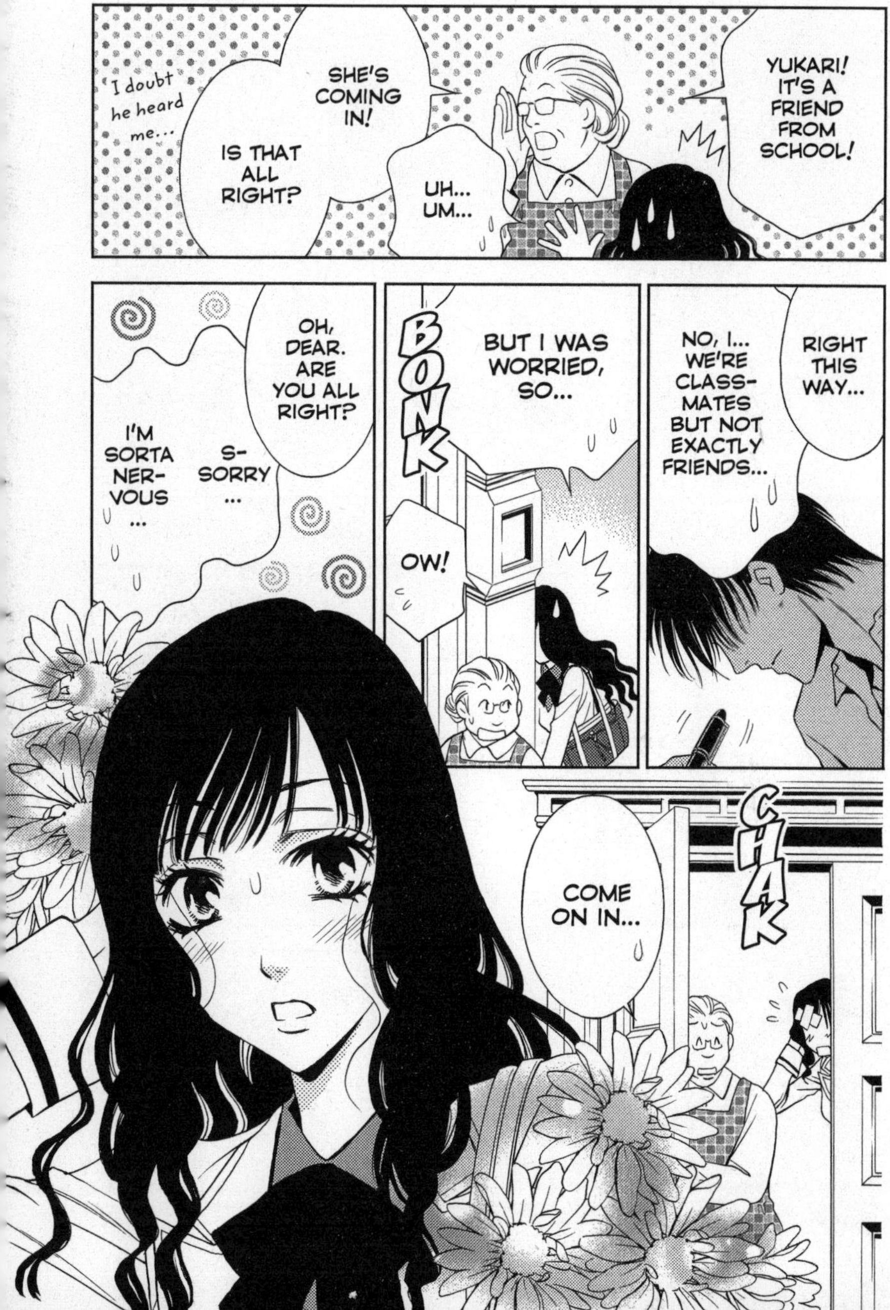
YUKARI! IT'S A FRIEND FROM SCHOOL!
SHE'S COMING IN!
UH... UM...
IS THAT ALL RIGHT?
I doubt he heard me...
RIGHT THIS WAY...
NO, I... WE'RE CLASS-MATES BUT NOT EXACTLY FRIENDS...
BUT I WAS WORRIED, SO...
BONK
OW!
OH, DEAR. ARE YOU ALL RIGHT?
S-SORRY...
I'M SORTA NER-VOUS...
CHAK
COME ON IN...

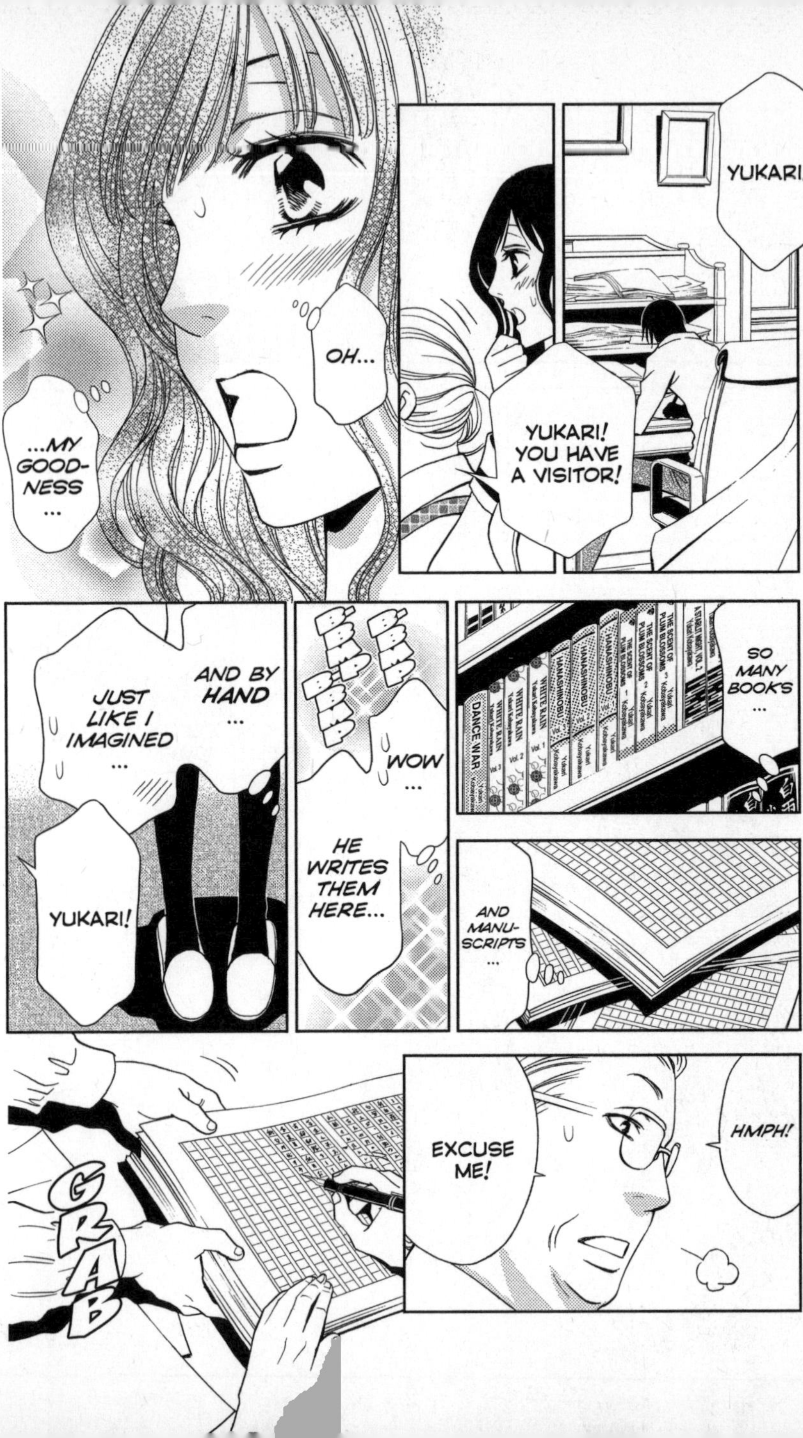
YUKARI!
YUKARI! YOU HAVE A VISITOR!
OH...
...MY GOODNESS...
SO MANY BOOKS...
A STARLIT NIGHT, VOL. 2 Yukari Kobayakawa
THE SCENT OF PLUM BLOSSOMS 3 Yukari Kobayakawa
THE SCENT OF PLUM BLOSSOMS 2 Yukari Kobayakawa
THE SCENT OF PLUM BLOSSOMS 1 Yukari Kobayakawa
HANASHINOBU Vol. 1 Yukari Kobayakawa
HANASHINOBU Vol. 2 Yukari Kobayakawa
HANASHINOBU Vol. 3 Yukari Kobayakawa
WHITE RAIN Yukari Kobayakawa Vol. 1
WHITE RAIN Yukari Kobayakawa Vol. 2
WHITE RAIN Yukari Kobayakawa Vol. 3
DANCE WAR Yukari Kobayakawa
AND MANU-SCRIPTS...
WOW...
HE WRITES THEM HERE...
AND BY HAND...
JUST LIKE I IMAGINED...
YUKARI!
HMPH!
EXCUSE ME!
GRAB

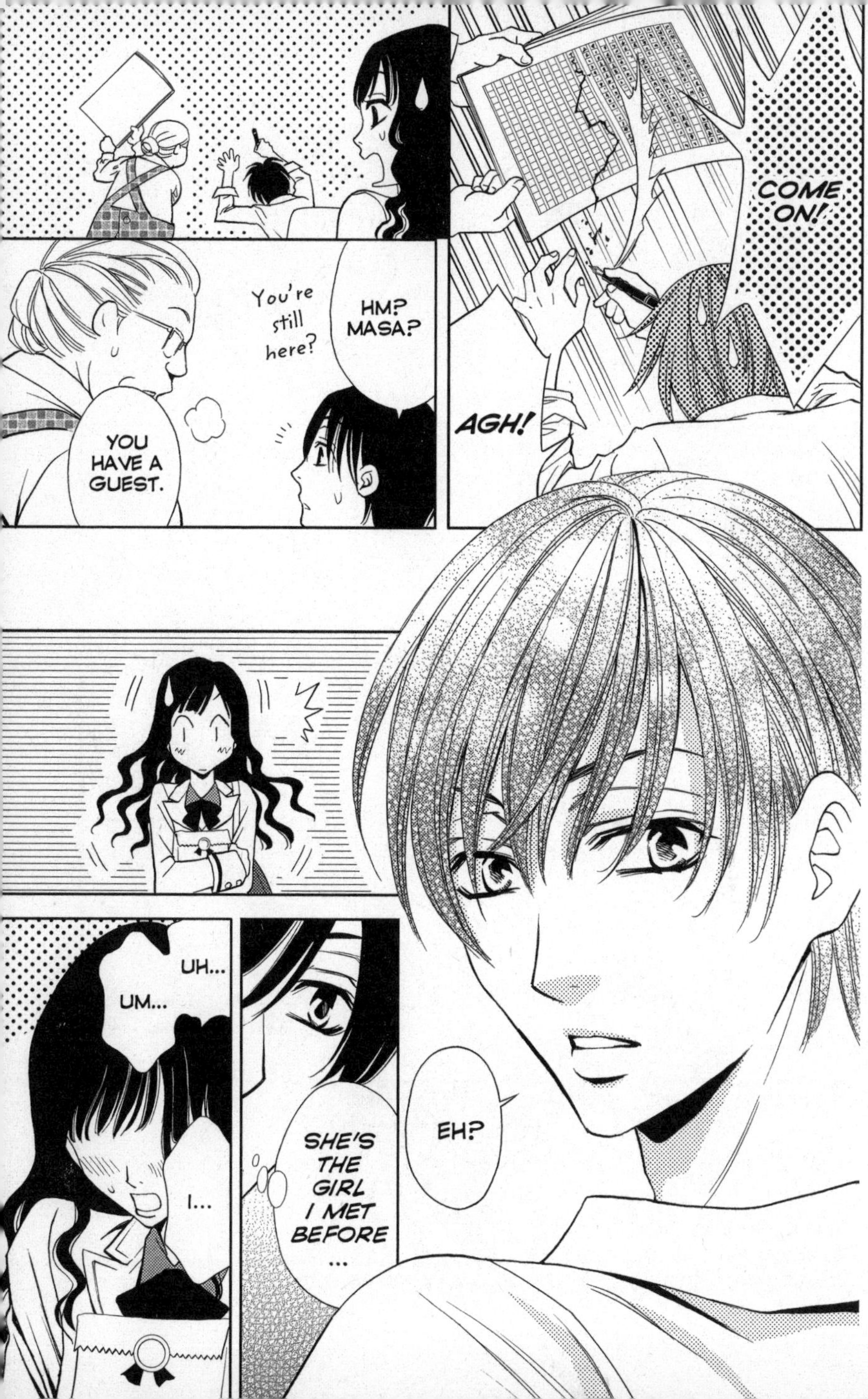
COME ON!
AGH!
HM? MASA?
You're still here?
YOU HAVE A GUEST.
EH?
SHE'S THE GIRL I MET BEFORE ...
UH...
UM...
I...

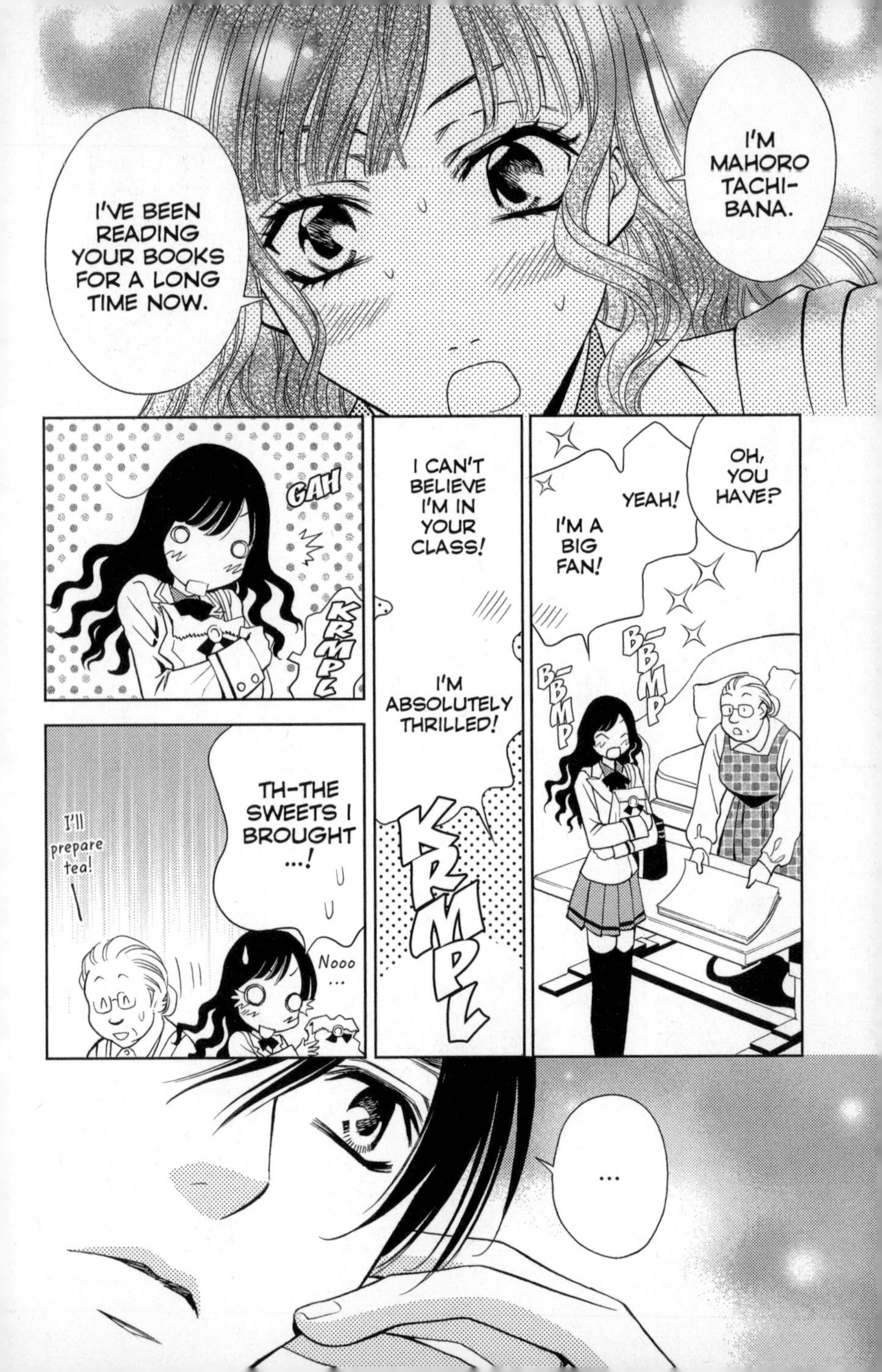
I'M MAHORO TACHIBANA.
I'VE BEEN READING YOUR BOOKS FOR A LONG TIME NOW.
OH, YOU HAVE?
YEAH!
I'M A BIG FAN!
B-BMP
B-BMP
I CAN'T BELIEVE I'M IN YOUR CLASS!
I'M ABSOLUTELY THRILLED!
KRMPL
GAH
KRMPL
TH-THE SWEETS I BROUGHT ...!
Nooo ...
I'll prepare tea!
...

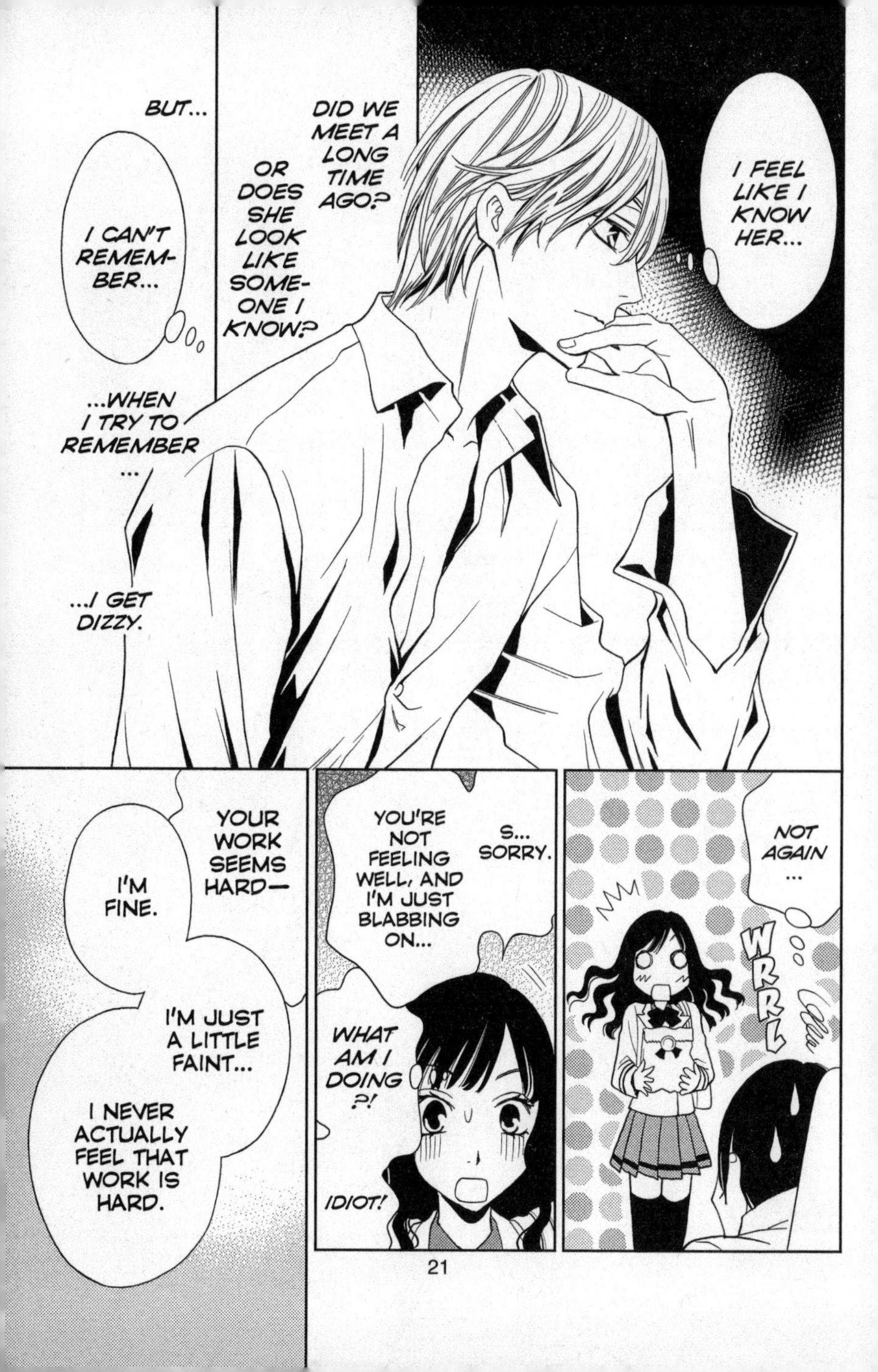
I FEEL LIKE I KNOW HER...
DID WE MEET A LONG TIME AGO?
OR DOES SHE LOOK LIKE SOMEONE I KNOW?
BUT...
I CAN'T REMEMBER...
...WHEN I TRY TO REMEMBER...
...I GET DIZZY.
NOT AGAIN...
WRRL
S... SORRY.
YOU'RE NOT FEELING WELL, AND I'M JUST BLABBING ON...
WHAT AM I DOING?!
IDIOT!
YOUR WORK SEEMS HARD—
I'M FINE.
I'M JUST A LITTLE FAINT...
I NEVER ACTUALLY FEEL THAT WORK IS HARD.

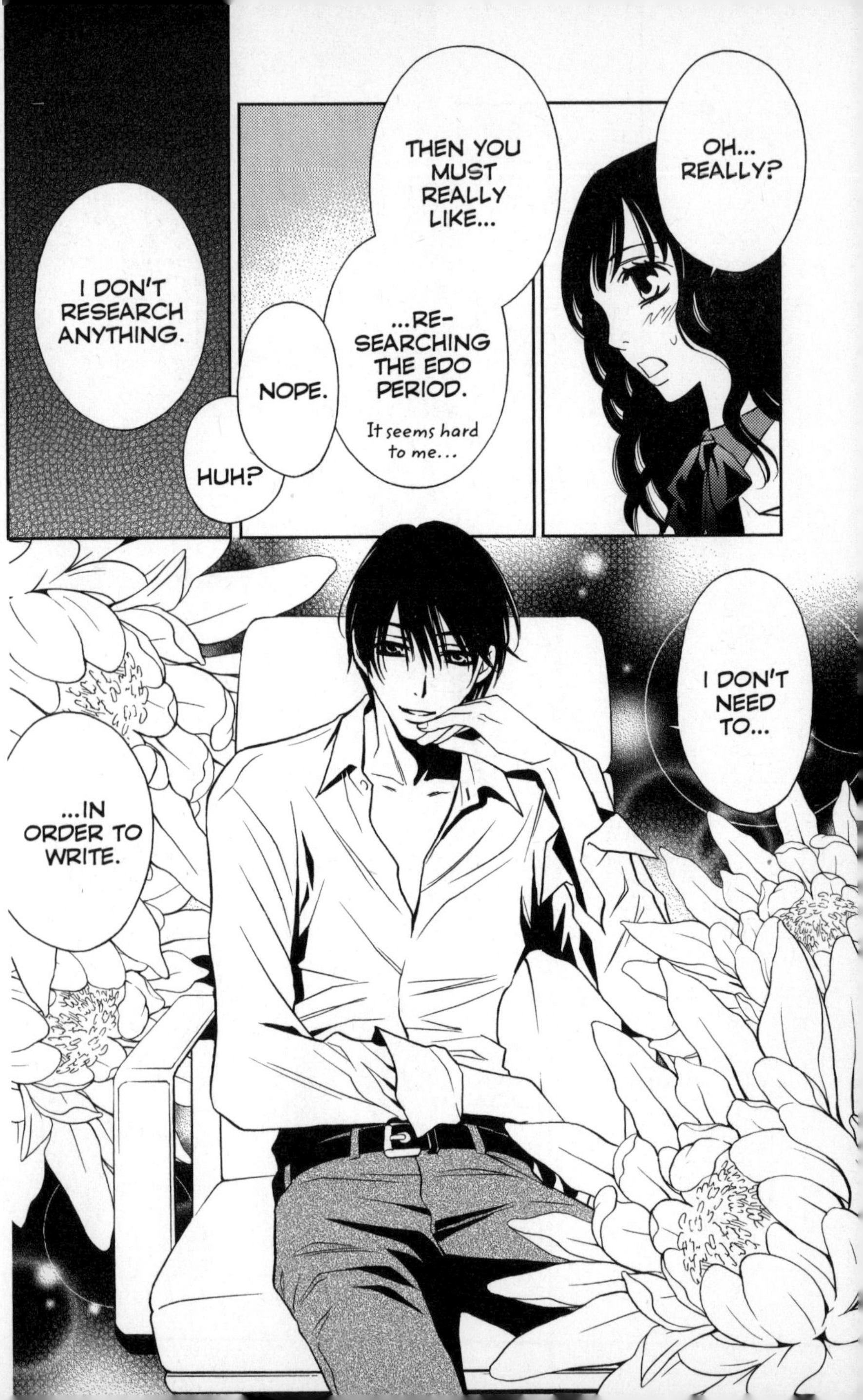
OH... REALLY?
THEN YOU MUST REALLY LIKE...
...RE-SEARCHING THE EDO PERIOD.
It seems hard to me...
NOPE.
HUH?
I DON'T RESEARCH ANYTHING.
I DON'T NEED TO...
...IN ORDER TO WRITE.

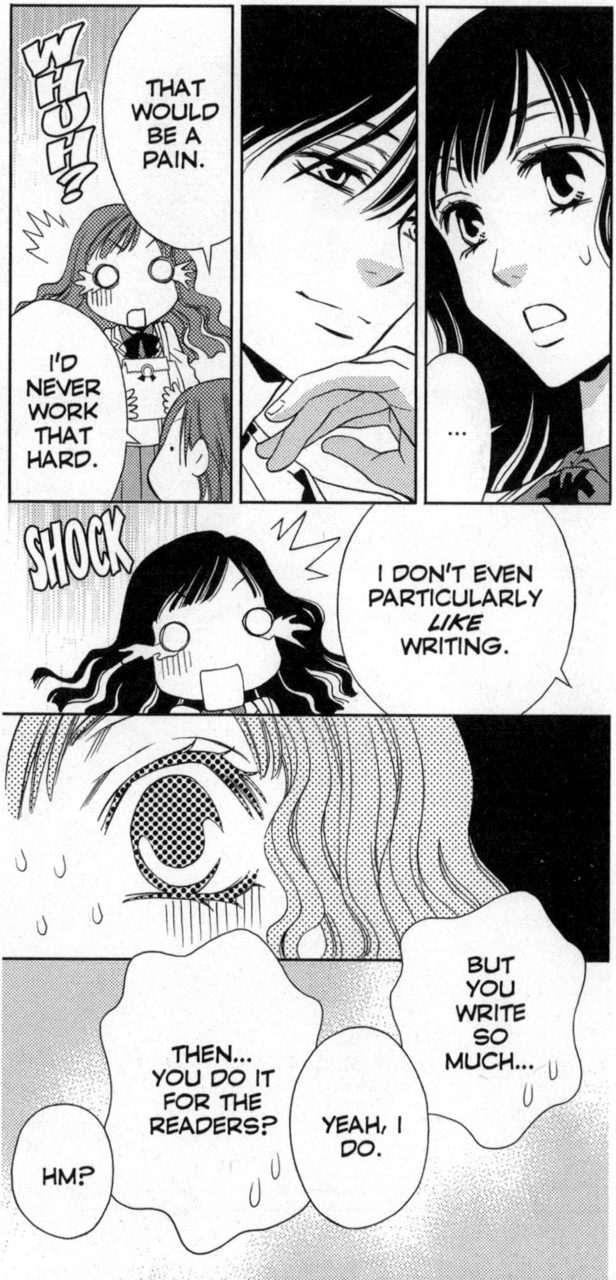
...
THAT WOULD BE A PAIN.
WHUH!?
I'D NEVER WORK THAT HARD.
I DON'T EVEN PARTICULARLY *LIKE* WRITING.
SHOCK
BUT YOU WRITE SO MUCH...
YEAH, I DO.
THEN... YOU DO IT FOR THE READERS?
HM?

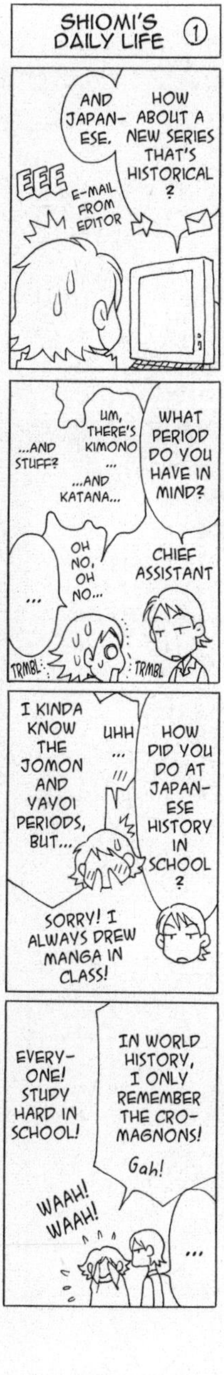
SHIOMI'S DAILY LIFE ①
HOW ABOUT A NEW SERIES THAT'S HISTORICAL?
AND JAPANESE.
EEE
E-MAIL FROM EDITOR
WHAT PERIOD DO YOU HAVE IN MIND?
UM, THERE'S KIMONO ... ...AND KATANA...
...AND STUFF?
CHIEF ASSISTANT
OH NO, OH NO...
...
TRMBL
TRMBL
HOW DID YOU DO AT JAPANESE HISTORY IN SCHOOL?
UHH ...
I KINDA KNOW THE JOMON AND YAYOI PERIODS, BUT...
SORRY! I ALWAYS DREW MANGA IN CLASS!
IN WORLD HISTORY, I ONLY REMEMBER THE CRO-MAGNONS!
EVERYONE! STUDY HARD IN SCHOOL!
Gah!
WAAH! WAAH!
...

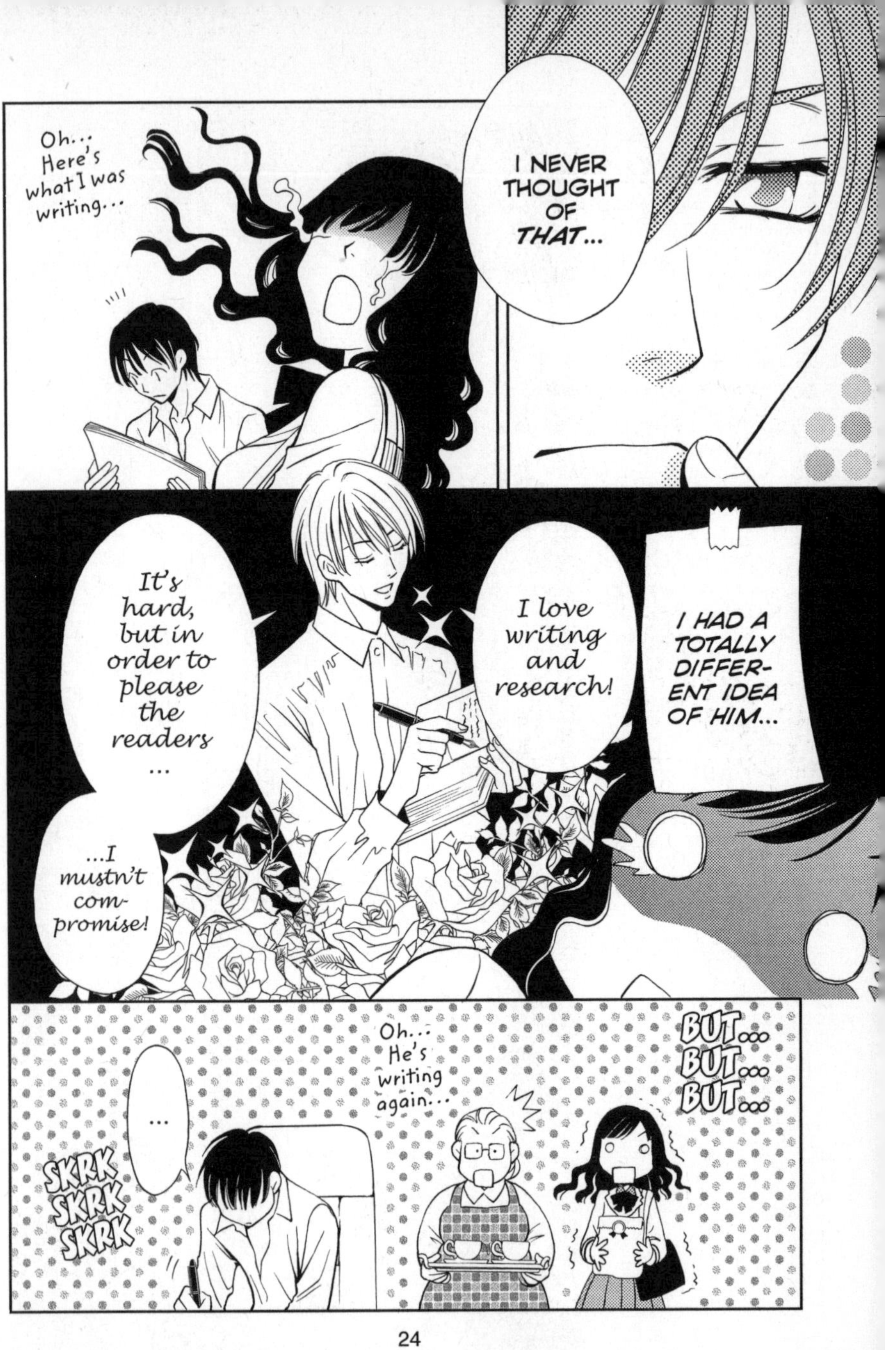
I NEVER THOUGHT OF *THAT*...
Oh... Here's what I was writing...
I HAD A TOTALLY DIFFER-ENT IDEA OF HIM...
I love writing and research!
It's hard, but in order to please the readers ...
...I mustn't com-promise!
BUT... BUT... BUT...
Oh... He's writing again...
...
SKRK SKRK SKRK

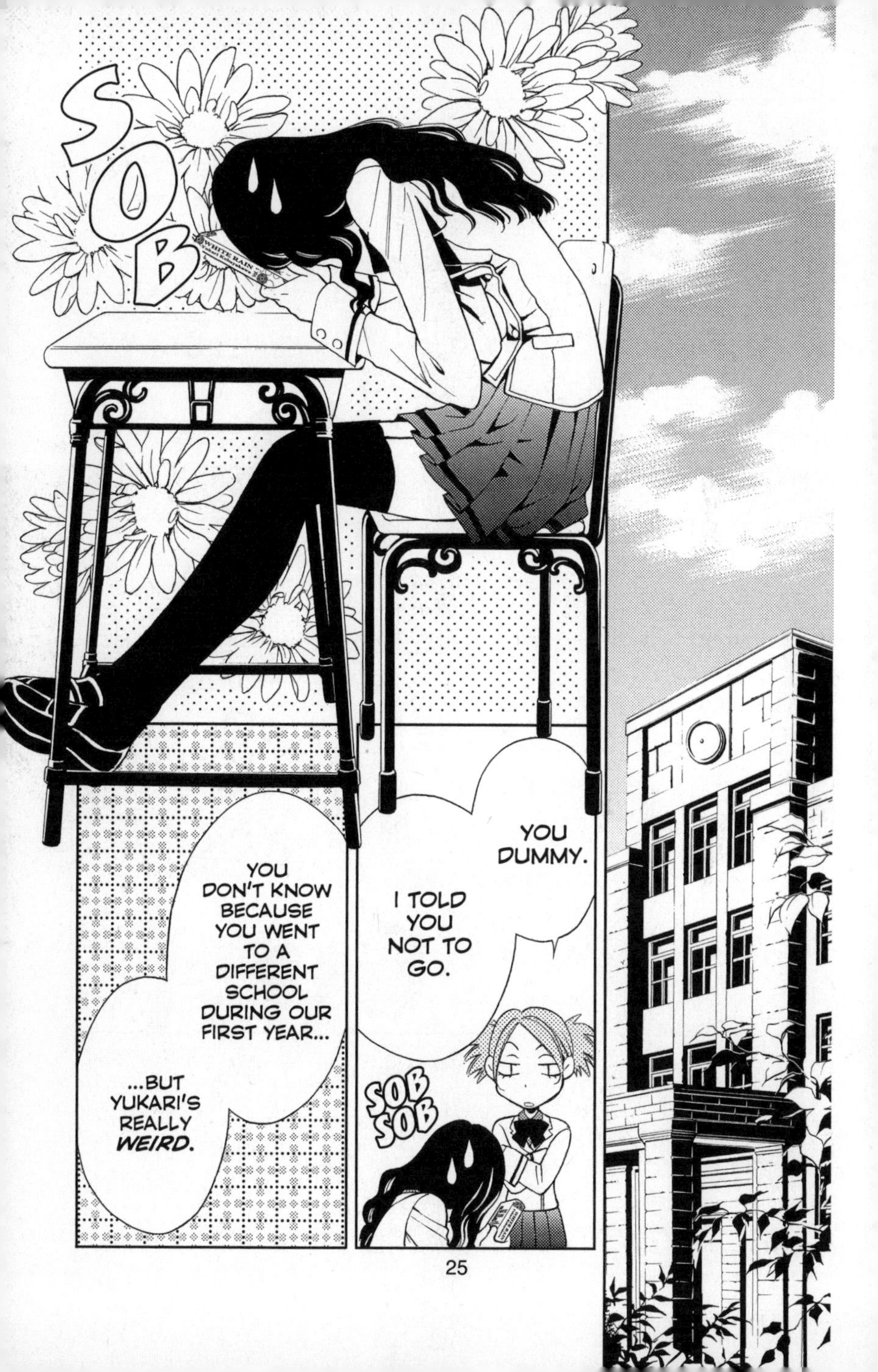
SOB
WHITE RAIN
YOU DUMMY.
I TOLD YOU NOT TO GO.
SOB SOB
YOU DON'T KNOW BECAUSE YOU WENT TO A DIFFERENT SCHOOL DURING OUR FIRST YEAR...
...BUT YUKARI'S REALLY *WEIRD*.

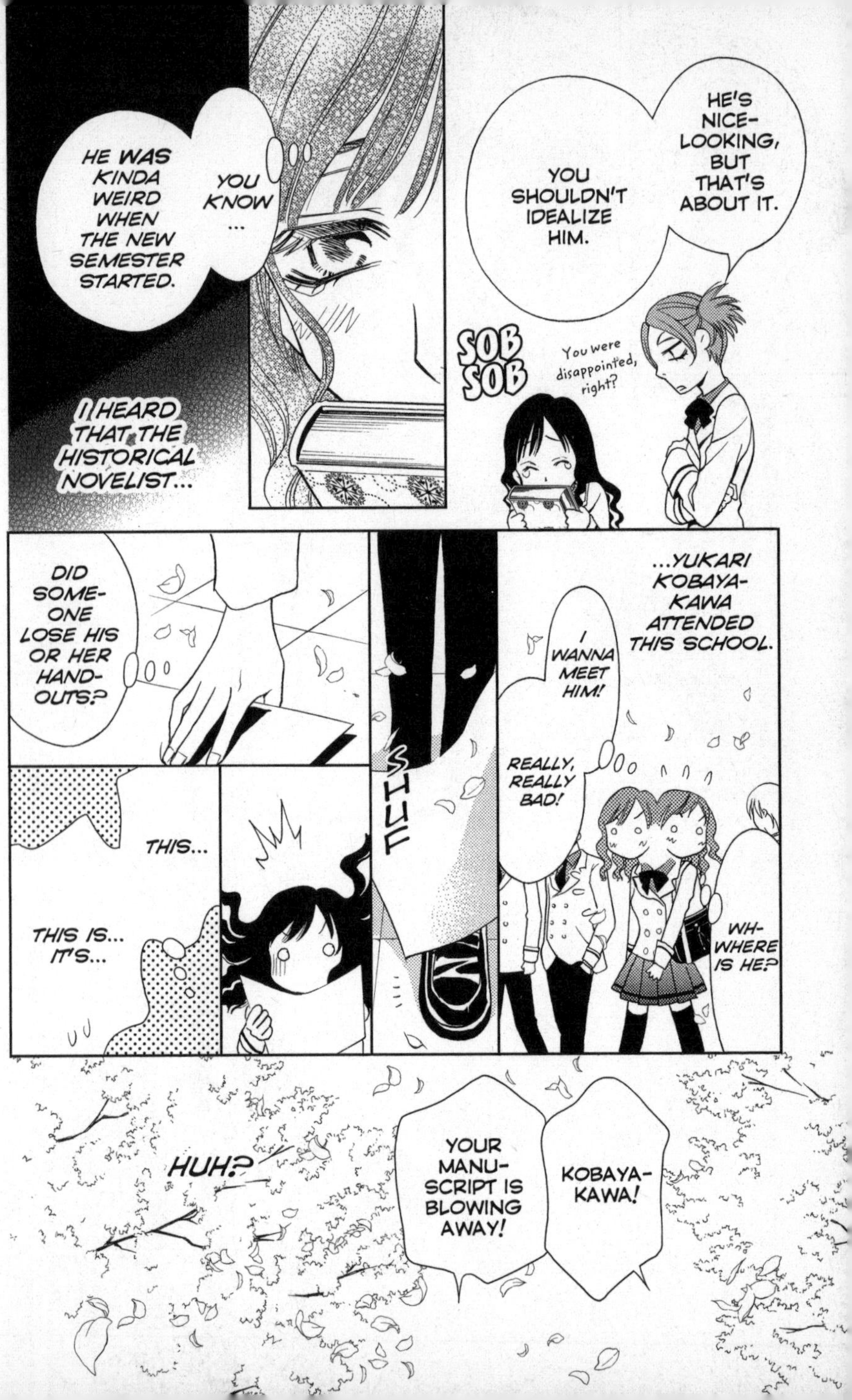
HE'S NICE-LOOKING, BUT THAT'S ABOUT IT.
YOU SHOULDN'T IDEALIZE HIM.
SOB SOB
You were disappointed, right?
YOU KNOW...
HE WAS KINDA WEIRD WHEN THE NEW SEMESTER STARTED.
I HEARD THAT THE HISTORICAL NOVELIST...
...YUKARI KOBAYA-KAWA ATTENDED THIS SCHOOL.
I WANNA MEET HIM!
REALLY, REALLY BAD!
WH-WHERE IS HE?
SHUF
DID SOME-ONE LOSE HIS OR HER HAND-OUTS?
THIS...
THIS IS... IT'S...
KOBAYA-KAWA!
YOUR MANU-SCRIPT IS BLOWING AWAY!
HUH?

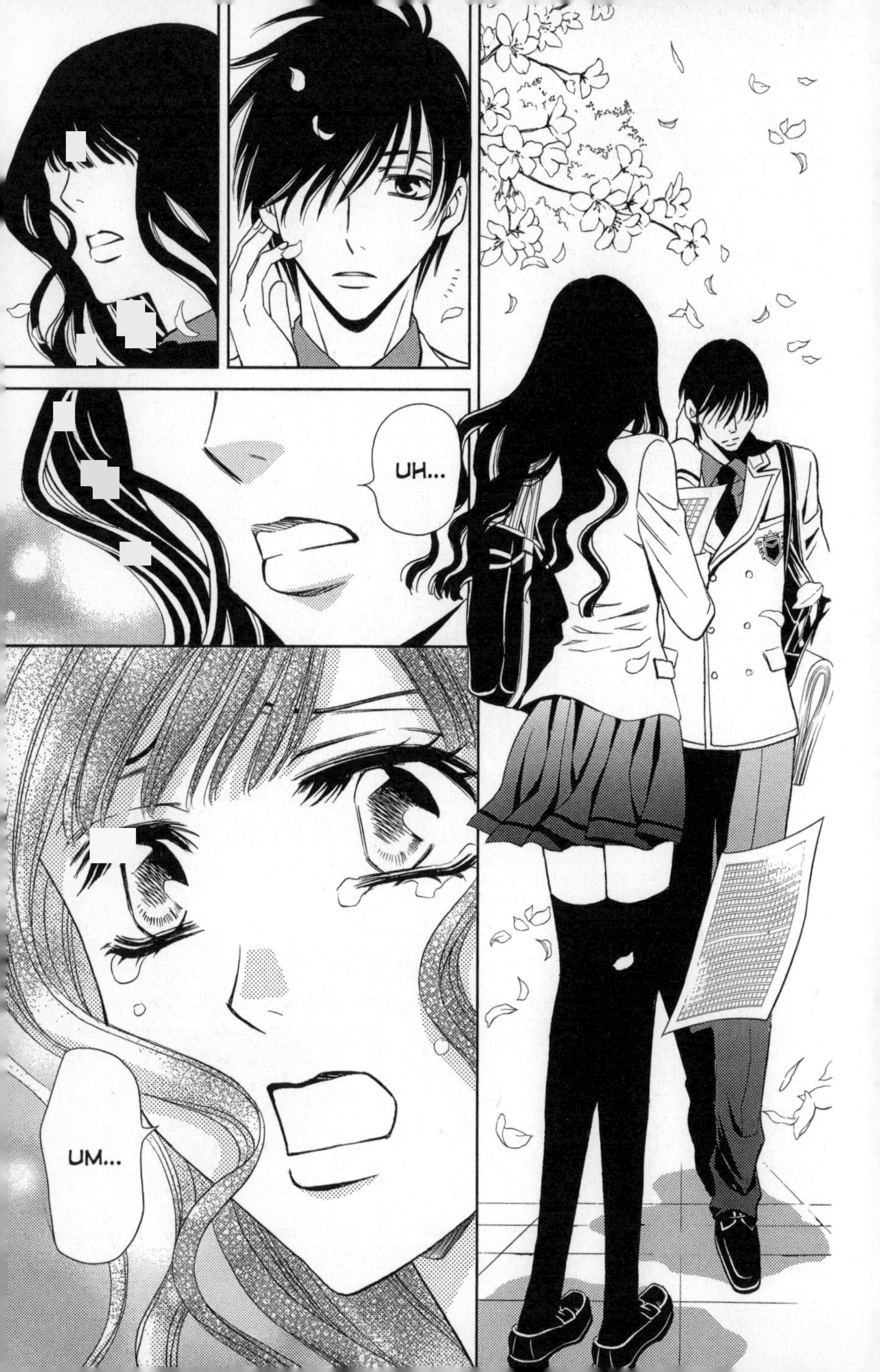
UH...
UM...

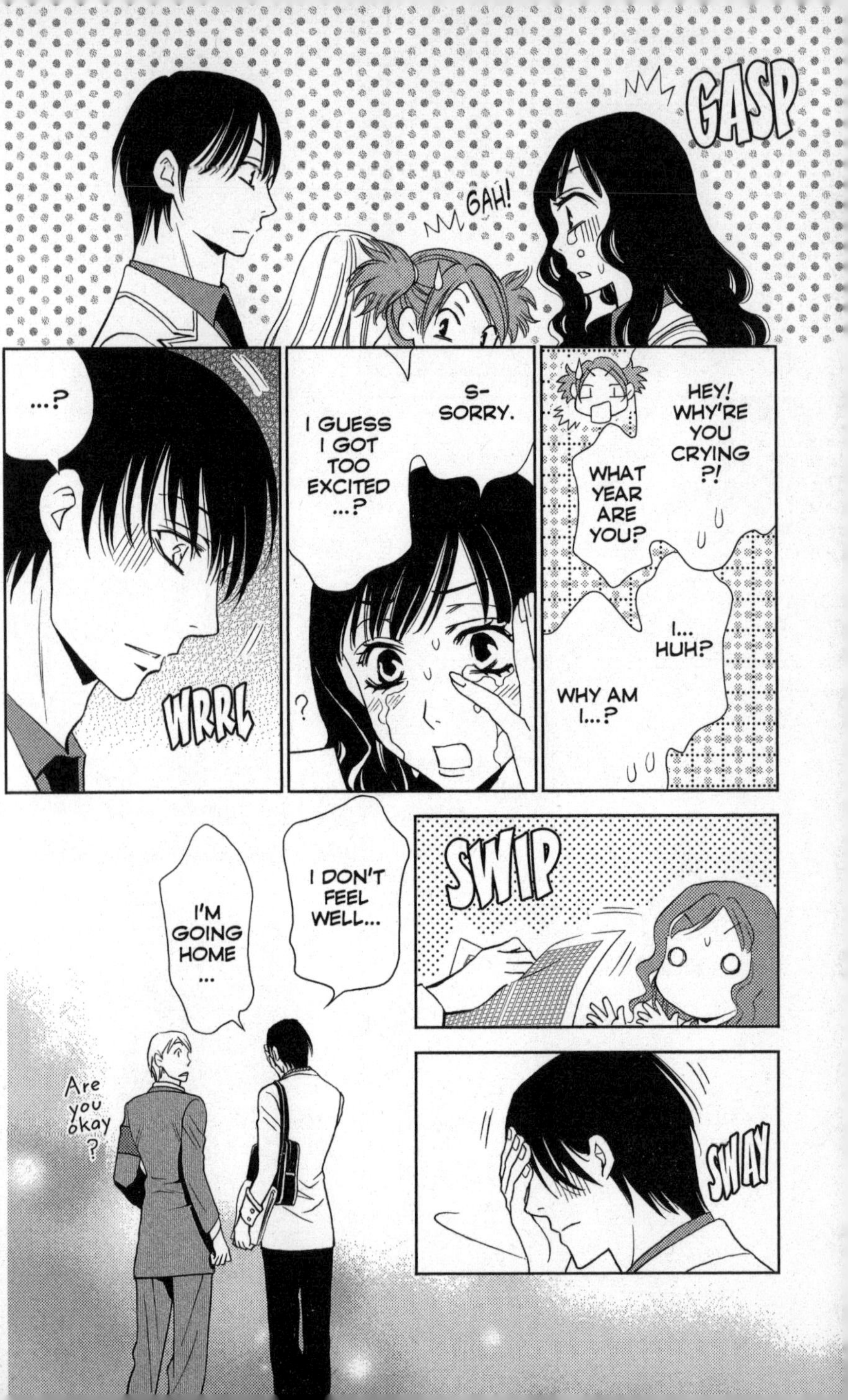
GASP
GAH!
HEY! WHY'RE YOU CRYING?!
WHAT YEAR ARE YOU?
I... HUH?
WHY AM I...?
S-SORRY.
I GUESS I GOT TOO EXCITED...?
?
...?
WRRL
SWIP
SWAY
I DON'T FEEL WELL...
I'M GOING HOME...
Are you okay?

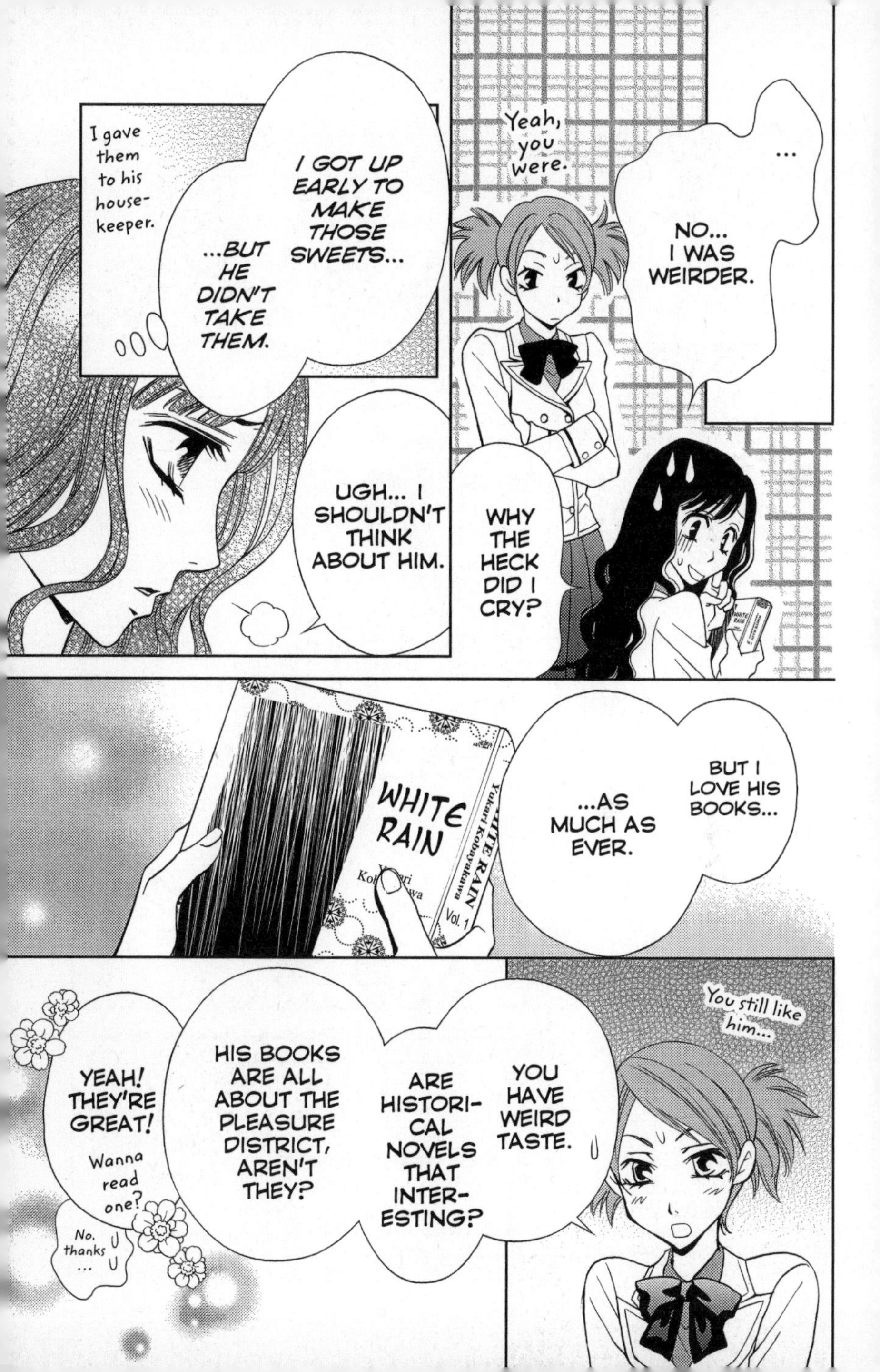
...
NO... I WAS WEIRDER.
Yeah, you were.
WHY THE HECK DID I CRY?
I GOT UP EARLY TO MAKE THOSE SWEETS...
...BUT HE DIDN'T TAKE THEM.
I gave them to his house-keeper.
UGH... I SHOULDN'T THINK ABOUT HIM.
BUT I LOVE HIS BOOKS...
...AS MUCH AS EVER.
WHITE RAIN
Yukari Kobayakawa
Vol. 1
You still like him...
YOU HAVE WEIRD TASTE.
ARE HISTORI-CAL NOVELS THAT INTER-ESTING?
HIS BOOKS ARE ALL ABOUT THE PLEASURE DISTRICT, AREN'T THEY?
YEAH! THEY'RE GREAT!
Wanna read one?
No, thanks...

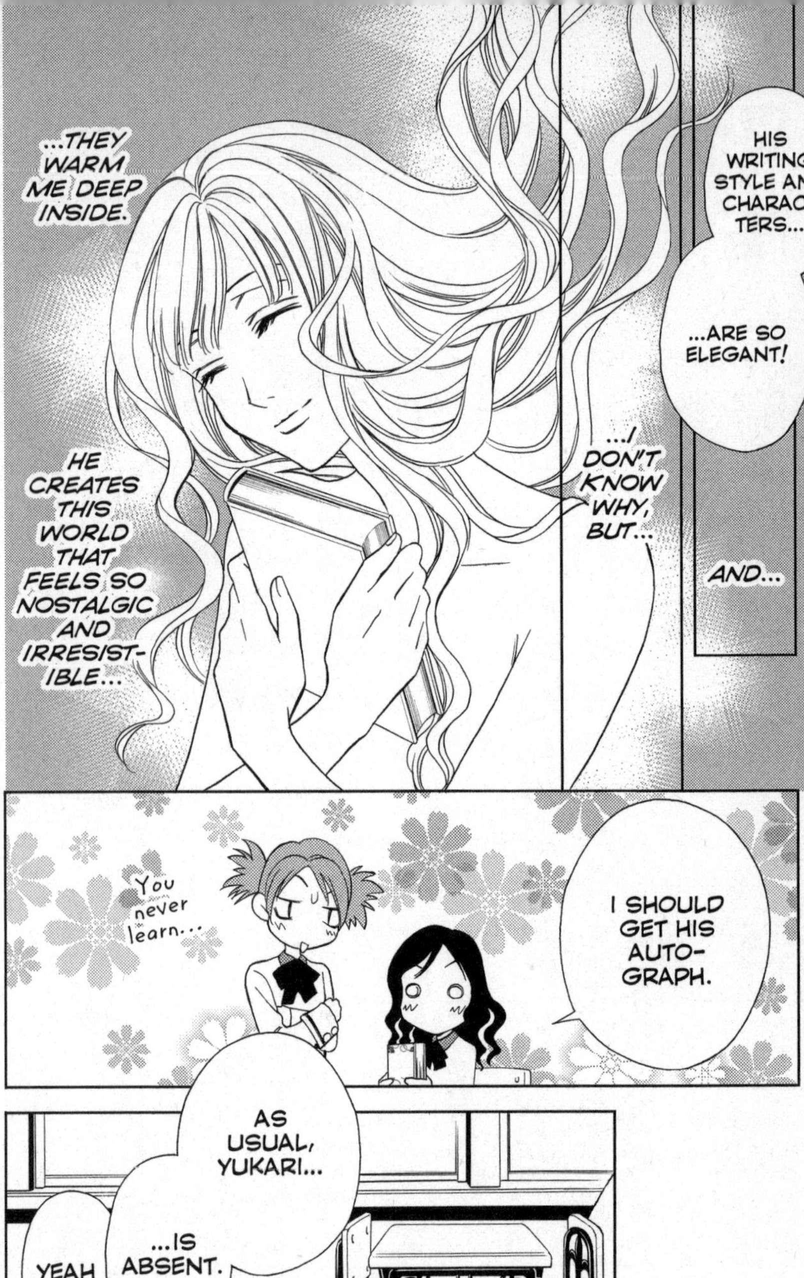
HIS WRITING STYLE AND CHARAC-TERS...
...ARE SO ELEGANT!
AND...
HE CREATES THIS WORLD THAT FEELS SO NOSTALGIC AND IRRESIST-IBLE...
...I DON'T KNOW WHY, BUT...
...THEY WARM ME DEEP INSIDE.
I SHOULD GET HIS AUTO-GRAPH.
You never learn...
AS USUAL, YUKARI...
...IS ABSENT.
YEAH ...

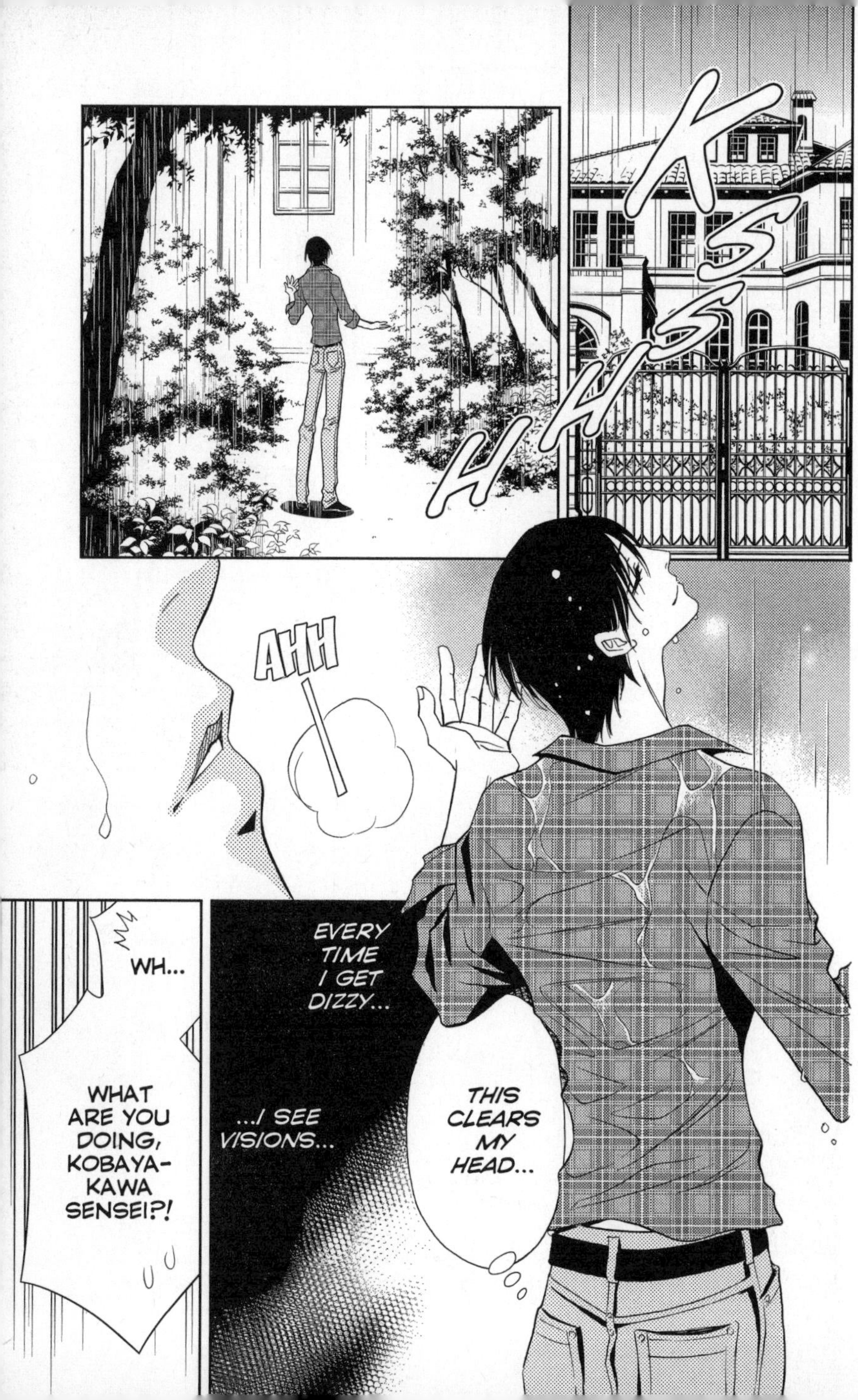
KSSHHH
AHH
EVERY TIME I GET DIZZY...
...I SEE VISIONS...
THIS CLEARS MY HEAD...
WH...
WHAT ARE YOU DOING, KOBAYA-KAWA SENSEI?!

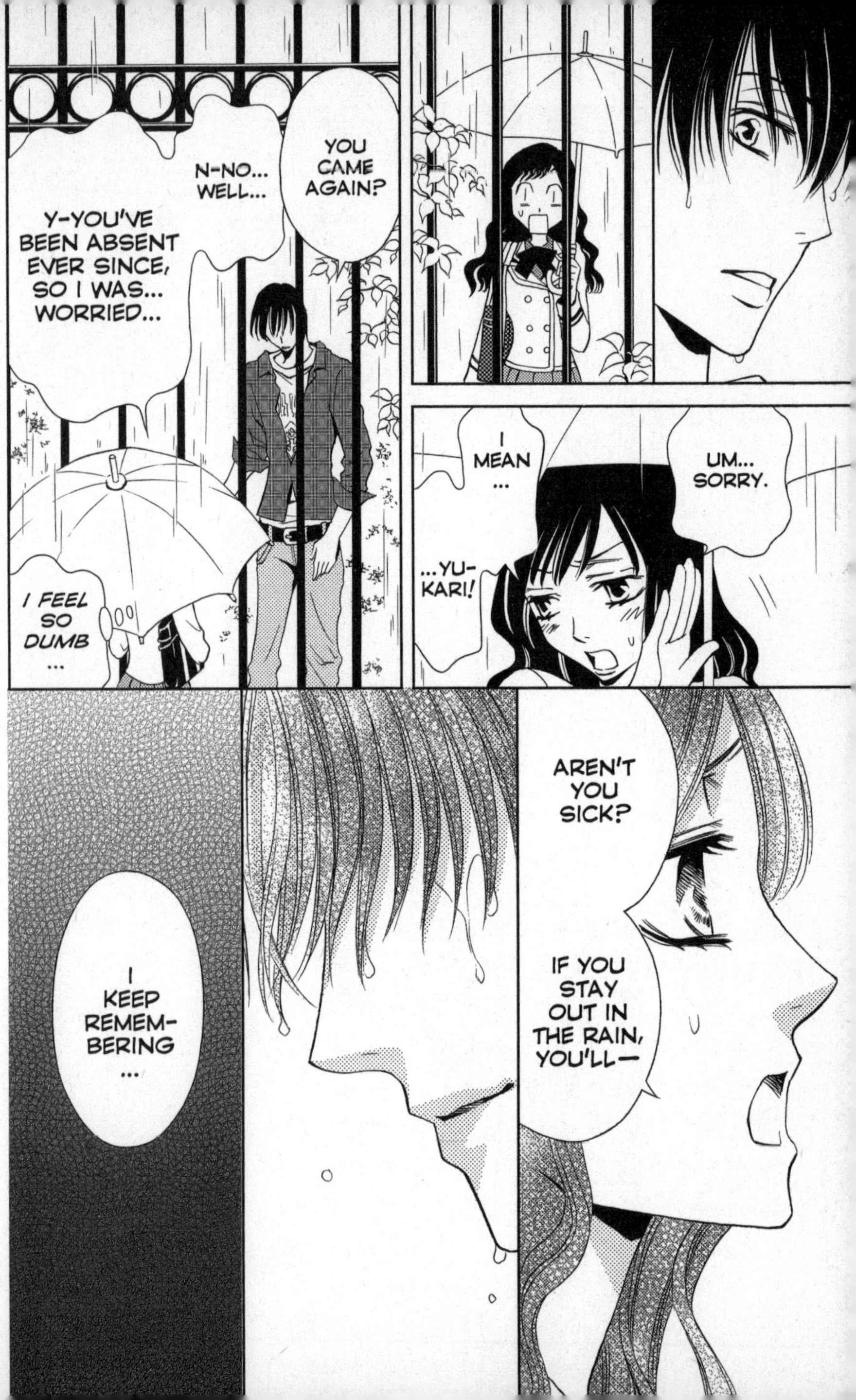
UM... SORRY.
I MEAN ...
...YU-KARI!
YOU CAME AGAIN?
N-NO... WELL...
Y-YOU'VE BEEN ABSENT EVER SINCE, SO I WAS... WORRIED...
I FEEL SO DUMB ...
AREN'T YOU SICK?
IF YOU STAY OUT IN THE RAIN, YOU'LL—
I KEEP REMEM-BERING ...

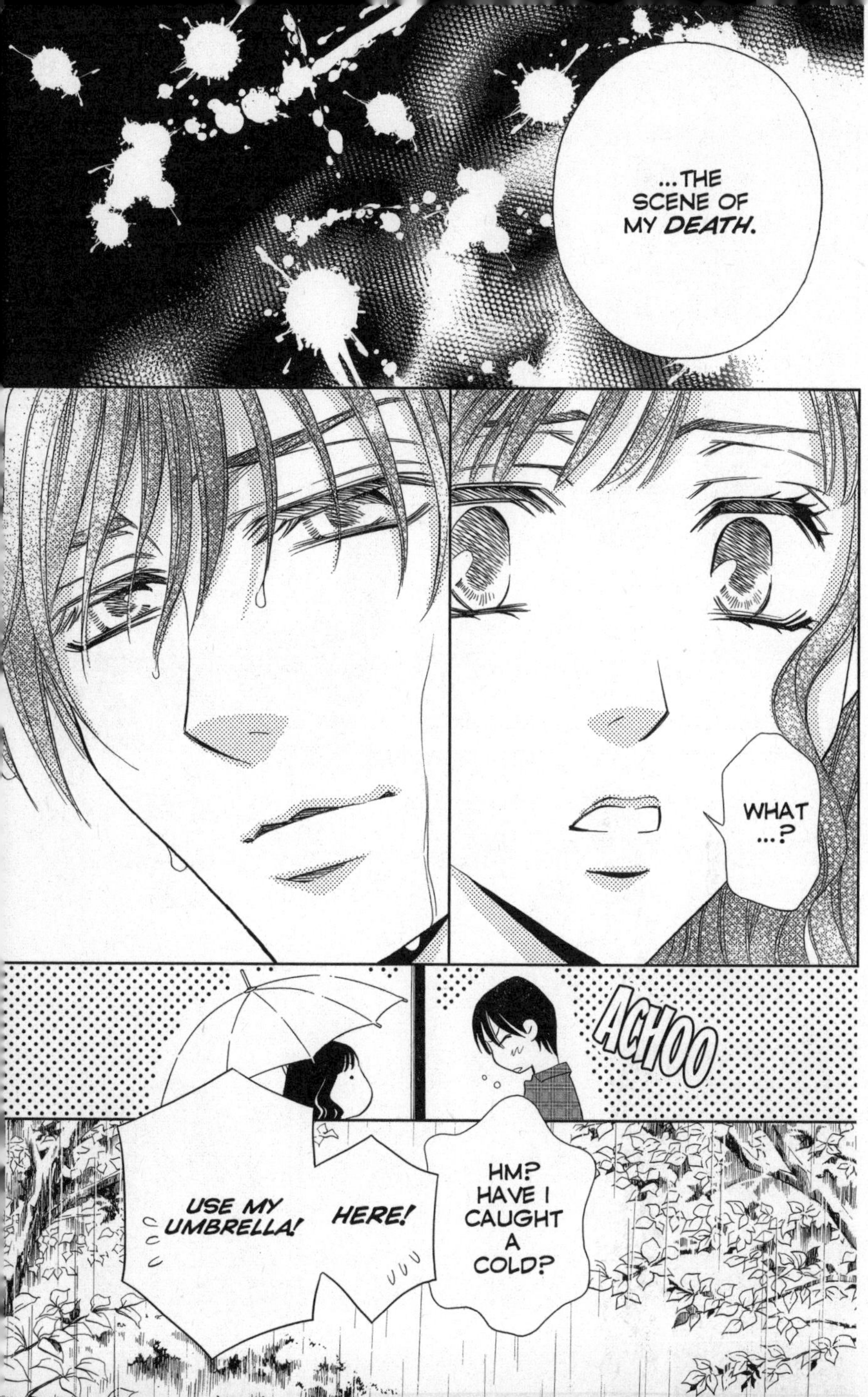
...THE SCENE OF MY DEATH.
WHAT ...?
ACHOO
HM? HAVE I CAUGHT A COLD?
HERE!
USE MY UMBRELLA!

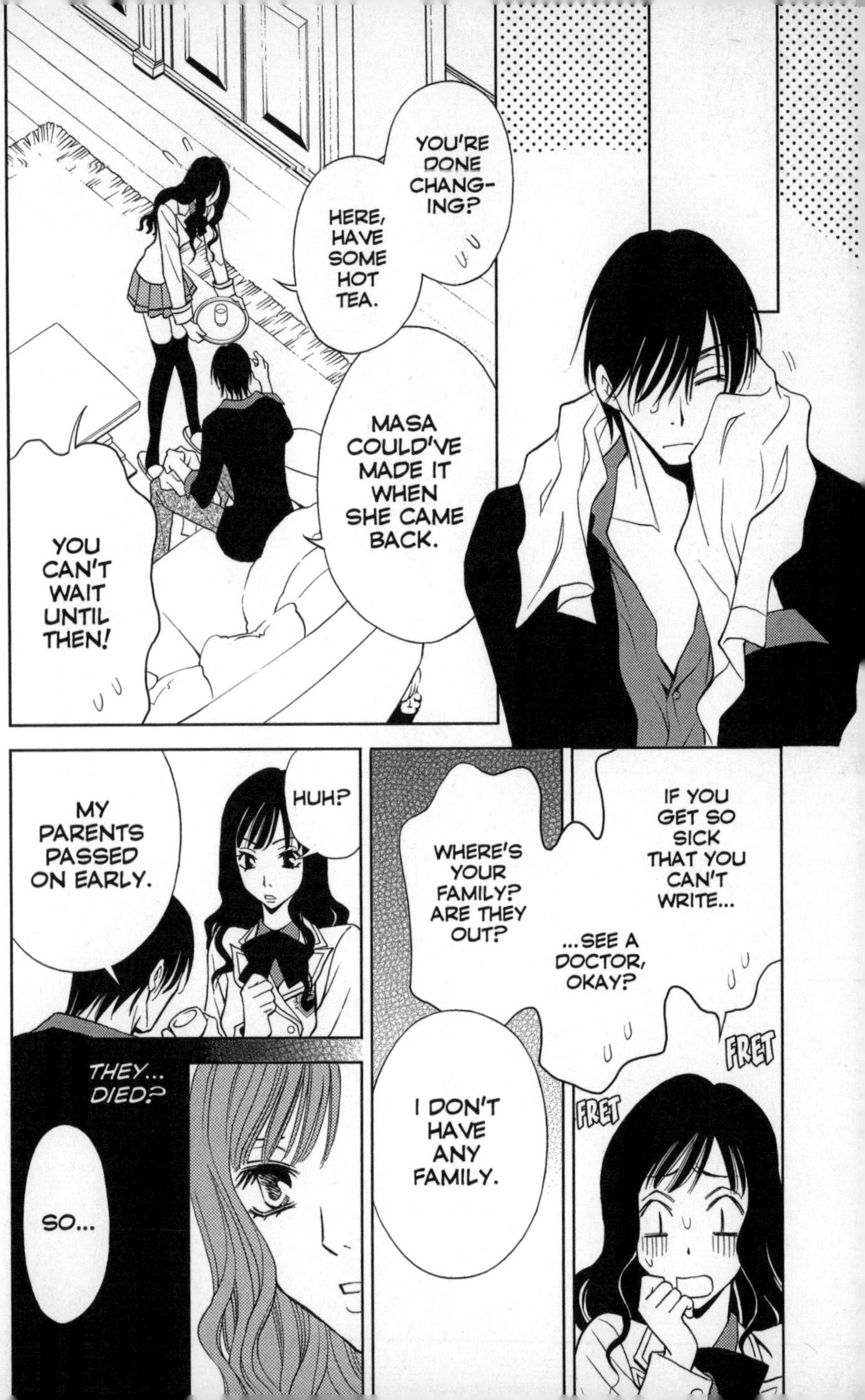
YOU'RE DONE CHANGING?
HERE, HAVE SOME HOT TEA.
MASA COULD'VE MADE IT WHEN SHE CAME BACK.
YOU CAN'T WAIT UNTIL THEN!
IF YOU GET SO SICK THAT YOU CAN'T WRITE...
...SEE A DOCTOR, OKAY?
WHERE'S YOUR FAMILY? ARE THEY OUT?
FRET
FRET
I DON'T HAVE ANY FAMILY.
HUH?
MY PARENTS PASSED ON EARLY.
THEY... DIED?
SO...

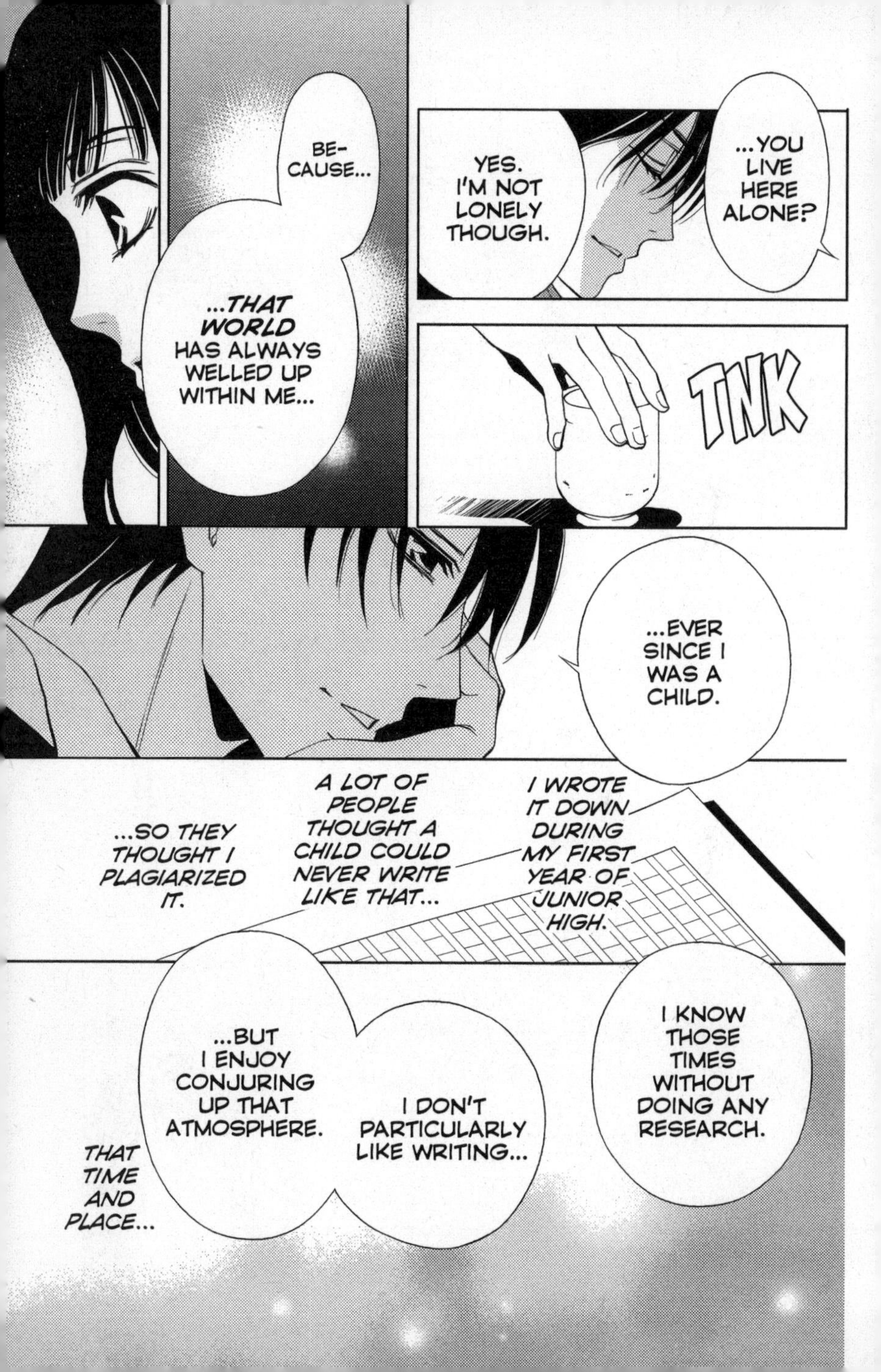
...YOU LIVE HERE ALONE?
YES. I'M NOT LONELY THOUGH.
TNK
BE-CAUSE...
...THAT WORLD HAS ALWAYS WELLED UP WITHIN ME...
...EVER SINCE I WAS A CHILD.
I WROTE IT DOWN DURING MY FIRST YEAR OF JUNIOR HIGH.
A LOT OF PEOPLE THOUGHT A CHILD COULD NEVER WRITE LIKE THAT...
...SO THEY THOUGHT I PLAGIARIZED IT.
I KNOW THOSE TIMES WITHOUT DOING ANY RESEARCH.
I DON'T PARTICULARLY LIKE WRITING...
...BUT I ENJOY CONJURING UP THAT ATMOSPHERE.
THAT TIME AND PLACE...

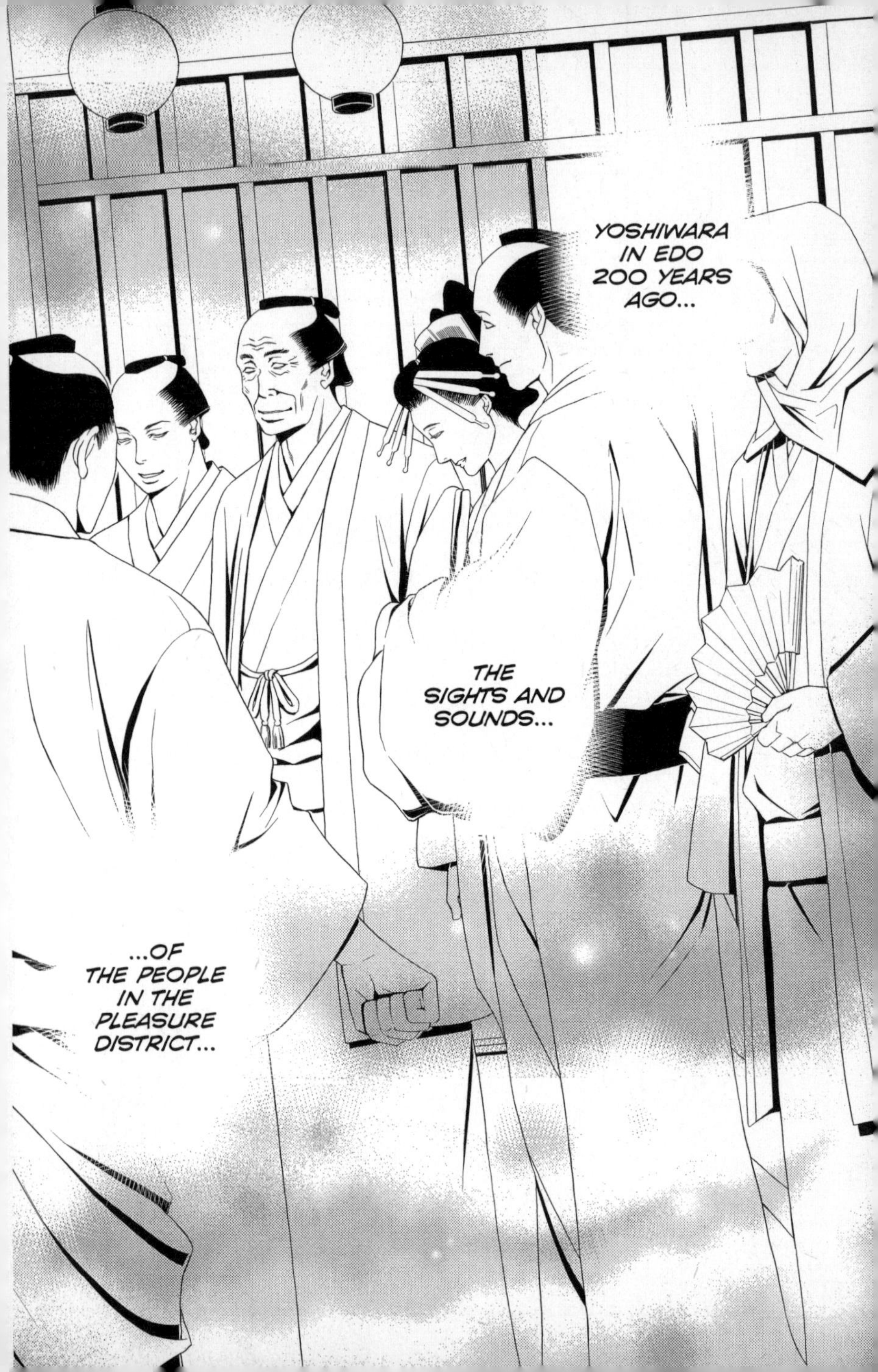
YOSHIWARA IN EDO 200 YEARS AGO...
THE SIGHTS AND SOUNDS...
...OF THE PEOPLE IN THE PLEASURE DISTRICT...

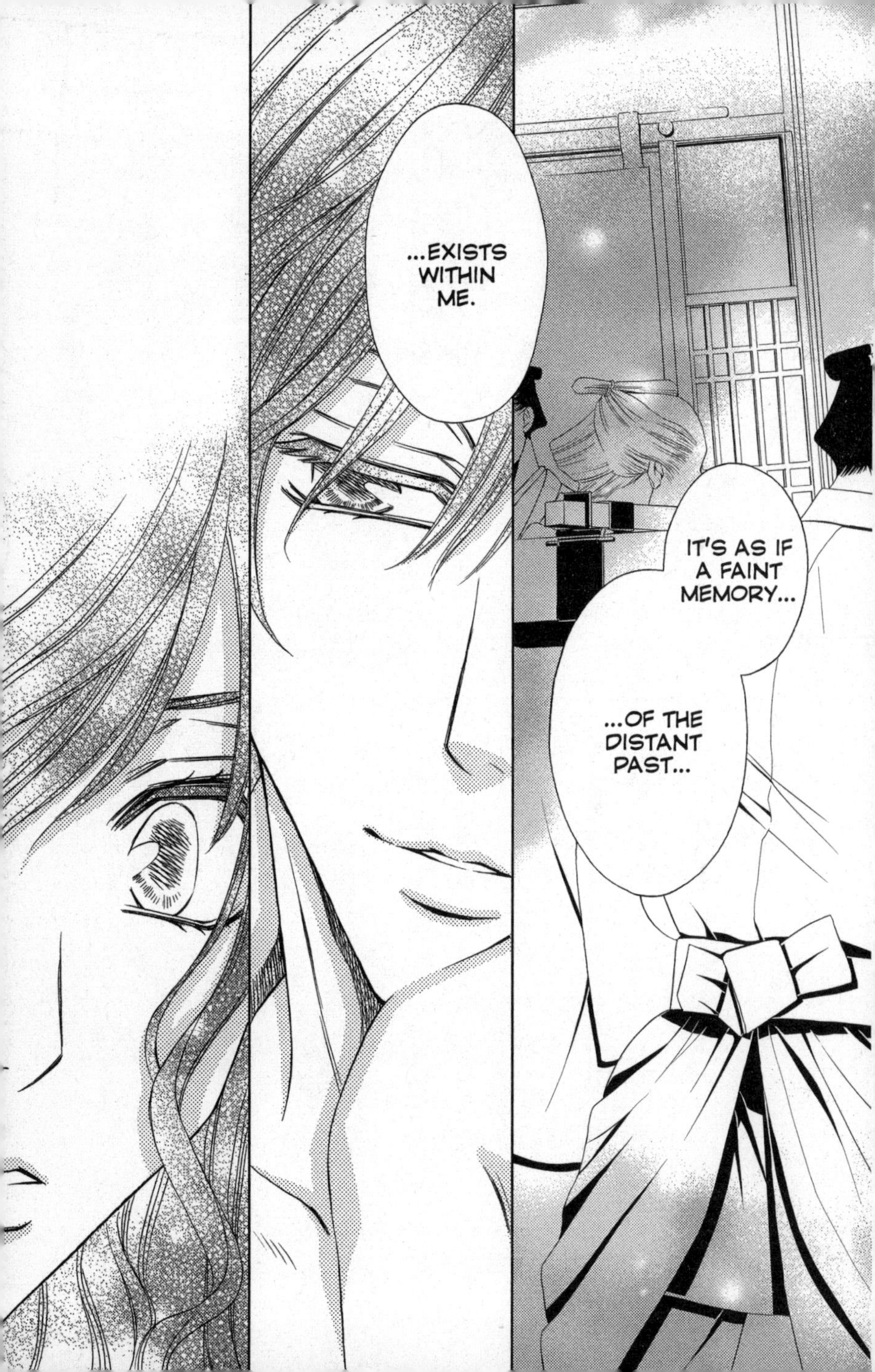
IT'S AS IF A FAINT MEMORY...
...OF THE DISTANT PAST...
...EXISTS WITHIN ME.

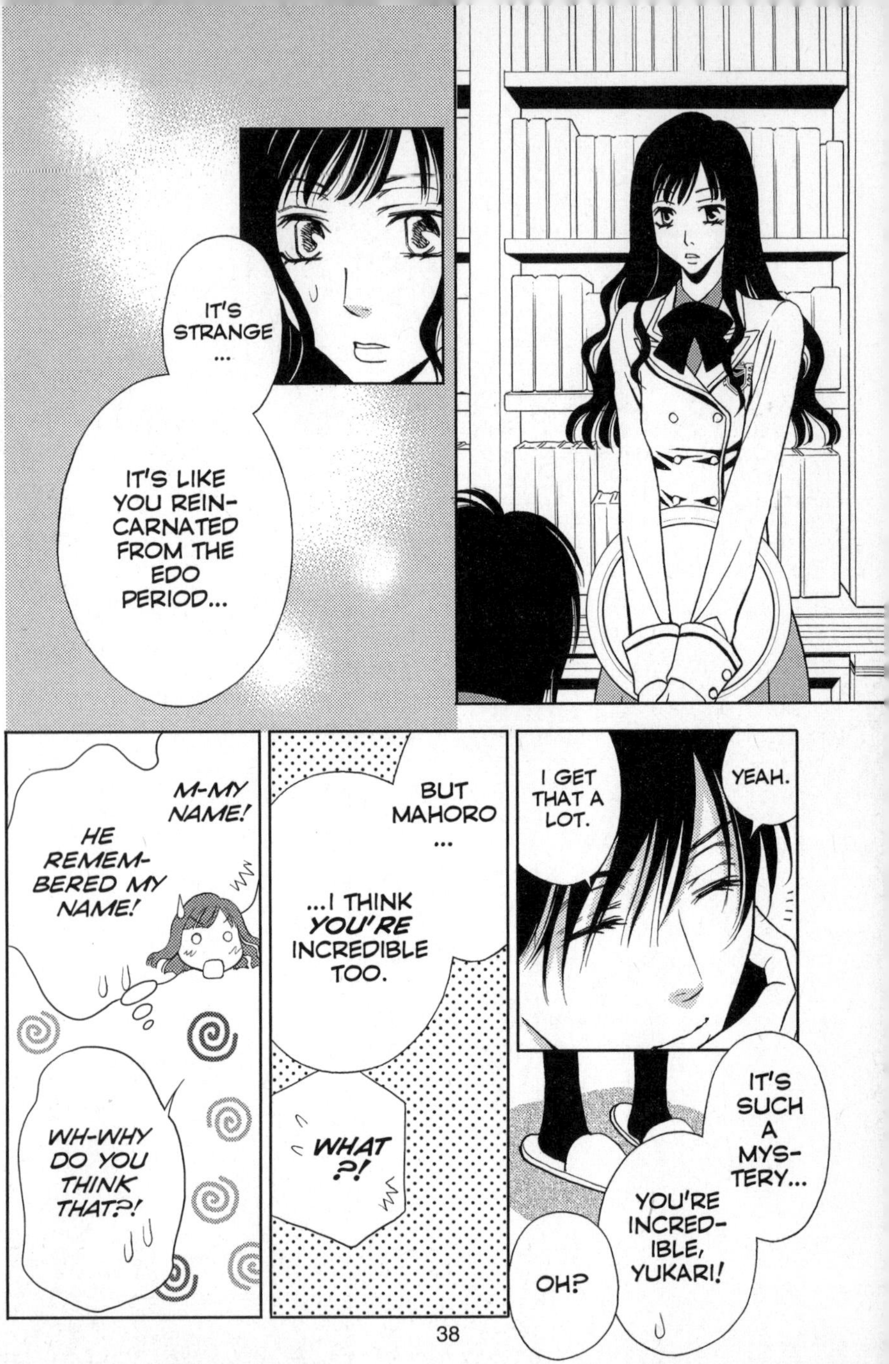
IT'S STRANGE...
IT'S LIKE YOU REINCARNATED FROM THE EDO PERIOD...
YEAH.
I GET THAT A LOT.
IT'S SUCH A MYSTERY...
YOU'RE INCREDIBLE, YUKARI!
OH?
BUT MAHORO...
...I THINK *YOU'RE* INCREDIBLE TOO.
WHAT?!
M-MY NAME!
HE REMEMBERED MY NAME!
WH-WHY DO YOU THINK THAT?!

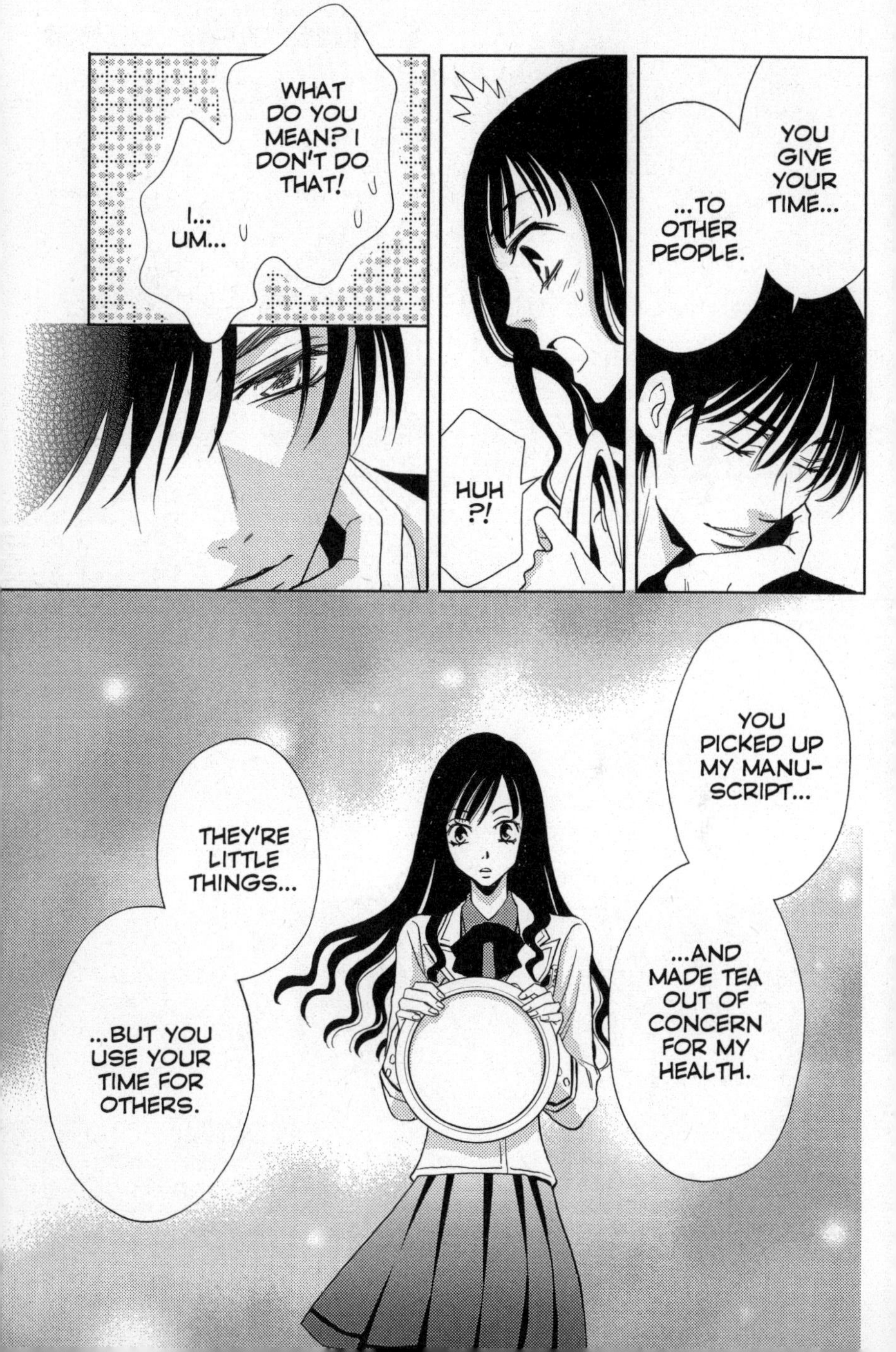
YOU GIVE YOUR TIME...
...TO OTHER PEOPLE.
HUH?!
WHAT DO YOU MEAN? I DON'T DO THAT!
I... UM...
YOU PICKED UP MY MANU-SCRIPT...
...AND MADE TEA OUT OF CONCERN FOR MY HEALTH.
THEY'RE LITTLE THINGS...
...BUT YOU USE YOUR TIME FOR OTHERS.

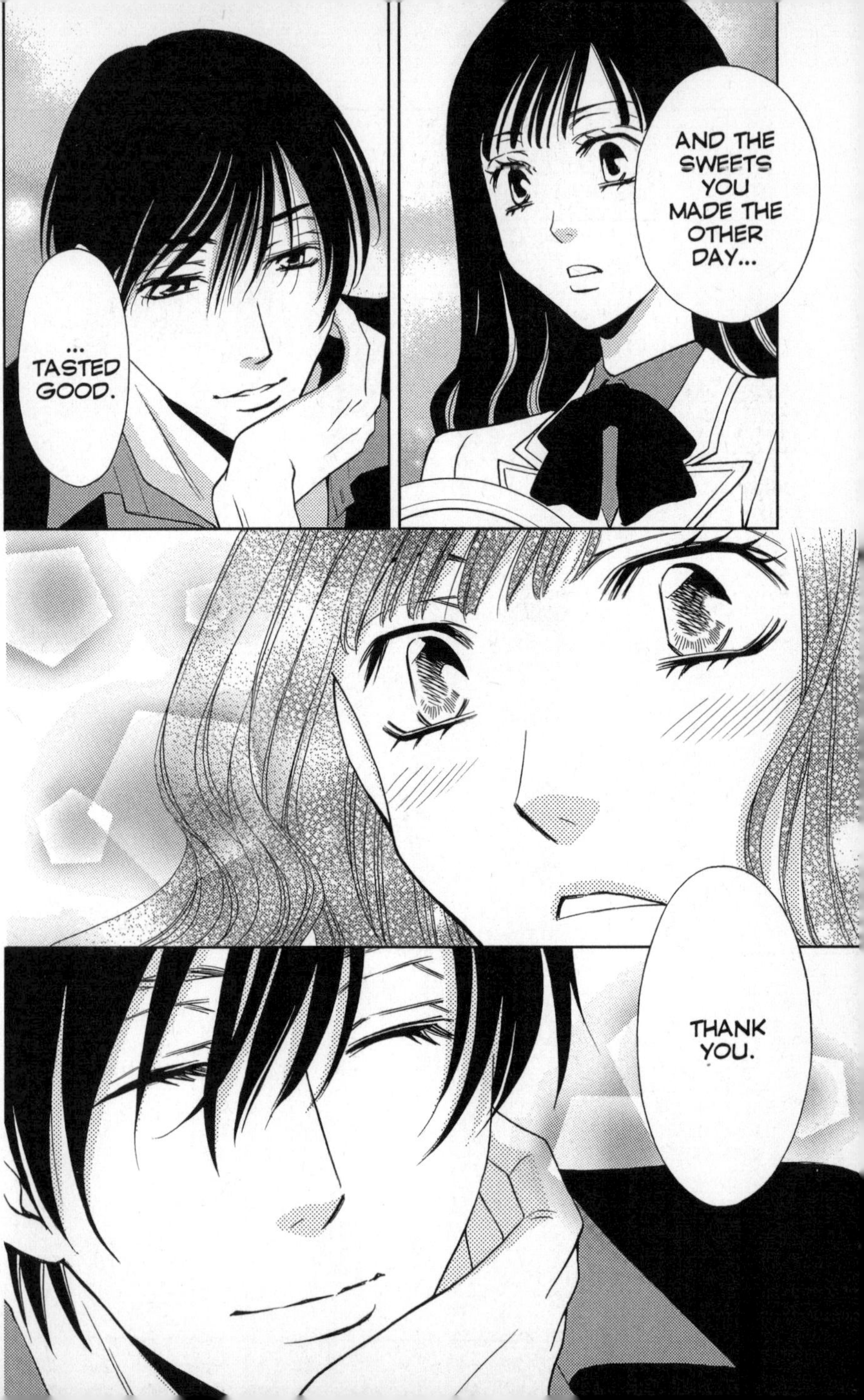
AND THE SWEETS YOU MADE THE OTHER DAY...
... TASTED GOOD.
THANK YOU.

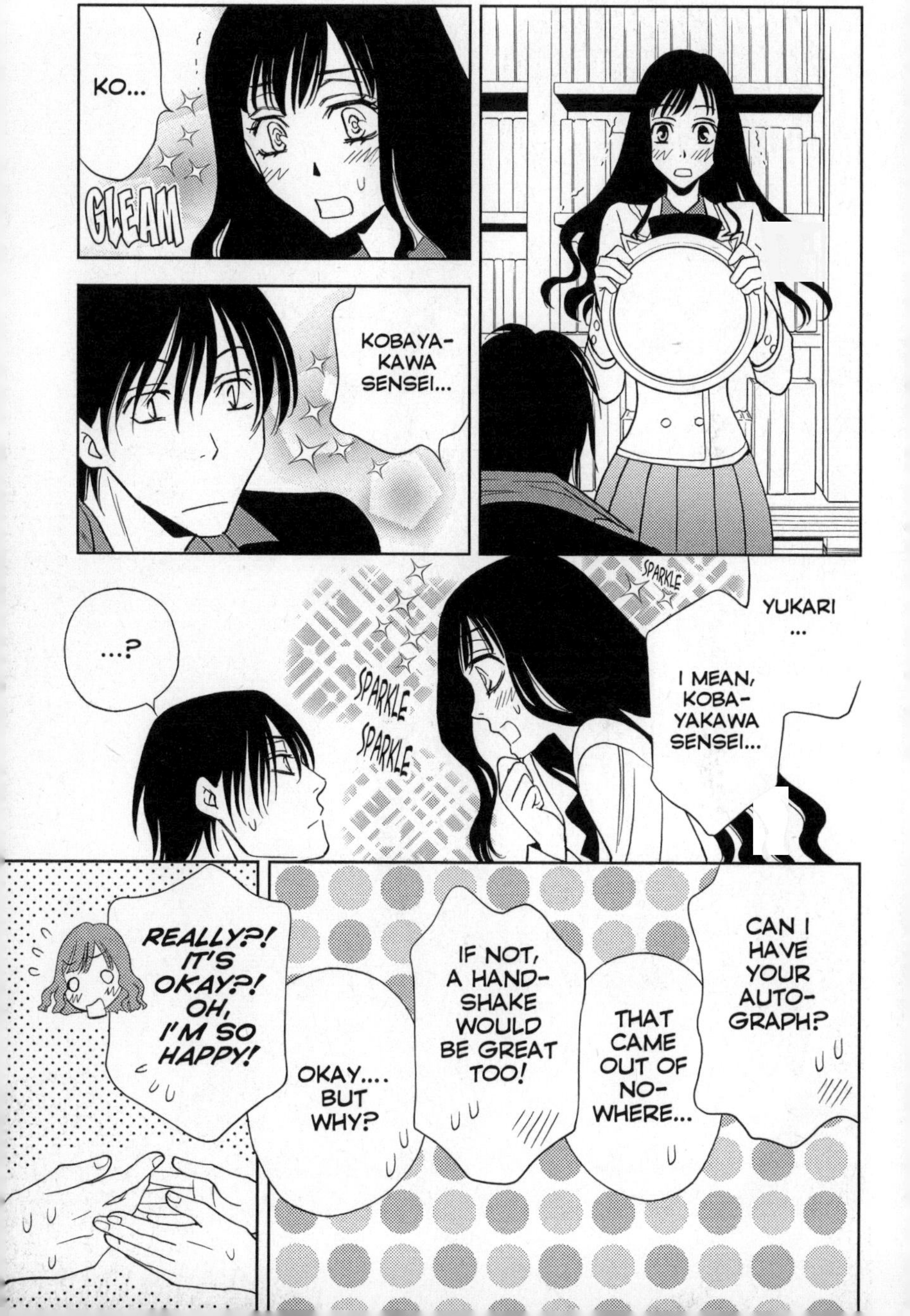
KO...
GLEAM
KOBAYA-KAWA SENSEI...
SPARKLE
YUKARI ...
I MEAN, KOBA-YAKAWA SENSEI...
SPARKLE SPARKLE
...?
CAN I HAVE YOUR AUTO-GRAPH?
THAT CAME OUT OF NO-WHERE...
IF NOT, A HAND-SHAKE WOULD BE GREAT TOO!
OKAY.... BUT WHY?
REALLY?! IT'S OKAY?! OH, I'M SO HAPPY!

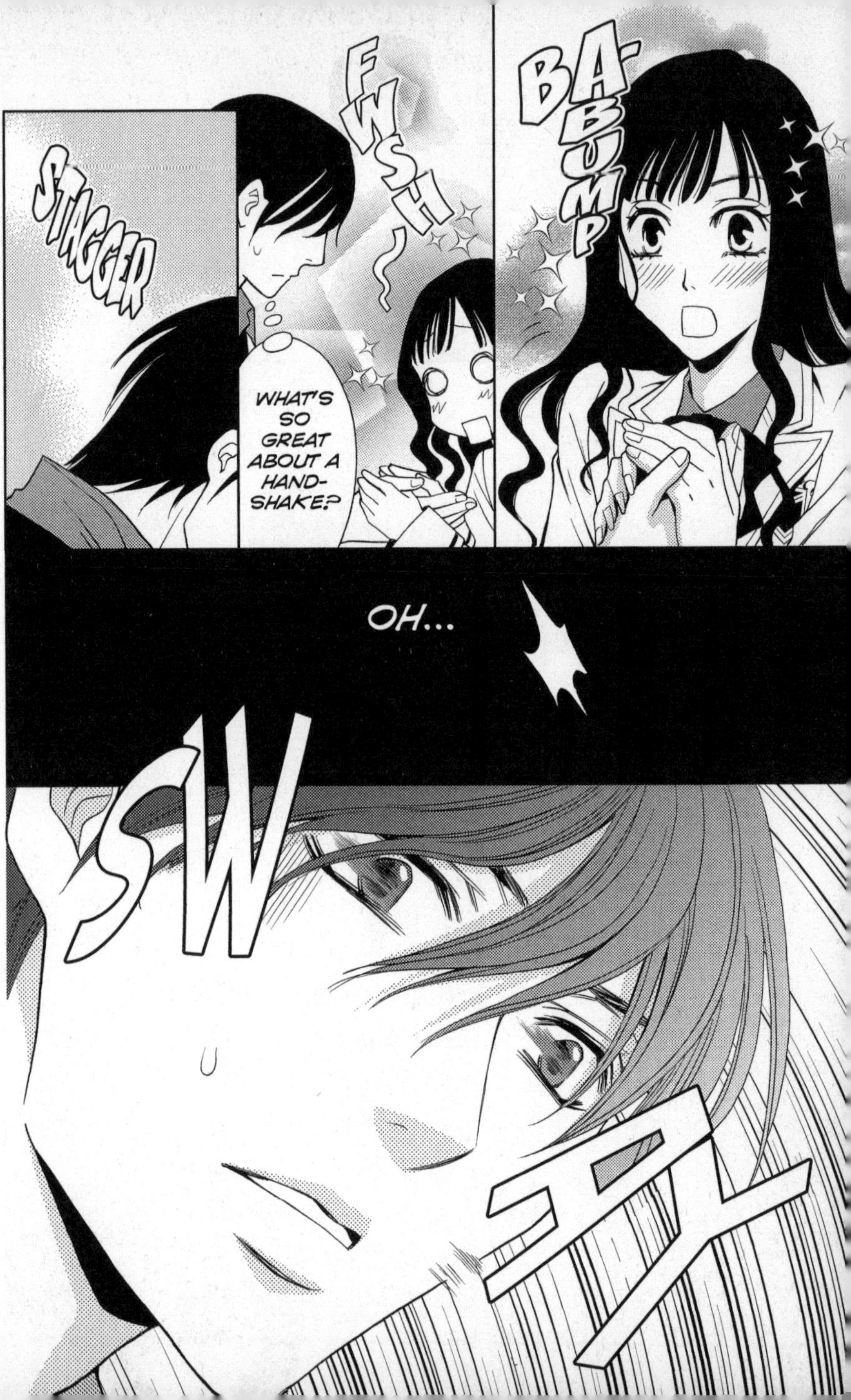
BA-BUMP
FWSH~
WHAT'S SO GREAT ABOUT A HAND-SHAKE?
STAGGER
OH...
SW

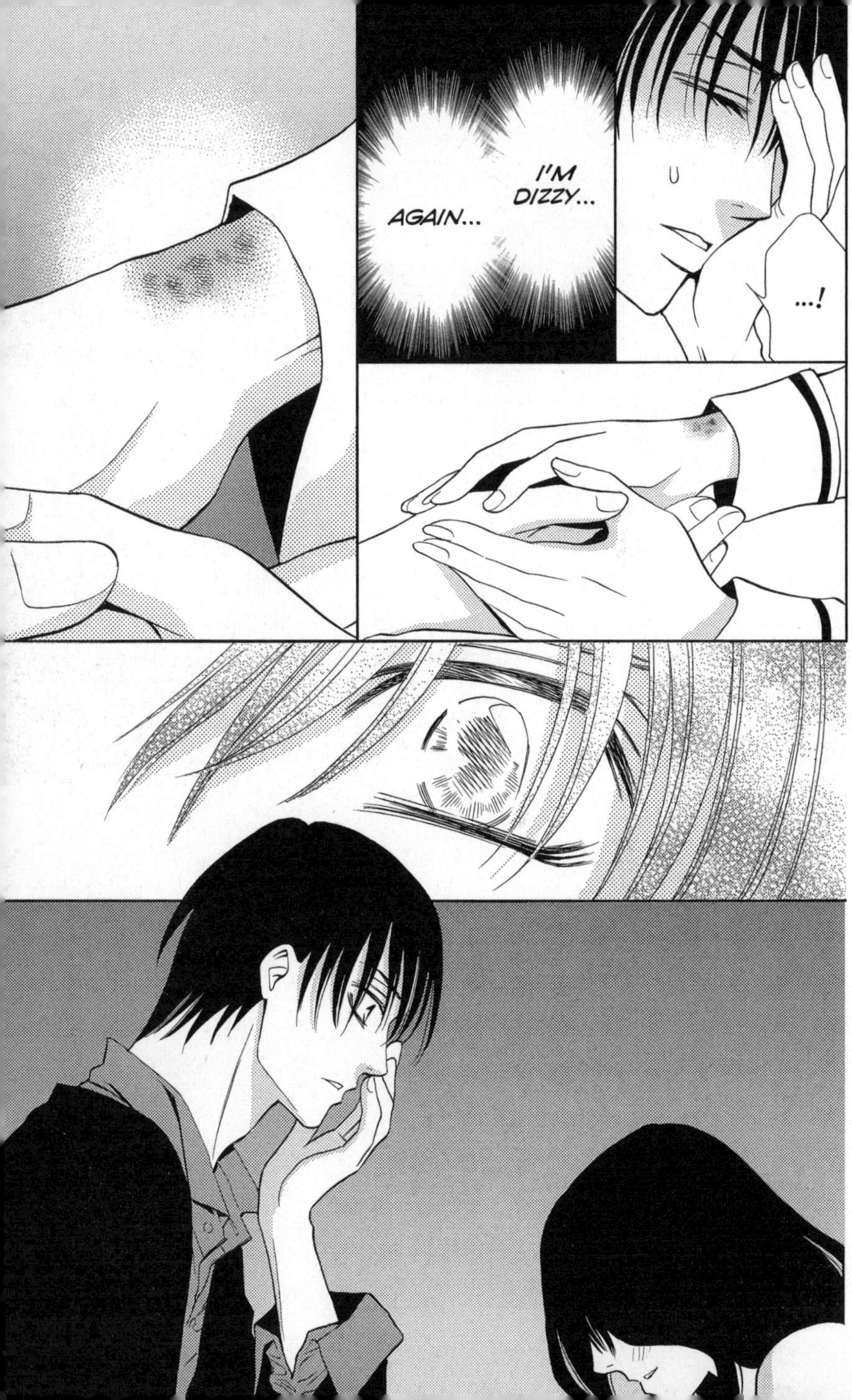
...!
I'M DIZZY...
AGAIN...

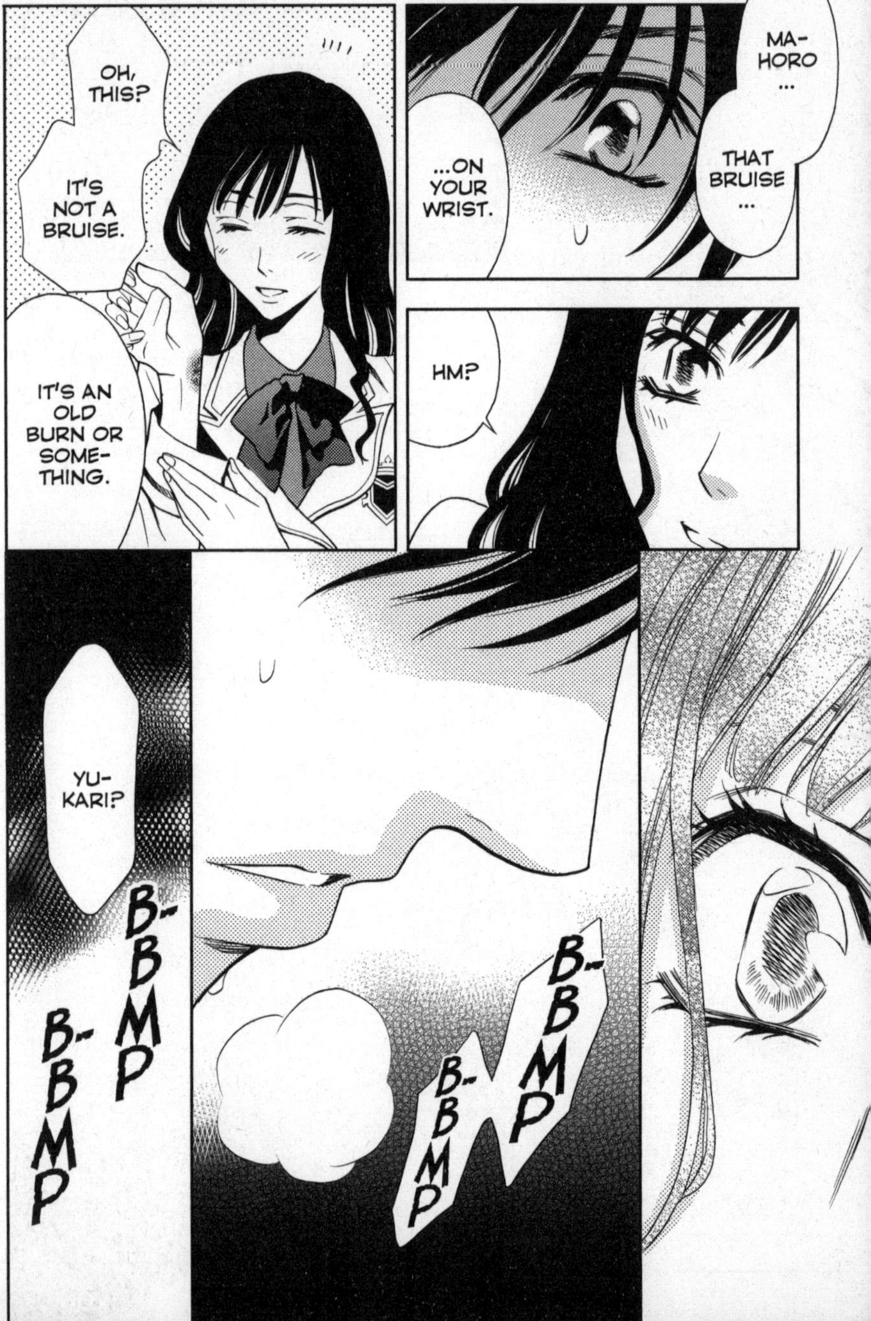
MA-HORO ...
THAT BRUISE ...
...ON YOUR WRIST.
HM?
OH, THIS?
IT'S NOT A BRUISE.
IT'S AN OLD BURN OR SOME-THING.
B-BBMP
B-BBMP
YU-KARI?
B-BBMP
B-BBMP

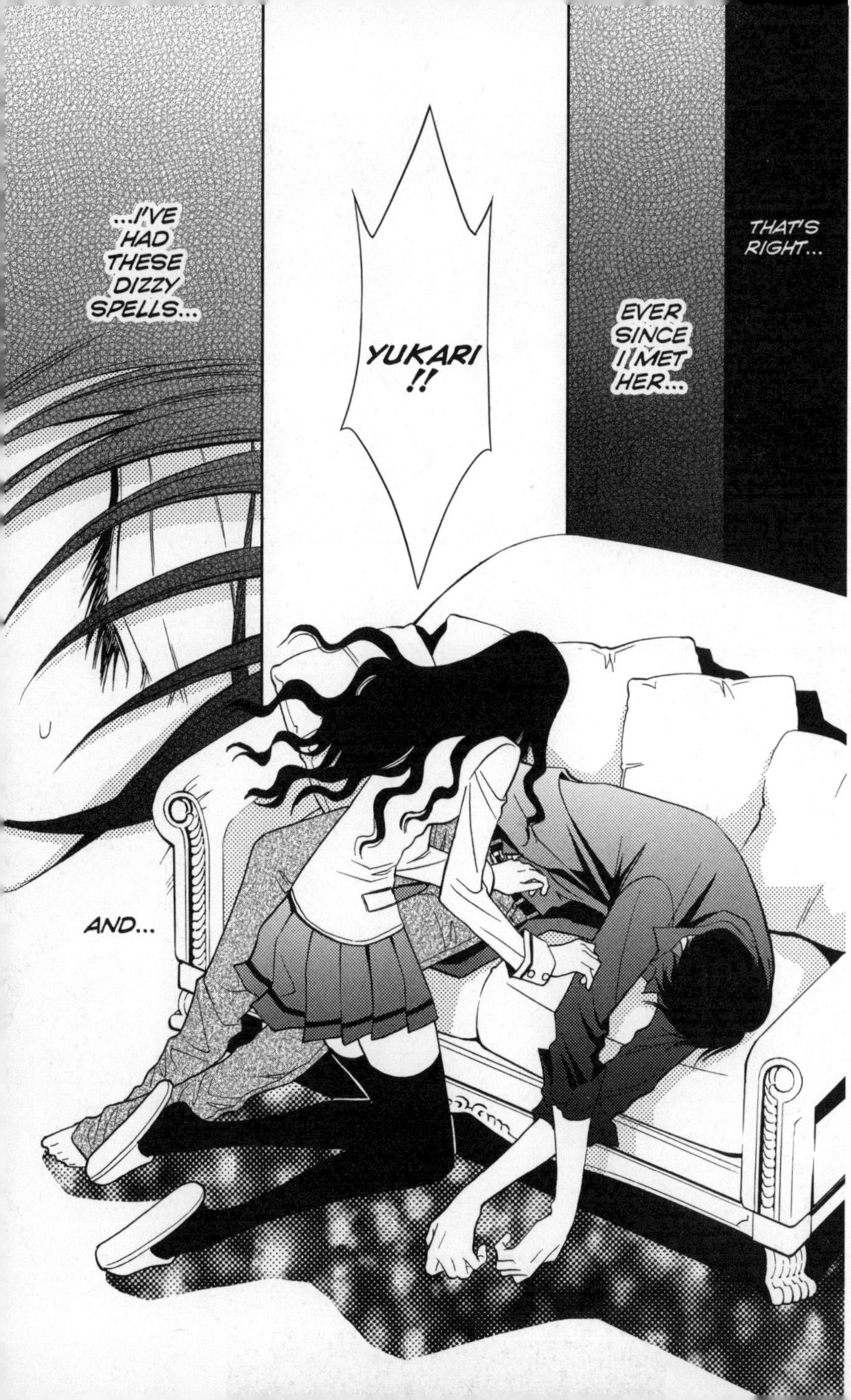
THAT'S RIGHT...
EVER SINCE I MET HER...
YUKARI !!
...I'VE HAD THESE DIZZY SPELLS...
AND...

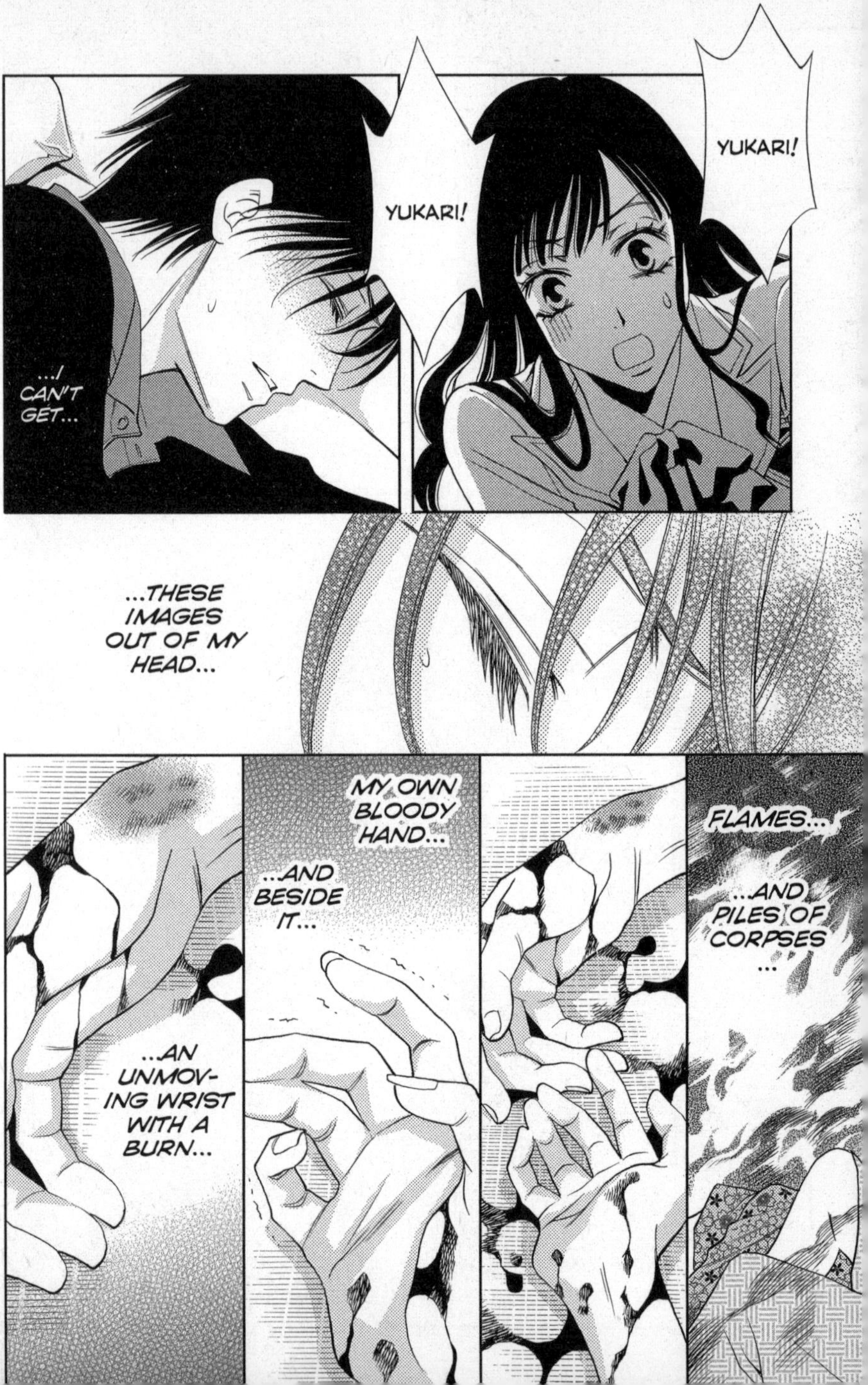
YUKARI!
YUKARI!
...I CAN'T GET...
...THESE IMAGES OUT OF MY HEAD...
FLAMES...
...AND PILES OF CORPSES ...
MY OWN BLOODY HAND...
...AND BESIDE IT...
...AN UNMOV-ING WRIST WITH A BURN...

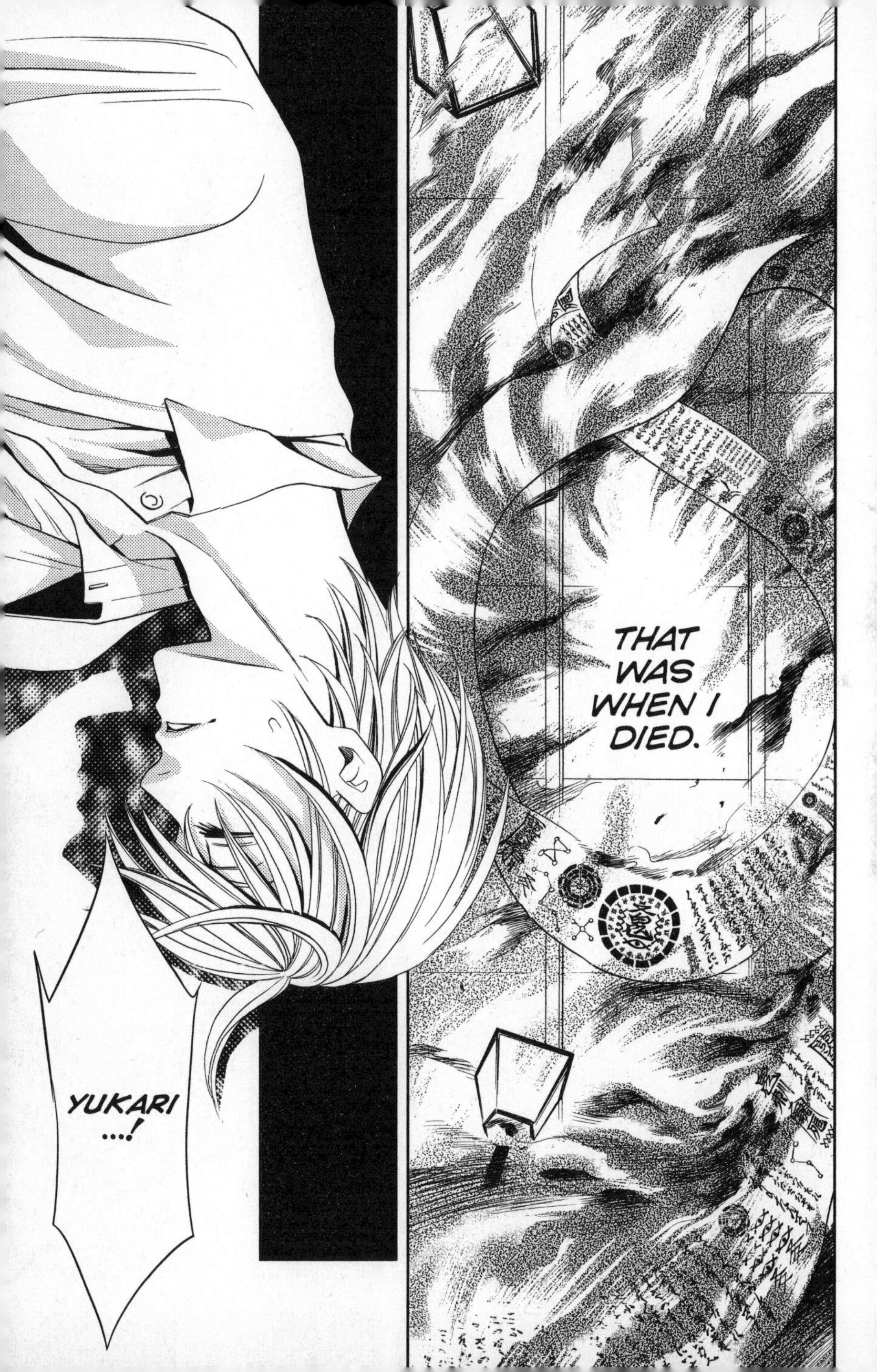
THAT WAS WHEN I DIED.
YUKARI ...!

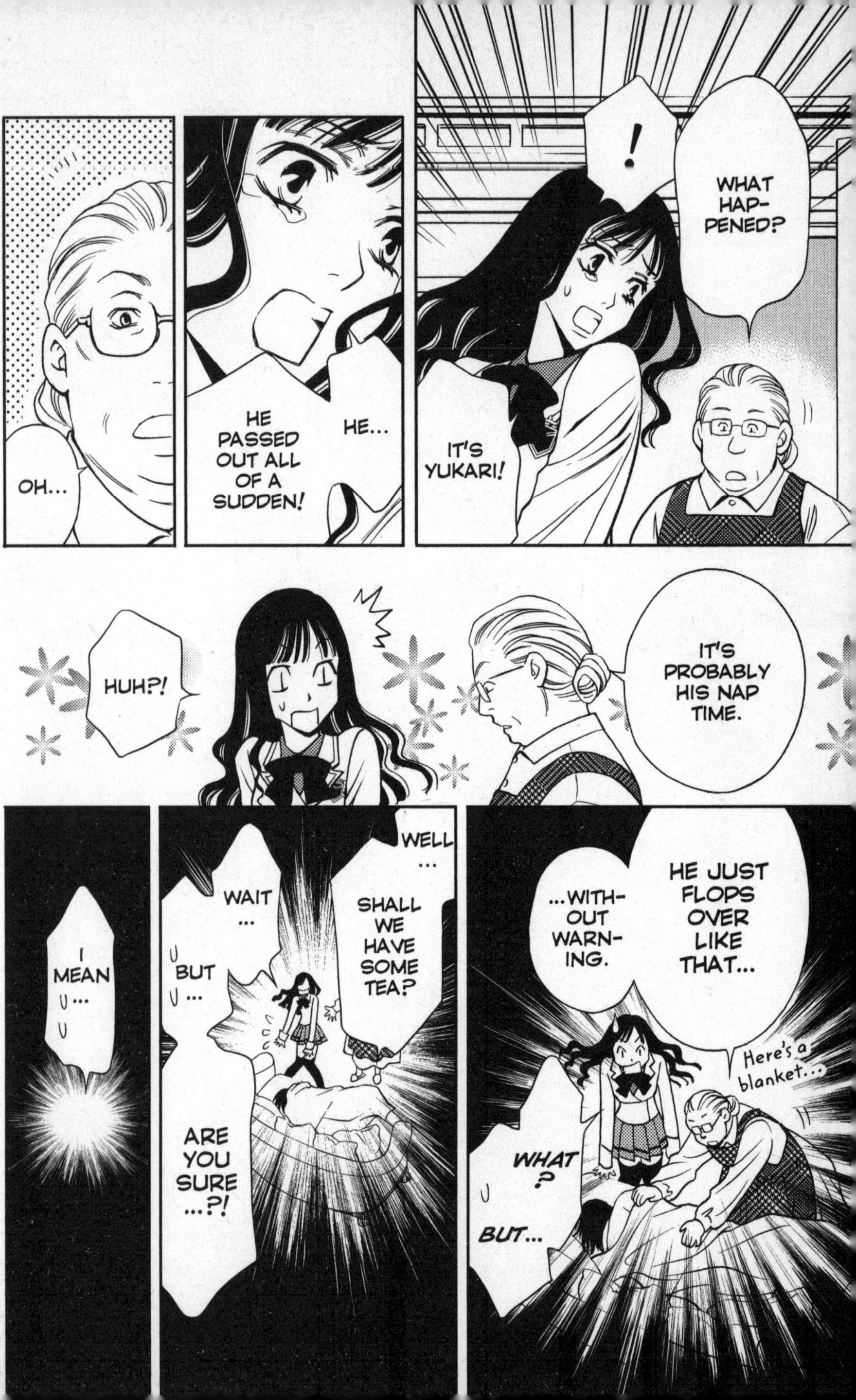
!
WHAT HAP-PENED?
IT'S YUKARI!
HE...
HE PASSED OUT ALL OF A SUDDEN!
OH...
IT'S PROBABLY HIS NAP TIME.
HUH?!
HE JUST FLOPS OVER LIKE THAT...
...WITH-OUT WARN-ING.
Here's a blanket...
WHAT?
BUT...
WELL...
SHALL WE HAVE SOME TEA?
WAIT...
BUT...
ARE YOU SURE...?!
I MEAN...

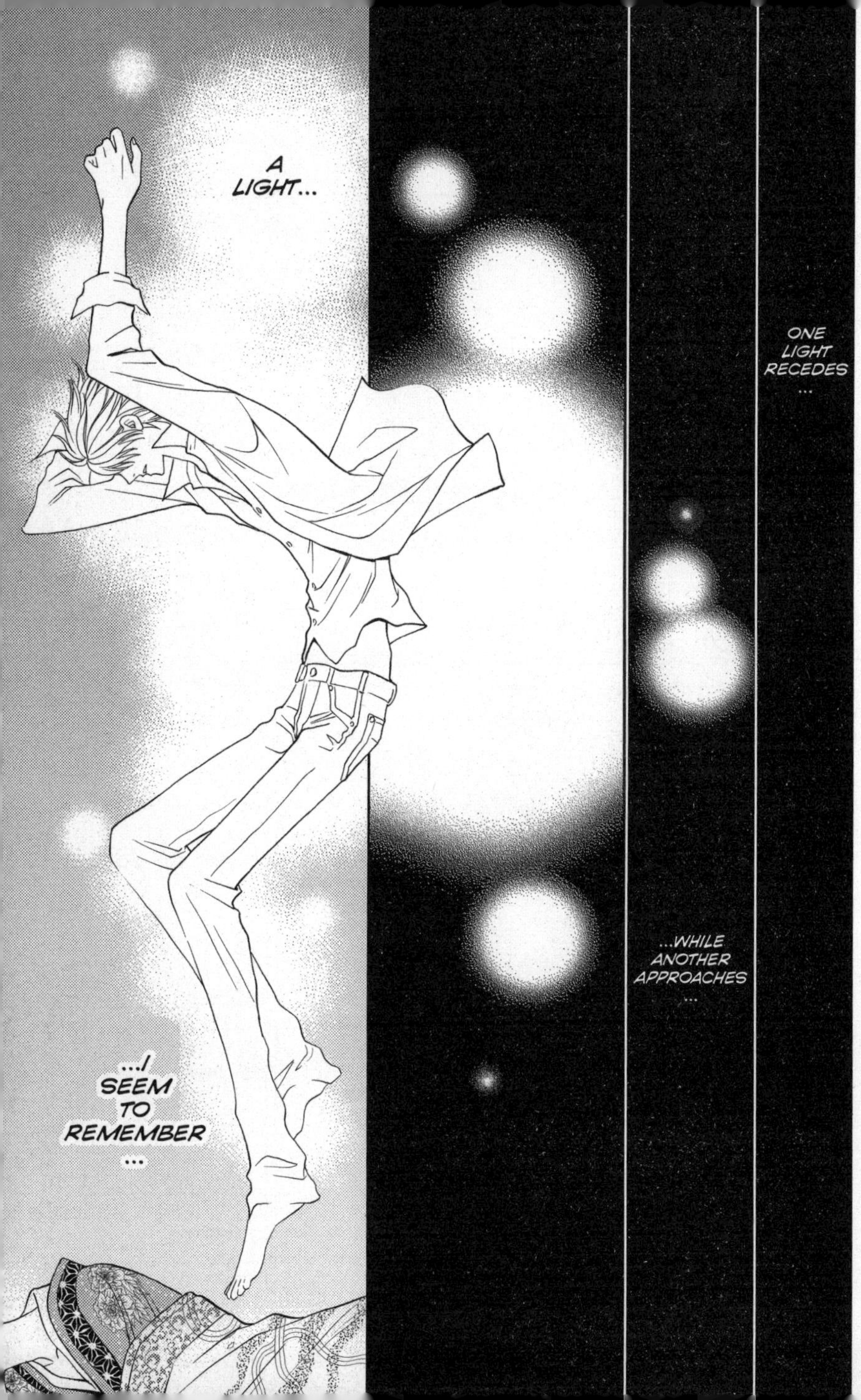
ONE LIGHT RECEDES ...
...WHILE ANOTHER APPROACHES ...
A LIGHT...
...I SEEM TO REMEMBER ...

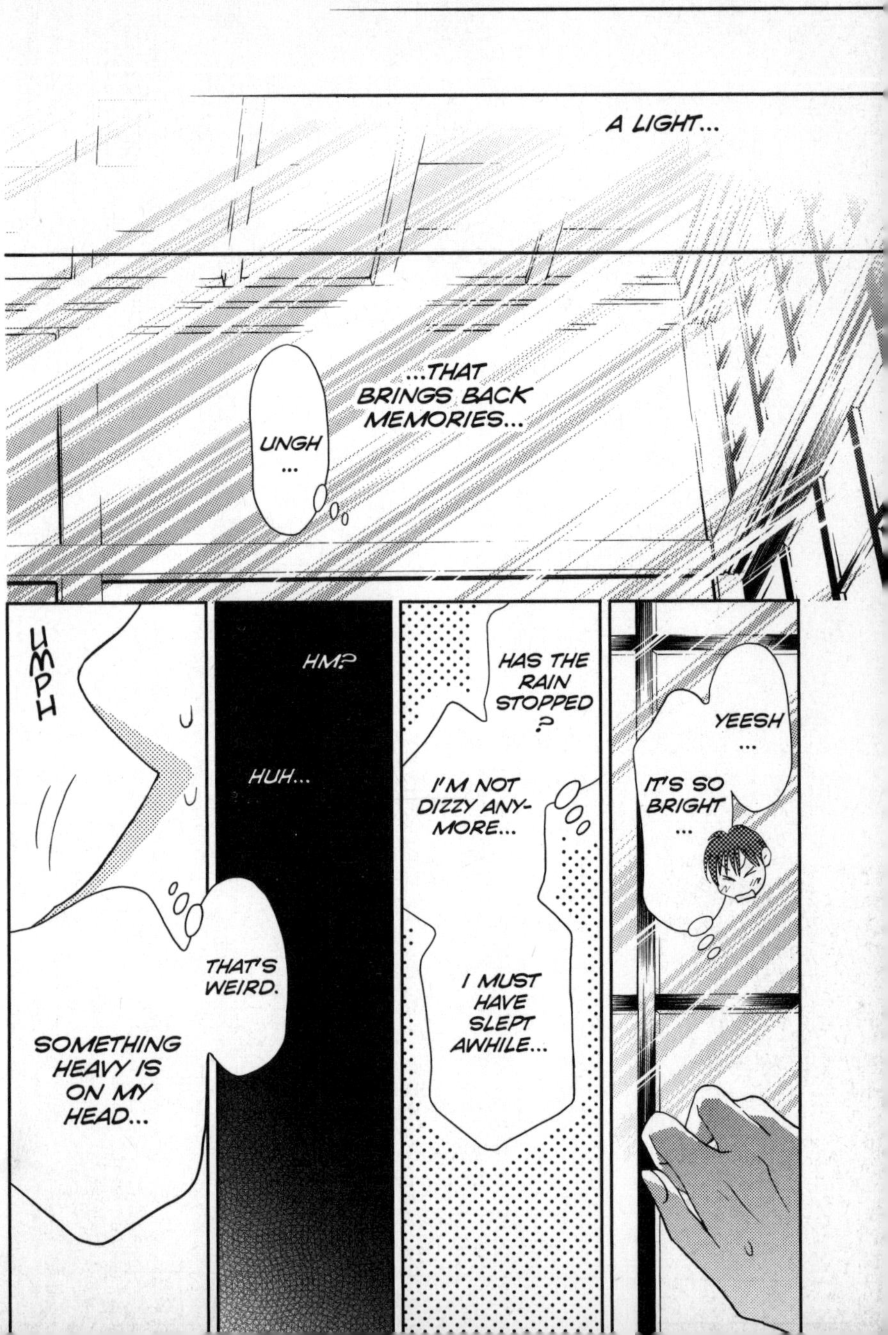
A LIGHT...
...THAT BRINGS BACK MEMORIES...
UNGH ...
YEESH ...
IT'S SO BRIGHT ...
HAS THE RAIN STOPPED ?
I'M NOT DIZZY ANY-MORE...
I MUST HAVE SLEPT AWHILE...
HM?
HUH...
UMPH
THAT'S WEIRD.
SOMETHING HEAVY IS ON MY HEAD...

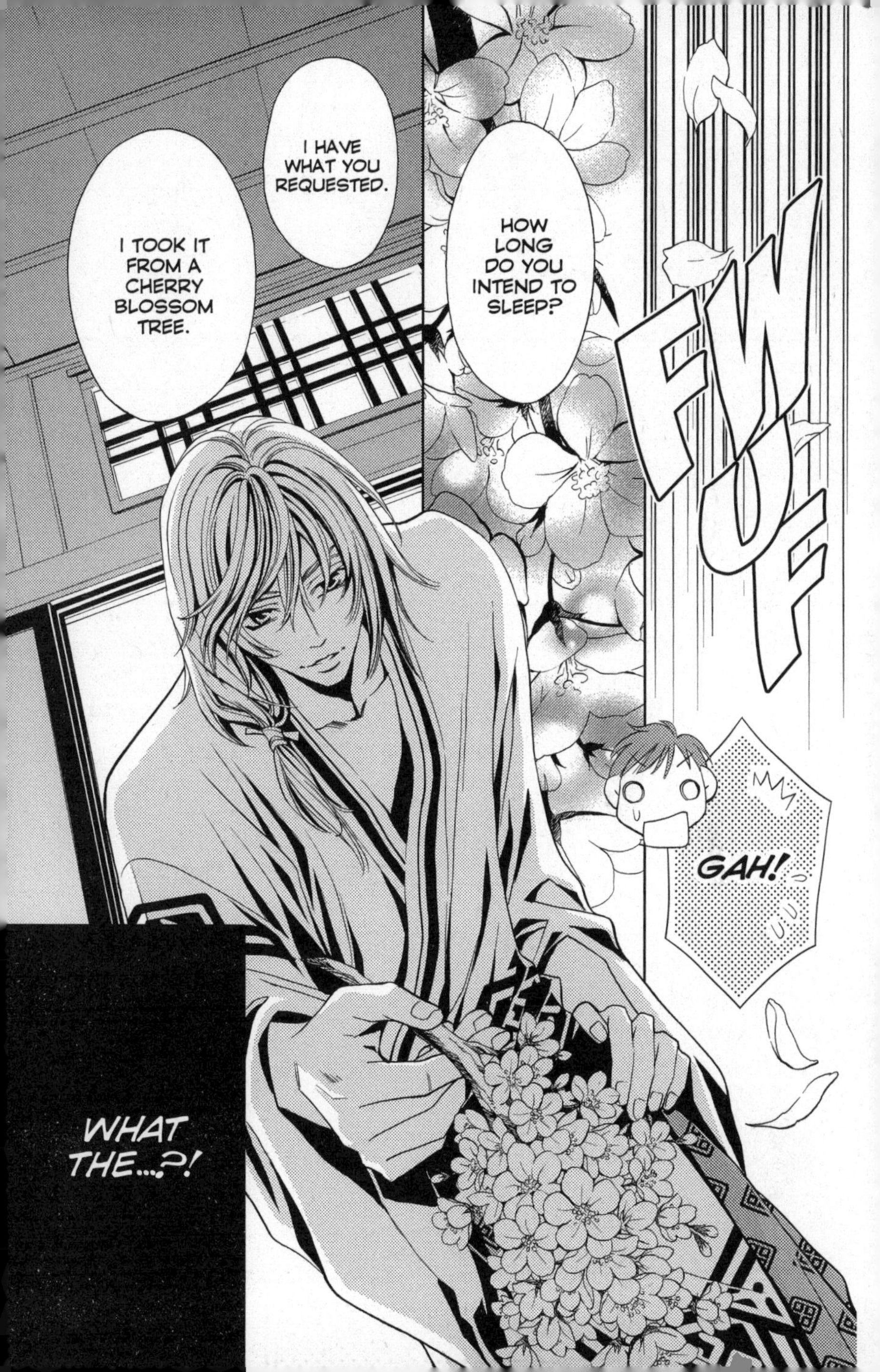
FWUF
GAH!
HOW LONG DO YOU INTEND TO SLEEP?
I HAVE WHAT YOU REQUESTED.
I TOOK IT FROM A CHERRY BLOSSOM TREE.
WHAT THE...?!

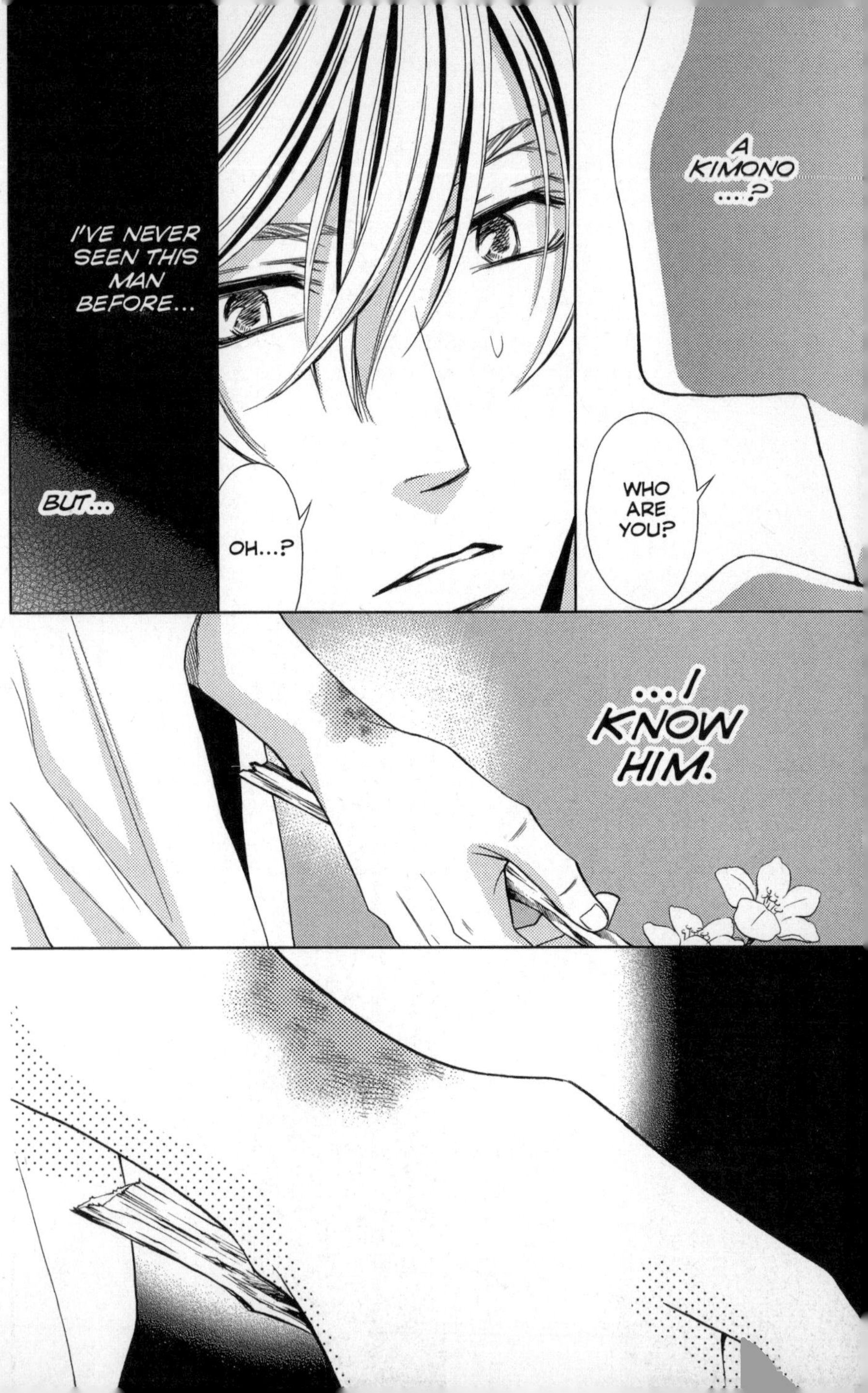
A KIMONO ...?
WHO ARE YOU?
OH...?
I'VE NEVER SEEN THIS MAN BEFORE...
BUT...
...I KNOW HIM.

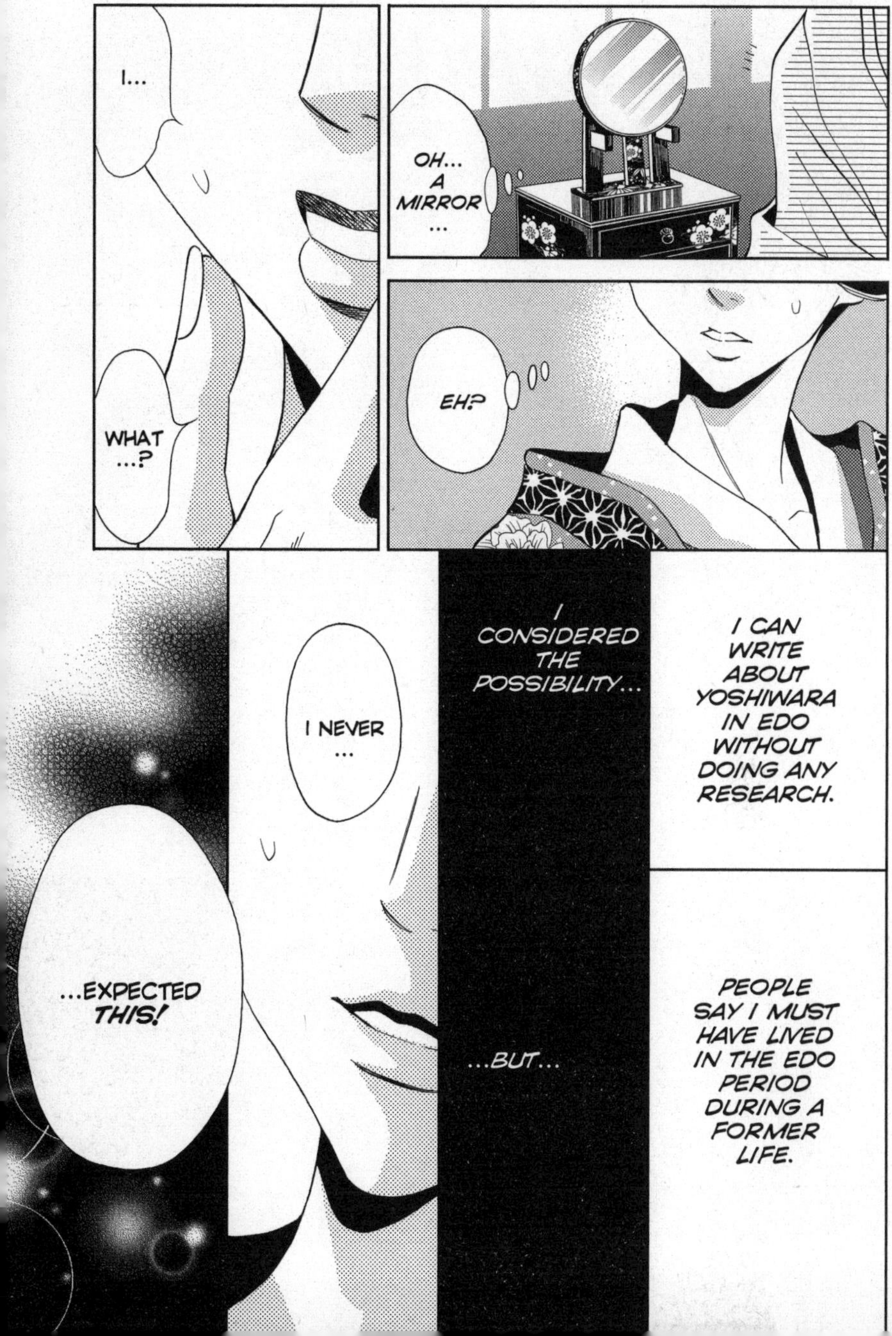
OH... A MIRROR ...
EH?
I...
WHAT ...?
I CAN WRITE ABOUT YOSHIWARA IN EDO WITHOUT DOING ANY RESEARCH.
PEOPLE SAY I MUST HAVE LIVED IN THE EDO PERIOD DURING A FORMER LIFE.
I CONSIDERED THE POSSIBILITY...
...BUT...
I NEVER ...
...EXPECTED THIS!

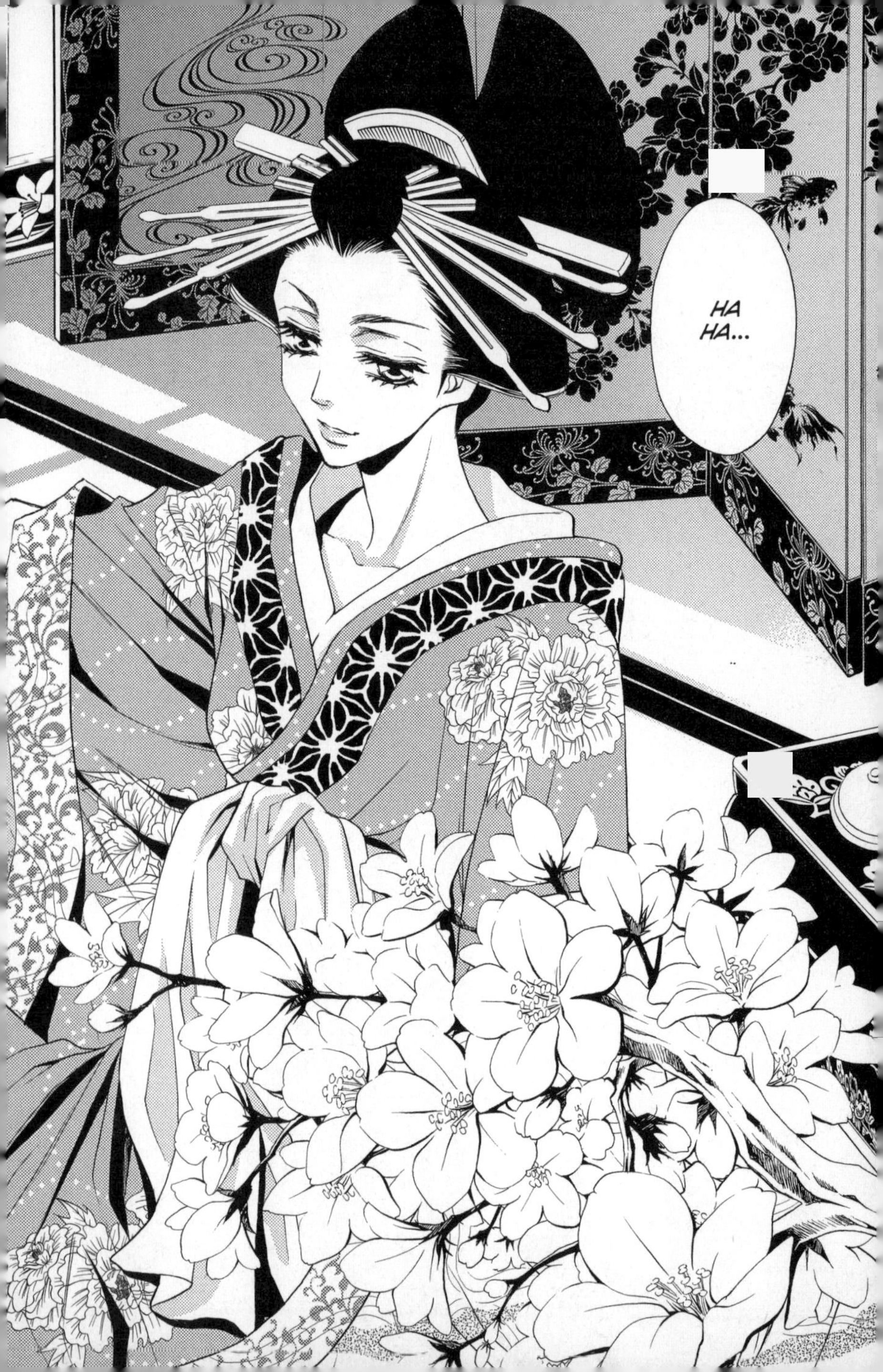
HA HA...

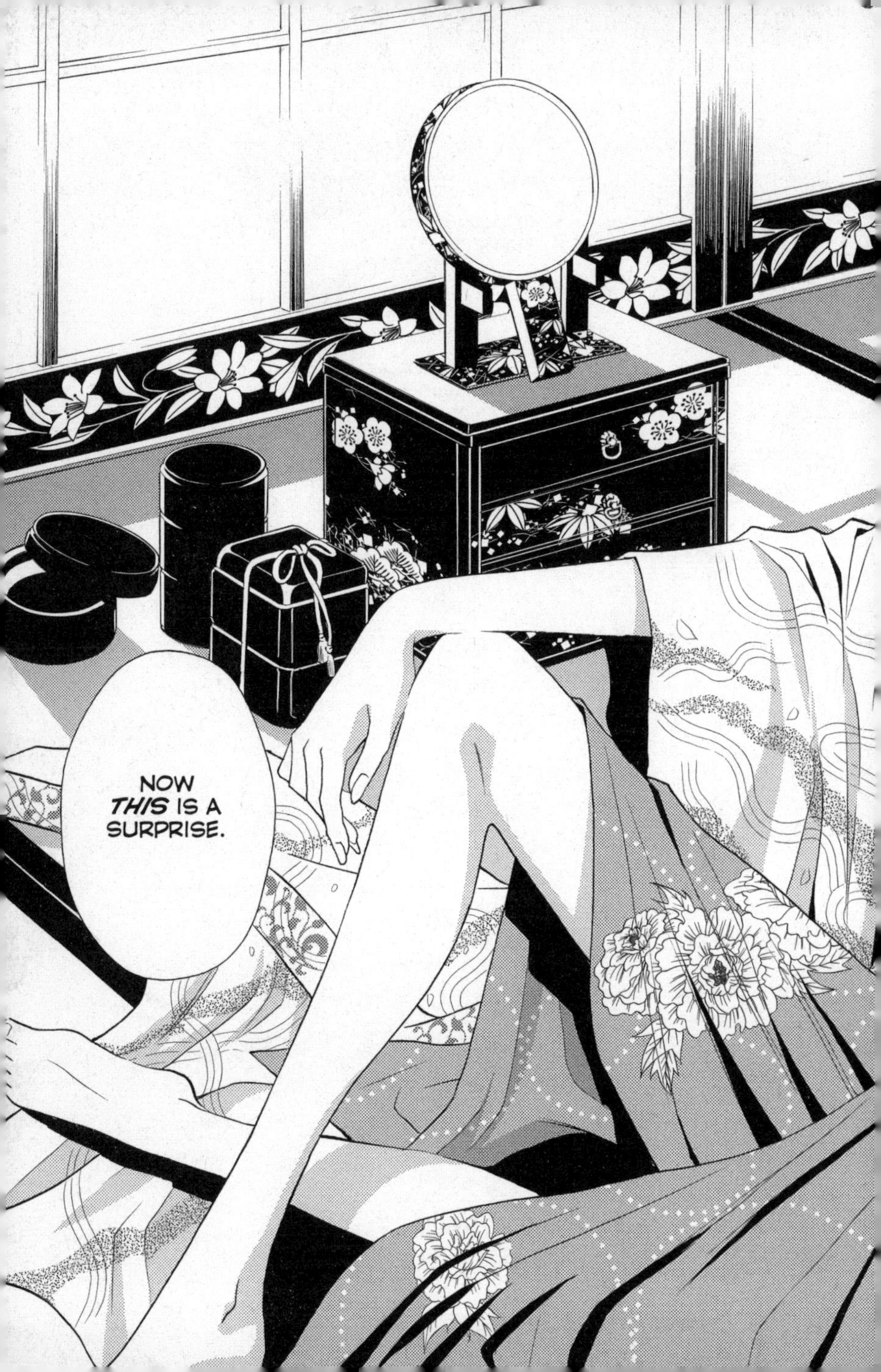
NOW *THIS* IS A SURPRISE.

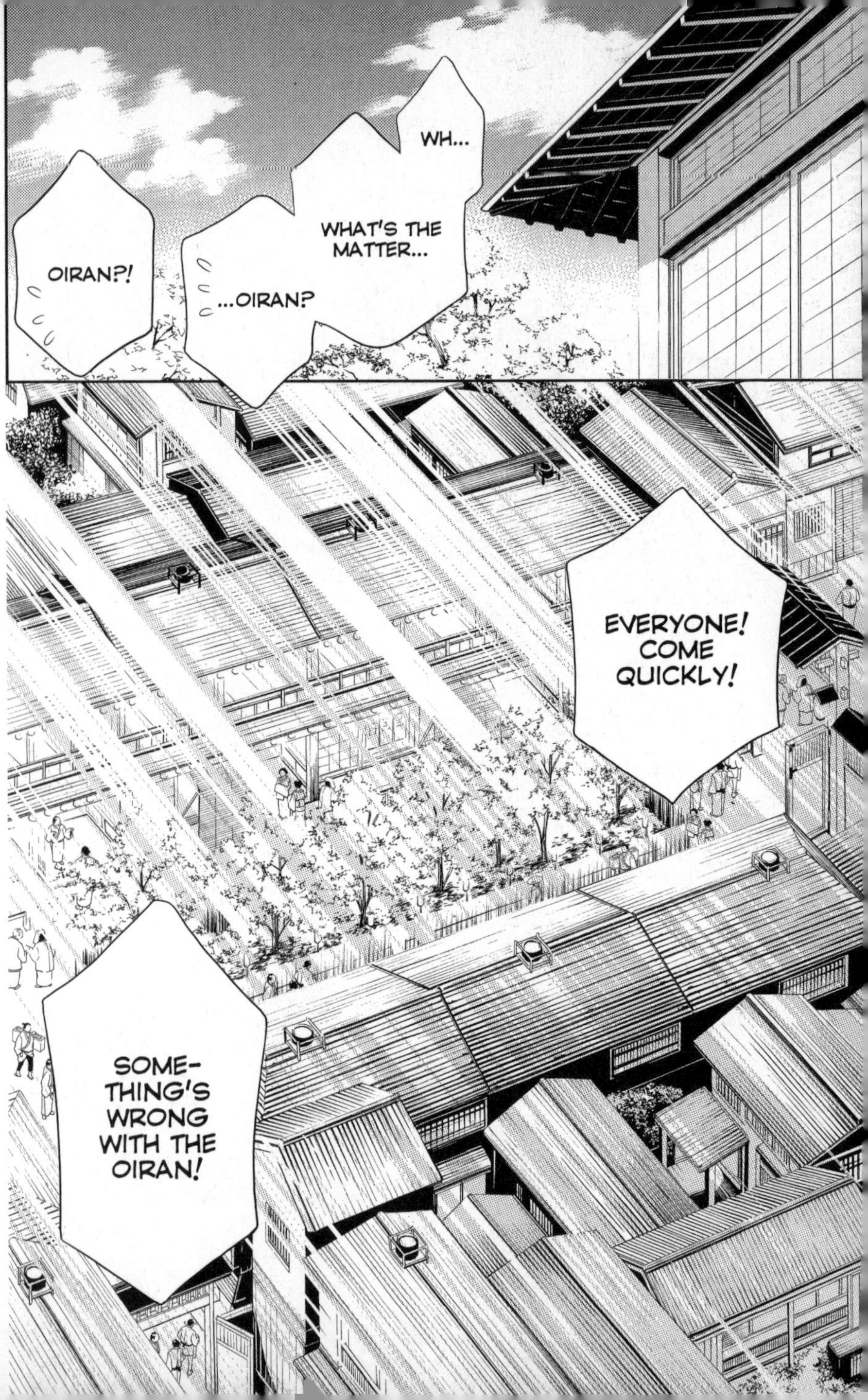
WH...
WHAT'S THE MATTER... ...OIRAN?
OIRAN?!
EVERYONE! COME QUICKLY!
SOME-THING'S WRONG WITH THE OIRAN!

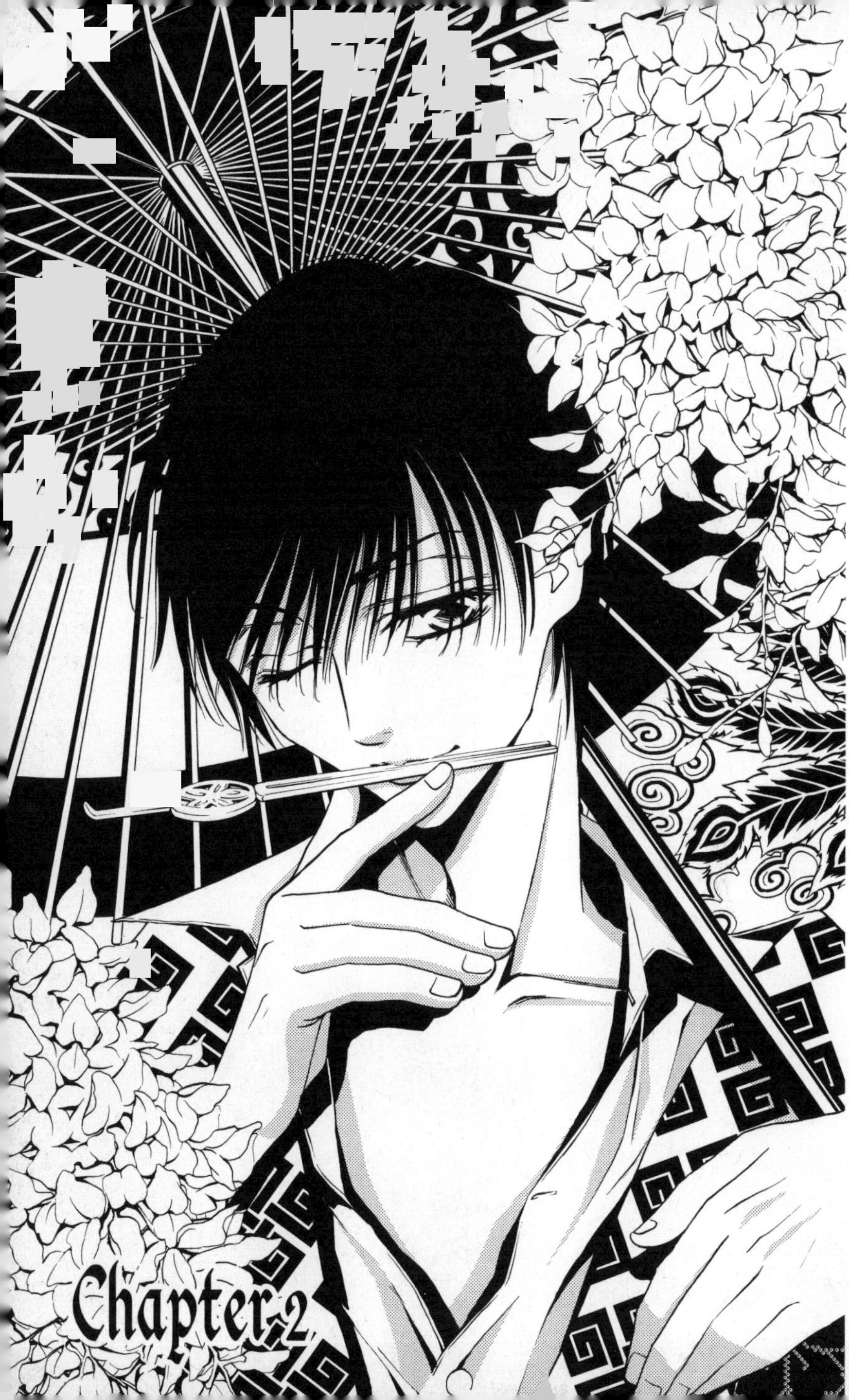
Chapter 2

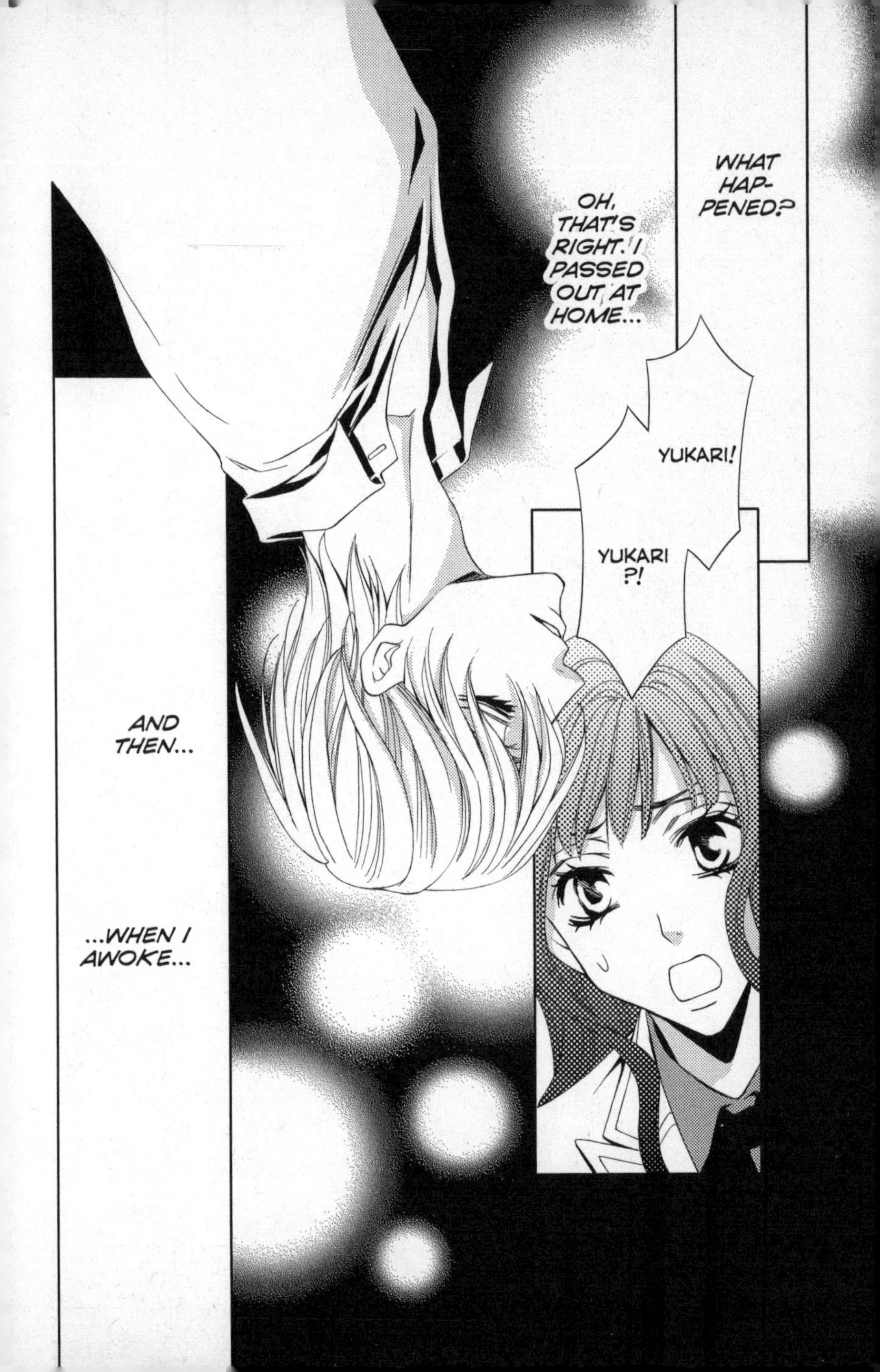
WHAT HAP-PENED?
OH, THAT'S RIGHT. I PASSED OUT AT HOME...
YUKARI!
YUKARI ?!
AND THEN...
...WHEN I AWOKE...

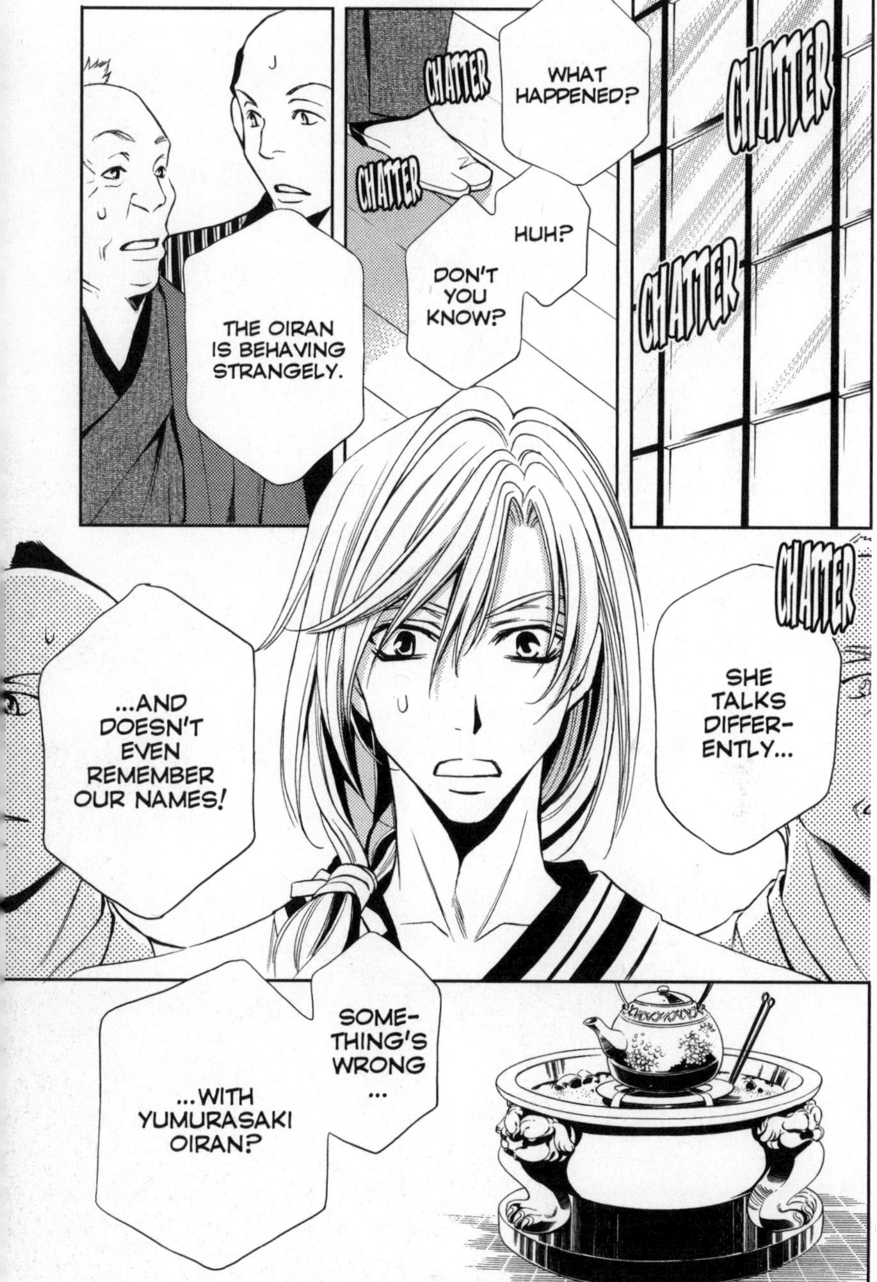
CHATTER
CHATTER
CHATTER
WHAT HAPPENED?
CHATTER
HUH?
DON'T YOU KNOW?
THE OIRAN IS BEHAVING STRANGELY.
CHATTER
SHE TALKS DIFFER-ENTLY...
...AND DOESN'T EVEN REMEMBER OUR NAMES!
SOME-THING'S WRONG ...
...WITH YUMURASAKI OIRAN?

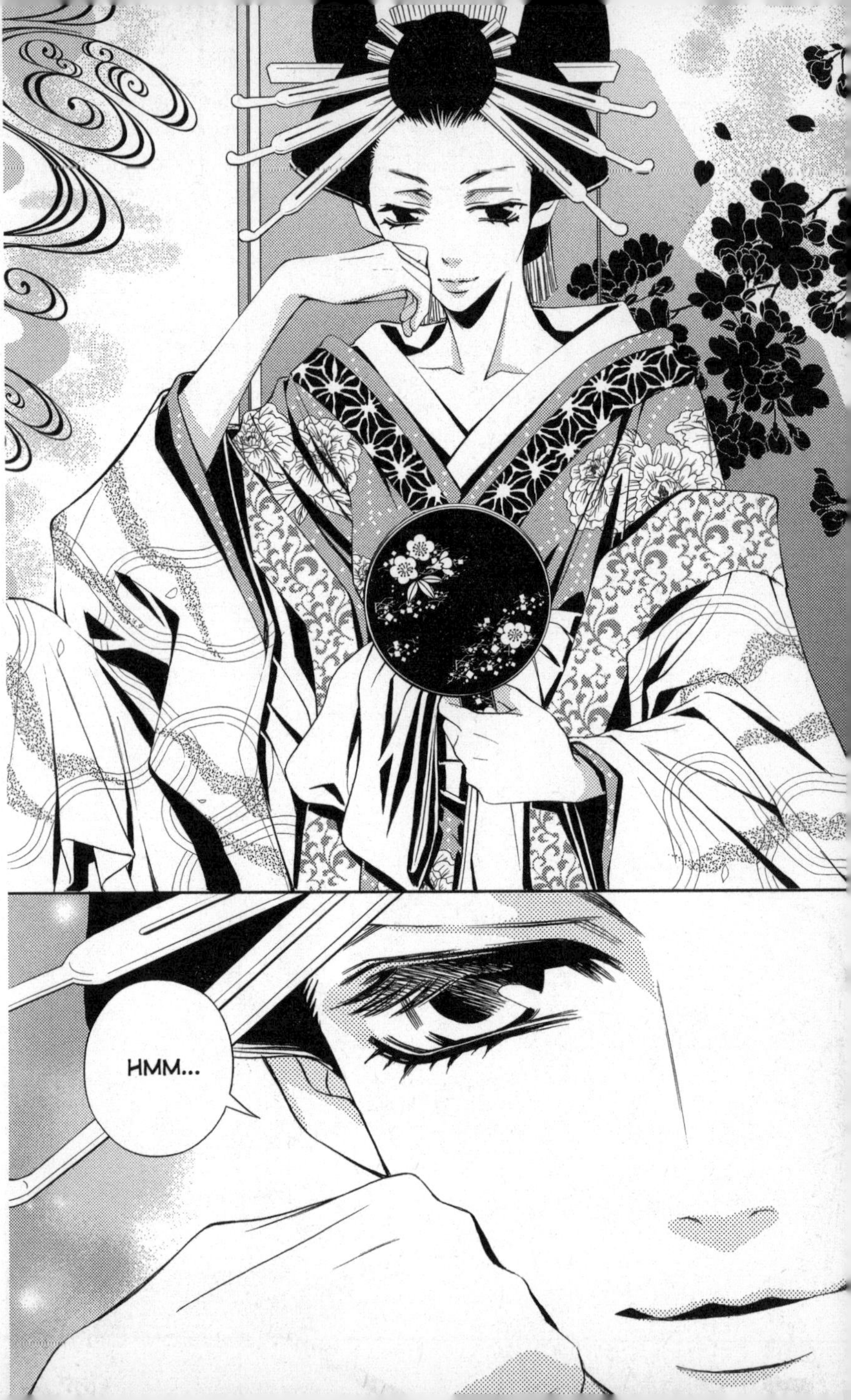
HMM...

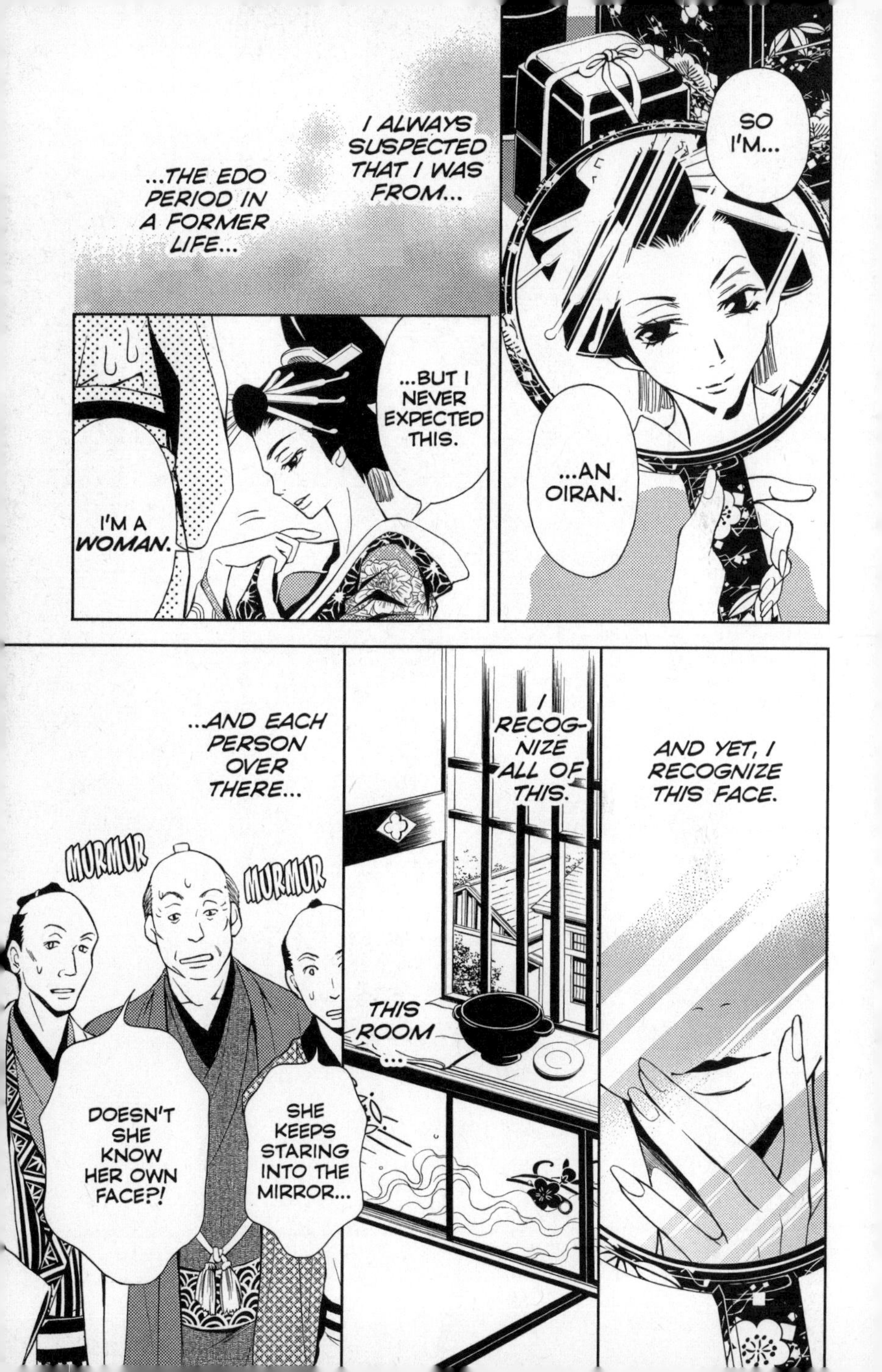
SO I'M...
...AN OIRAN.
I ALWAYS SUSPECTED THAT I WAS FROM...
...THE EDO PERIOD IN A FORMER LIFE...
...BUT I NEVER EXPECTED THIS.
I'M A *WOMAN.*
AND YET, I RECOGNIZE THIS FACE.
I RECOGNIZE ALL OF THIS.
THIS ROOM...
...AND EACH PERSON OVER THERE...
MURMUR
MURMUR
SHE KEEPS STARING INTO THE MIRROR...
DOESN'T SHE KNOW HER OWN FACE?!

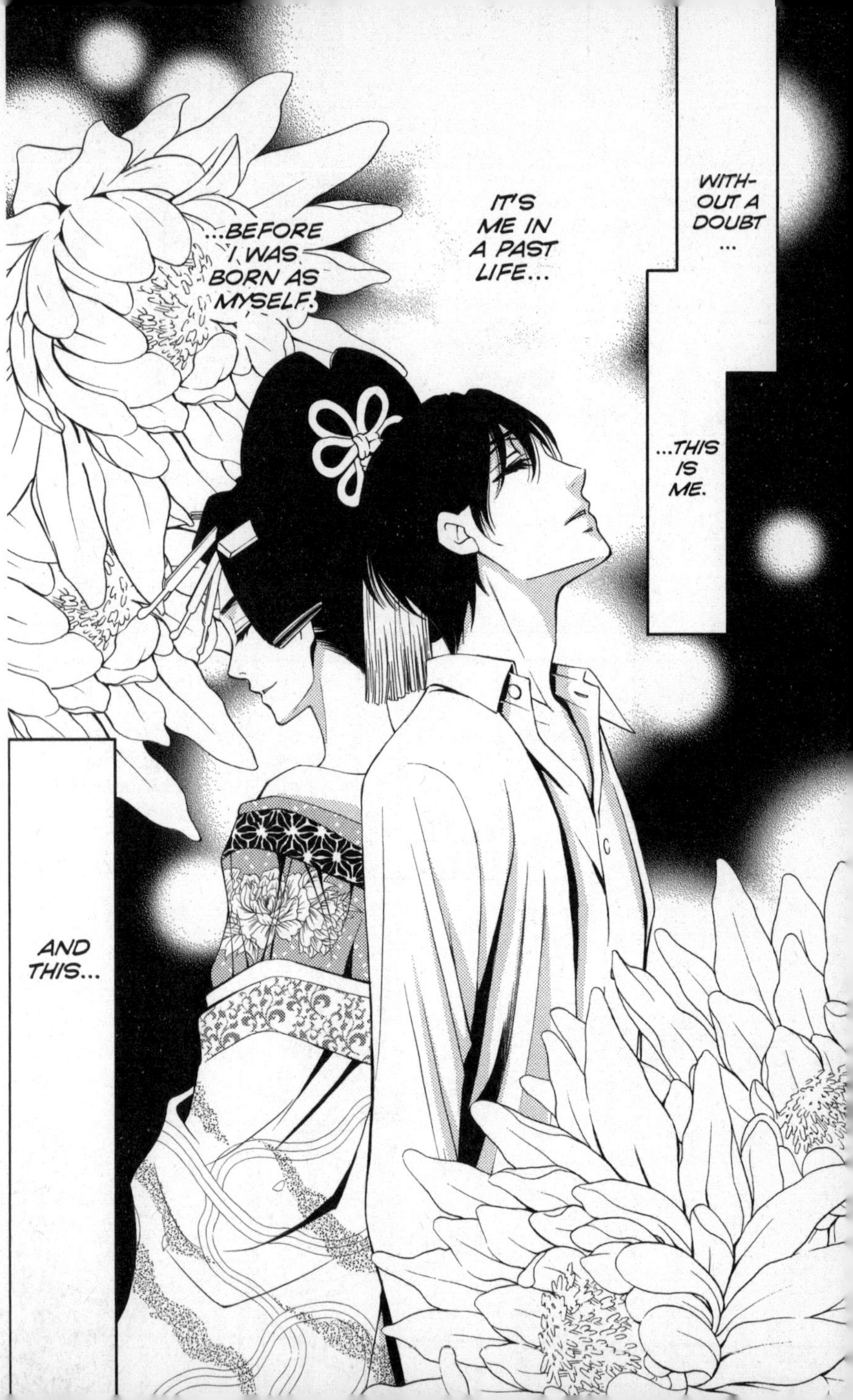
WITH-OUT A DOUBT...
...THIS IS ME.
IT'S ME IN A PAST LIFE...
...BEFORE I WAS BORN AS MYSELF.
AND THIS...

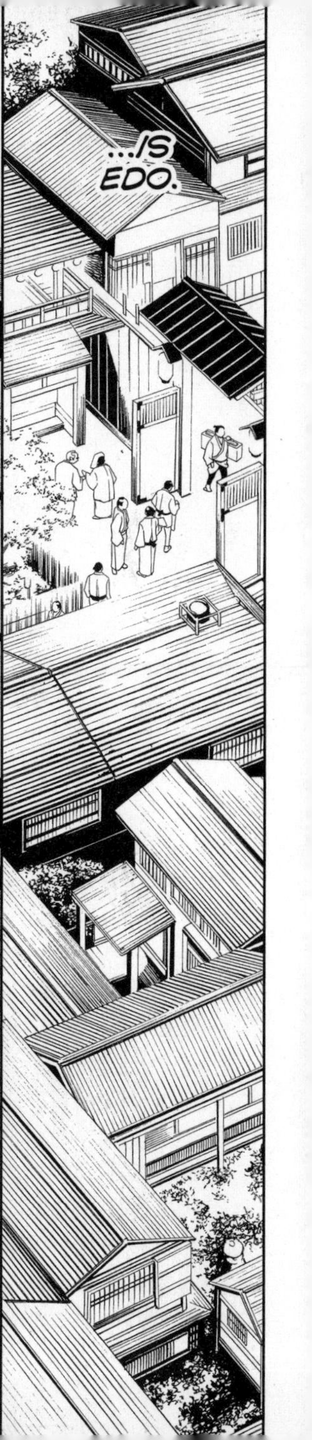
...IS EDO.

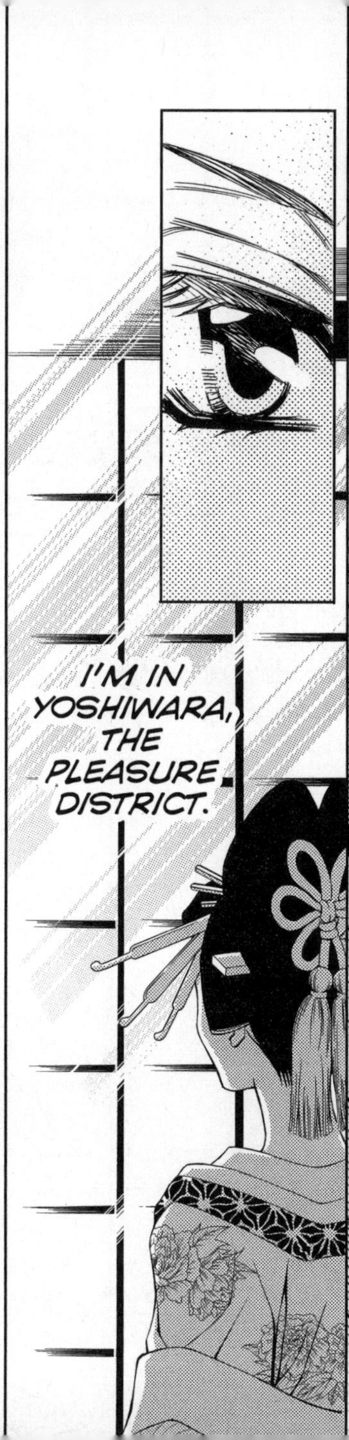
I'M IN YOSHIWARA, THE PLEASURE DISTRICT.

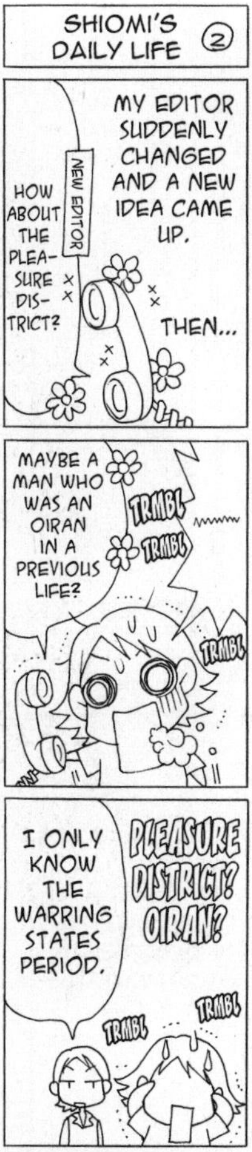
SHIOMI'S DAILY LIFE ②
MY EDITOR SUDDENLY CHANGED AND A NEW IDEA CAME UP.
NEW EDITOR
HOW ABOUT THE PLEA-SURE DIS-TRICT?
THEN...
TRMBL
TRMBL
TRMBL
MAYBE A MAN WHO WAS AN OIRAN IN A PREVIOUS LIFE?
PLEASURE DISTRICT? OIRAN?
I ONLY KNOW THE WARRING STATES PERIOD.
TRMBL
TRMBL
I BOUGHT A DOLL...
I GOTTA DRAW THIS?
CAN'T SOME-ONE ELSE DO IT?
TRMBL TRMBL
AM I GONNA DRAW THE HAIRPINS?

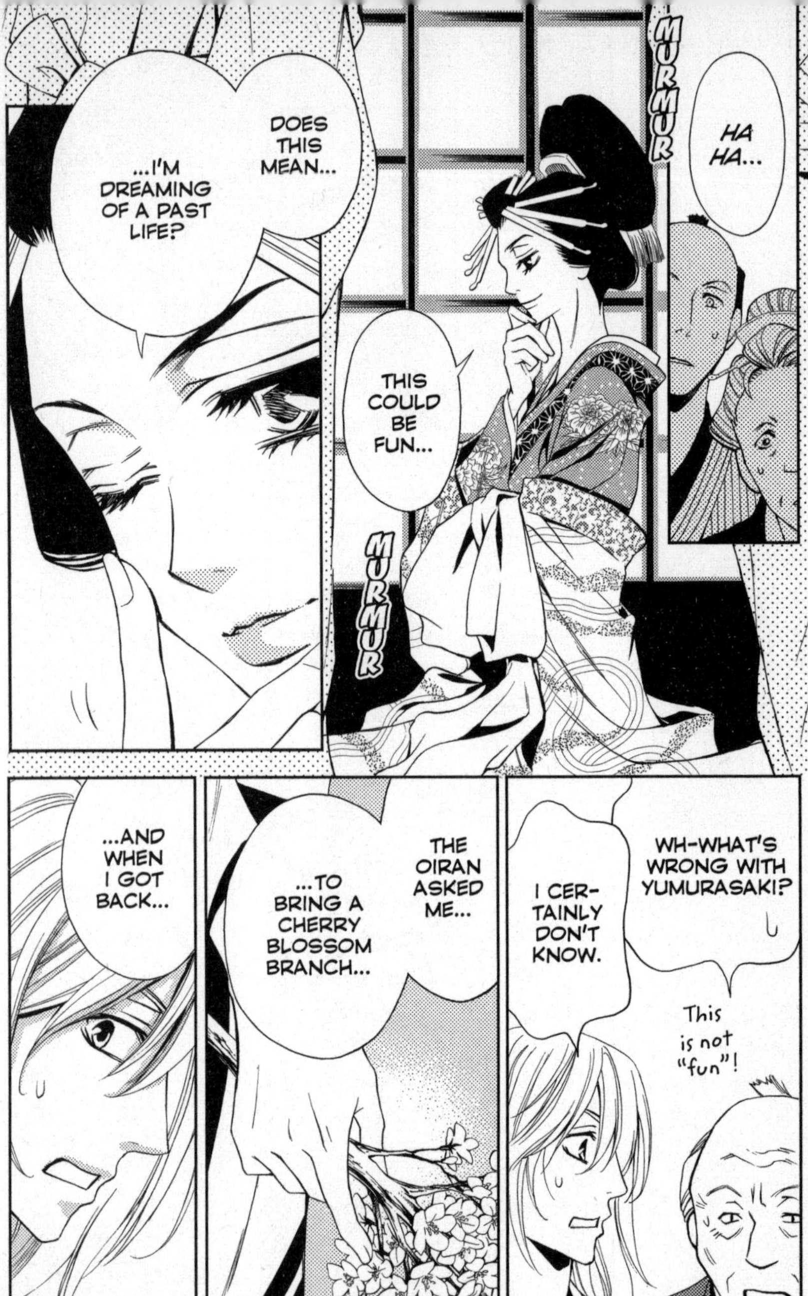
MURMUR
HA HA...
THIS COULD BE FUN...
MURMUR
DOES THIS MEAN...
...I'M DREAMING OF A PAST LIFE?
WH-WHAT'S WRONG WITH YUMURASAKI?
I CER-TAINLY DON'T KNOW.
This is not "fun"!
THE OIRAN ASKED ME...
...TO BRING A CHERRY BLOSSOM BRANCH...
...AND WHEN I GOT BACK...

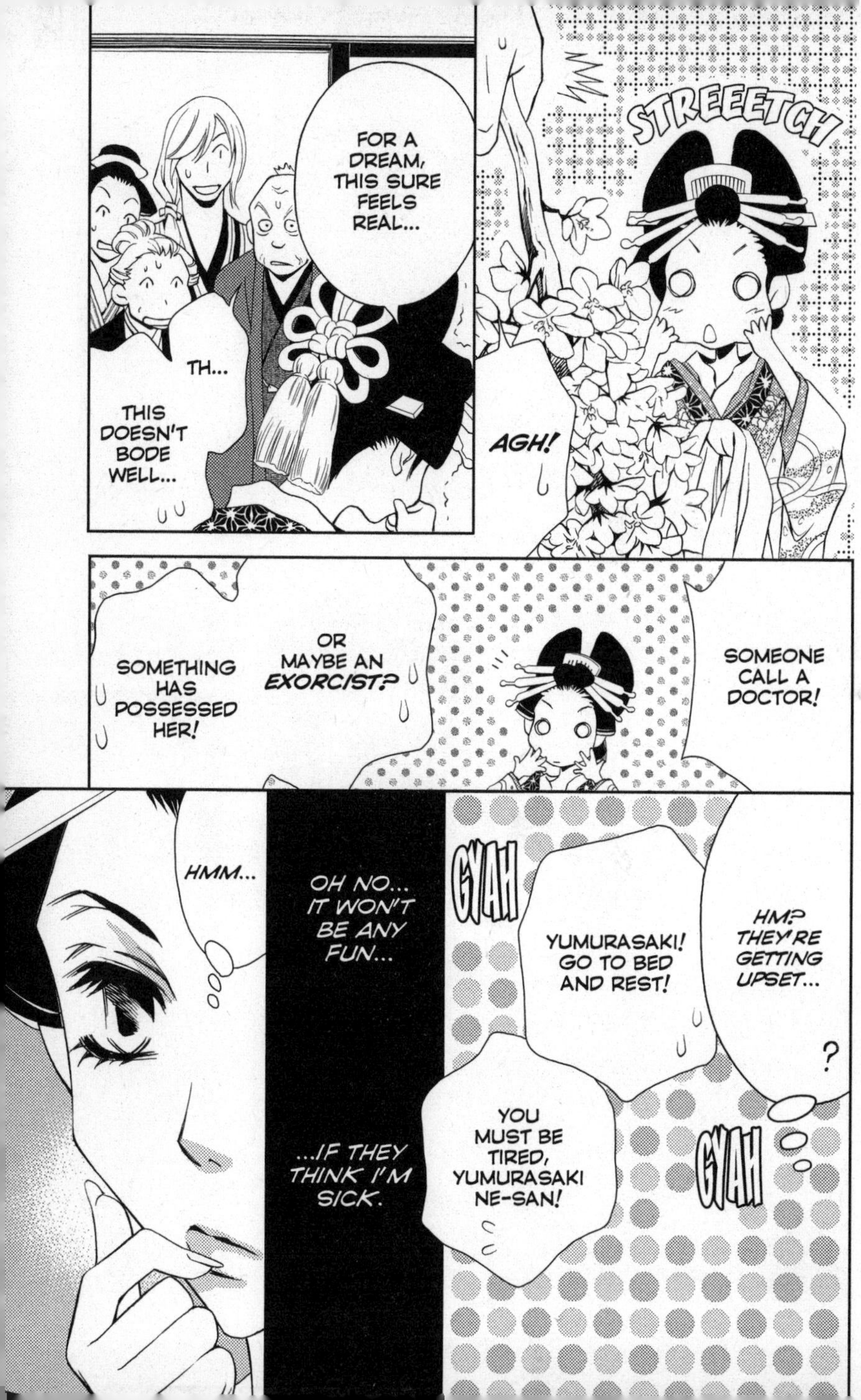
STREEETCH
AGH!
FOR A DREAM, THIS SURE FEELS REAL...
TH...
THIS DOESN'T BODE WELL...
SOMEONE CALL A DOCTOR!
OR MAYBE AN *EXORCIST?*
SOMETHING HAS POSSESSED HER!
HM? THEY'RE GETTING UPSET...
?
GYAH
YUMURASAKI! GO TO BED AND REST!
GYAH
YOU MUST BE TIRED, YUMURASAKI NE-SAN!
OH NO... IT WON'T BE ANY FUN...
...IF THEY THINK I'M SICK.
HMM...

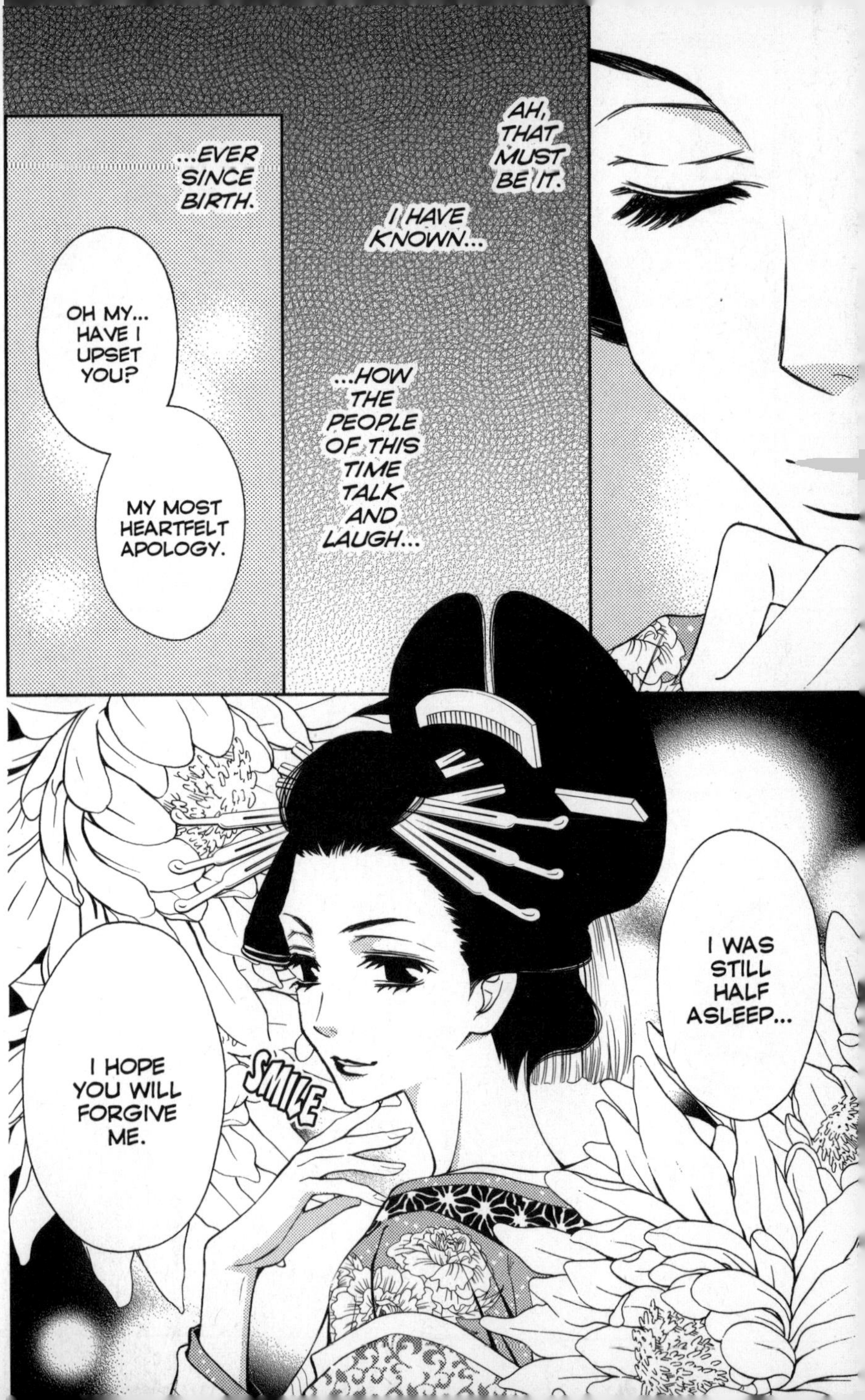
AH, THAT MUST BE IT.
I HAVE KNOWN...
...HOW THE PEOPLE OF THIS TIME TALK AND LAUGH...
...EVER SINCE BIRTH.
OH MY... HAVE I UPSET YOU?
MY MOST HEARTFELT APOLOGY.
I WAS STILL HALF ASLEEP...
SMILE
I HOPE YOU WILL FORGIVE ME.

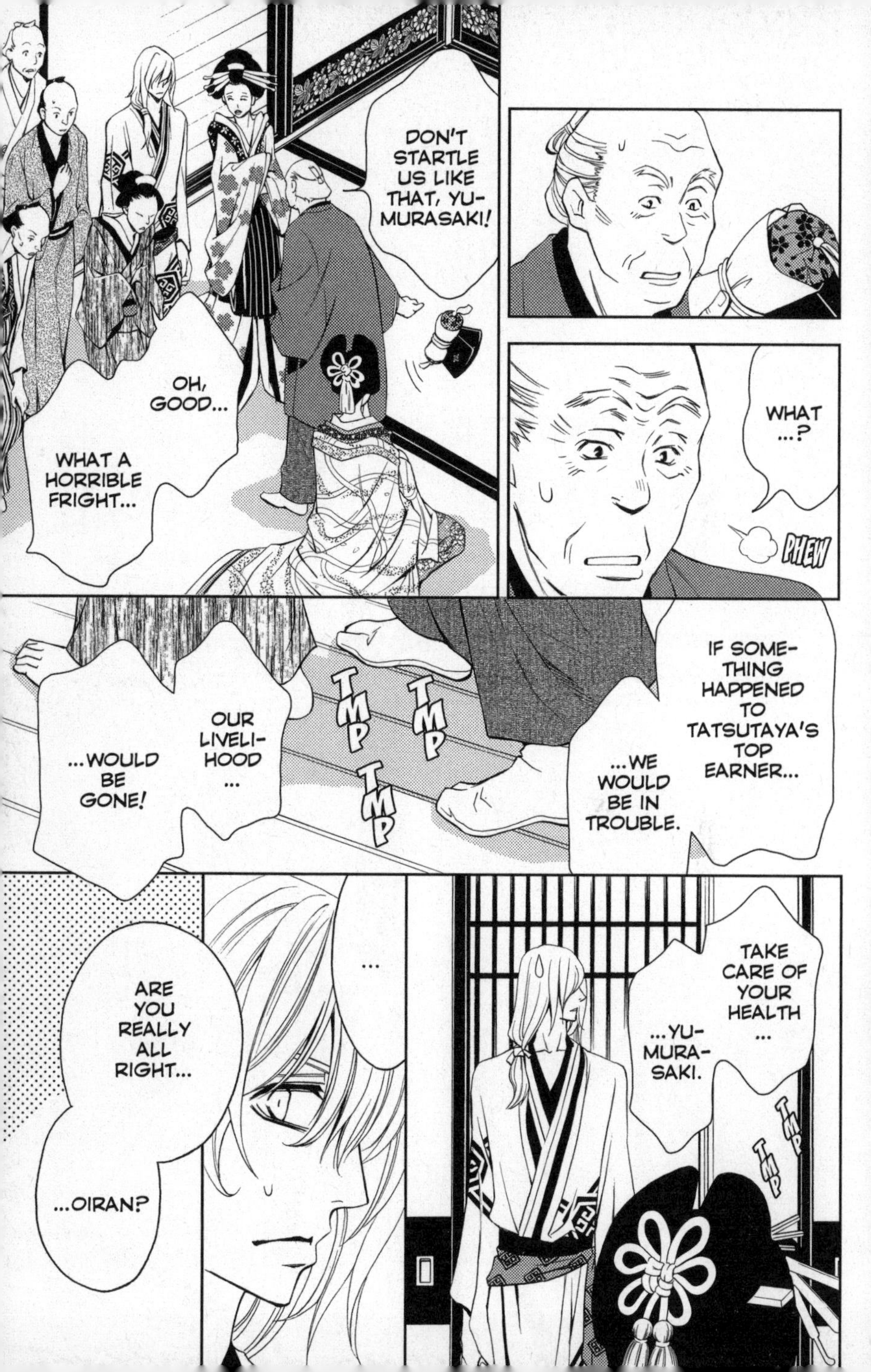
WHAT ...?
PHEW
DON'T STARTLE US LIKE THAT, YU-MURASAKI!
OH, GOOD...
WHAT A HORRIBLE FRIGHT...
IF SOMETHING HAPPENED TO TATSUTAYA'S TOP EARNER...
...WE WOULD BE IN TROUBLE.
TMP TMP
TMP
OUR LIVELIHOOD...
...WOULD BE GONE!
TAKE CARE OF YOUR HEALTH...
...YU-MURASAKI.
TMP TMP
...
ARE YOU REALLY ALL RIGHT...
...OIRAN?

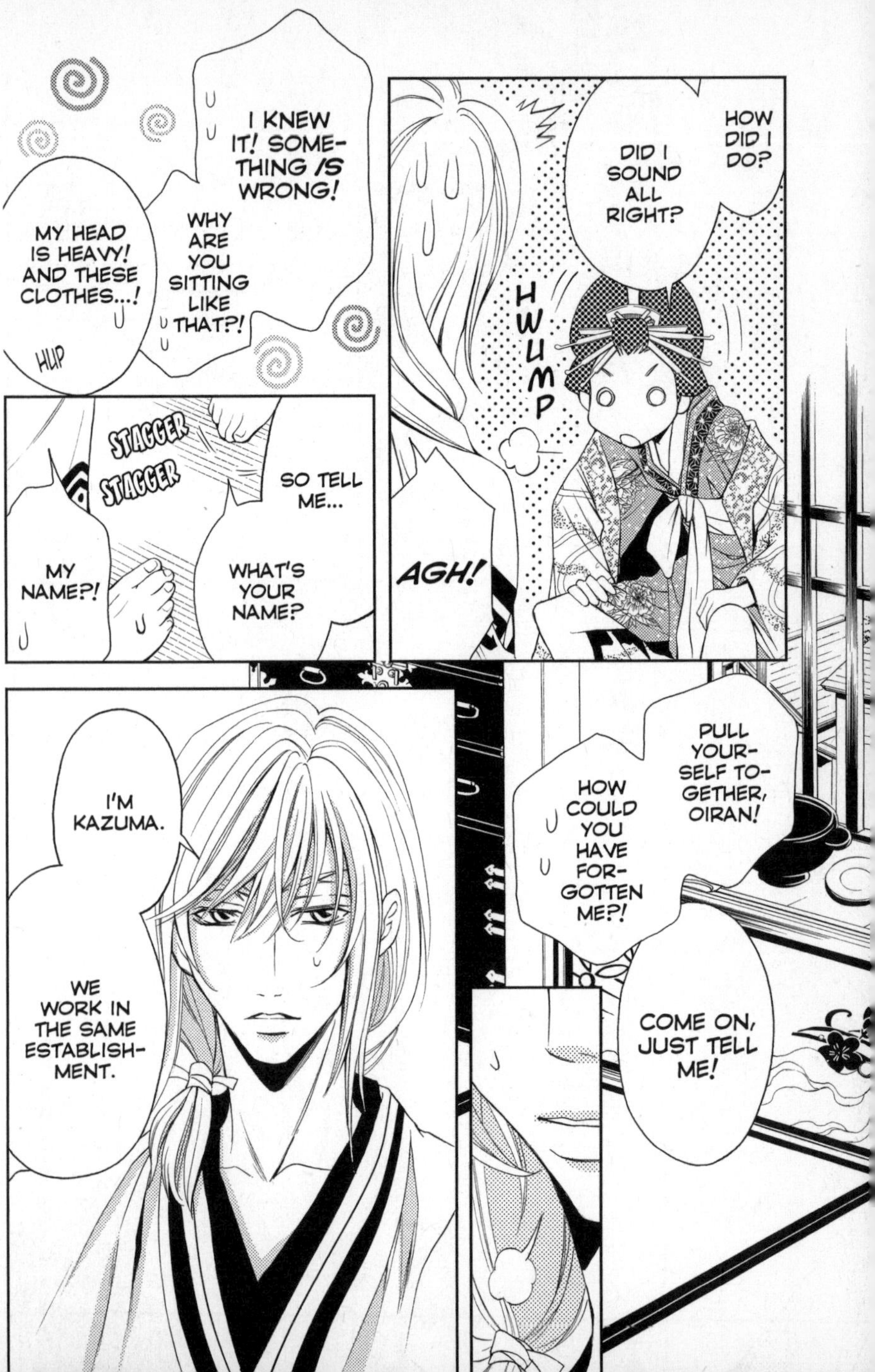
HOW DID I DO?
DID I SOUND ALL RIGHT?
HWUMP
AGH!
I KNEW IT! SOMETHING IS WRONG!
WHY ARE YOU SITTING LIKE THAT?!
MY HEAD IS HEAVY! AND THESE CLOTHES...!
HUP
STAGGER
STAGGER
SO TELL ME...
WHAT'S YOUR NAME?
MY NAME?!
PULL YOURSELF TOGETHER, OIRAN!
HOW COULD YOU HAVE FORGOTTEN ME?!
COME ON, JUST TELL ME!
I'M KAZUMA.
WE WORK IN THE SAME ESTABLISHMENT.

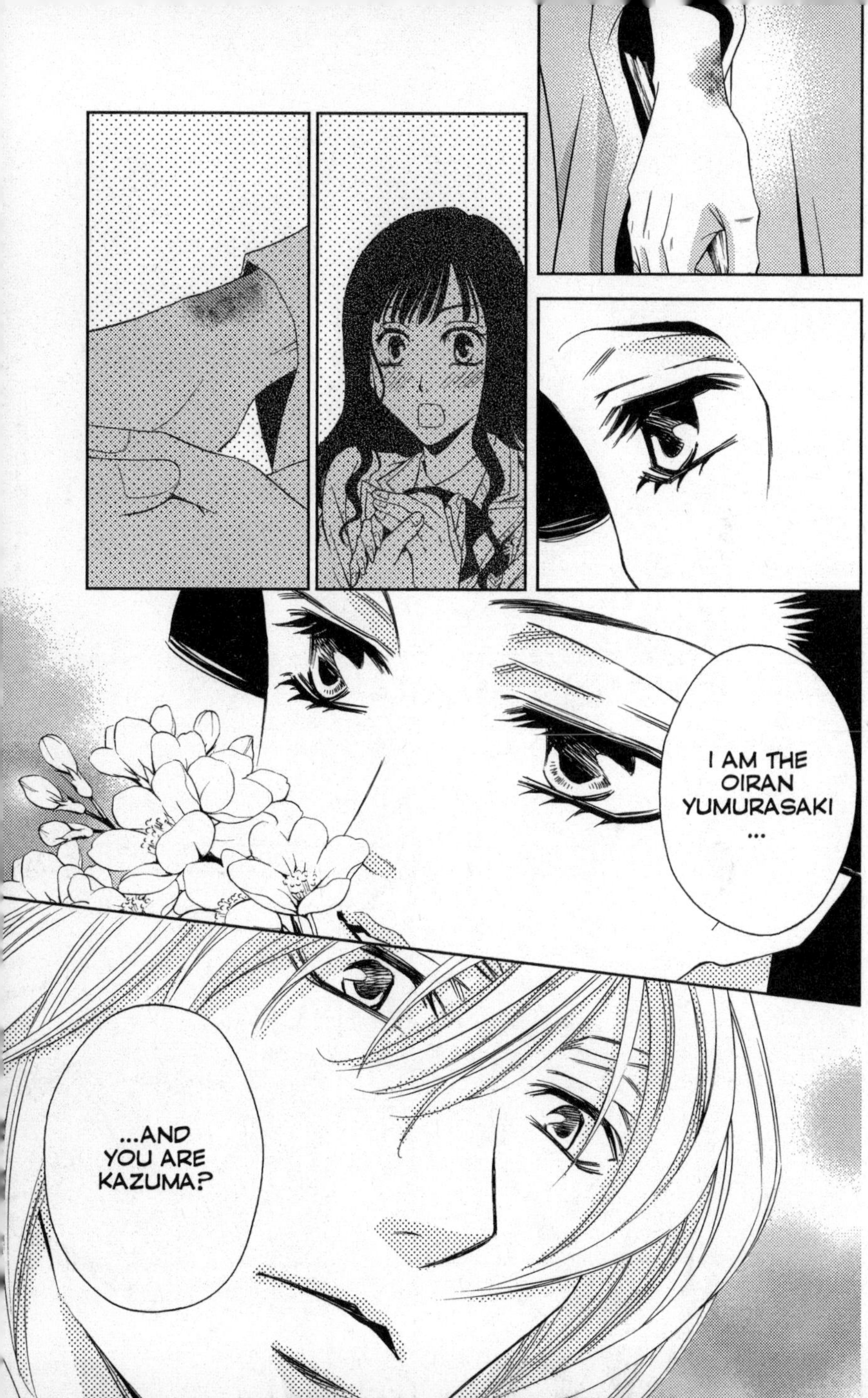
I AM THE OIRAN YUMURASAKI ...
...AND YOU ARE KAZUMA?

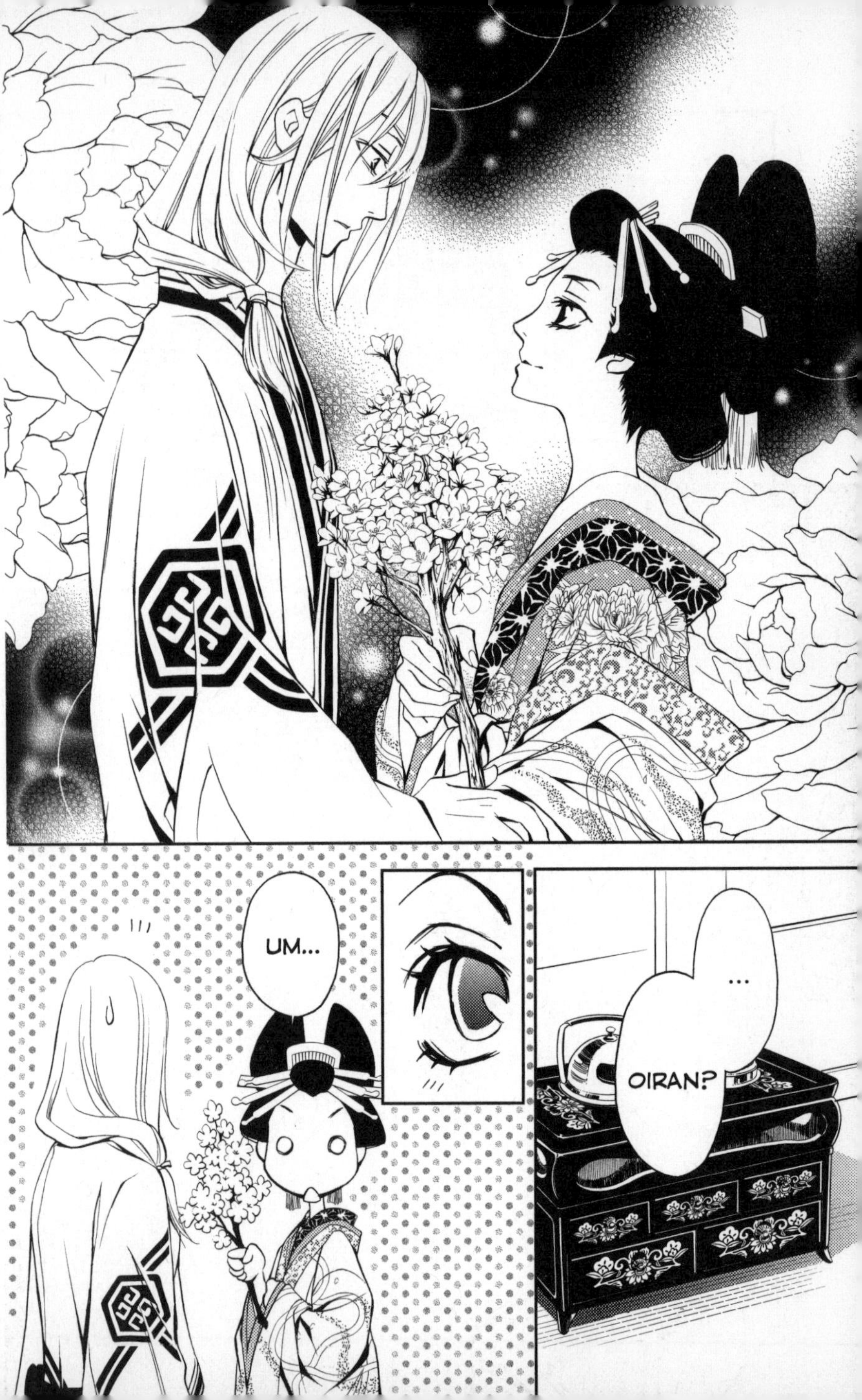
... OIRAN?
UM...

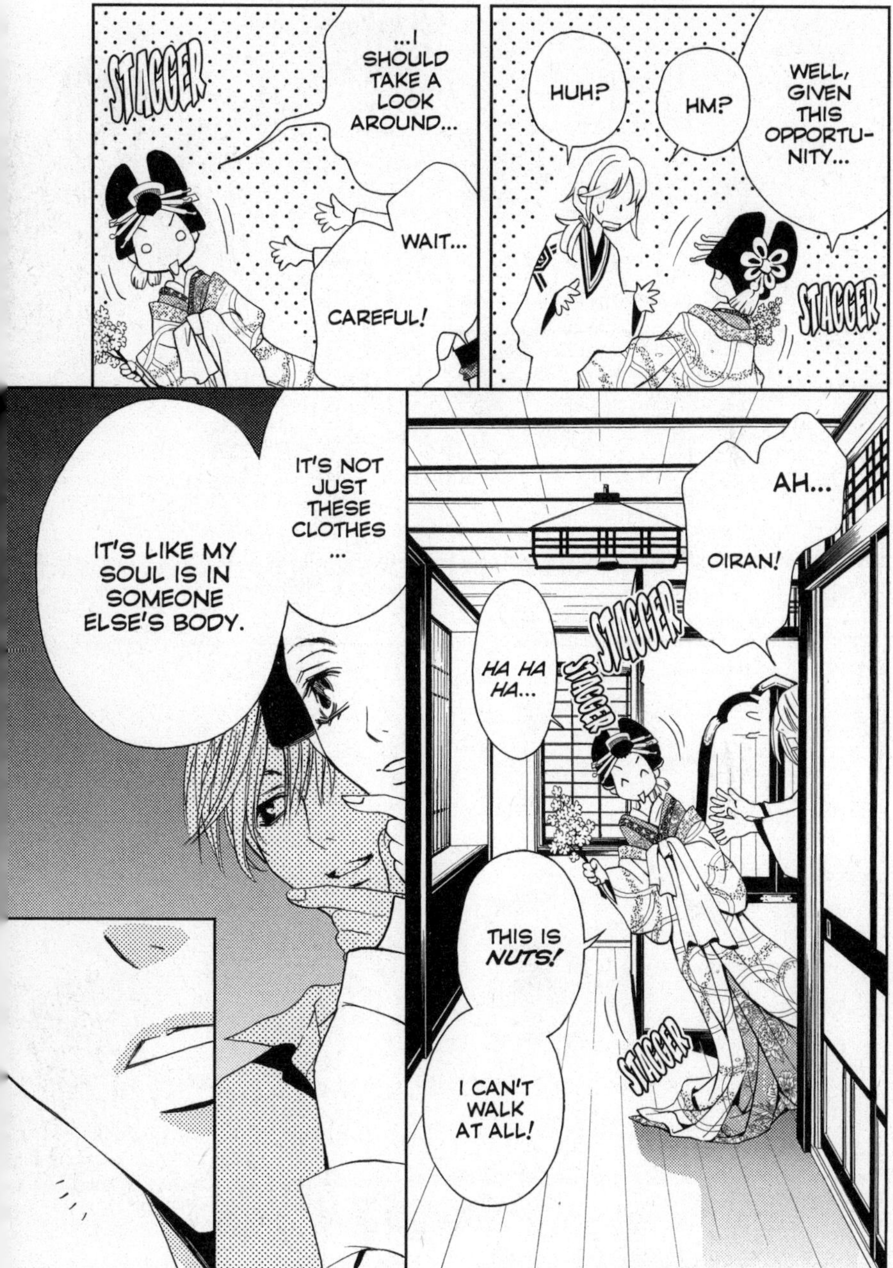
WELL, GIVEN THIS OPPORTUNITY...
HM?
HUH?
STAGGER
...I SHOULD TAKE A LOOK AROUND...
WAIT...
CAREFUL!
STAGGER
AH...
OIRAN!
STAGGER
STAGGER
HA HA HA...
THIS IS NUTS!
I CAN'T WALK AT ALL!
STAGGER
IT'S NOT JUST THESE CLOTHES...
IT'S LIKE MY SOUL IS IN SOMEONE ELSE'S BODY.

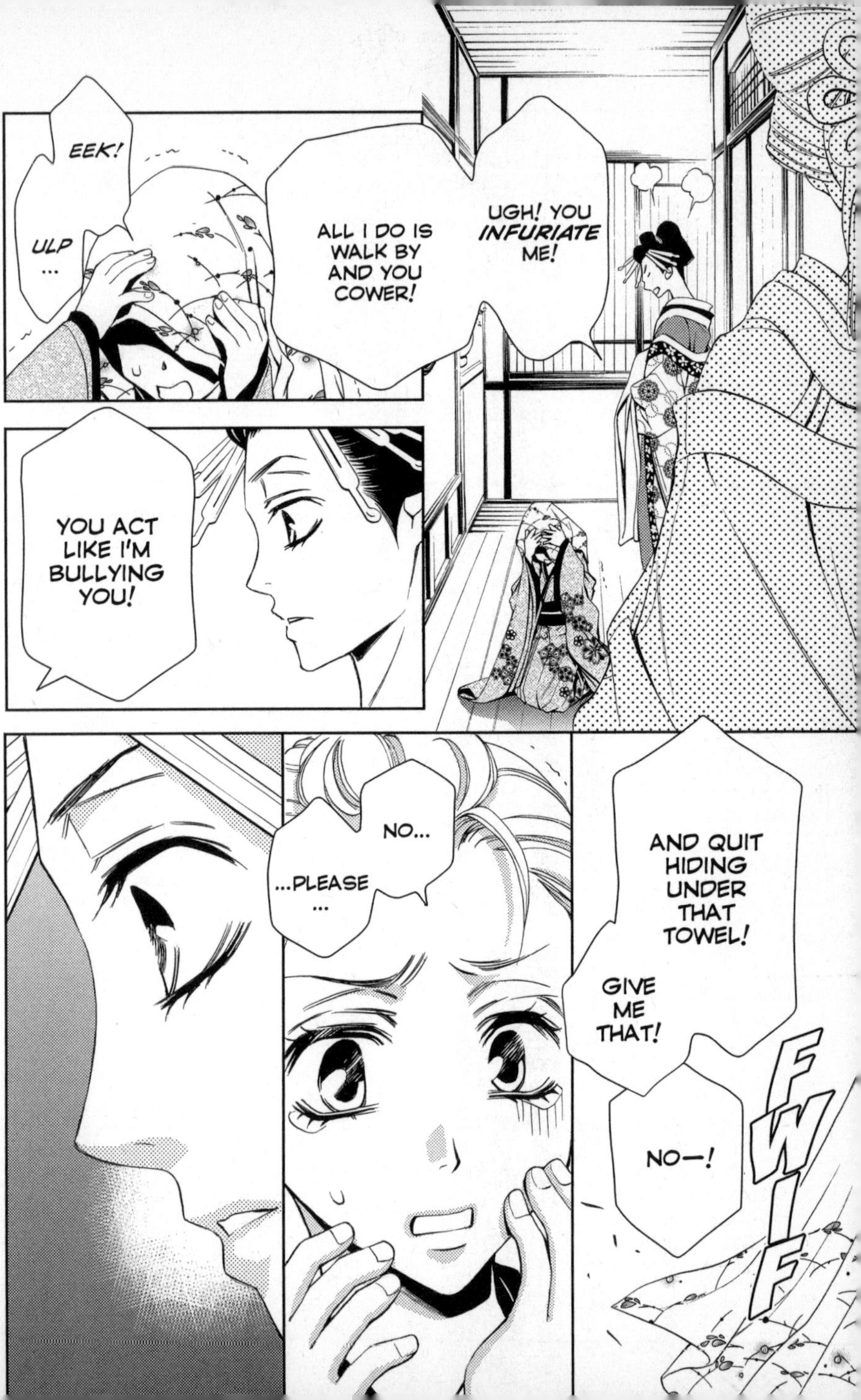
UGH! YOU *INFURIATE* ME!
ALL I DO IS WALK BY AND YOU COWER!
EEK!
ULP ...
YOU ACT LIKE I'M BULLYING YOU!
AND QUIT HIDING UNDER THAT TOWEL!
GIVE ME THAT!
NO—!
FWIF
NO...
...PLEASE ...

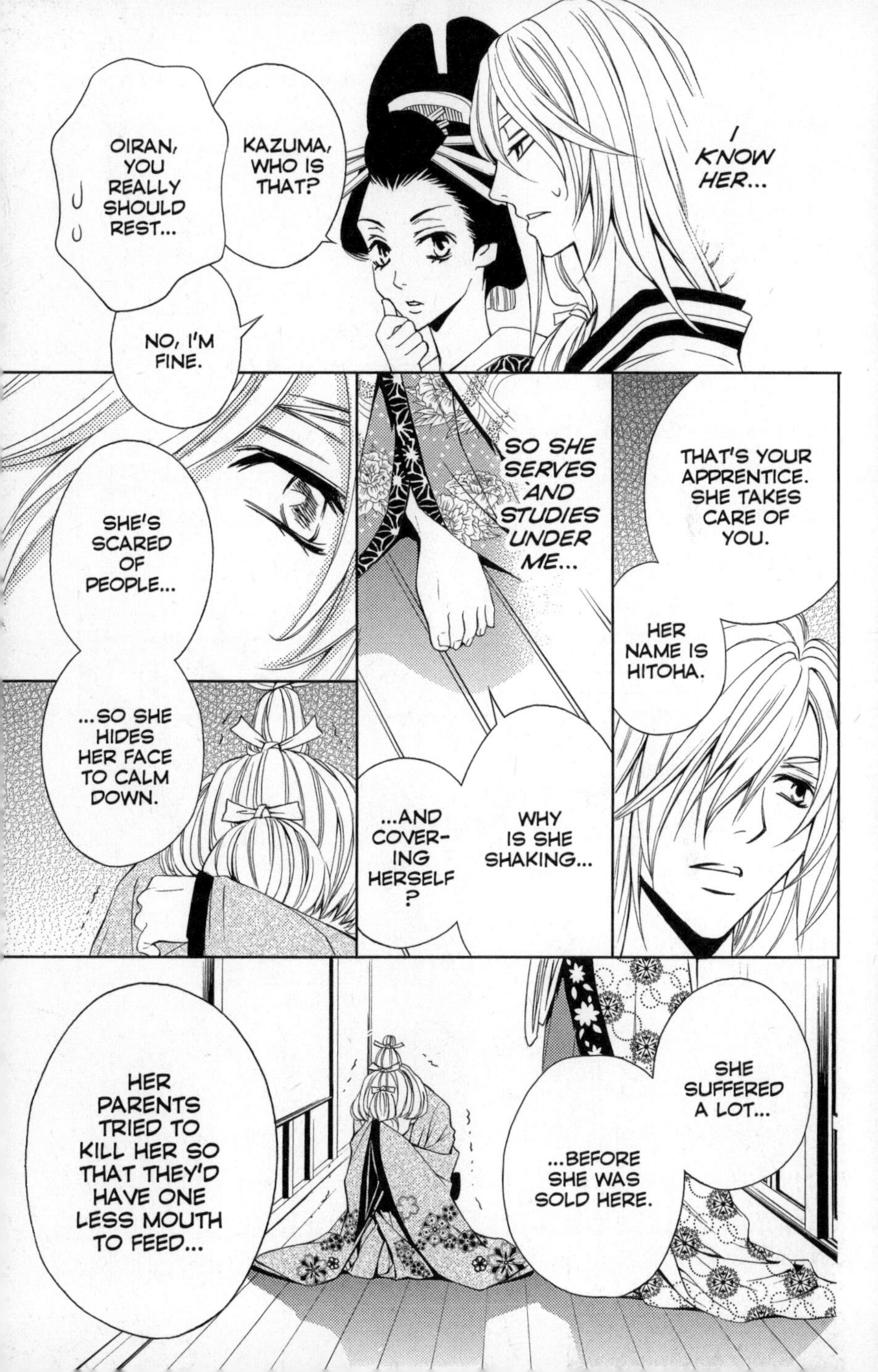
I KNOW HER...
KAZUMA, WHO IS THAT?
OIRAN, YOU REALLY SHOULD REST...
NO, I'M FINE.
THAT'S YOUR APPRENTICE. SHE TAKES CARE OF YOU.
HER NAME IS HITOHA.
SO SHE SERVES AND STUDIES UNDER ME...
WHY IS SHE SHAKING...
...AND COVER-ING HERSELF?
SHE'S SCARED OF PEOPLE...
...SO SHE HIDES HER FACE TO CALM DOWN.
SHE SUFFERED A LOT...
...BEFORE SHE WAS SOLD HERE.
HER PARENTS TRIED TO KILL HER SO THAT THEY'D HAVE ONE LESS MOUTH TO FEED...

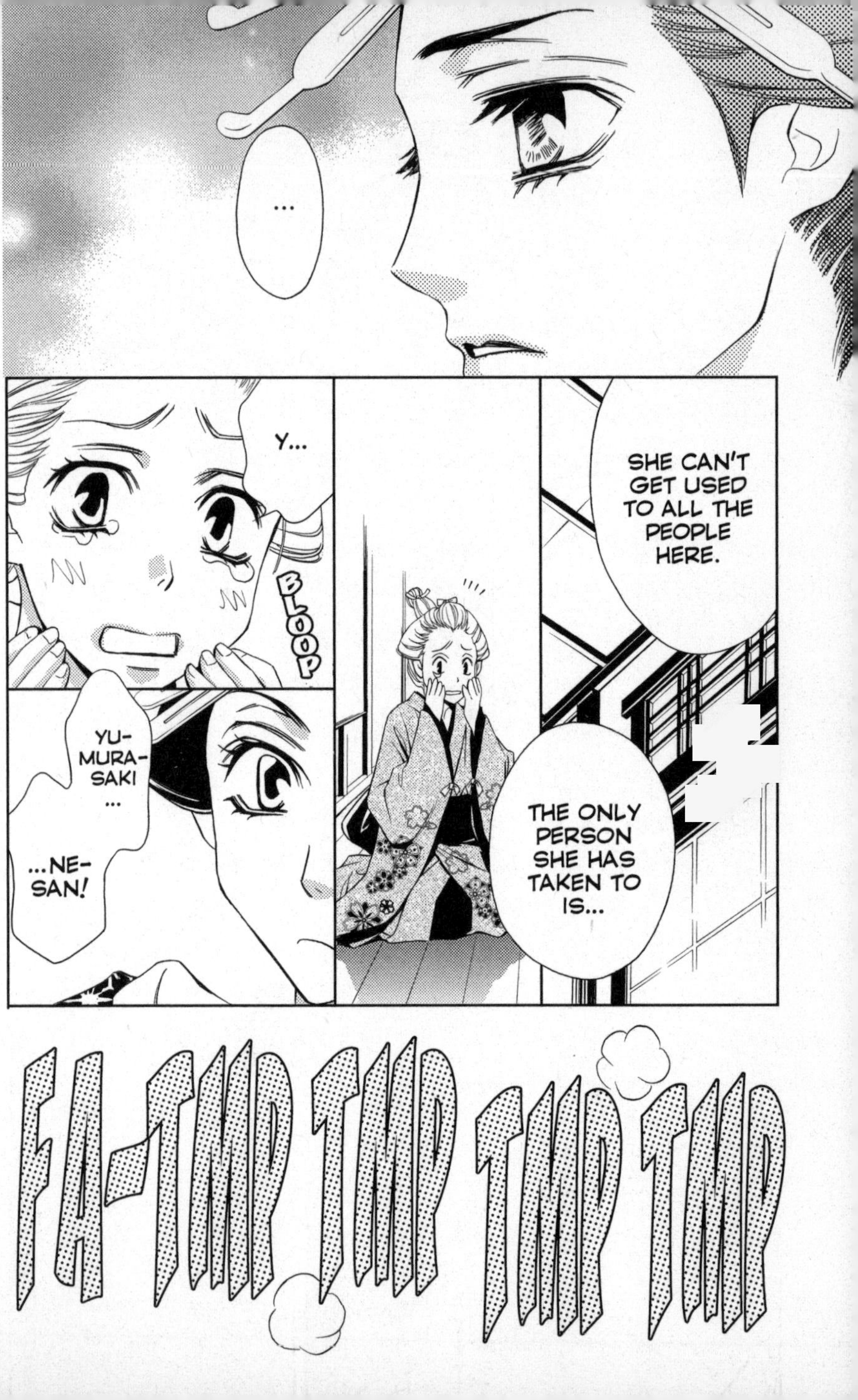
...
SHE CAN'T GET USED TO ALL THE PEOPLE HERE.
THE ONLY PERSON SHE HAS TAKEN TO IS...
Y...
BLOOP
YU-MURASAKI...
...NE-SAN!
FA-TMP TMP TMP TMP

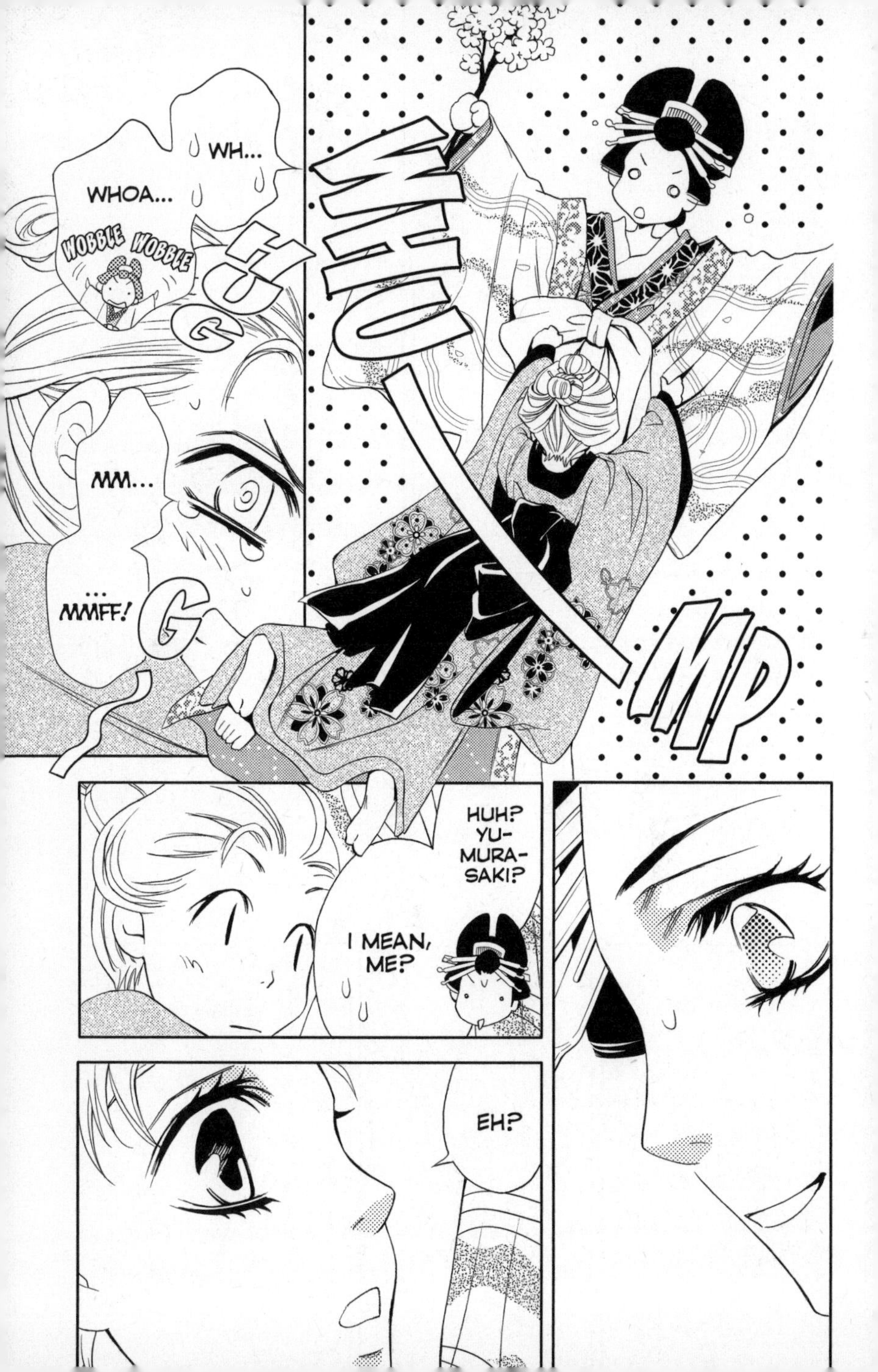
WHU—MP
WH...
WHOA...
WOBBLE WOBBLE
HUG
MM...
...MMFF!
HUH? YU-MURA-SAKI?
I MEAN, ME?
EH?

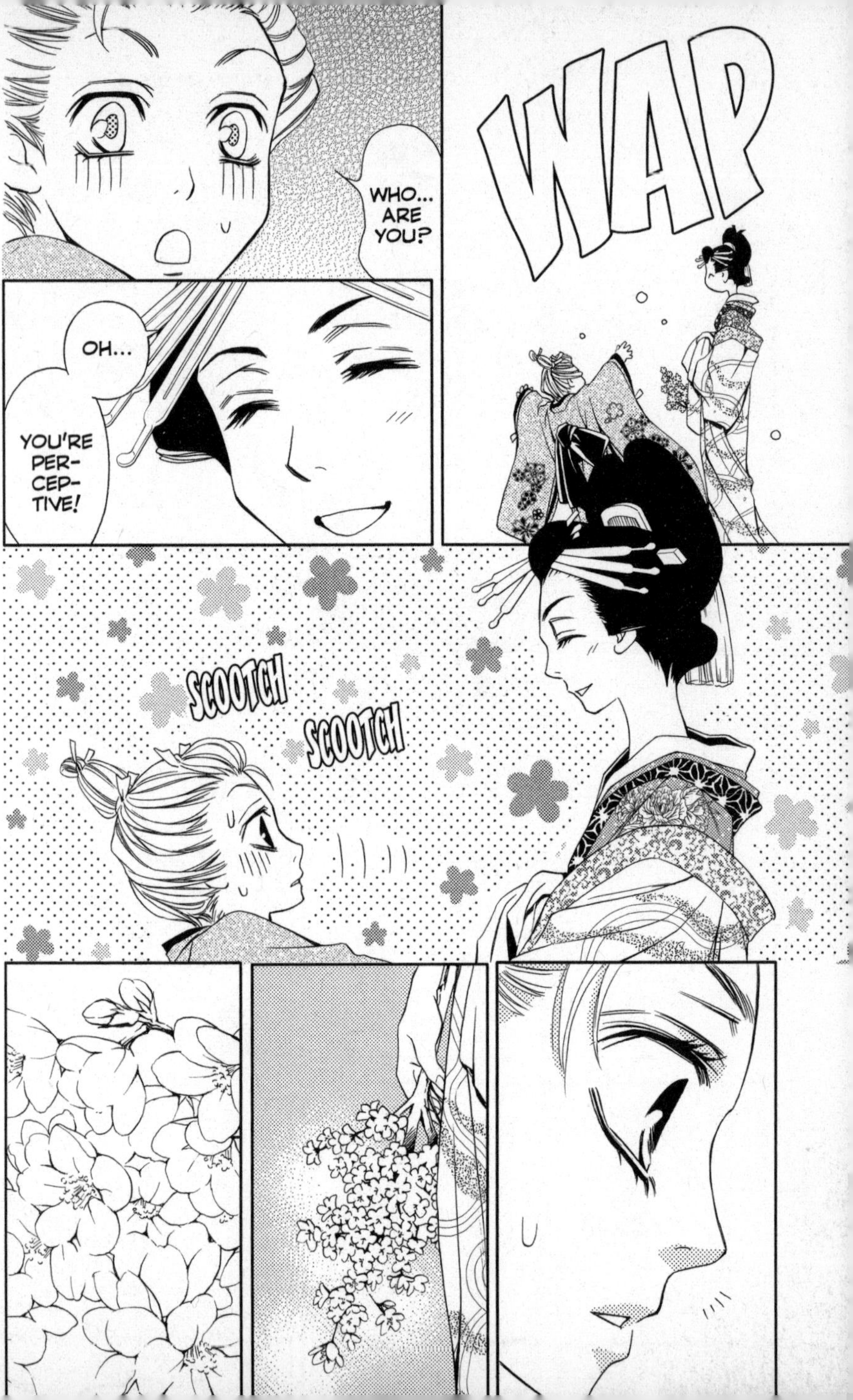
WAP
WHO... ARE YOU?
OH...
YOU'RE PER-CEP-TIVE!
SCOOTCH
SCOOTCH

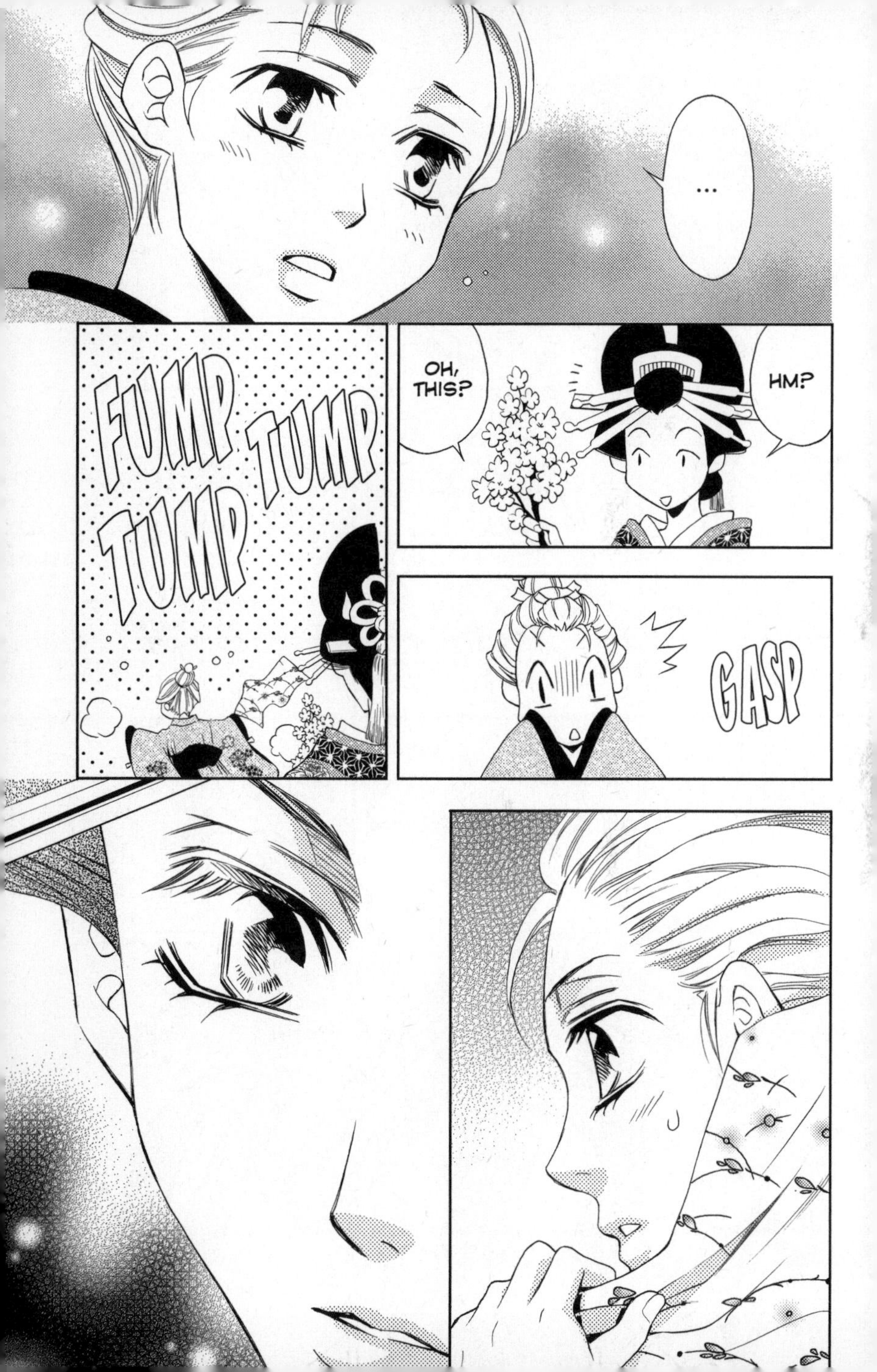
...
HM?
OH, THIS?
GASP
TUMP
FUMP
TUMP

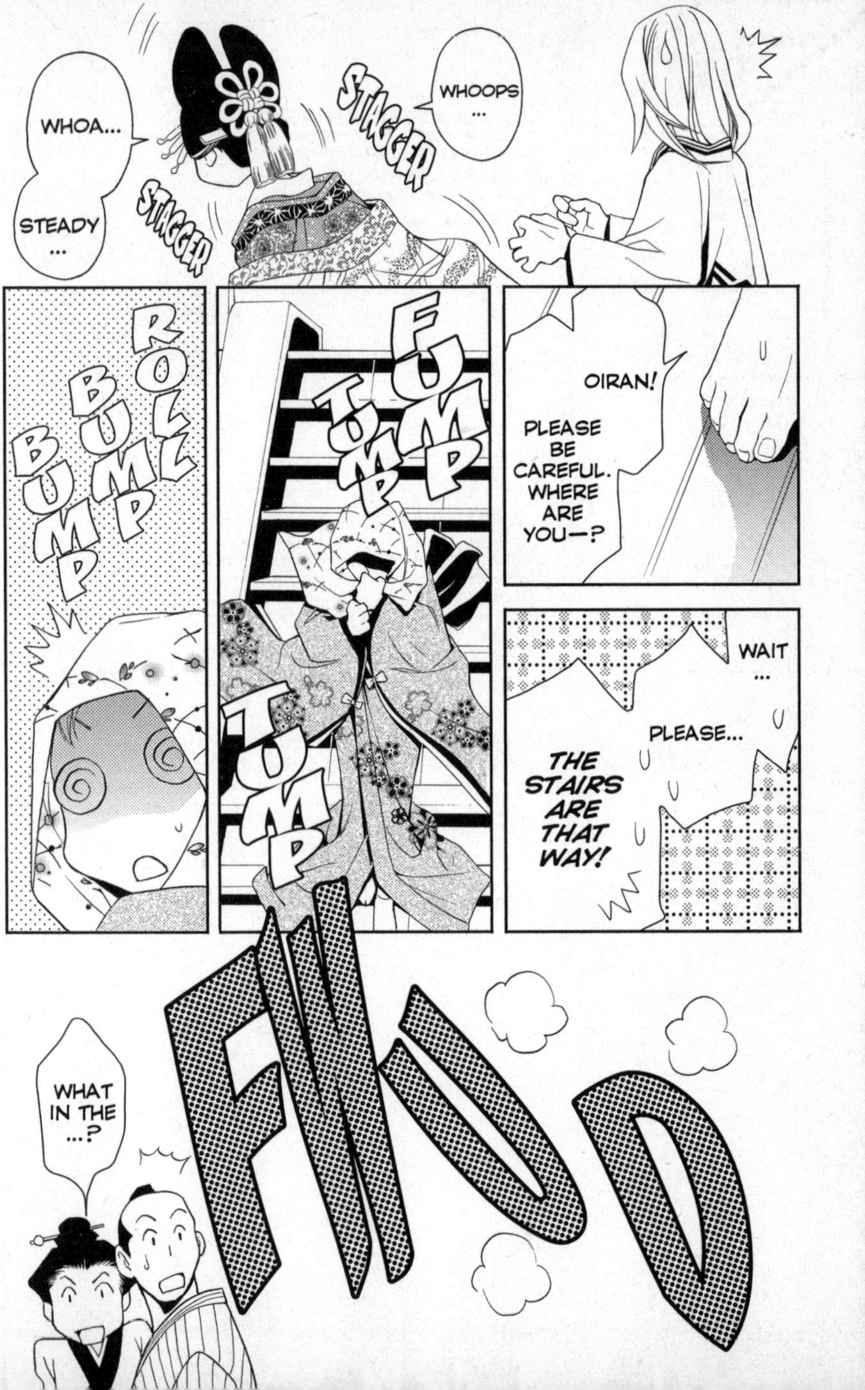
WHOOPS ...
STAGGER
WHOA...
STEADY ...
STAGGER
OIRAN!
PLEASE BE CAREFUL. WHERE ARE YOU—?
WAIT ...
PLEASE...
THE STAIRS ARE THAT WAY!
FUMP
TOMP
TOMP
ROLL
BUMP
BUMP
FWUD
WHAT IN THE ...?

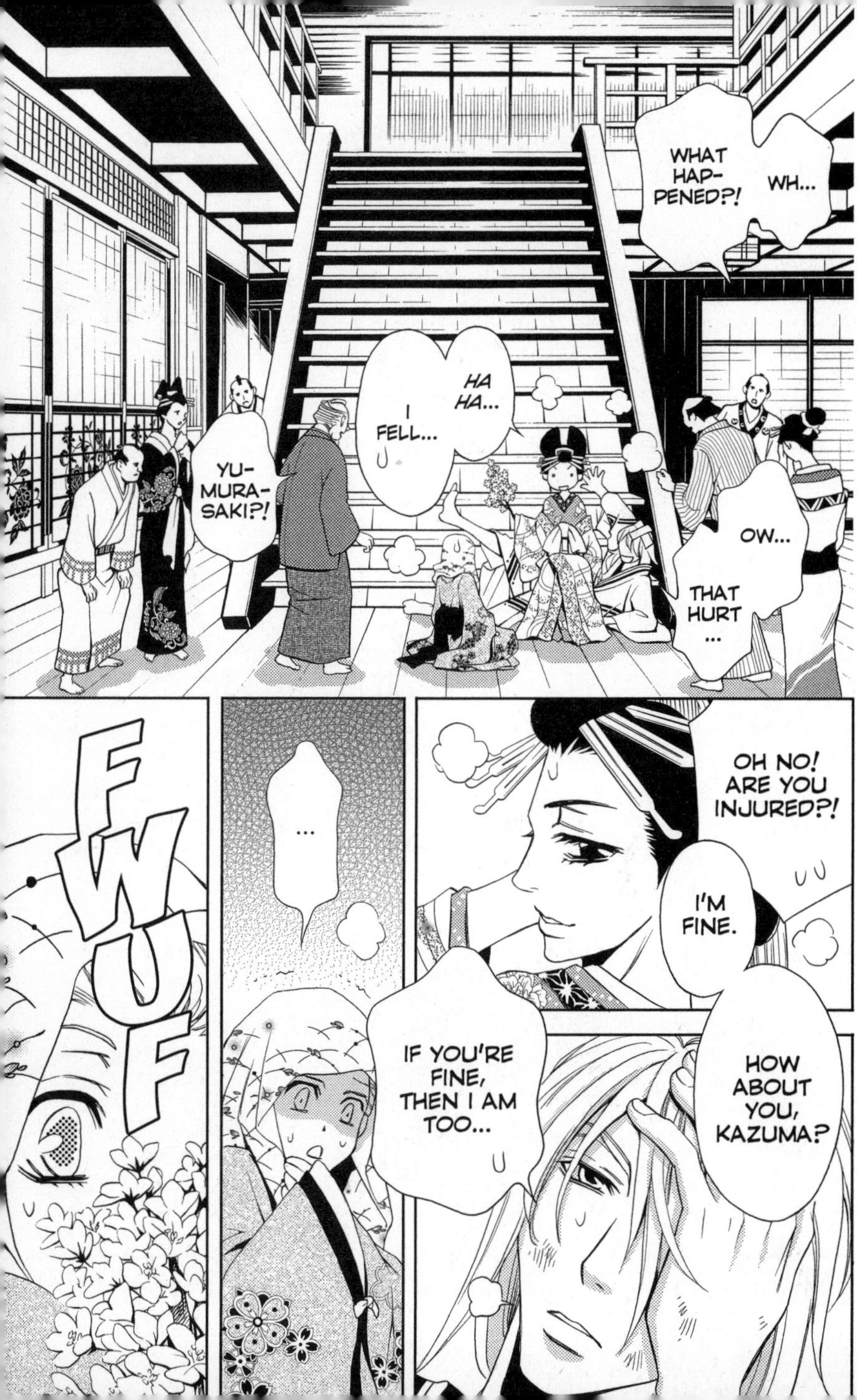
WH...
WHAT HAP-PENED?!
OW... THAT HURT...
HA HA... I FELL...
YU-MURA-SAKI?!
OH NO! ARE YOU INJURED?!
I'M FINE.
HOW ABOUT YOU, KAZUMA?
IF YOU'RE FINE, THEN I AM TOO...
...
FWUF

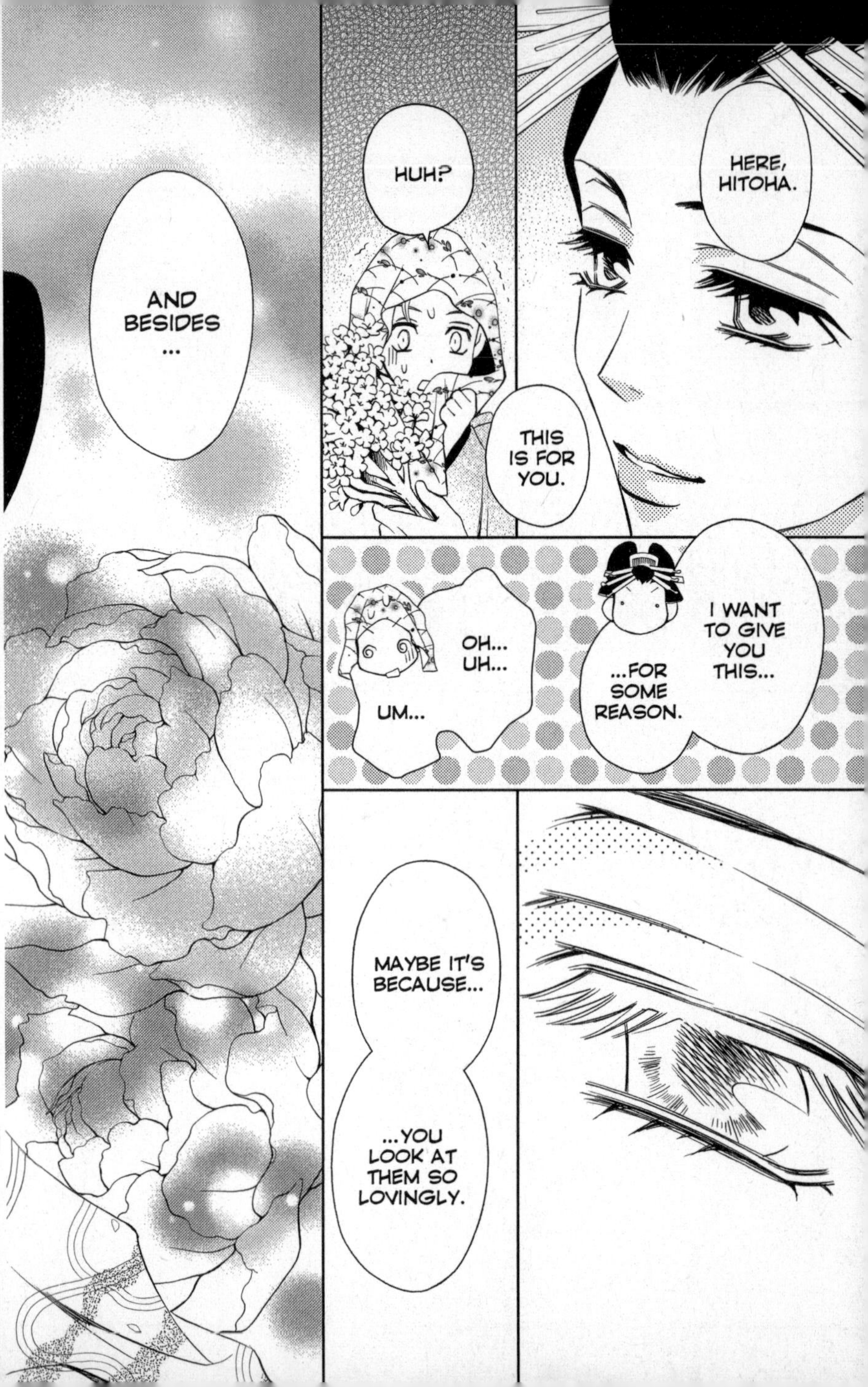
HERE, HITOHA.
THIS IS FOR YOU.
HUH?
I WANT TO GIVE YOU THIS...
...FOR SOME REASON.
OH... UH...
UM...
MAYBE IT'S BECAUSE...
...YOU LOOK AT THEM SO LOVINGLY.
AND BESIDES...

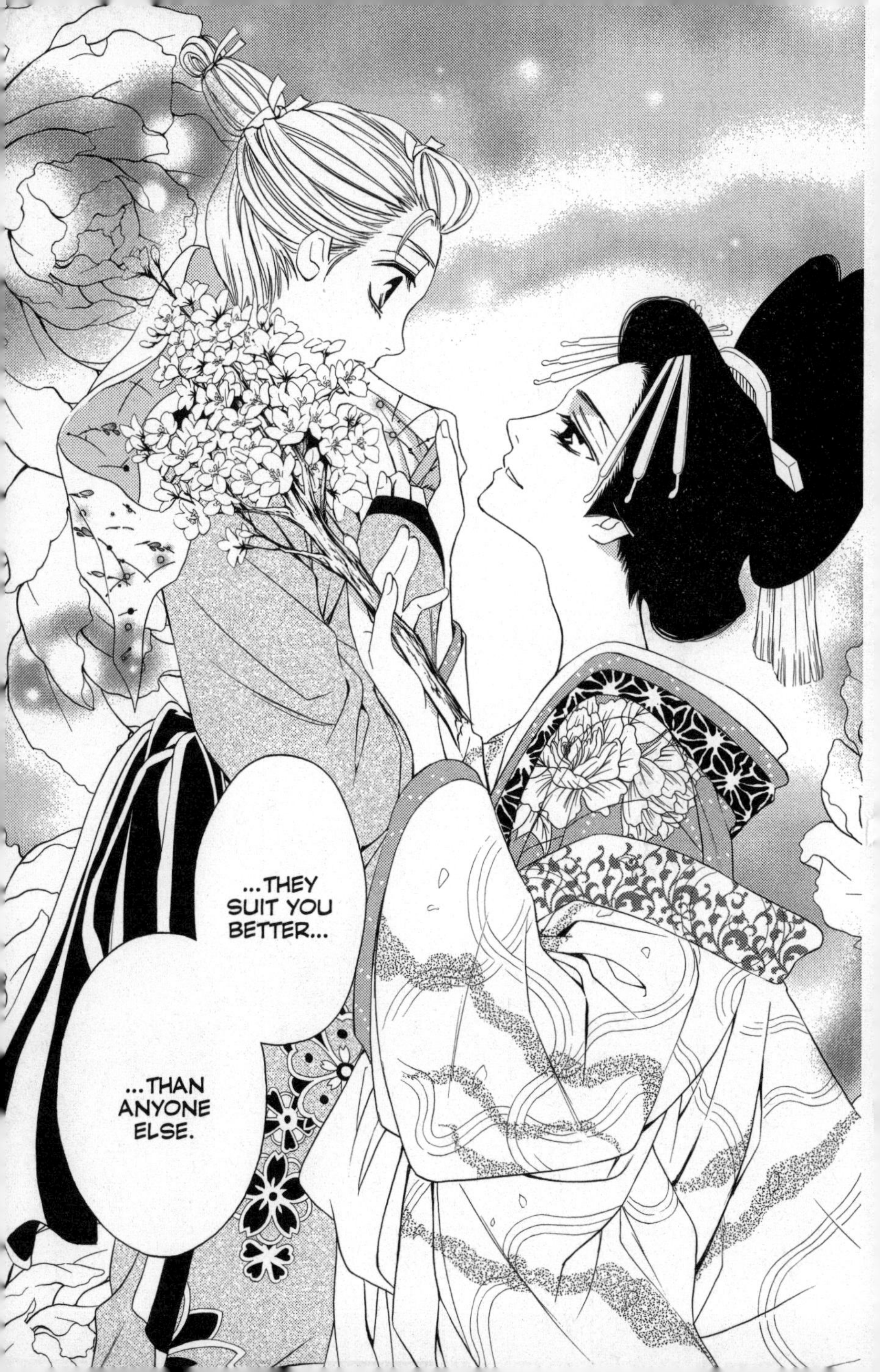
...THEY SUIT YOU BETTER...
...THAN ANYONE ELSE.

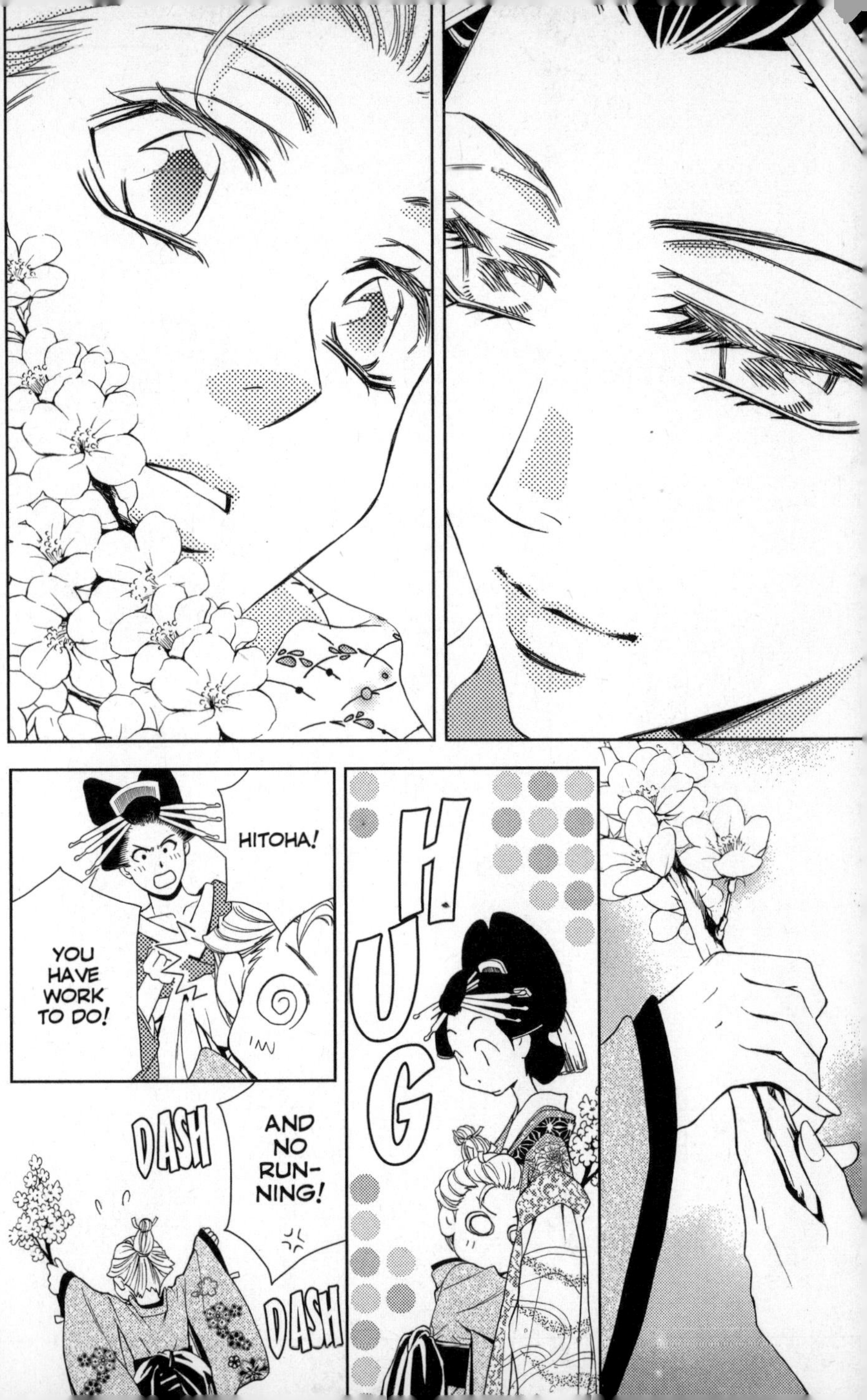
HUG
HITOHA!
YOU HAVE WORK TO DO!
DASH
AND NO RUN-NING!
DASH

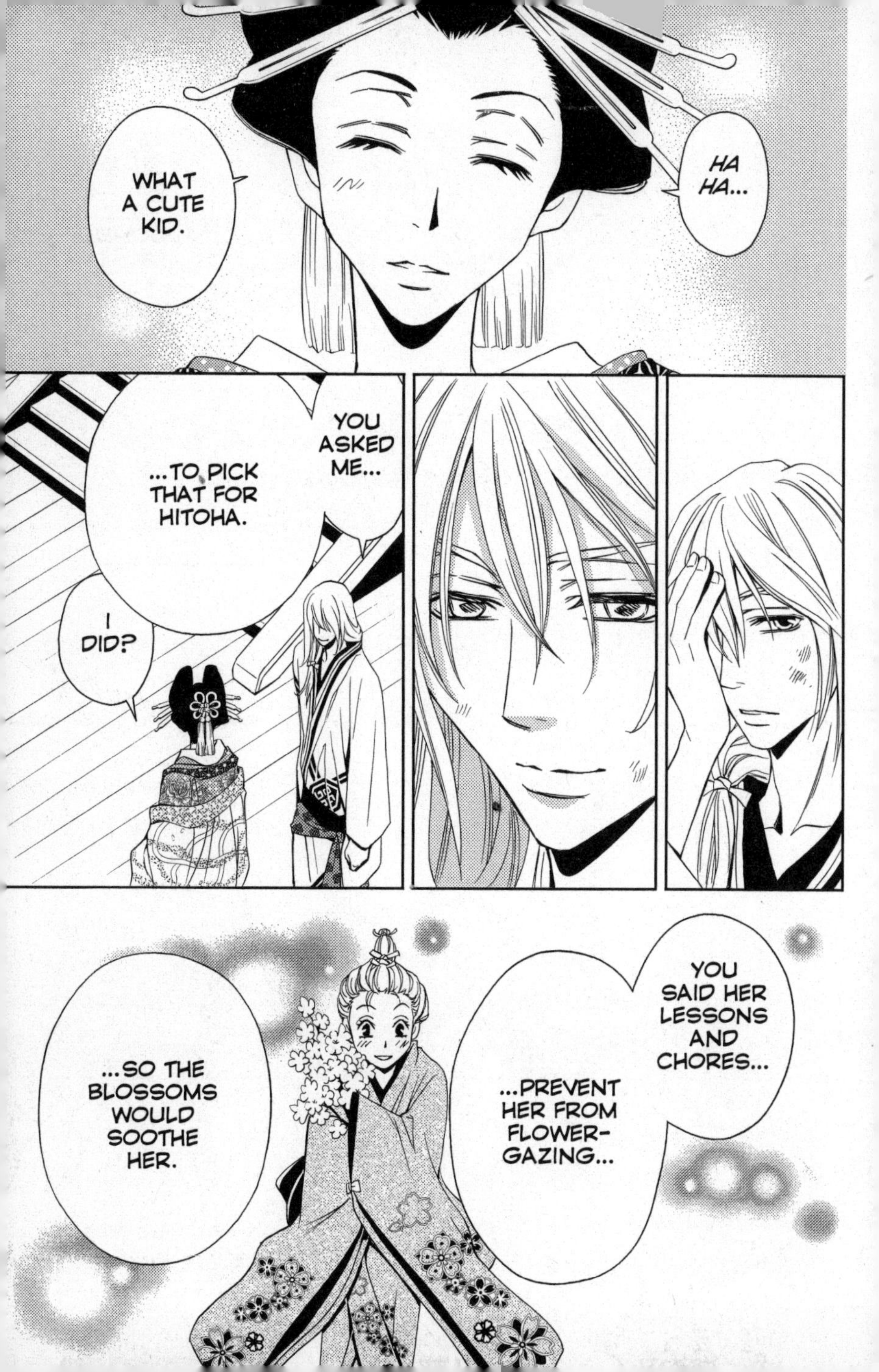
HA HA...
WHAT A CUTE KID.
YOU ASKED ME...
...TO PICK THAT FOR HITOHA.
I DID?
YOU SAID HER LESSONS AND CHORES...
...PREVENT HER FROM FLOWER-GAZING...
...SO THE BLOSSOMS WOULD SOOTHE HER.

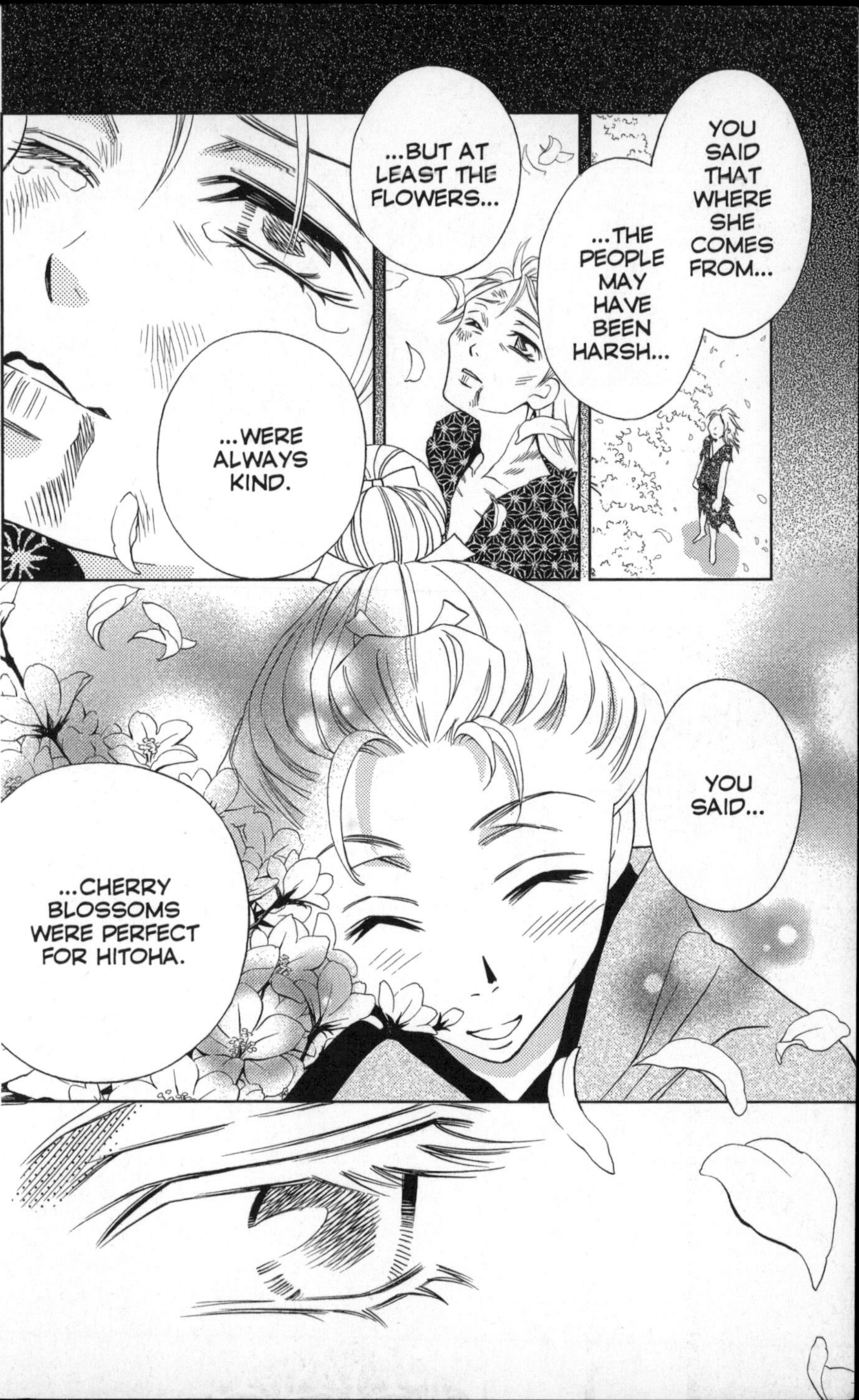
YOU SAID THAT WHERE SHE COMES FROM...
...THE PEOPLE MAY HAVE BEEN HARSH...
...BUT AT LEAST THE FLOWERS...
...WERE ALWAYS KIND.
YOU SAID...
...CHERRY BLOSSOMS WERE PERFECT FOR HITOHA.

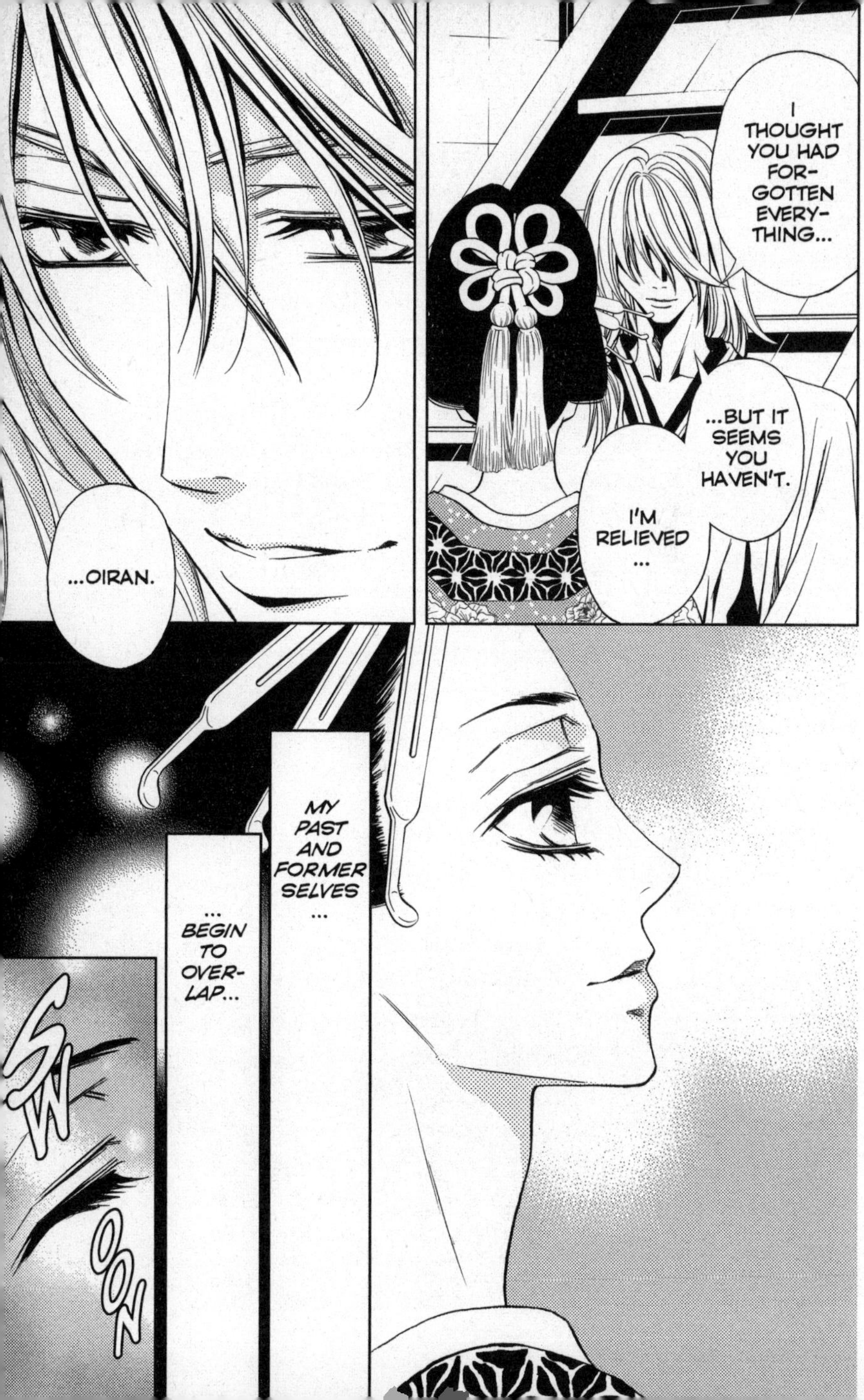
I THOUGHT YOU HAD FOR-GOTTEN EVERY-THING...
...BUT IT SEEMS YOU HAVEN'T.
I'M RELIEVED ...
...OIRAN.
MY PAST AND FORMER SELVES ...
... BEGIN TO OVER-LAP...
SWOON

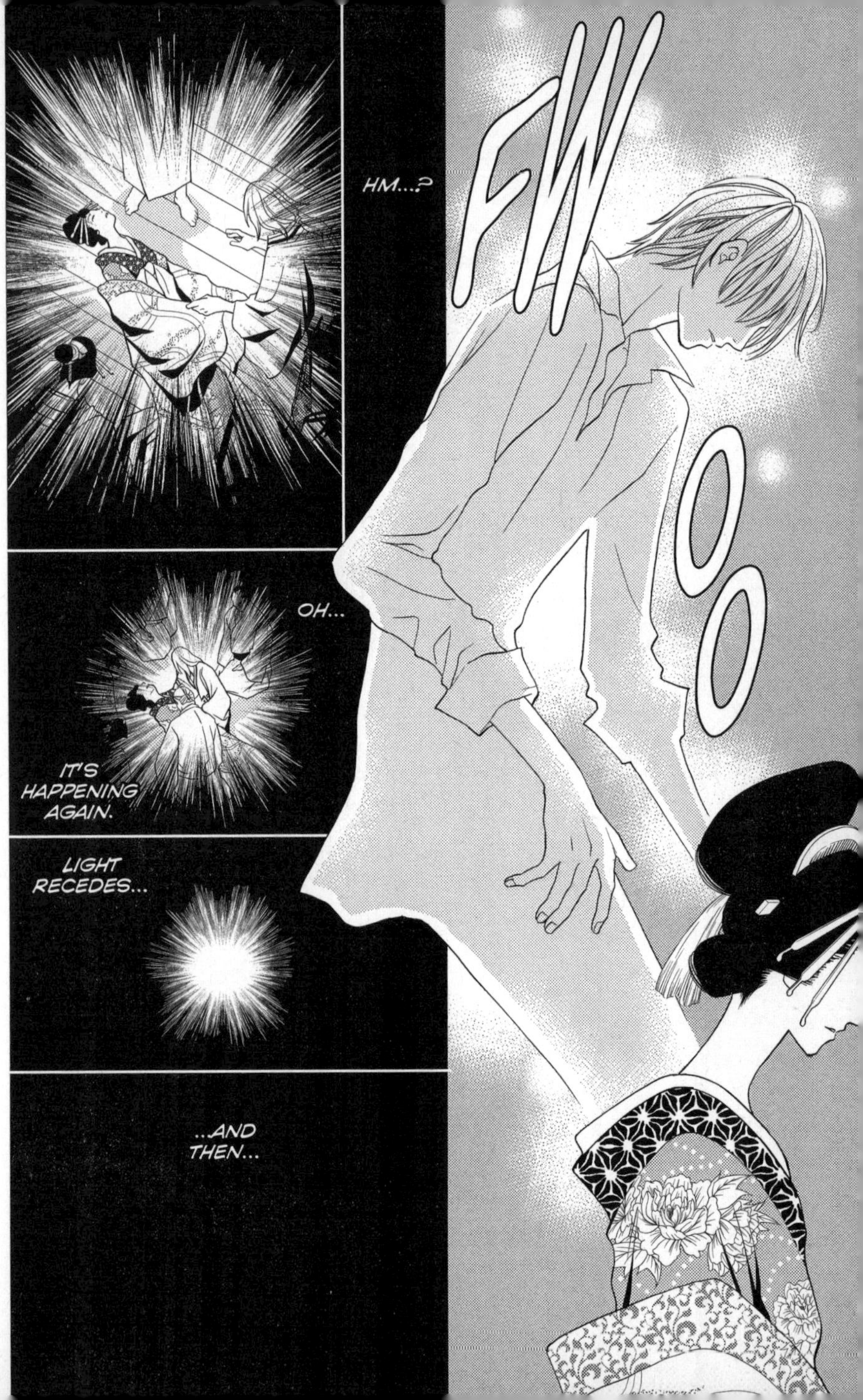
FWOOO
HM...?
OH...
IT'S HAPPENING AGAIN.
LIGHT RECEDES...
...AND THEN...

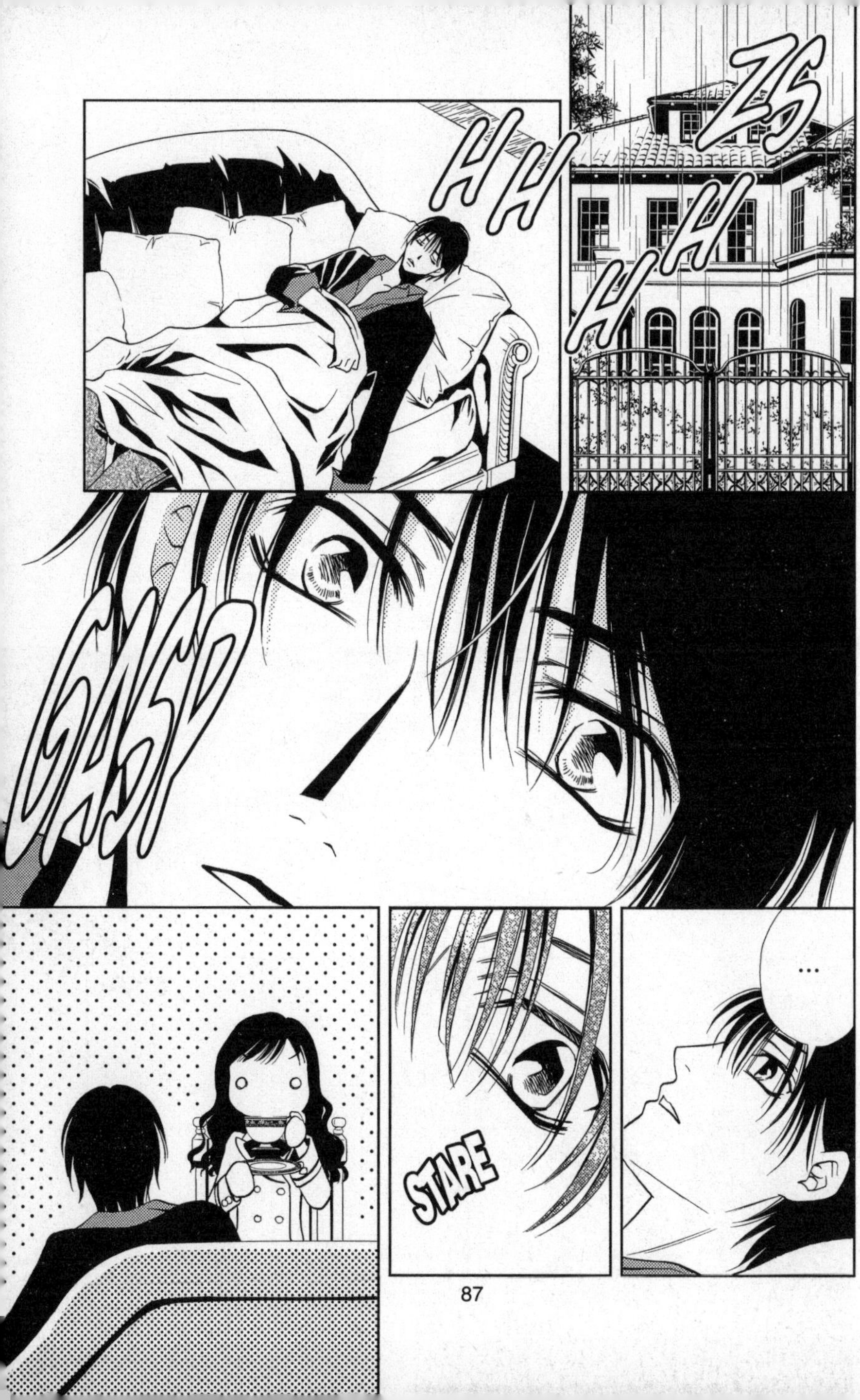
ZSHHHH
GASP
...
STARE

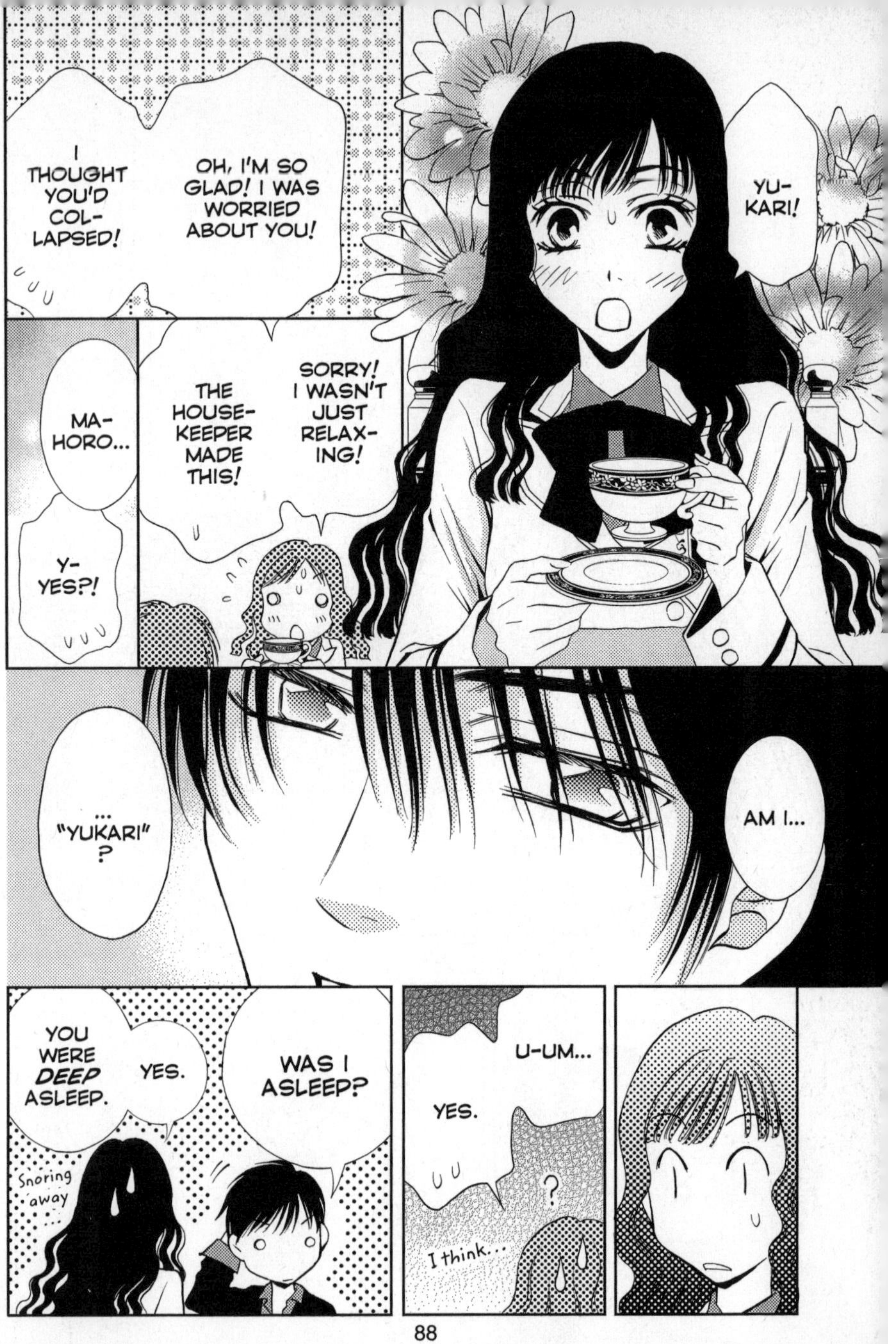
YU-KARI!
OH, I'M SO GLAD! I WAS WORRIED ABOUT YOU!
I THOUGHT YOU'D COL-LAPSED!
SORRY! I WASN'T JUST RELAX-ING!
THE HOUSE-KEEPER MADE THIS!
MA-HORO...
Y-YES?!
AM I...
... "YUKARI" ?
U-UM...
YES.
?
I think...
WAS I ASLEEP?
YES.
YOU WERE *DEEP* ASLEEP.
Snoring away...

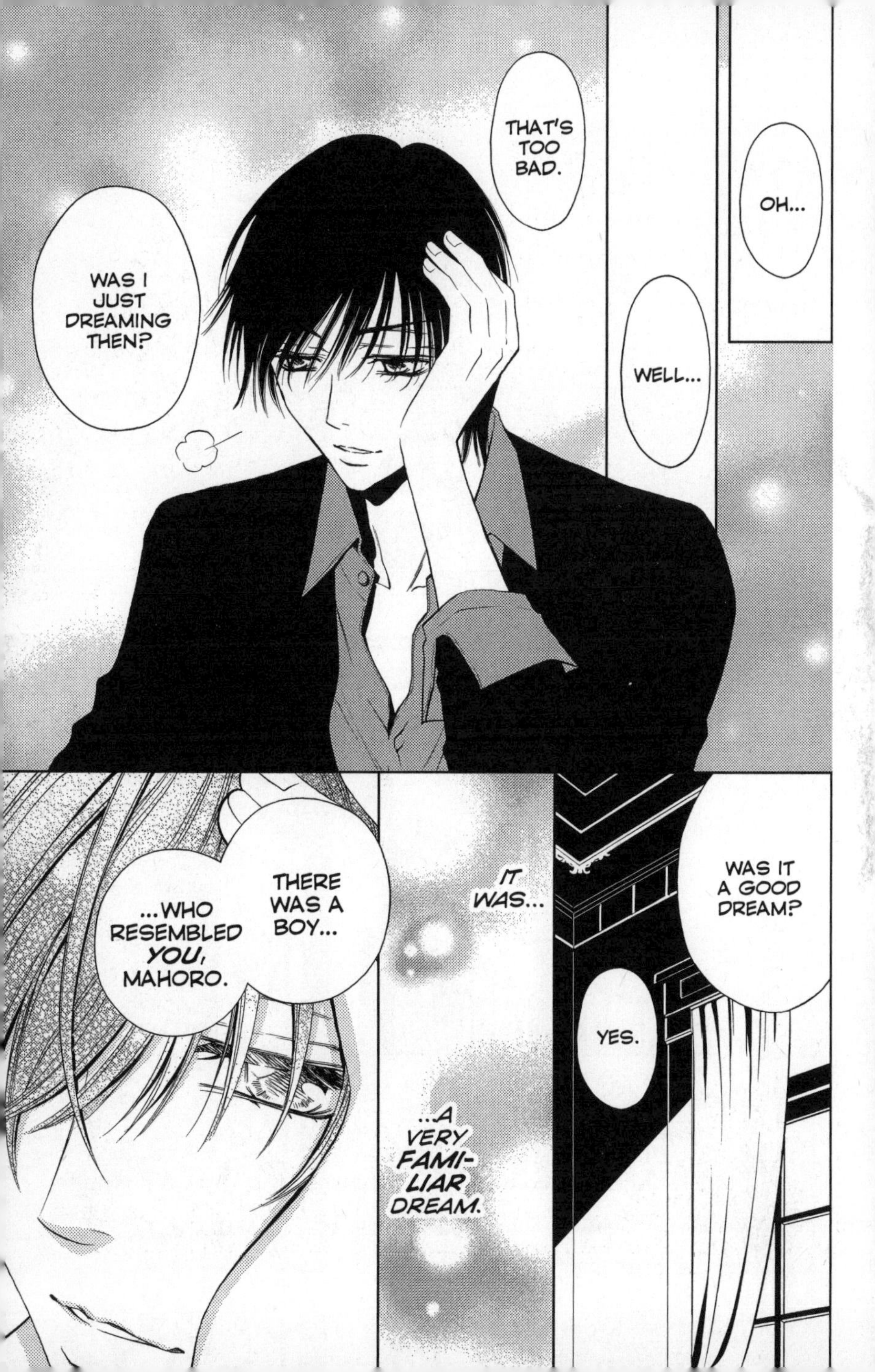
OH...
WELL...
THAT'S TOO BAD.
WAS I JUST DREAMING THEN?
WAS IT A GOOD DREAM?
YES.
IT WAS...
...A VERY FAMILIAR DREAM.
THERE WAS A BOY...
...WHO RESEMBLED YOU, MAHORO.

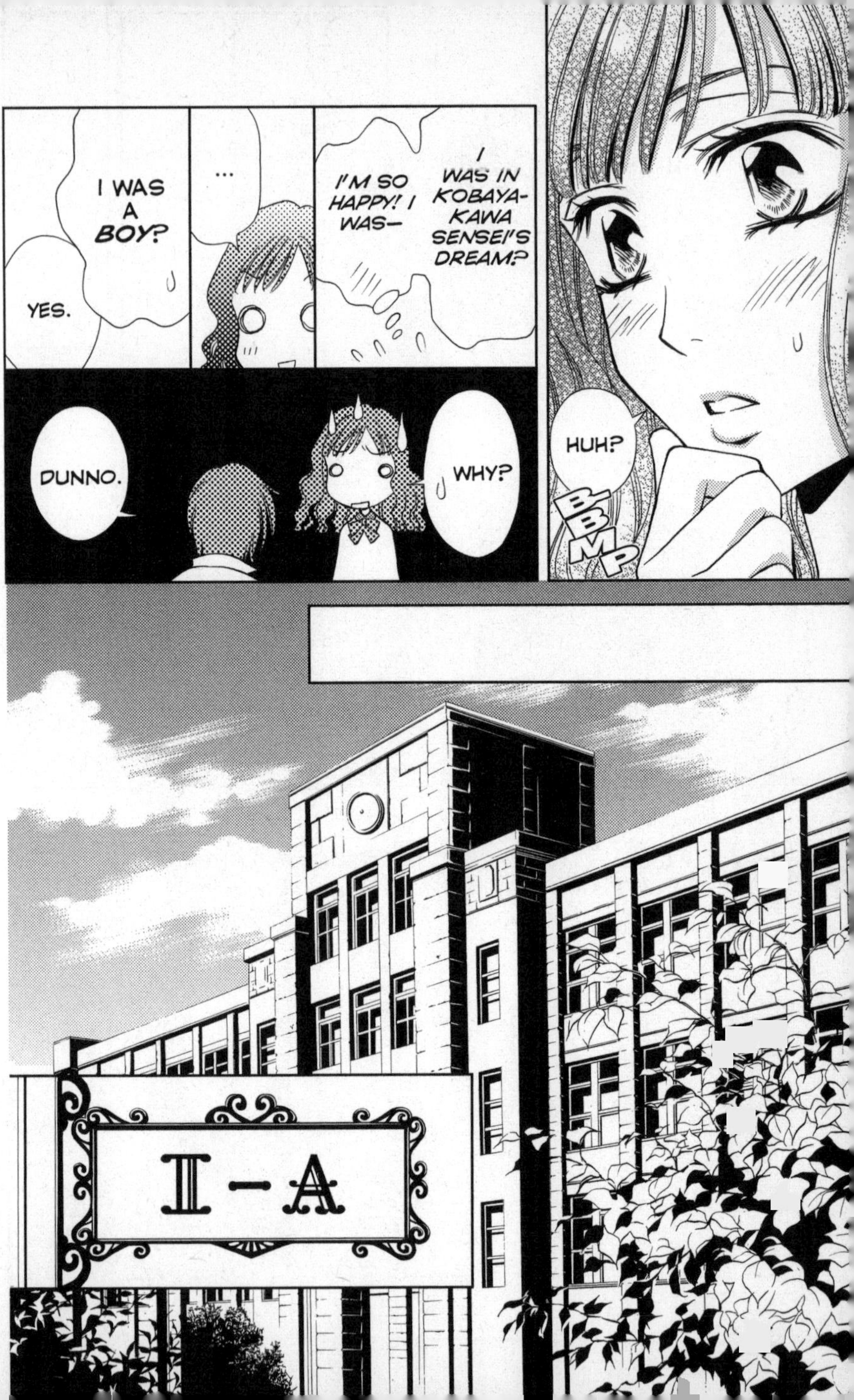
HUH?
B-BMP
I WAS IN KOBAYA-KAWA SENSEI'S DREAM?
I'M SO HAPPY! I WAS—
...
I WAS A *BOY?*
YES.
WHY?
DUNNO.
II-A

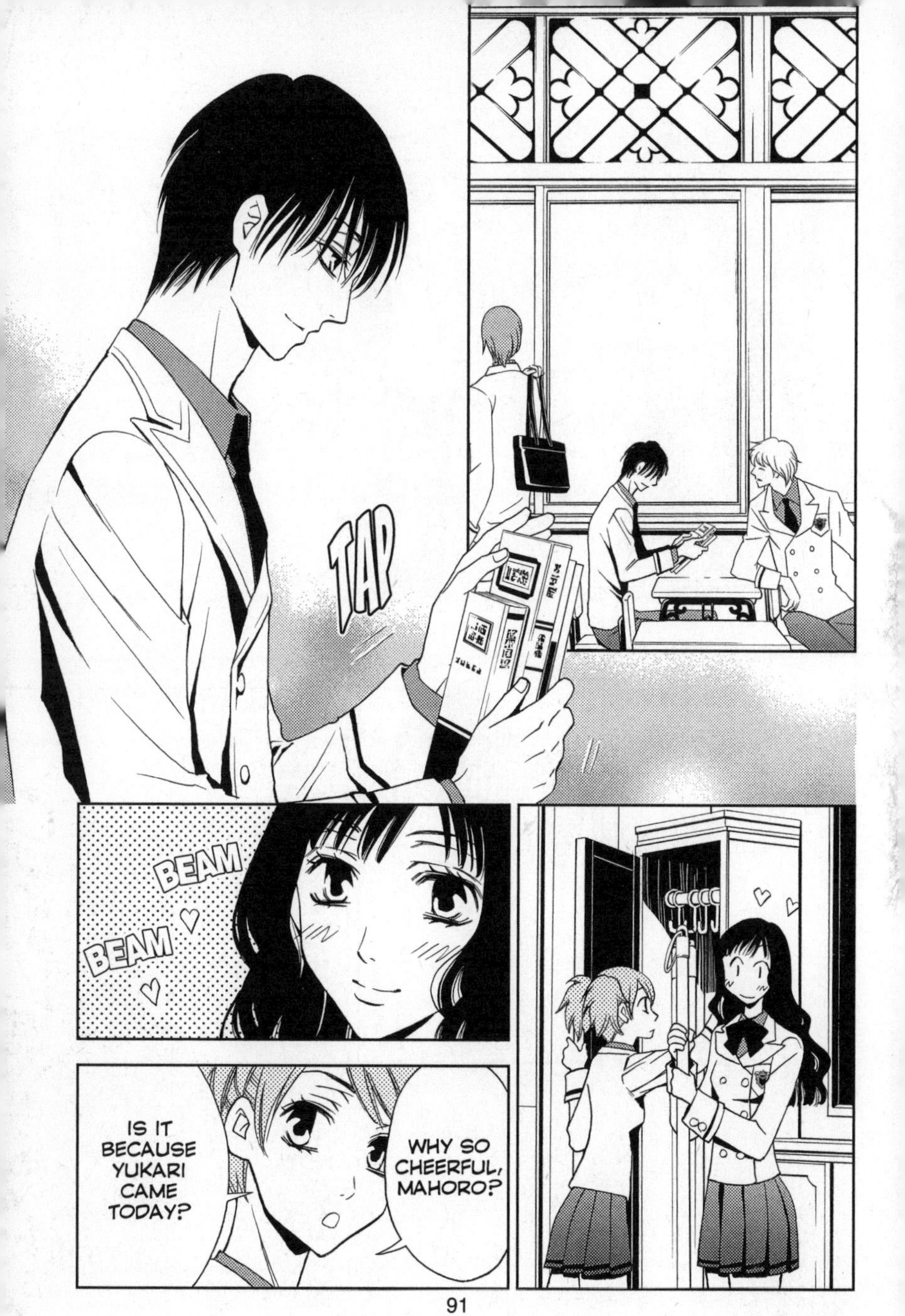
TAP
BEAM
BEAM
WHY SO CHEERFUL, MAHORO?
IS IT BECAUSE YUKARI CAME TODAY?

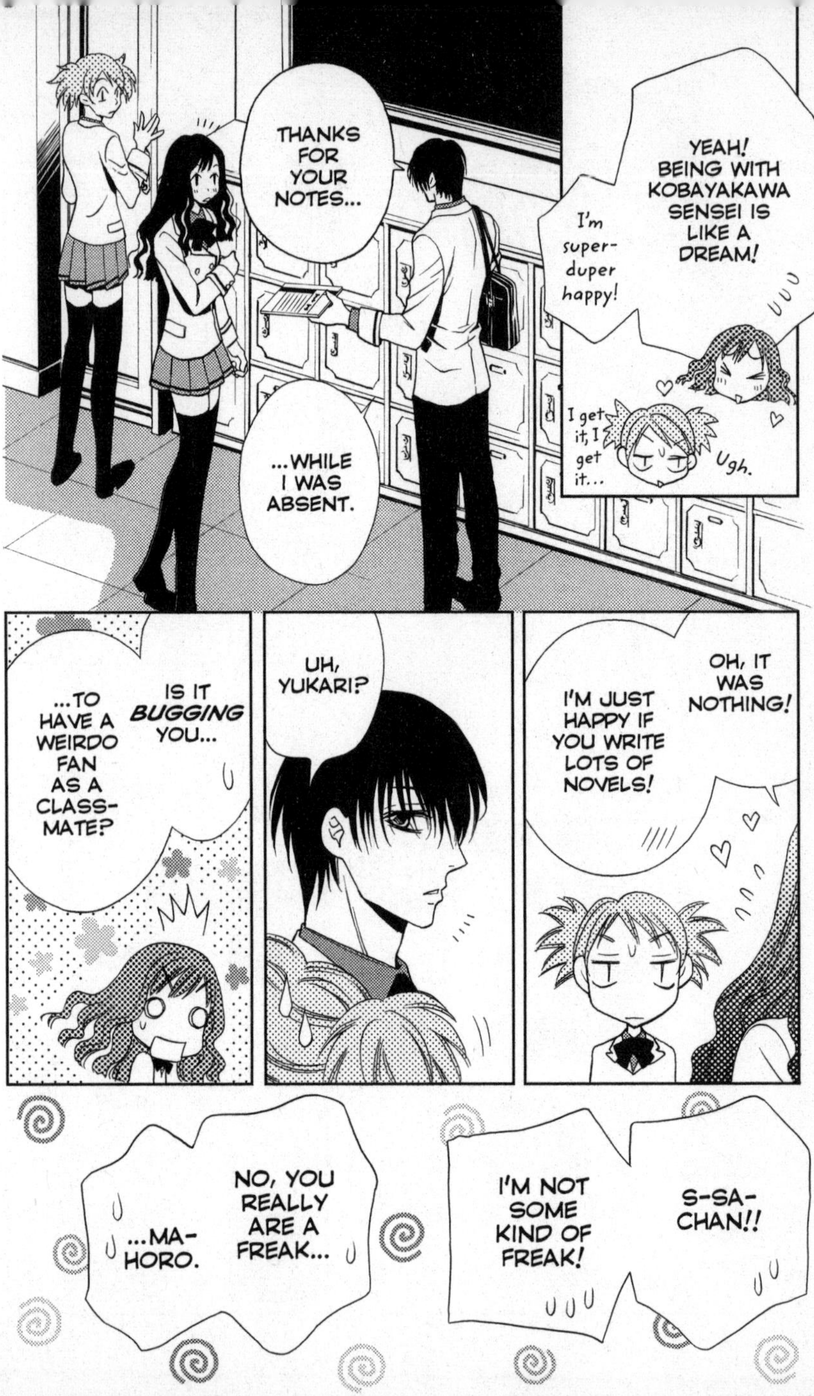
YEAH! BEING WITH KOBAYAKAWA SENSEI IS LIKE A DREAM!
I'm super-duper happy!
I get it, I get it...
Ugh.
THANKS FOR YOUR NOTES...
...WHILE I WAS ABSENT.
OH, IT WAS NOTHING!
I'M JUST HAPPY IF YOU WRITE LOTS OF NOVELS!
UH, YUKARI?
IS IT *BUGGING* YOU...
...TO HAVE A WEIRDO FAN AS A CLASS-MATE?
S-SA-CHAN!!
I'M NOT SOME KIND OF FREAK!
NO, YOU REALLY ARE A FREAK...
...MA-HORO.

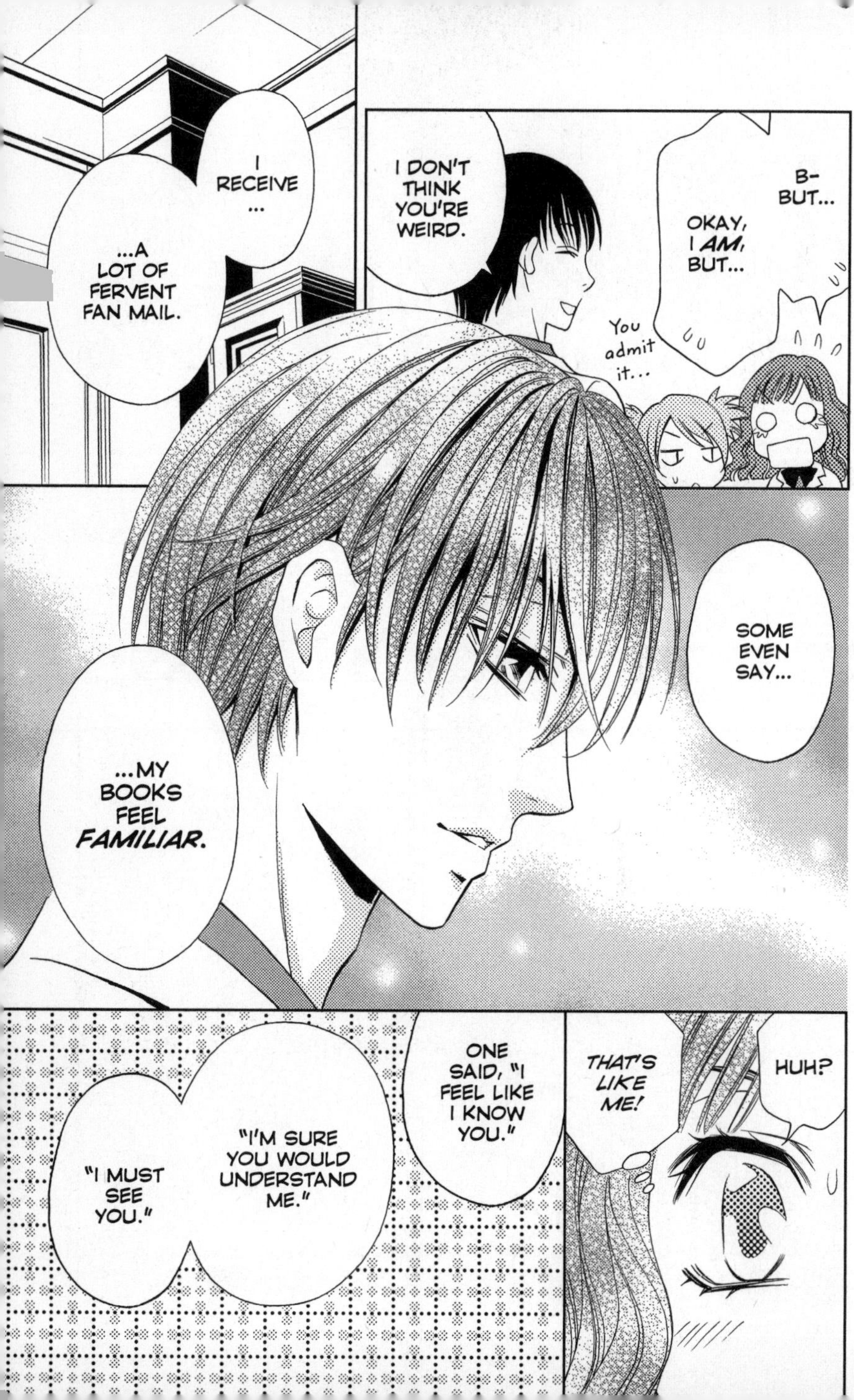
I DON'T THINK YOU'RE WEIRD.
B-BUT... OKAY, I *AM*, BUT...
You admit it...
I RECEIVE...
...A LOT OF FERVENT FAN MAIL.
SOME EVEN SAY...
...MY BOOKS FEEL *FAMILIAR*.
HUH?
THAT'S LIKE ME!
ONE SAID, "I FEEL LIKE I KNOW YOU."
"I'M SURE YOU WOULD UNDERSTAND ME."
"I MUST SEE YOU."

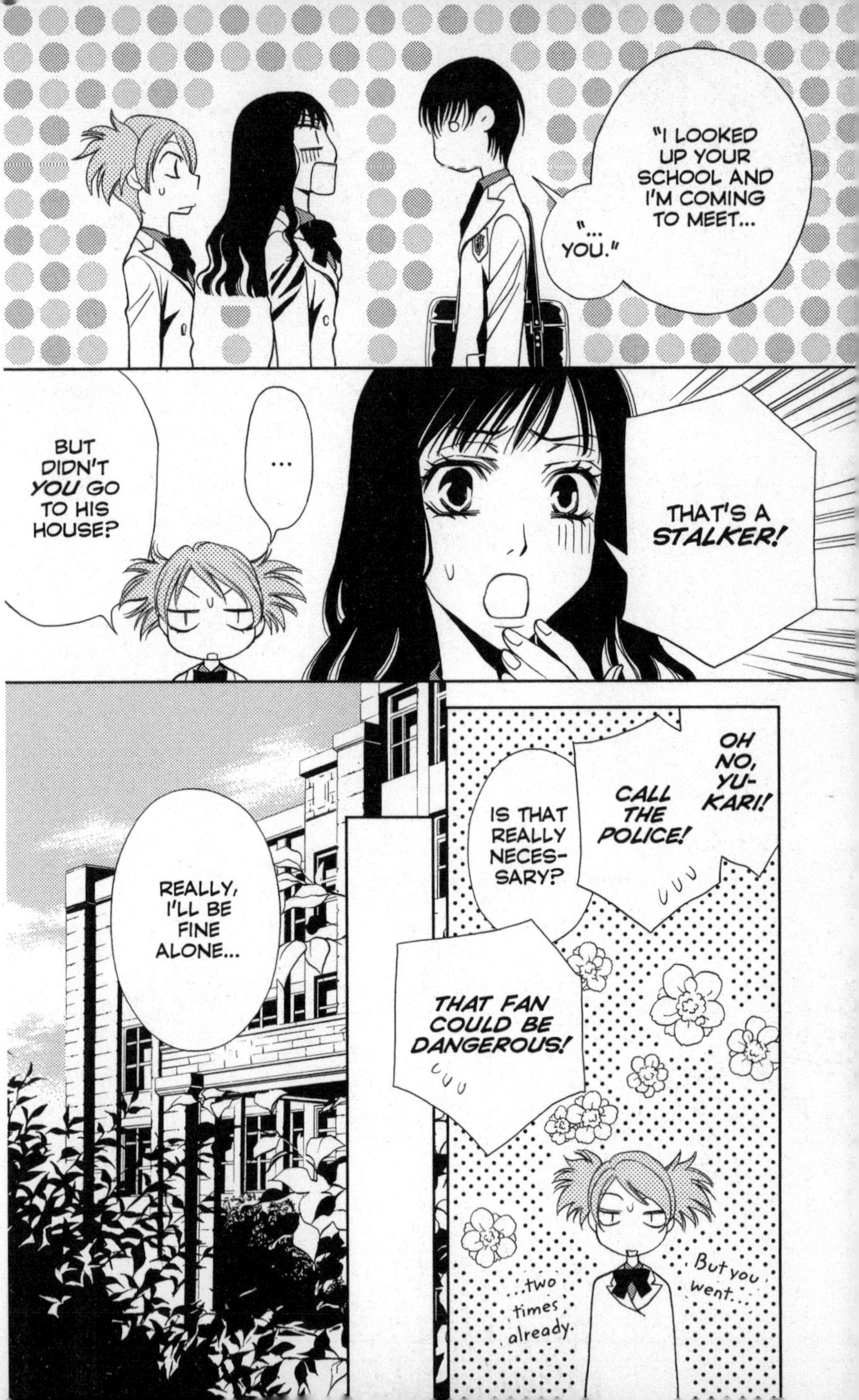
"I LOOKED UP YOUR SCHOOL AND I'M COMING TO MEET...
"... YOU."
THAT'S A STALKER!
...
BUT DIDN'T YOU GO TO HIS HOUSE?
OH NO, YU-KARI!
CALL THE POLICE!
IS THAT REALLY NECES-SARY?
THAT FAN COULD BE DANGEROUS!
But you went...
...two times already.
REALLY, I'LL BE FINE ALONE...

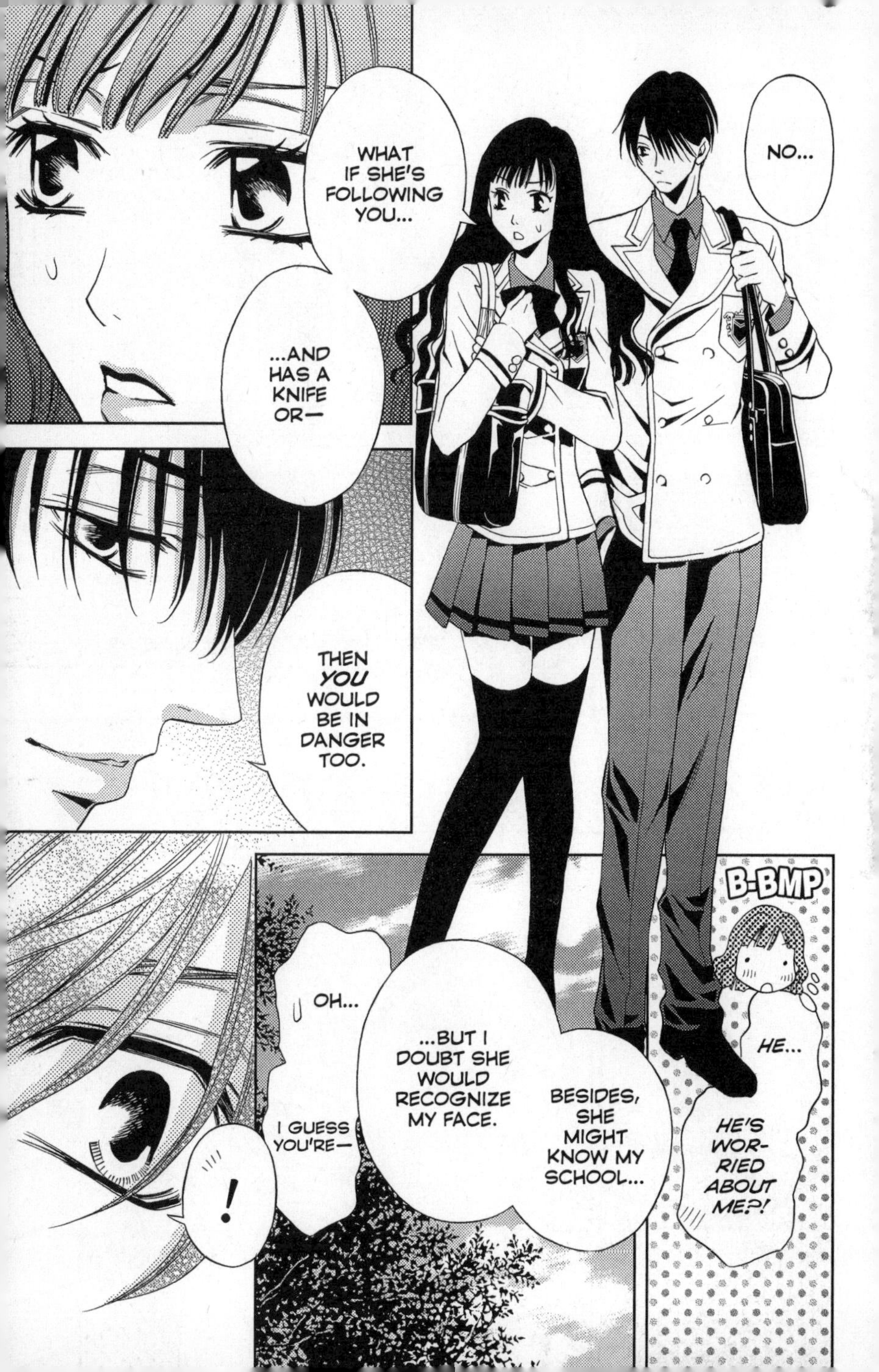
NO...
WHAT IF SHE'S FOLLOWING YOU...
...AND HAS A KNIFE OR—
THEN *YOU* WOULD BE IN DANGER TOO.
B-BMP
HE...
HE'S WORRIED ABOUT ME?!
BESIDES, SHE MIGHT KNOW MY SCHOOL...
...BUT I DOUBT SHE WOULD RECOGNIZE MY FACE.
OH...
I GUESS YOU'RE—
!

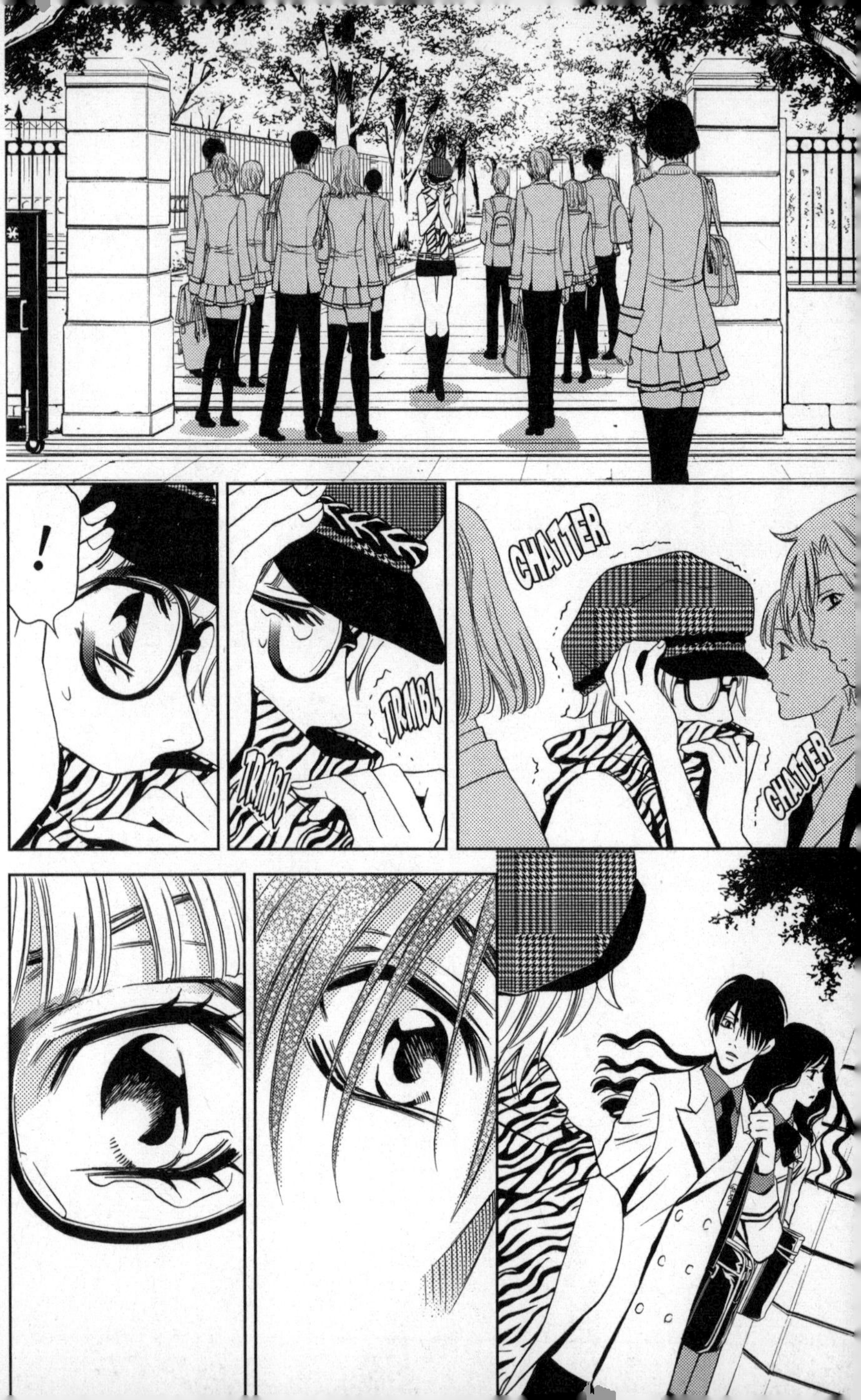
CHATTER
CHATTER
TRMBL
TRMBL
!

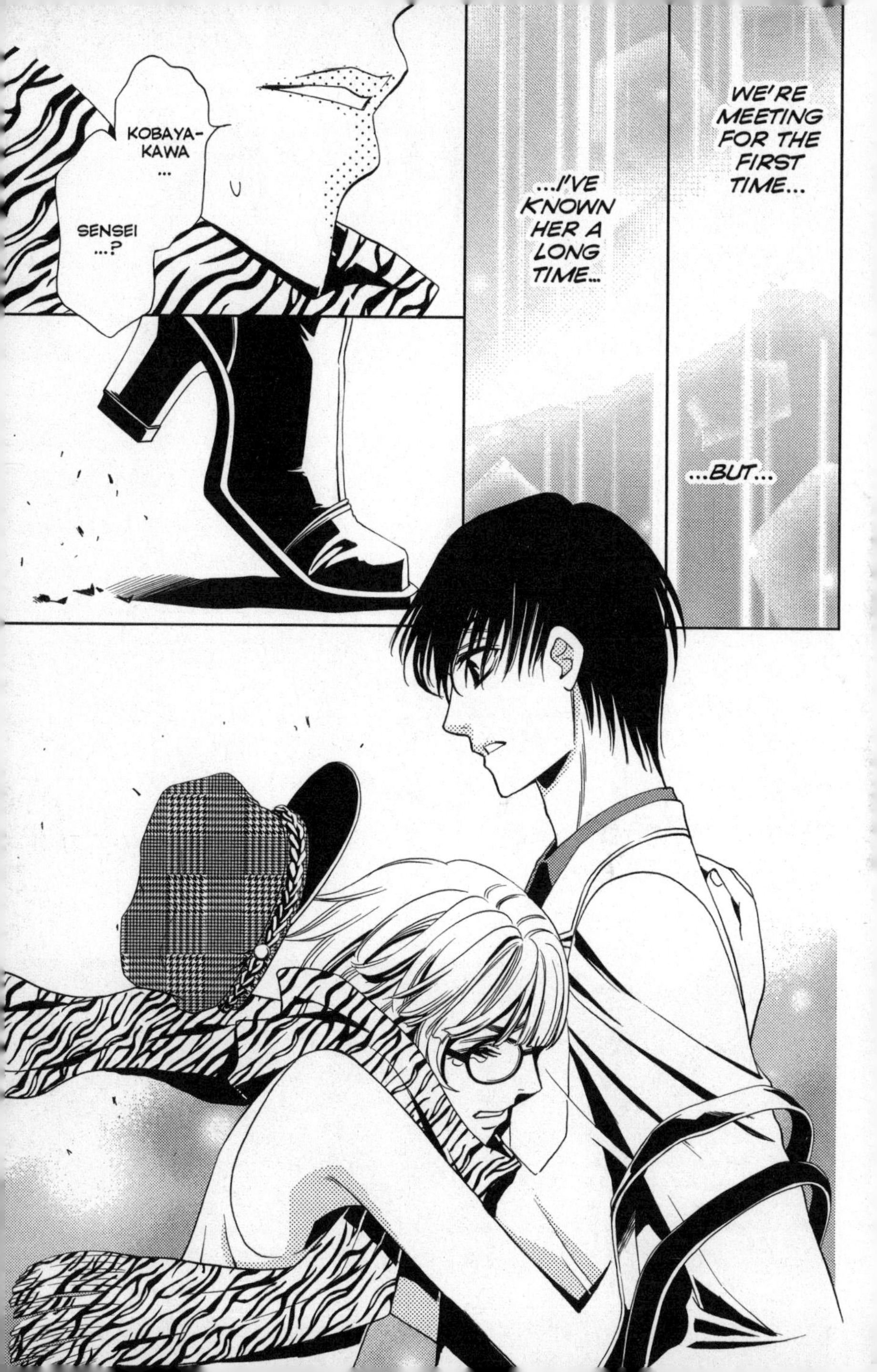
WE'RE MEETING FOR THE FIRST TIME...
...I'VE KNOWN HER A LONG TIME...
...BUT...
KOBAYA-KAWA ... SENSEI ...?

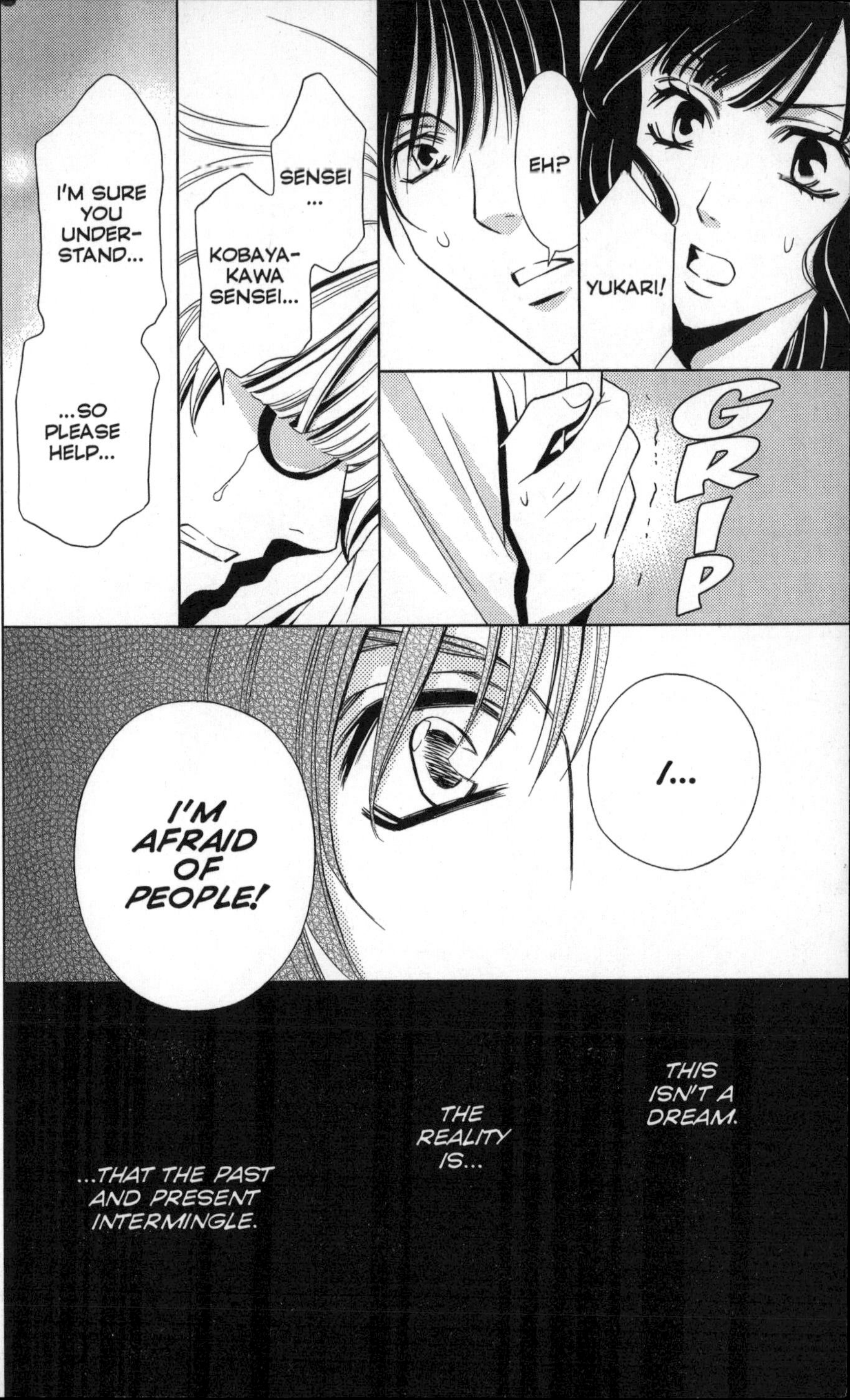
YUKARI!
EH?
GRIP
SENSEI ...
KOBAYA-KAWA SENSEI...
I'M SURE YOU UNDER-STAND...
...SO PLEASE HELP...
I...
I'M AFRAID OF PEOPLE!
THIS ISN'T A DREAM.
THE REALITY IS...
...THAT THE PAST AND PRESENT INTERMINGLE.

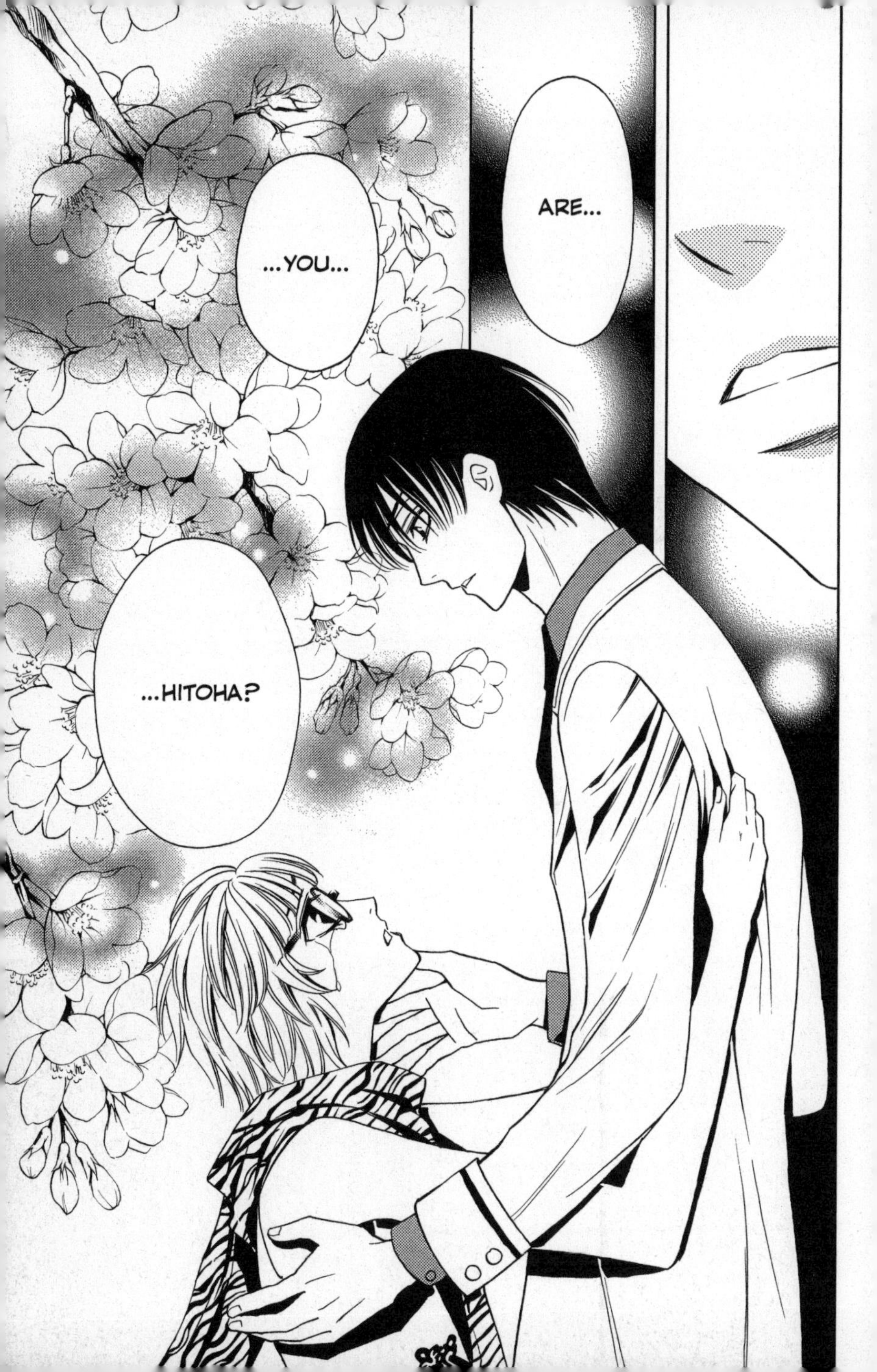
ARE...
...YOU...
...HITOHA?

Chapter 3

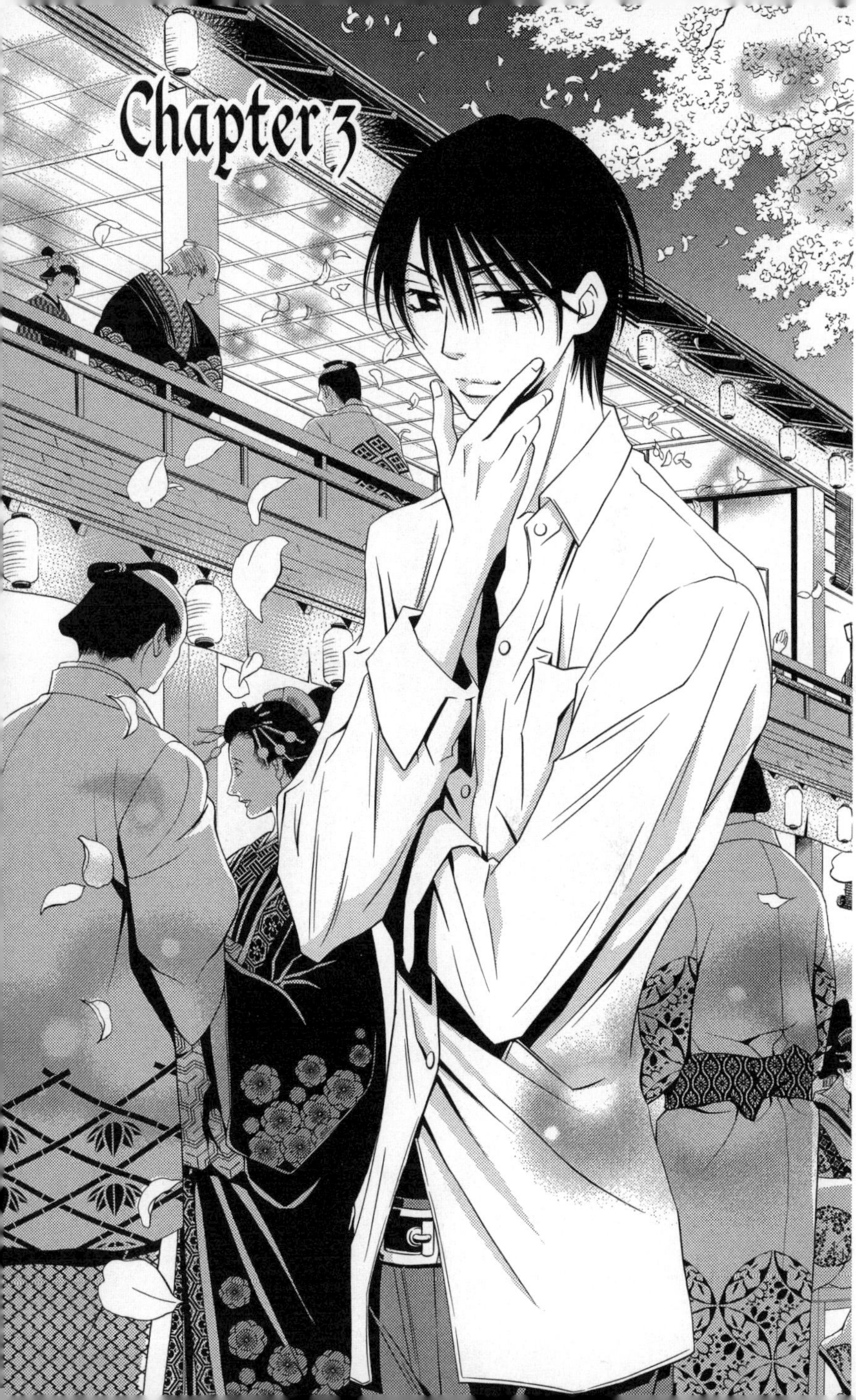

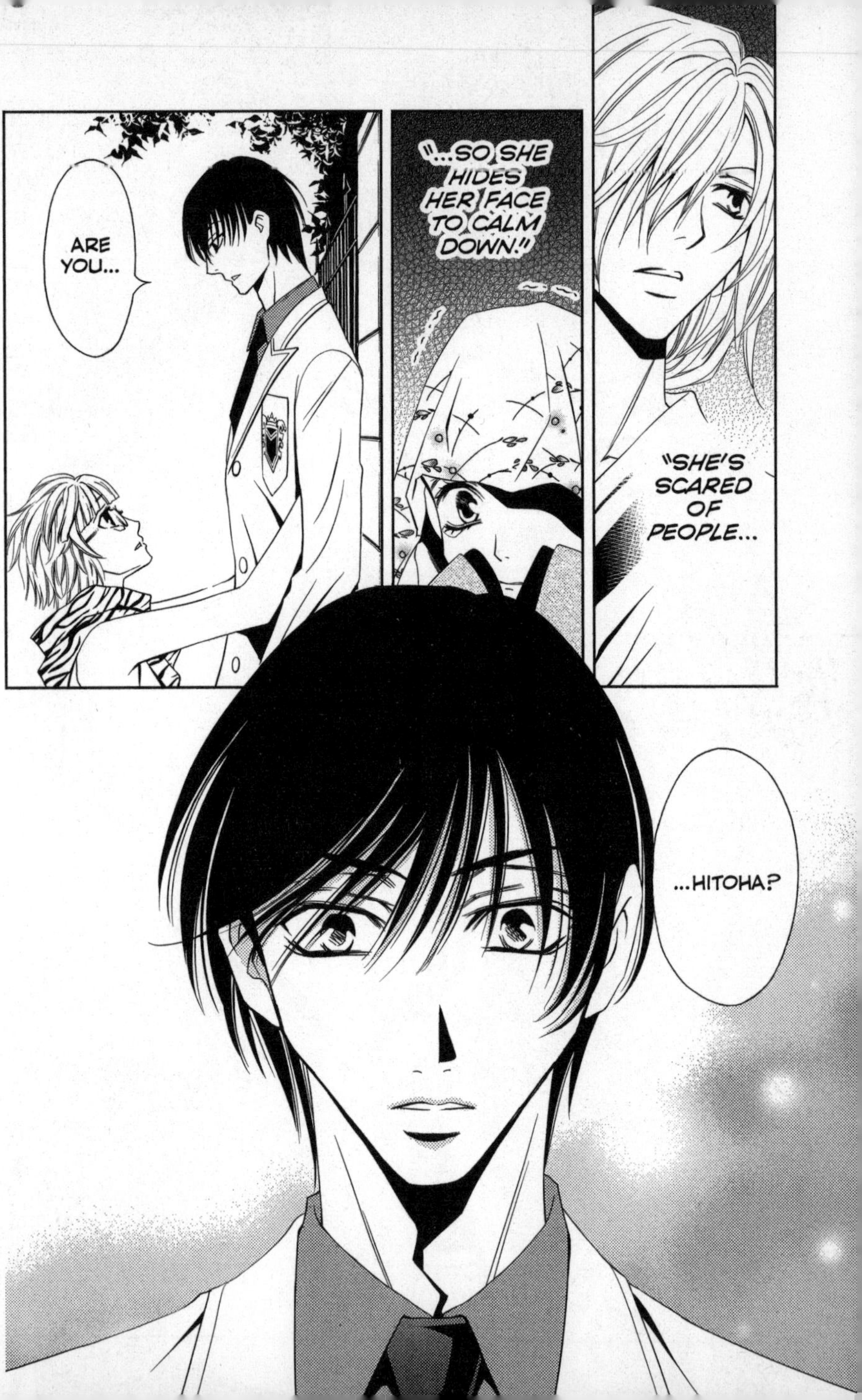
"SHE'S SCARED OF PEOPLE...
"...SO SHE HIDES HER FACE TO CALM DOWN."
ARE YOU...
...HITOHA?

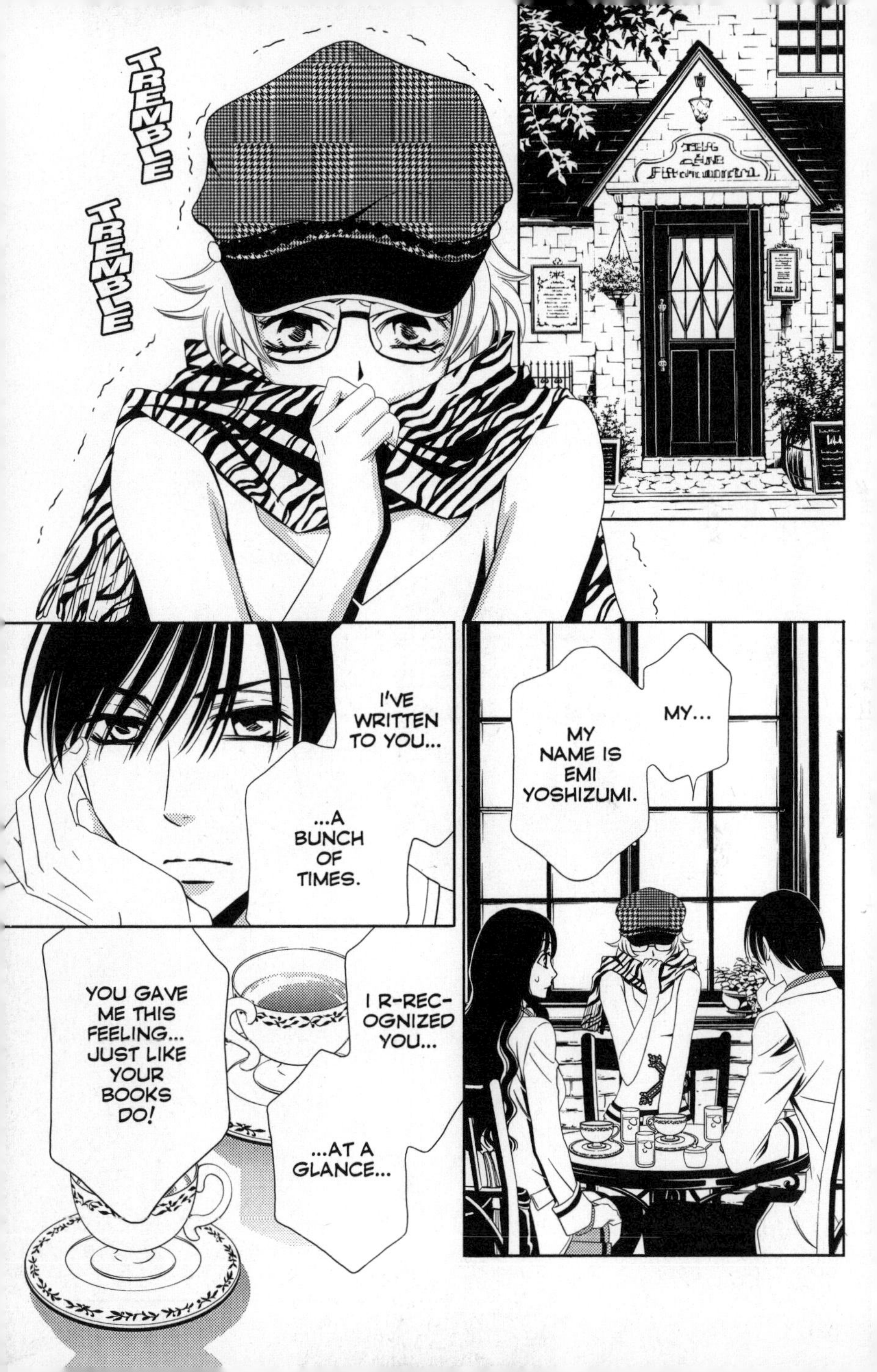
TREMBLE
TREMBLE
MY...
MY NAME IS EMI YOSHIZUMI.
I'VE WRITTEN TO YOU...
...A BUNCH OF TIMES.
I R-RECOGNIZED YOU...
...AT A GLANCE...
YOU GAVE ME THIS FEELING... JUST LIKE YOUR BOOKS DO!

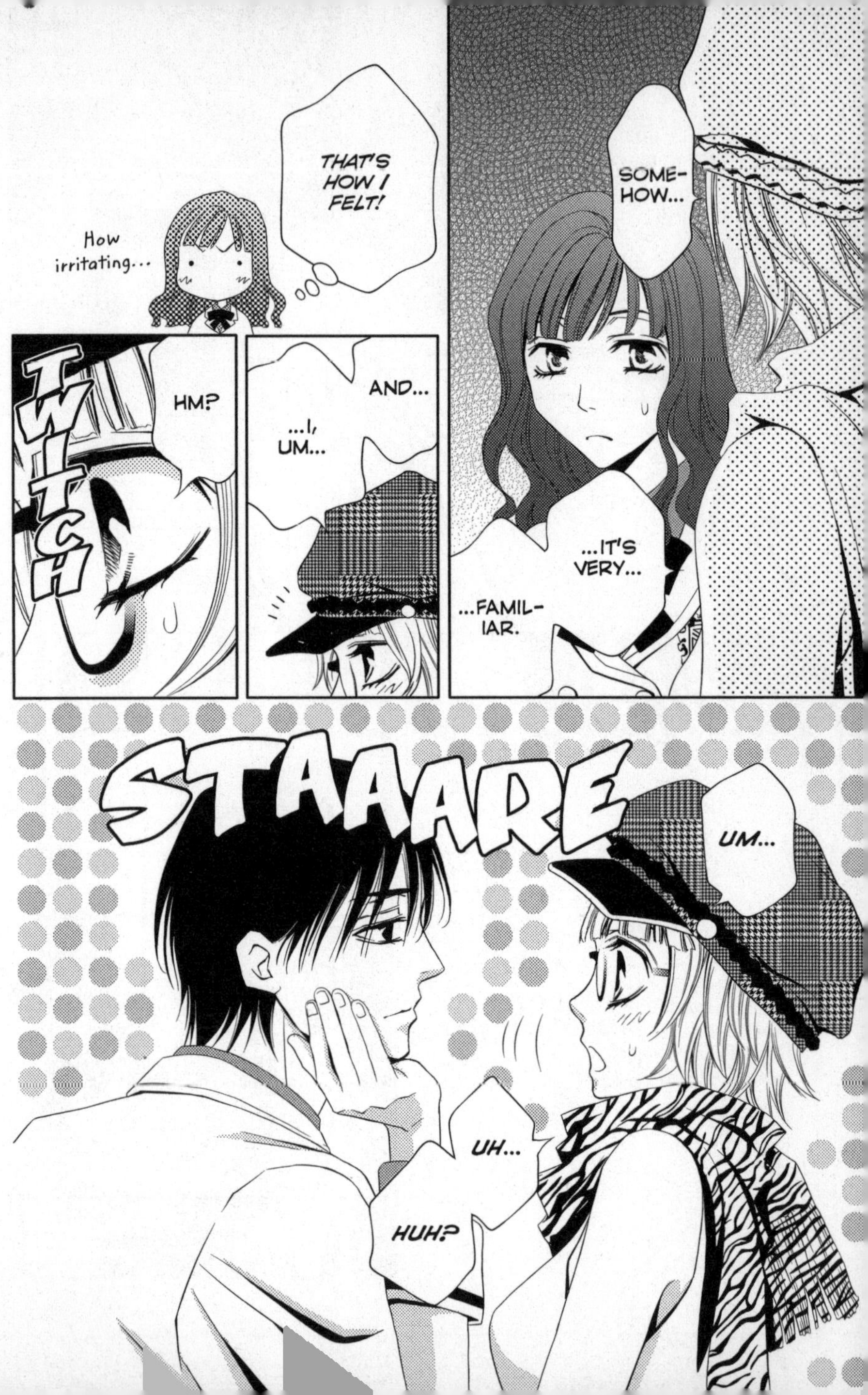
SOME-HOW...
...IT'S VERY...
...FAMIL-IAR.
THAT'S HOW I FELT!
How irritating...
AND...
...I, UM...
HM?
TWITCH
STAAARE
UM...
UH...
HUH?

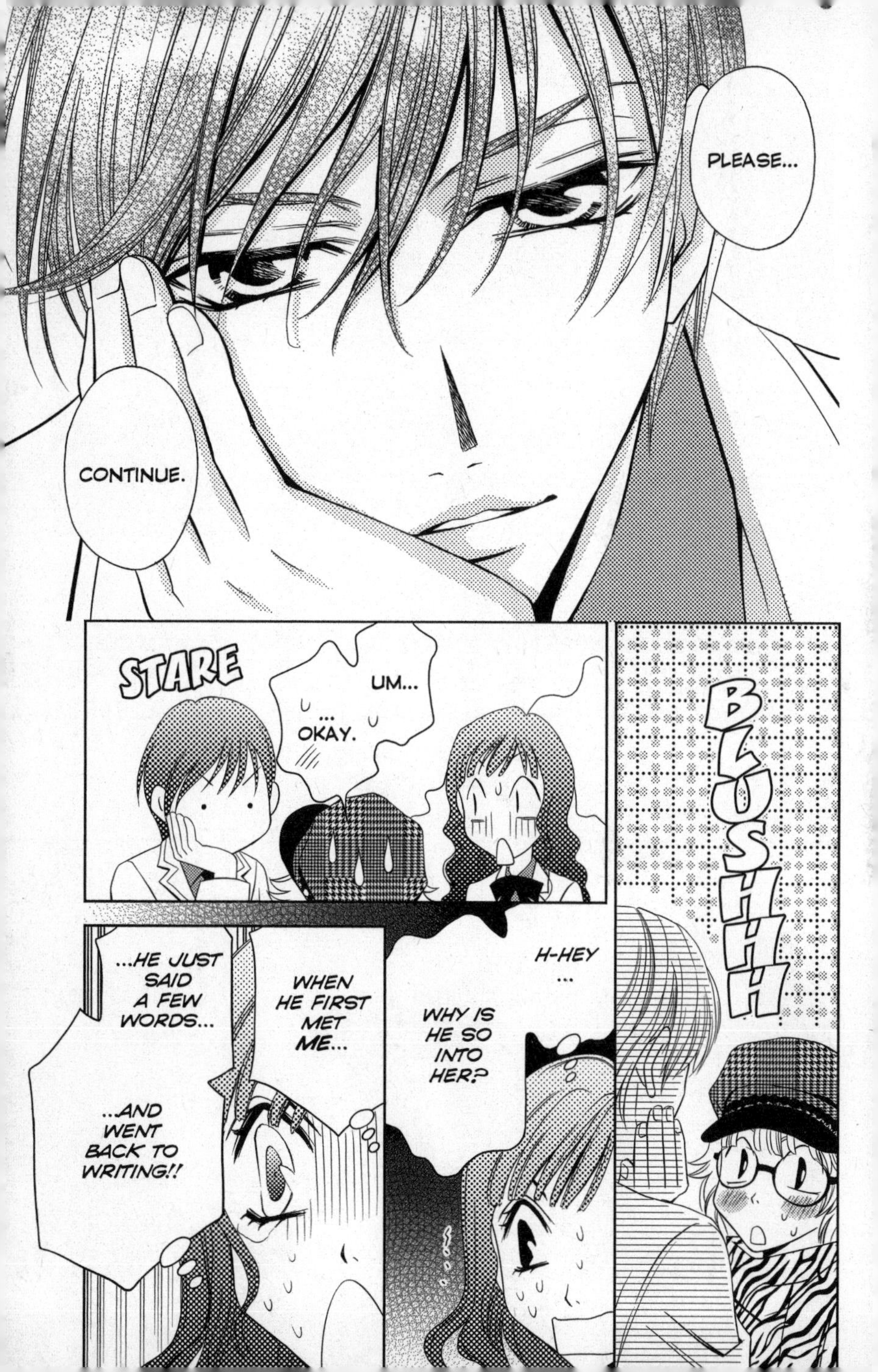
PLEASE...
CONTINUE.
BLUSHHH
STARE
UM...
...OKAY.
H-HEY...
WHY IS HE SO INTO HER?
WHEN HE FIRST MET ME...
...HE JUST SAID A FEW WORDS...
...AND WENT BACK TO WRITING!!

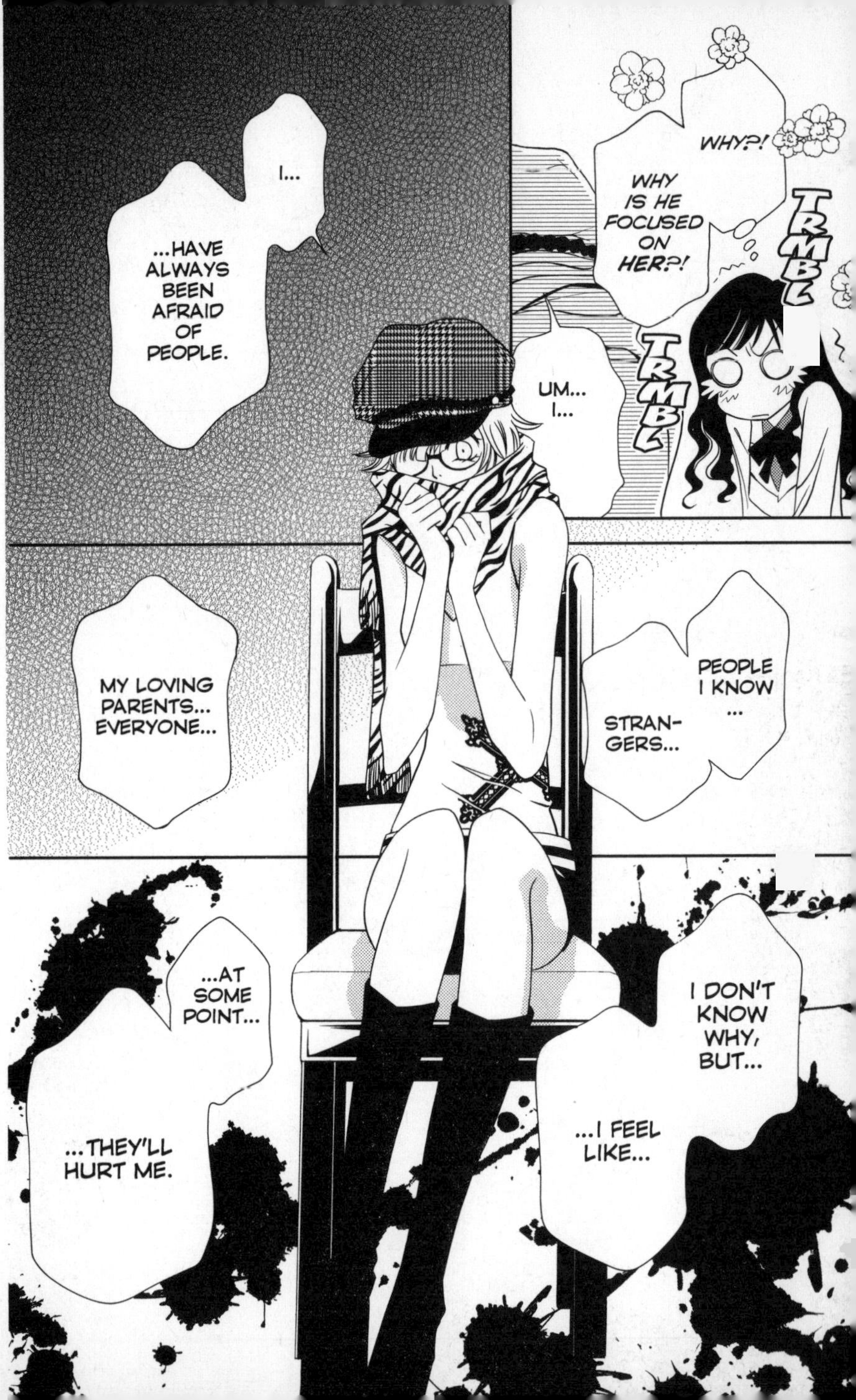
WHY?!
WHY IS HE FOCUSED ON HER?!
TRMBL
TRMBL
UM... I...
I...
...HAVE ALWAYS BEEN AFRAID OF PEOPLE.
PEOPLE I KNOW...
STRANGERS...
MY LOVING PARENTS... EVERYONE...
I DON'T KNOW WHY, BUT...
...I FEEL LIKE...
...AT SOME POINT...
...THEY'LL HURT ME.

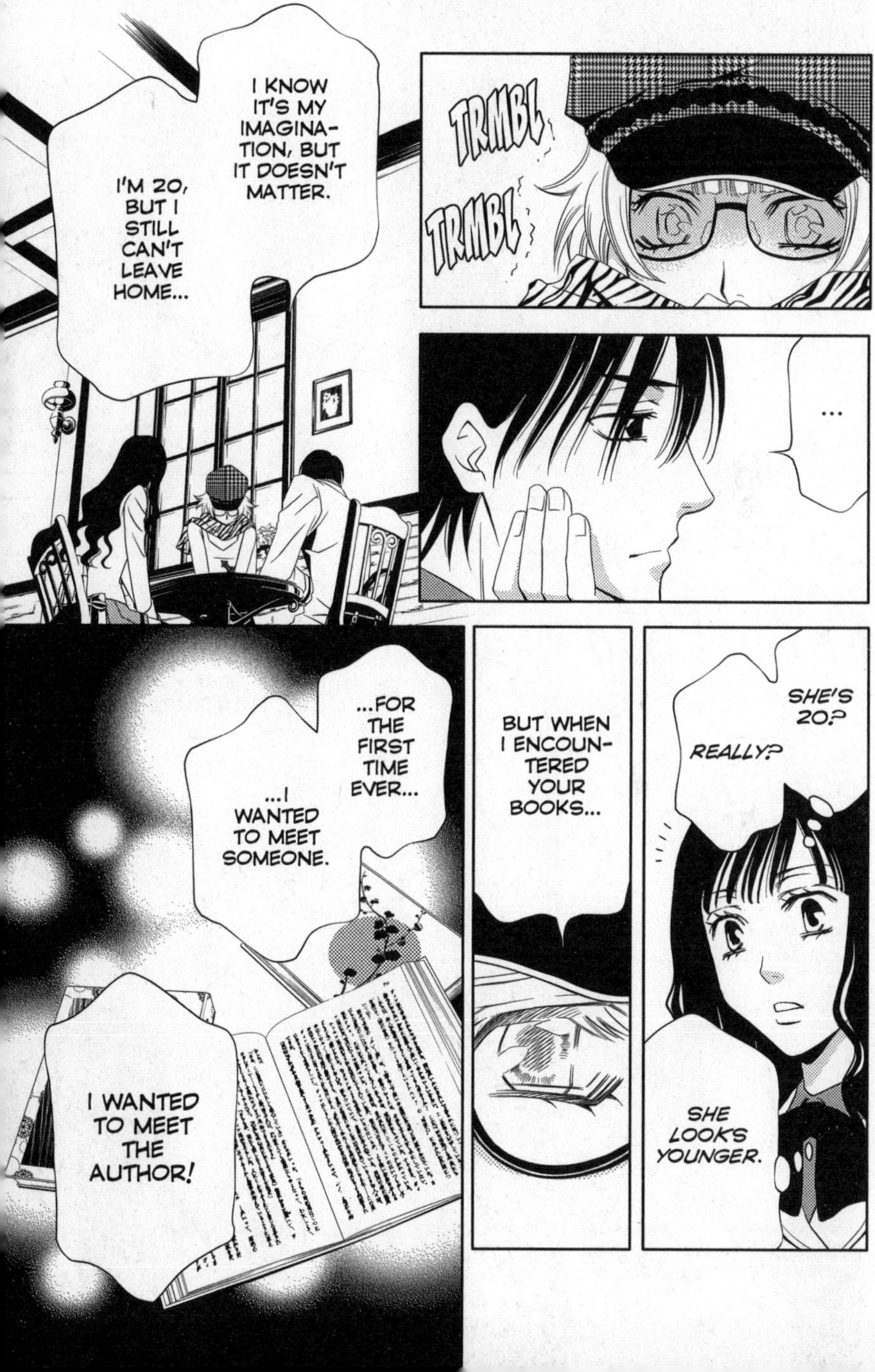
TRMBL
TRMBL
...
I KNOW IT'S MY IMAGINATION, BUT IT DOESN'T MATTER.
I'M 20, BUT I STILL CAN'T LEAVE HOME...
SHE'S 20?
REALLY?
SHE LOOKS YOUNGER.
BUT WHEN I ENCOUNTERED YOUR BOOKS...
...FOR THE FIRST TIME EVER...
...I WANTED TO MEET SOMEONE.
I WANTED TO MEET THE AUTHOR!

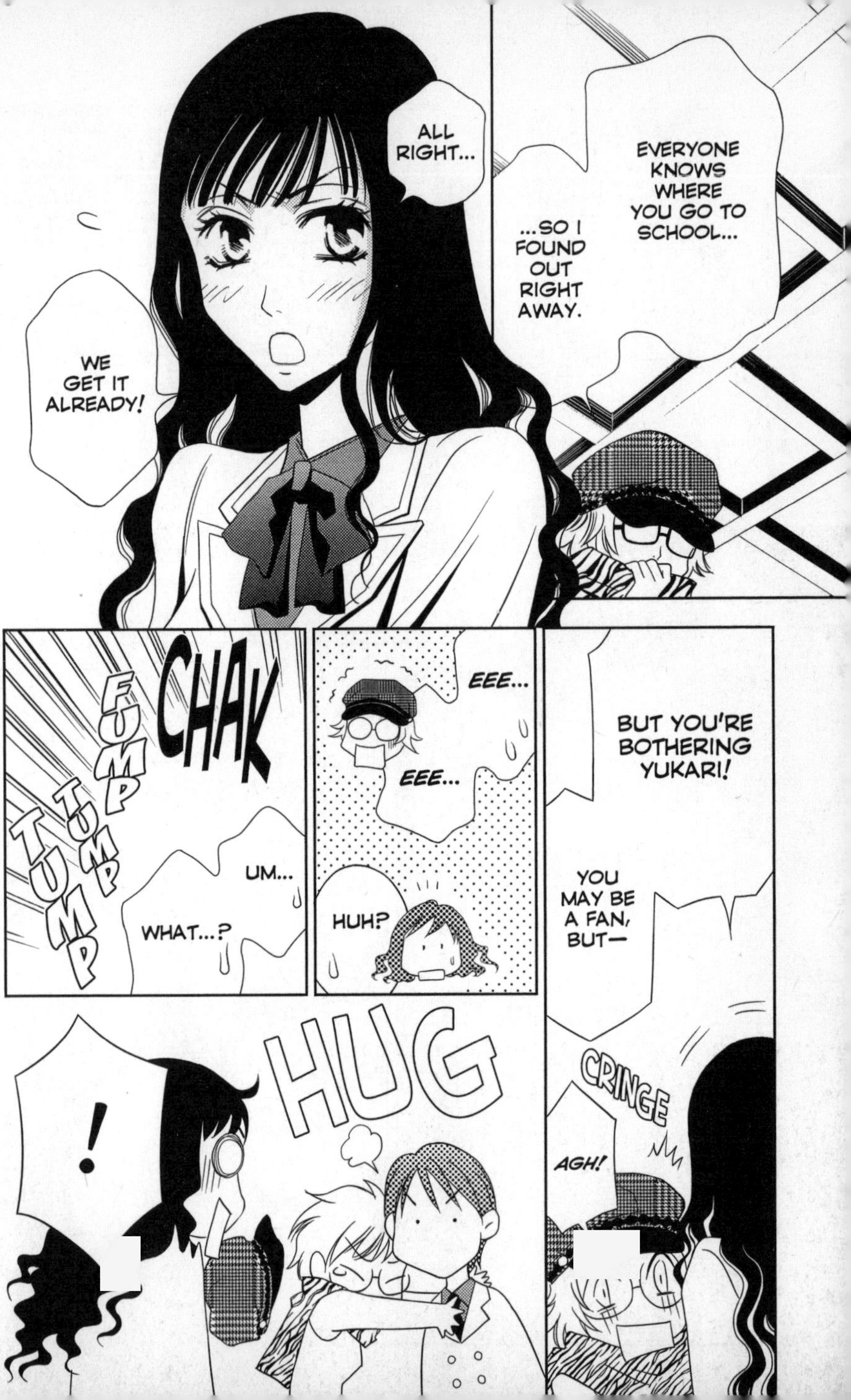
EVERYONE KNOWS WHERE YOU GO TO SCHOOL...
...SO I FOUND OUT RIGHT AWAY.
ALL RIGHT...
WE GET IT ALREADY!
BUT YOU'RE BOTHERING YUKARI!
YOU MAY BE A FAN, BUT—
CRINGE
AGH!
EEE...
EEE...
HUH?
CHAK
FUMP
TUMP
TUMP
UM...
WHAT...?
HUG
!

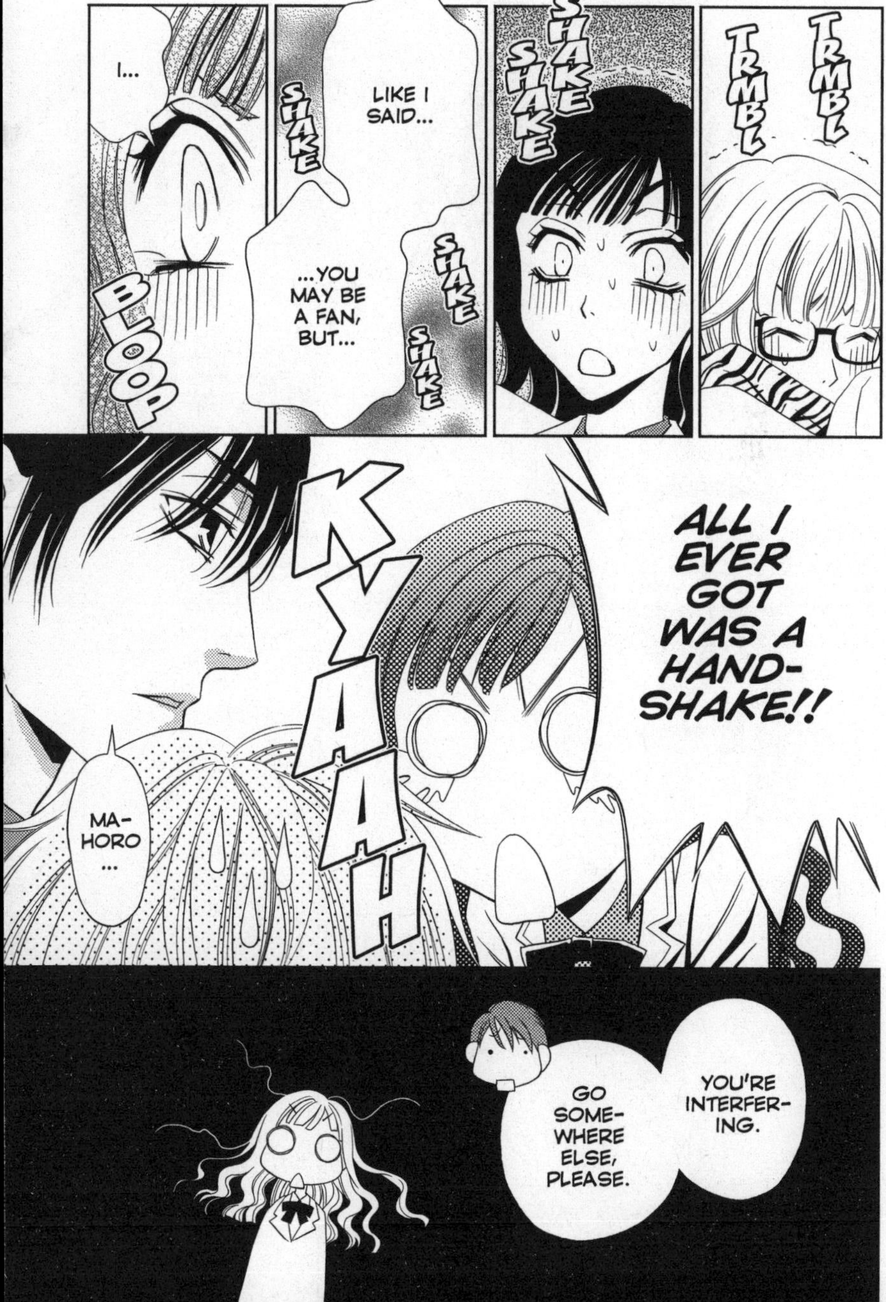
TRMBL
TRMBL
SHAKE
SHAKE
SHAKE
LIKE I SAID...
...YOU MAY BE A FAN, BUT...
SHAKE
SHAKE
SHAKE
I...
BLOOP
ALL I EVER GOT WAS A HAND-SHAKE!!
KYAAAH
MA-HORO...
YOU'RE INTERFER-ING.
GO SOME-WHERE ELSE, PLEASE.

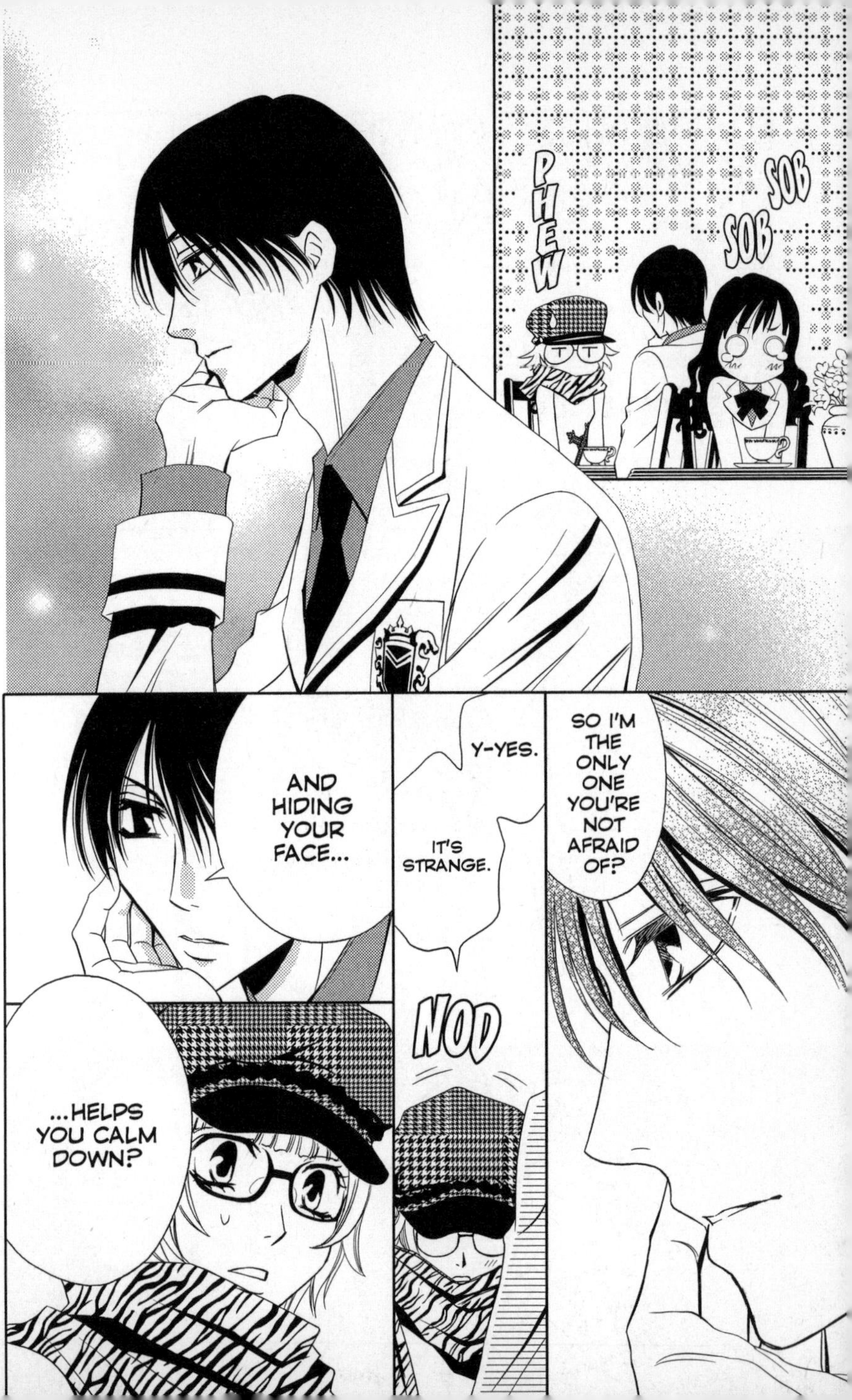
PHEW
SOB
SOB
SO I'M THE ONLY ONE YOU'RE NOT AFRAID OF?
Y-YES.
IT'S STRANGE.
AND HIDING YOUR FACE...
NOD
...HELPS YOU CALM DOWN?

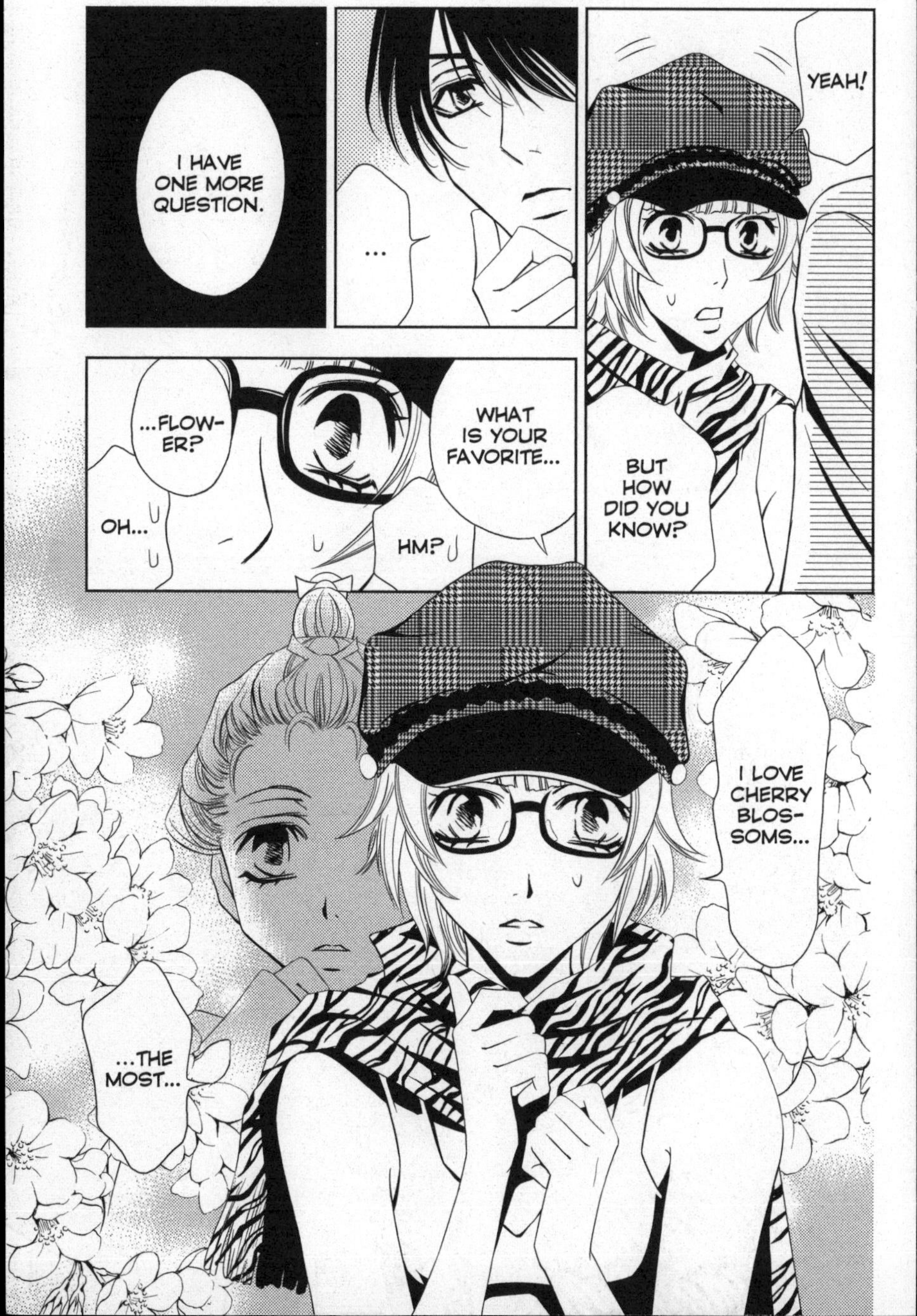
YEAH!
BUT HOW DID YOU KNOW?
...
I HAVE ONE MORE QUESTION.
WHAT IS YOUR FAVORITE...
HM?
...FLOWER?
OH...
I LOVE CHERRY BLOS-SOMS...
...THE MOST...

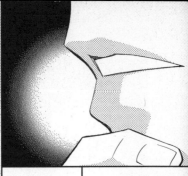

SHE'S A REINCARNATION OF THAT APPRENTICE IN THE PLEASURE DISTRICT...

...WHO FEARED PEOPLE BUT LIKED YUMURASAKI.

...IS HITOHA.

AHH...

THIS GIRL...

I KNEW IT.

SO WHEN I SAW THE PLEASURE DISTRICT...

...IN THE EDO PERIOD...

...IT WASN'T JUST A DREAM.

HA HA...

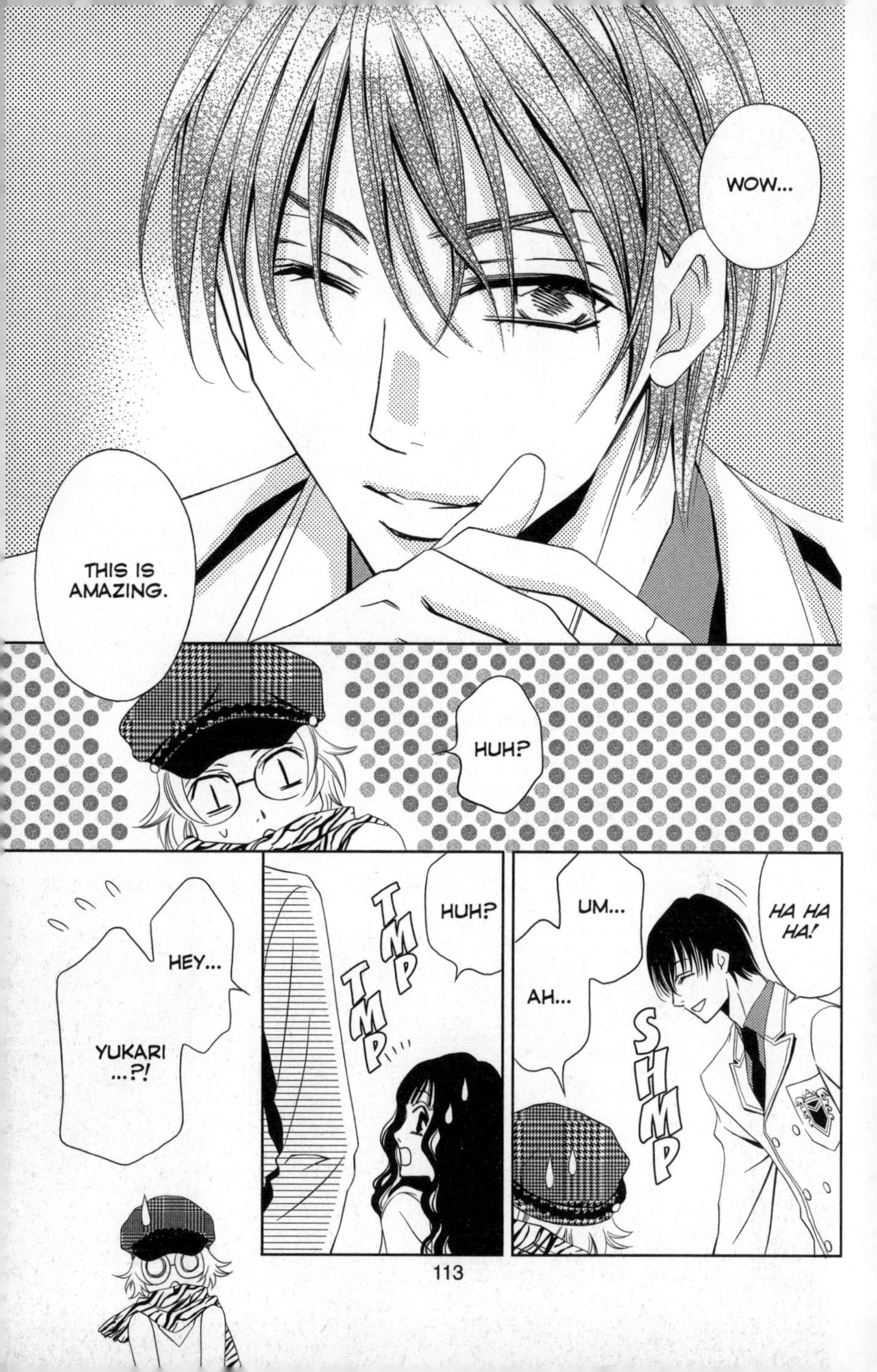
WOW...
THIS IS AMAZING.
HUH?
HA HA HA!
UM...
AH...
SHMP
HUH?
TMP
TMP
HEY...
YUKARI ...?!

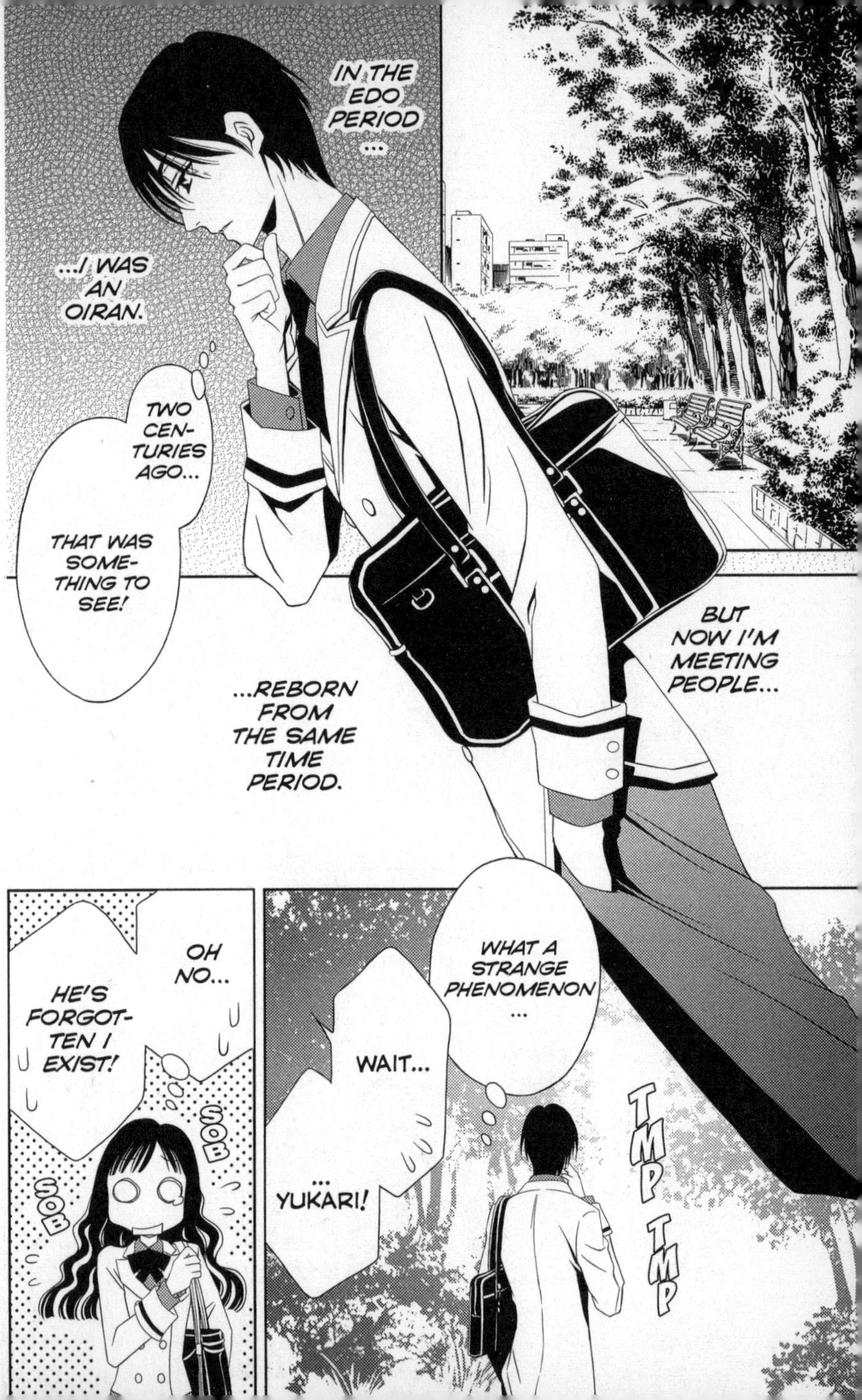
IN THE EDO PERIOD...
...I WAS AN OIRAN.
TWO CENTURIES AGO...
THAT WAS SOMETHING TO SEE!
BUT NOW I'M MEETING PEOPLE...
...REBORN FROM THE SAME TIME PERIOD.
WHAT A STRANGE PHENOMENON...
WAIT...
...YUKARI!
TMP TMP
OH NO...
HE'S FORGOTTEN I EXIST!
SOB
SOB

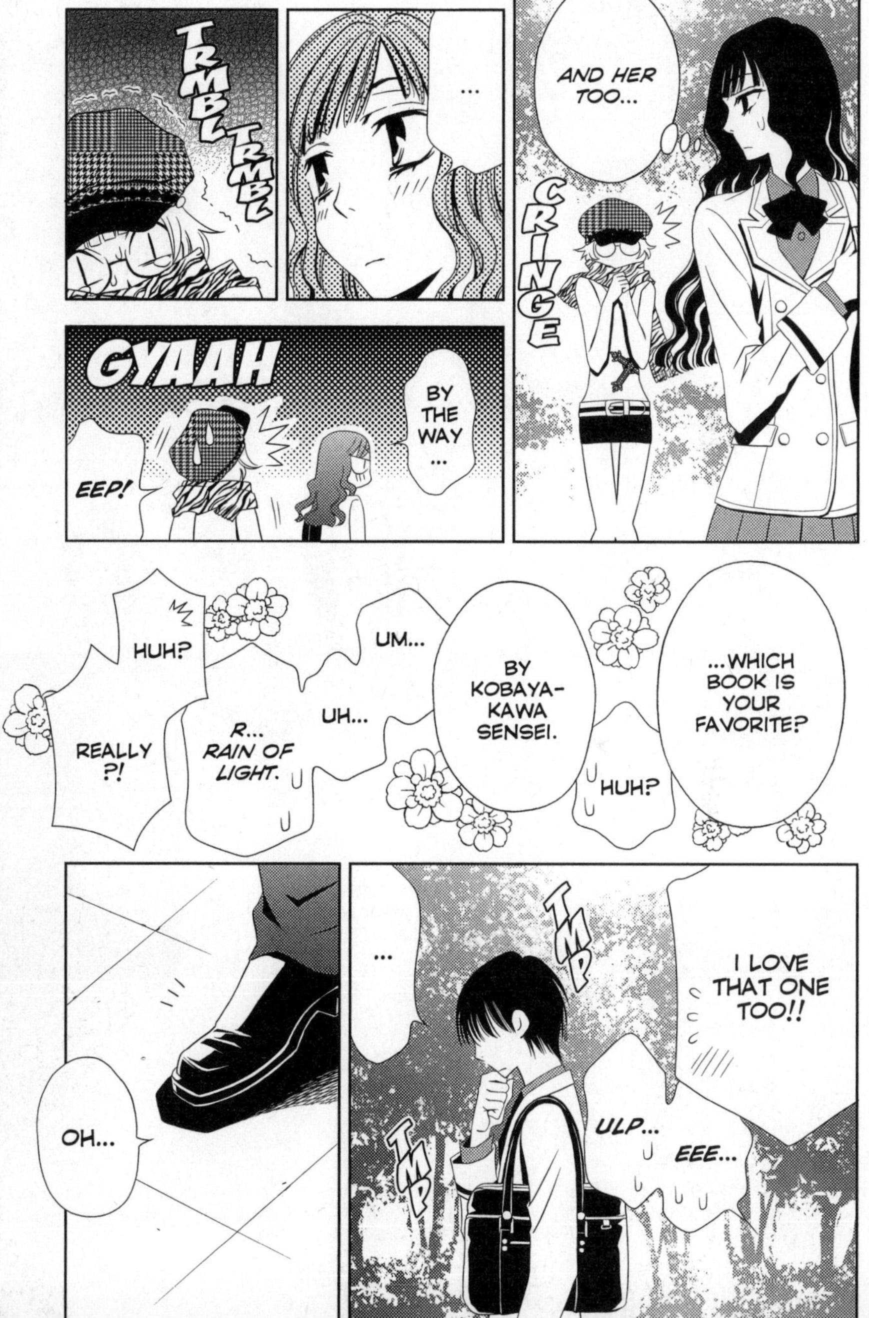
AND HER TOO...
CRINGE
...
TRMBL TRMBL
BY THE WAY...
GYAAH
EEP!
...WHICH BOOK IS YOUR FAVORITE?
HUH?
BY KOBAYA-KAWA SENSEI.
UH...
UM...
R... RAIN OF LIGHT.
HUH?
REALLY?!
I LOVE THAT ONE TOO!!
TMP
...
EEE...
ULP...
TMP
OH...

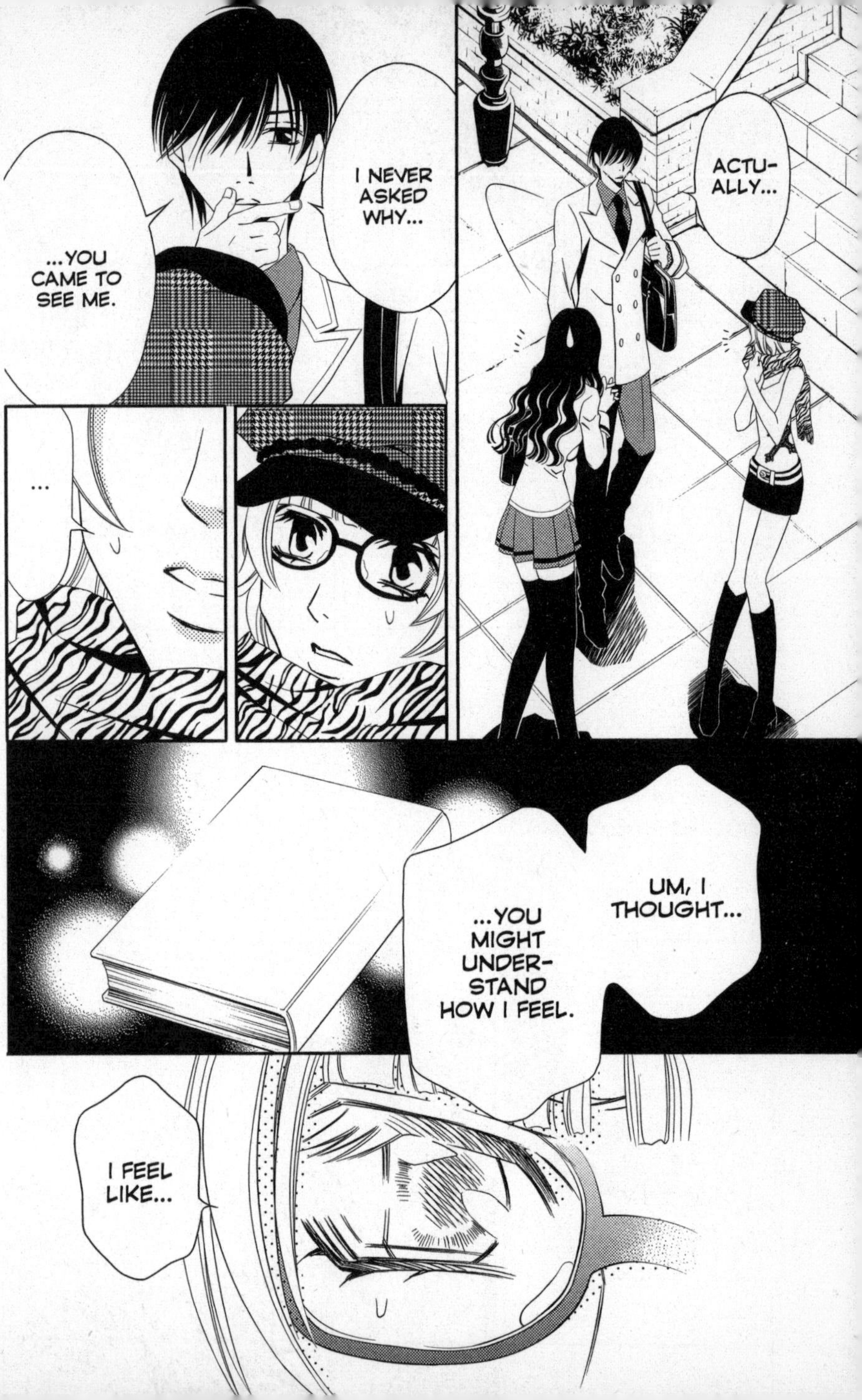
ACTU-ALLY...
I NEVER ASKED WHY...
...YOU CAME TO SEE ME.
...
UM, I THOUGHT...
...YOU MIGHT UNDER-STAND HOW I FEEL.
I FEEL LIKE...

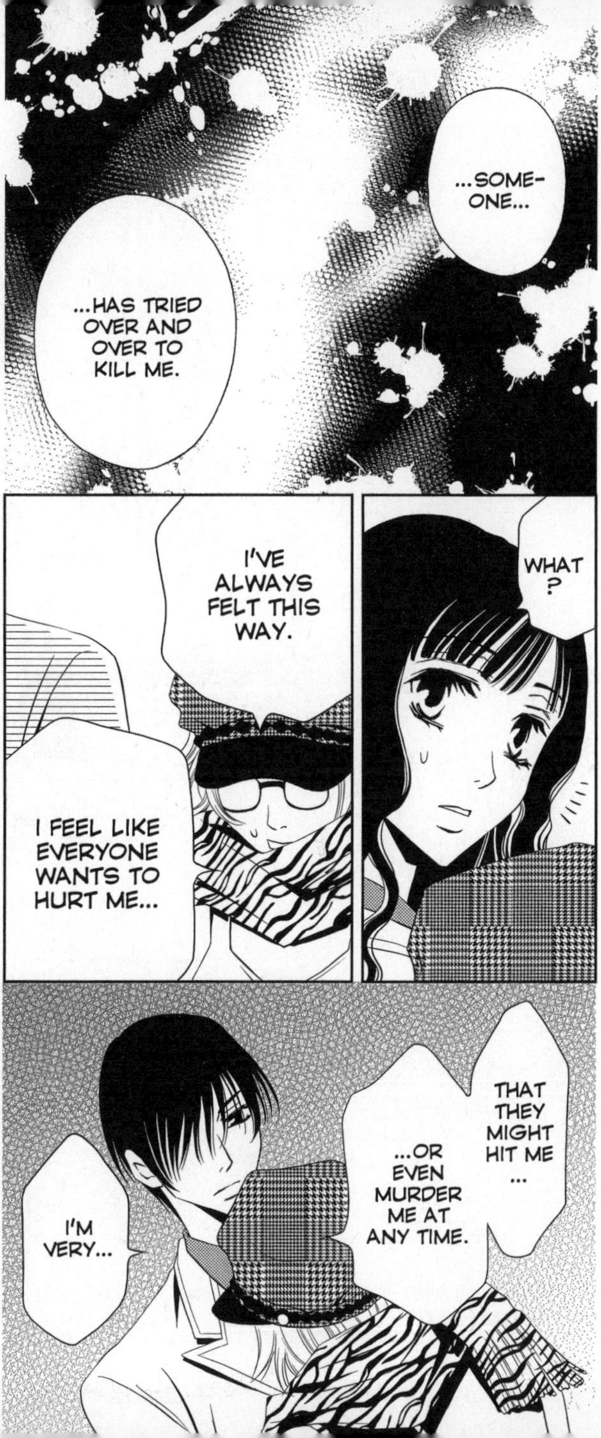
...SOME-ONE...
...HAS TRIED OVER AND OVER TO KILL ME.
WHAT?
I'VE ALWAYS FELT THIS WAY.
I FEEL LIKE EVERYONE WANTS TO HURT ME...
THAT THEY MIGHT HIT ME...
...OR EVEN MURDER ME AT ANY TIME.
I'M VERY...

SHIOMI'S DAILY LIFE ③

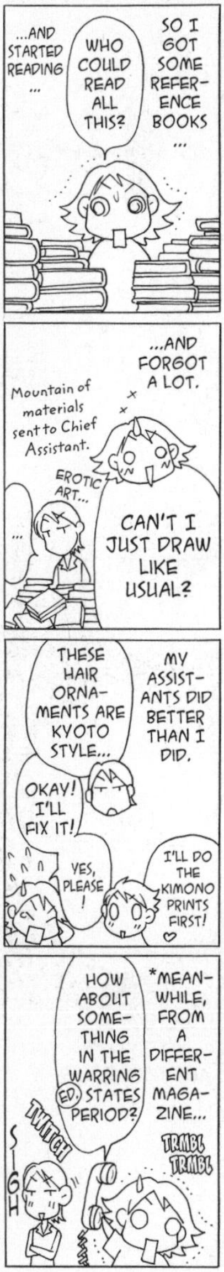
SO I GOT SOME REFERENCE BOOKS...
WHO COULD READ ALL THIS?
...AND STARTED READING...
...AND FORGOT A LOT.
Mountain of materials sent to Chief Assistant.
EROTIC ART...
CAN'T I JUST DRAW LIKE USUAL?
...
MY ASSISTANTS DID BETTER THAN I DID.
THESE HAIR ORNAMENTS ARE KYOTO STYLE...
OKAY! I'LL FIX IT!
I'LL DO THE KIMONO PRINTS FIRST!
YES, PLEASE!
*MEANWHILE, FROM A DIFFERENT MAGAZINE...
HOW ABOUT SOMETHING IN THE WARRING STATES PERIOD?
ED.
TRMBL TRMBL
TWITCH
SIGH

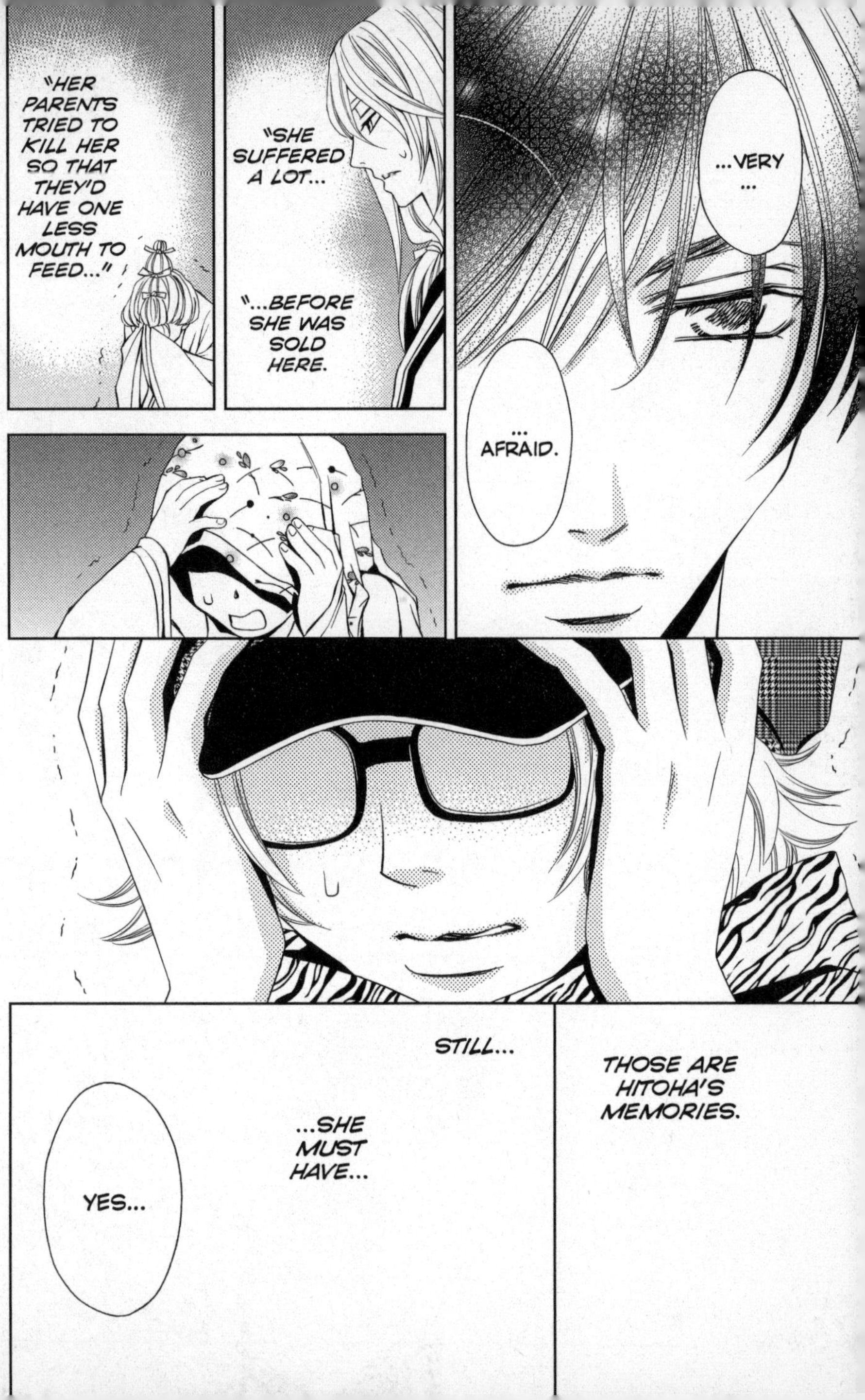
...VERY ...
... AFRAID.
“SHE SUFFERED A LOT...
“...BEFORE SHE WAS SOLD HERE.
“HER PARENTS TRIED TO KILL HER SO THAT THEY'D HAVE ONE LESS MOUTH TO FEED...”
THOSE ARE HITOHA'S MEMORIES.
STILL...
...SHE MUST HAVE...
YES...

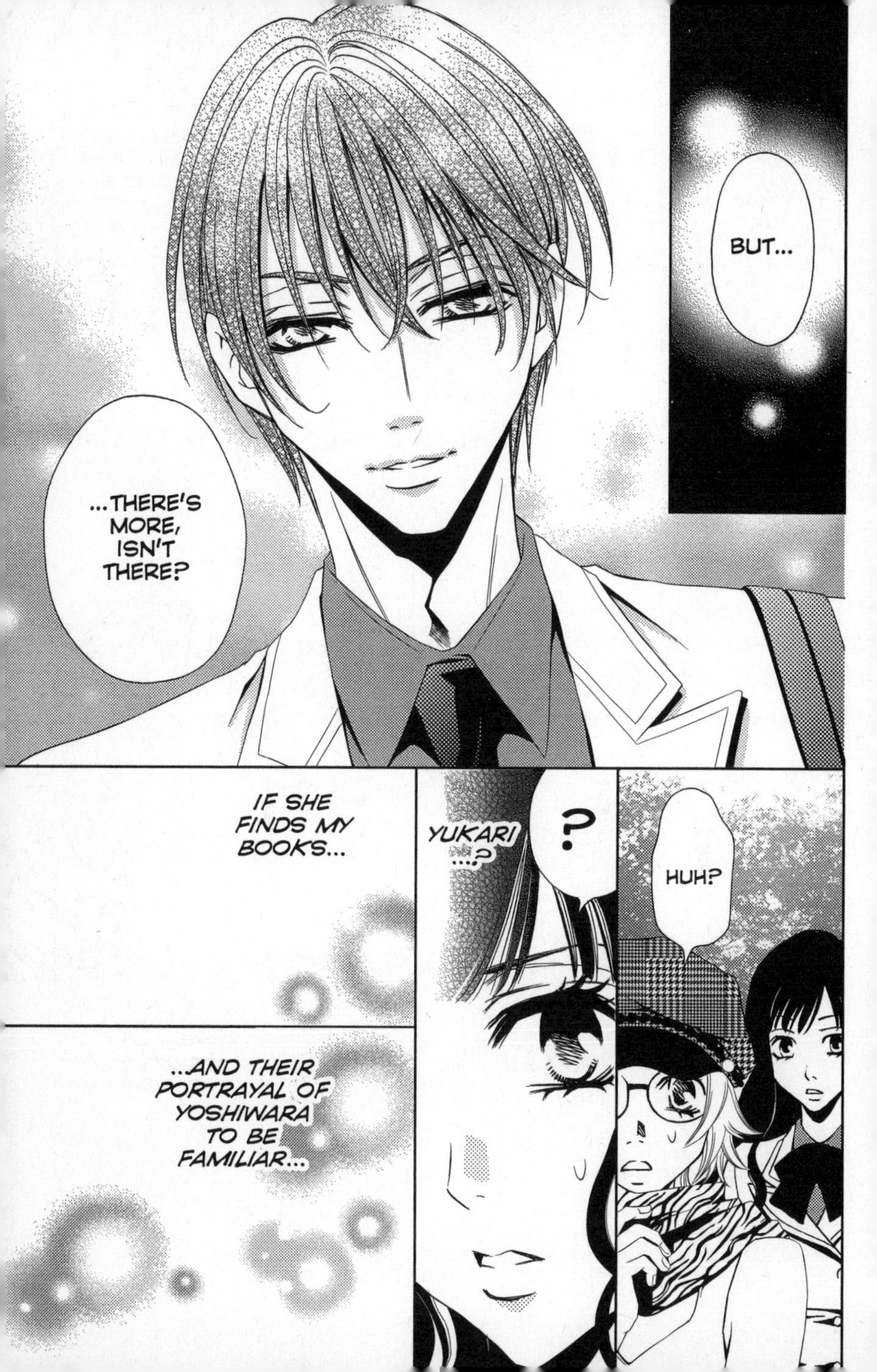
BUT...
...THERE'S MORE, ISN'T THERE?
HUH?
?
YUKARI ...?
IF SHE FINDS MY BOOKS...
...AND THEIR PORTRAYAL OF YOSHIWARA TO BE FAMILIAR...

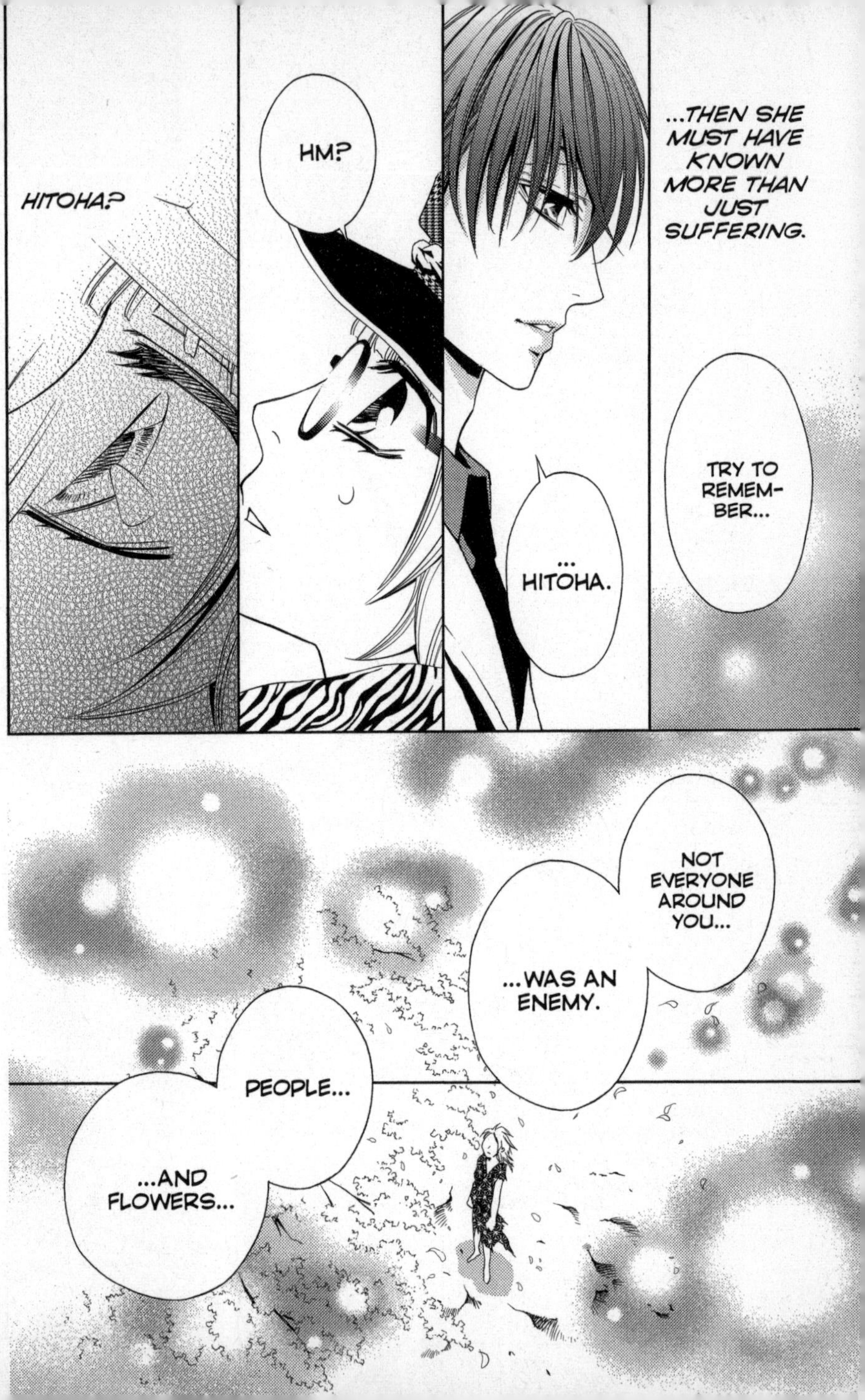
...THEN SHE MUST HAVE KNOWN MORE THAN JUST SUFFERING.
TRY TO REMEMBER...
... HITOHA.
HM?
HITOHA?
NOT EVERYONE AROUND YOU...
...WAS AN ENEMY.
PEOPLE...
...AND FLOWERS...

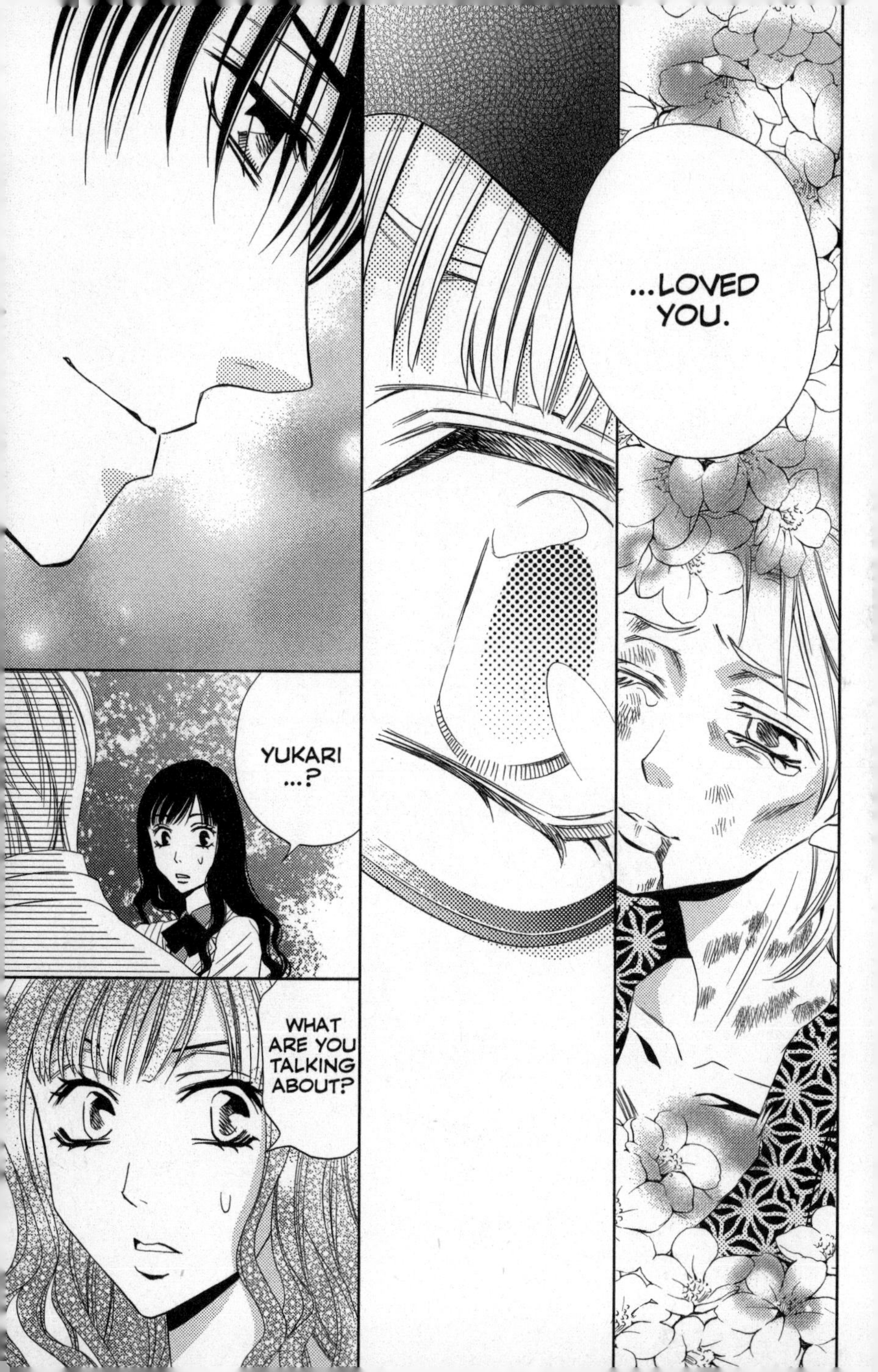
...LOVED YOU.
YUKARI ...?
WHAT ARE YOU TALKING ABOUT?

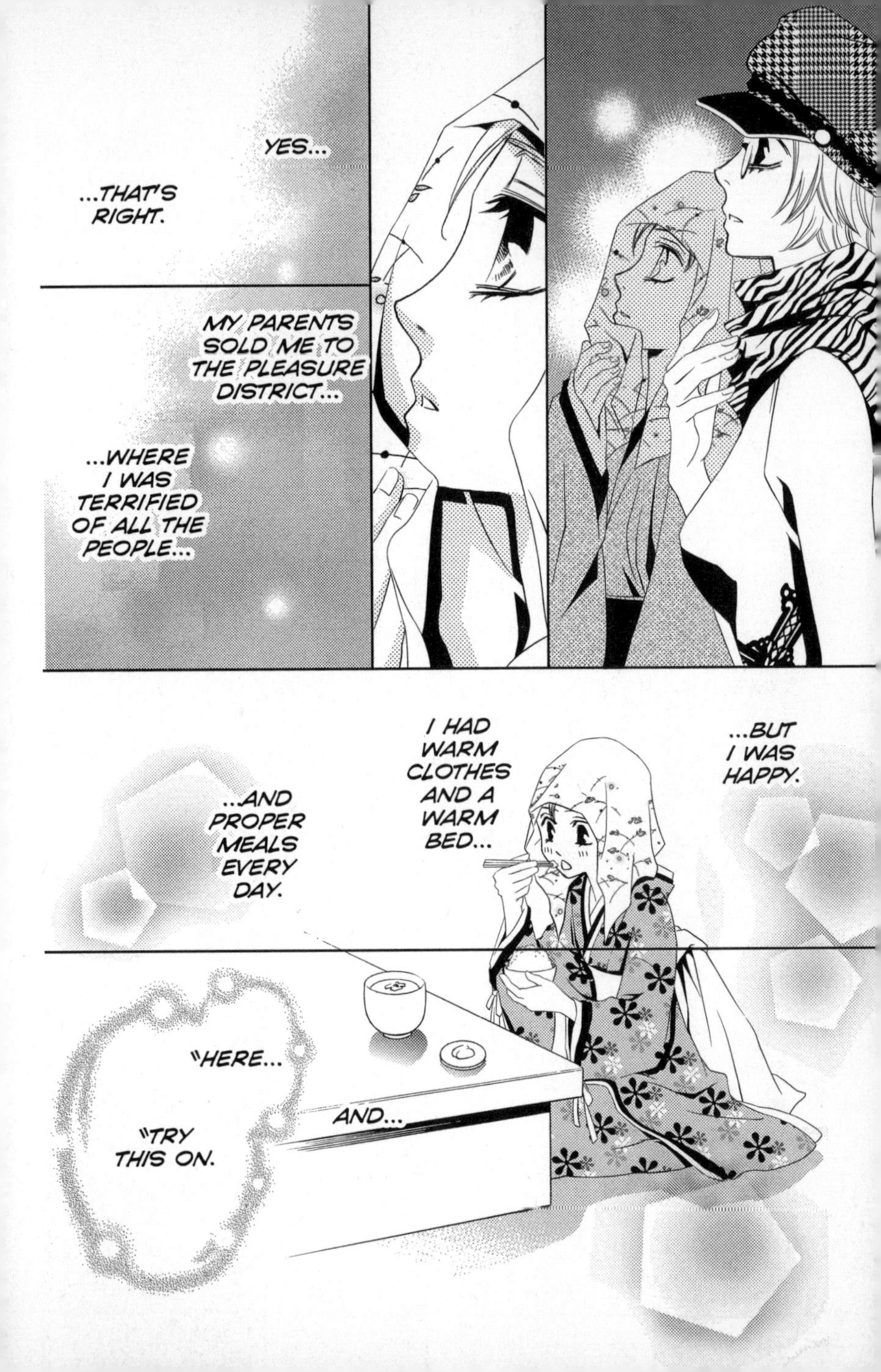
YES...
...THAT'S RIGHT.
MY PARENTS SOLD ME TO THE PLEASURE DISTRICT...
...WHERE I WAS TERRIFIED OF ALL THE PEOPLE...
...BUT I WAS HAPPY.
I HAD WARM CLOTHES AND A WARM BED...
...AND PROPER MEALS EVERY DAY.
AND...
"HERE...
"TRY THIS ON.

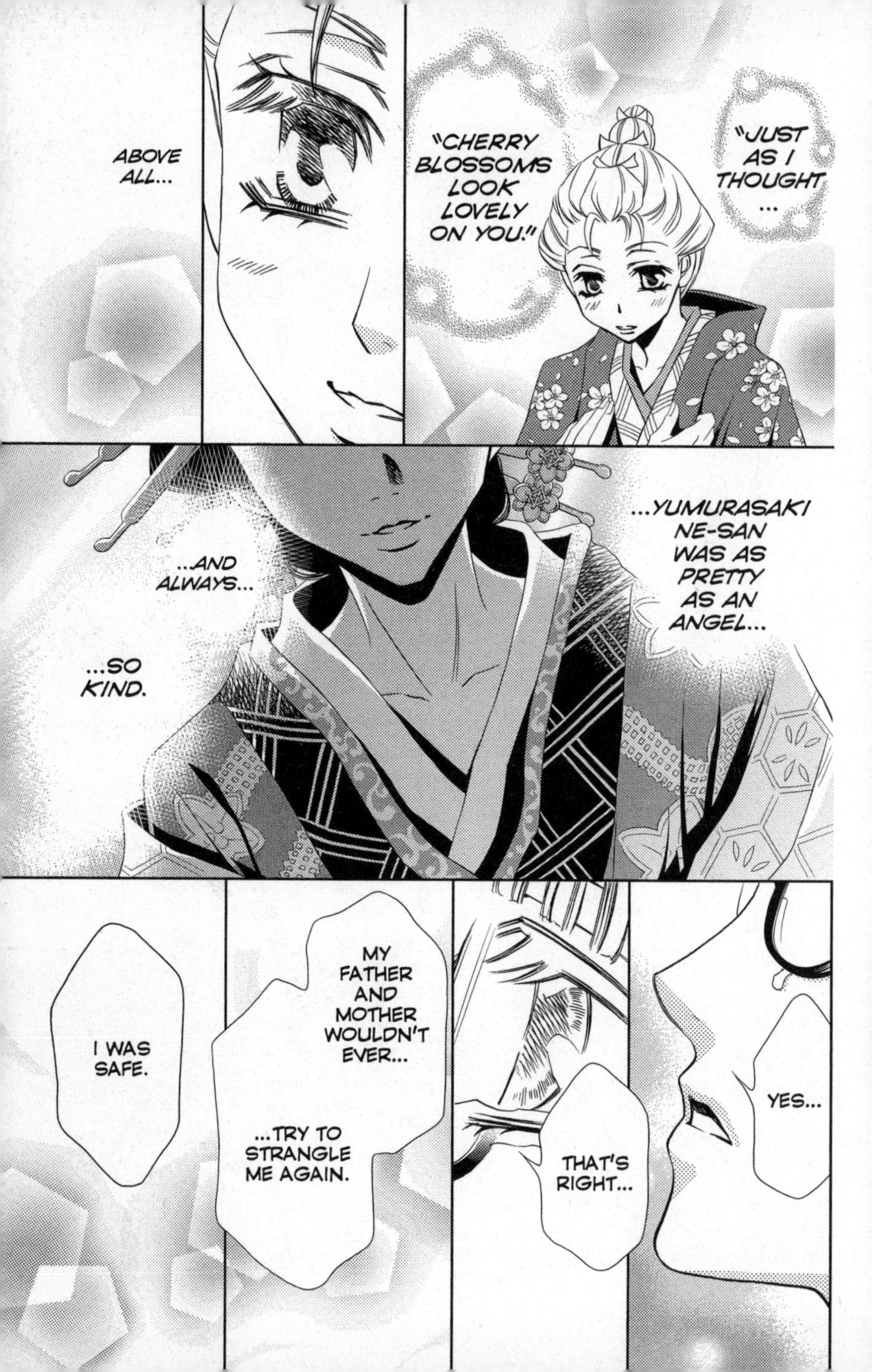
"JUST AS I THOUGHT...
"CHERRY BLOSSOMS LOOK LOVELY ON YOU."
ABOVE ALL...
...YUMURASAKI NE-SAN WAS AS PRETTY AS AN ANGEL...
...AND ALWAYS...
...SO KIND.
YES...
THAT'S RIGHT...
MY FATHER AND MOTHER WOULDN'T EVER...
...TRY TO STRANGLE ME AGAIN.
I WAS SAFE.

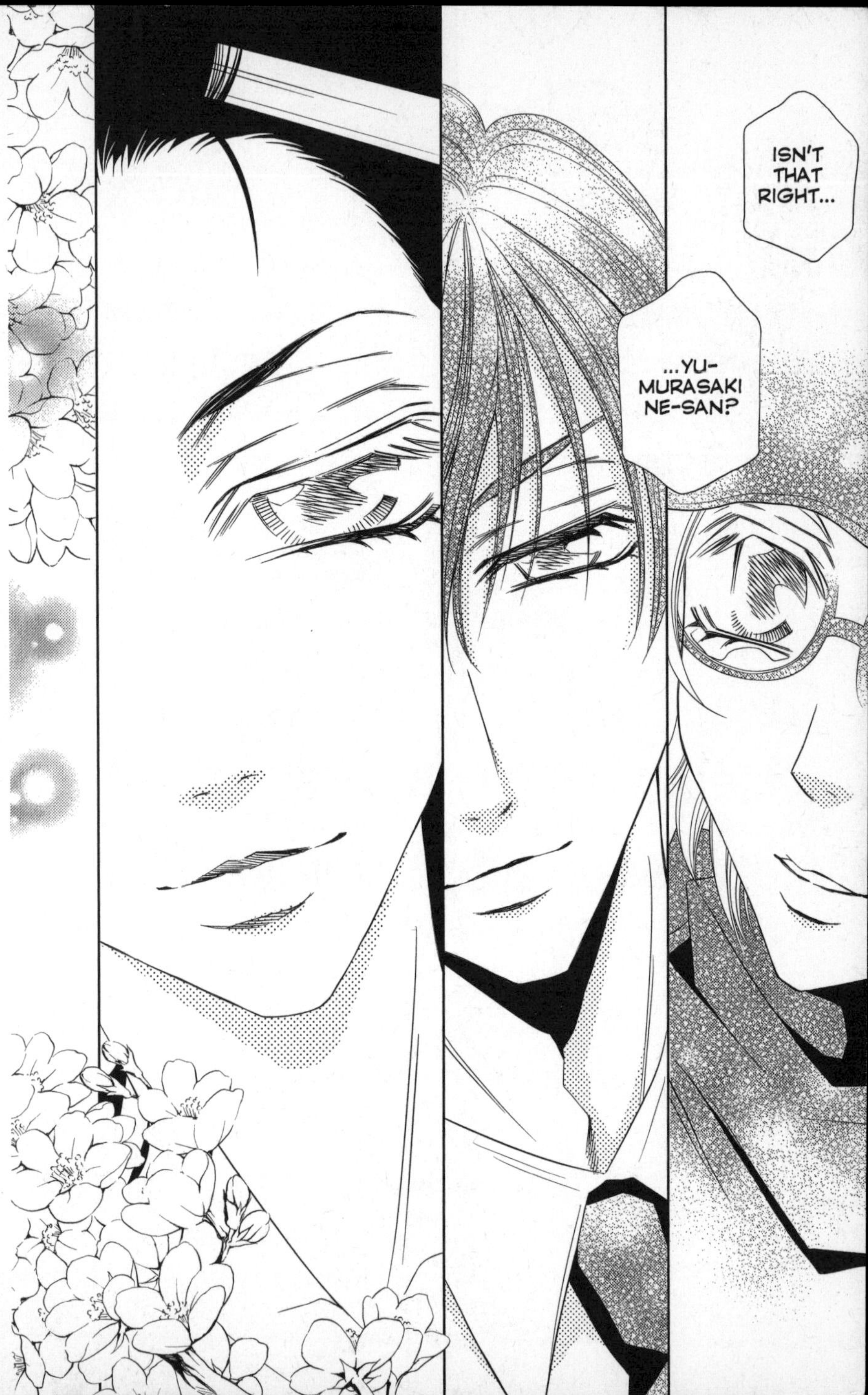
ISN'T THAT RIGHT...
...YU-MURASAKI NE-SAN?

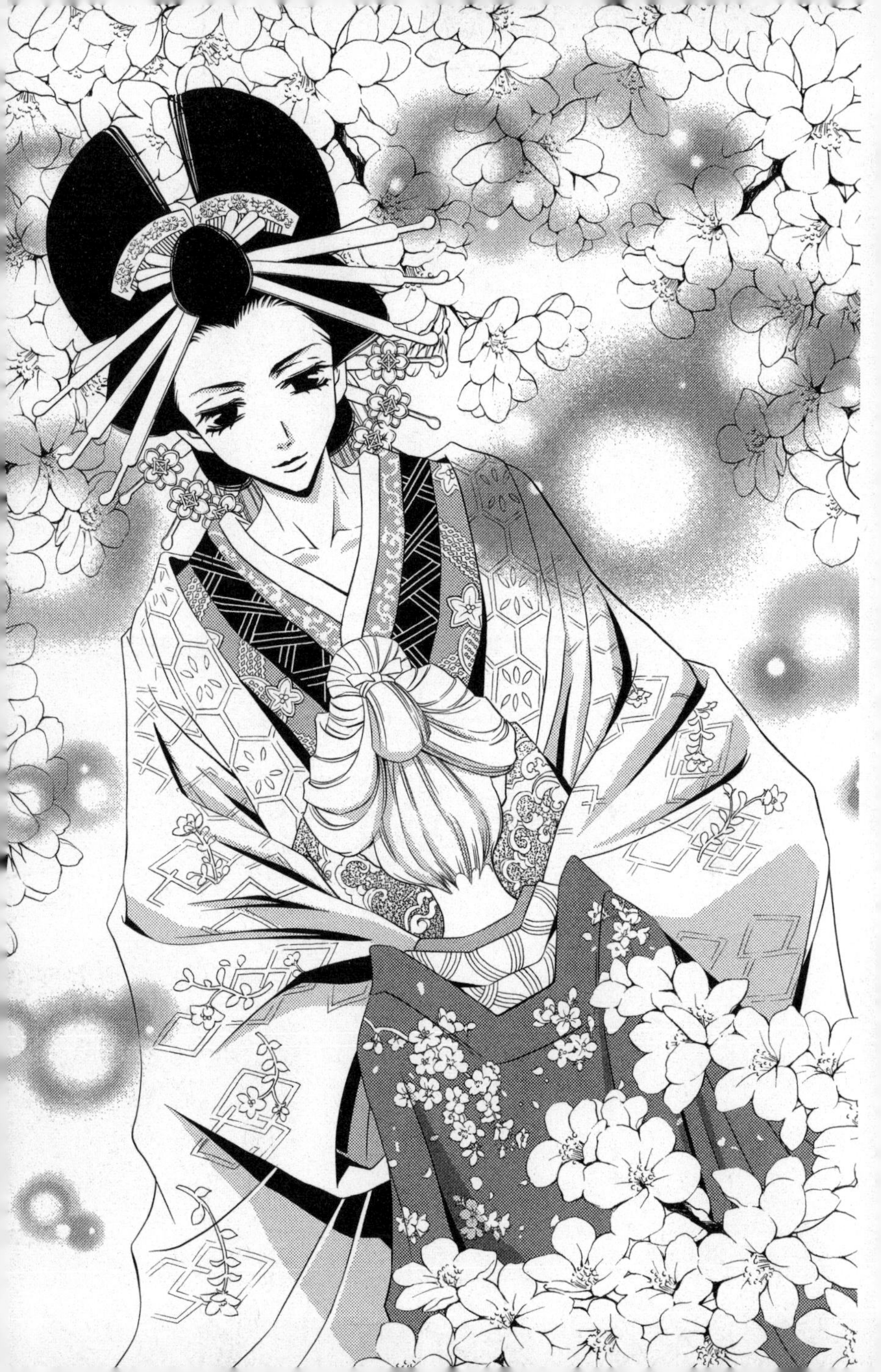

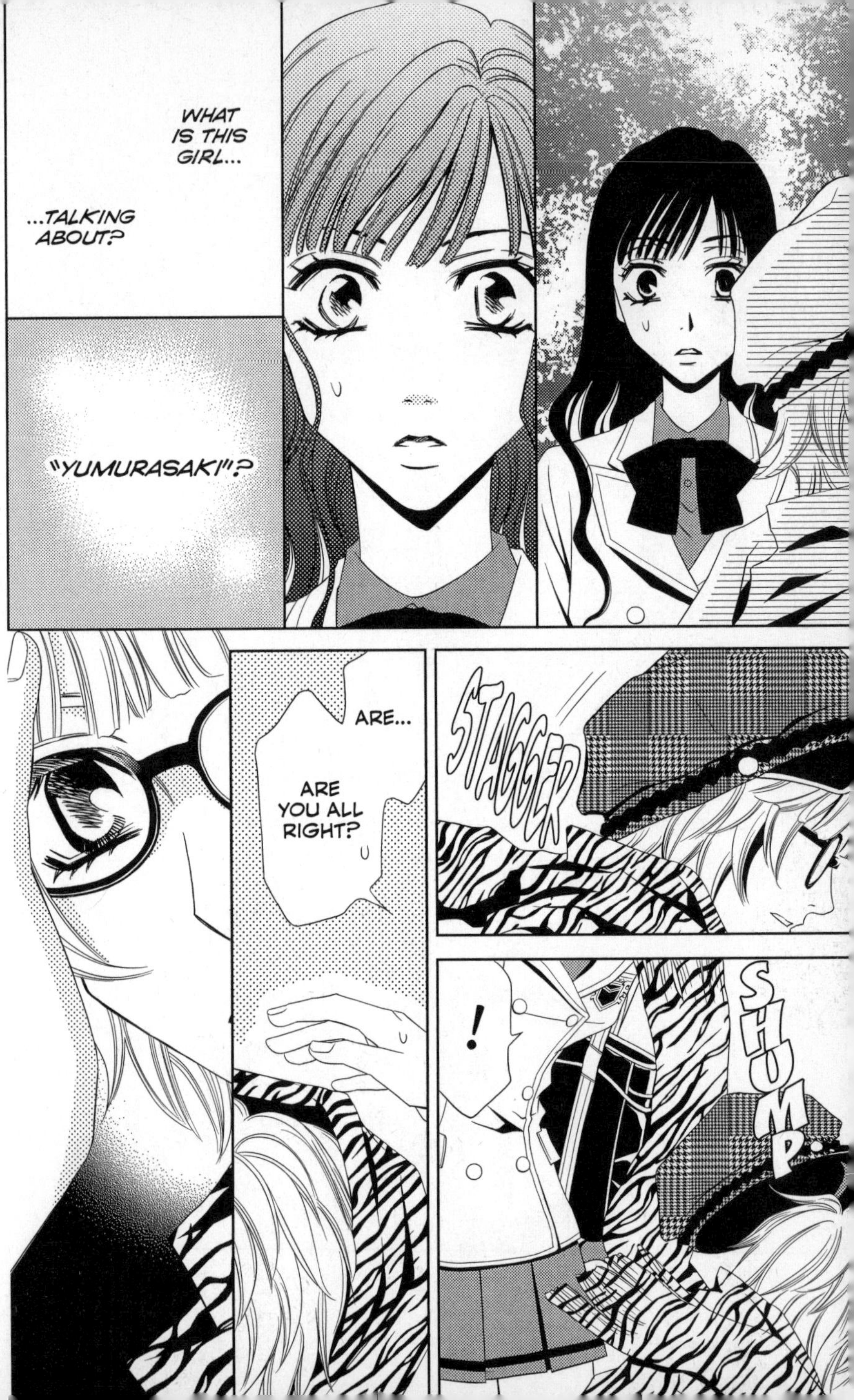
WHAT IS THIS GIRL...
...TALKING ABOUT?
"YUMURASAKI"?
STAGGER
SHUMP
!
ARE...
ARE YOU ALL RIGHT?

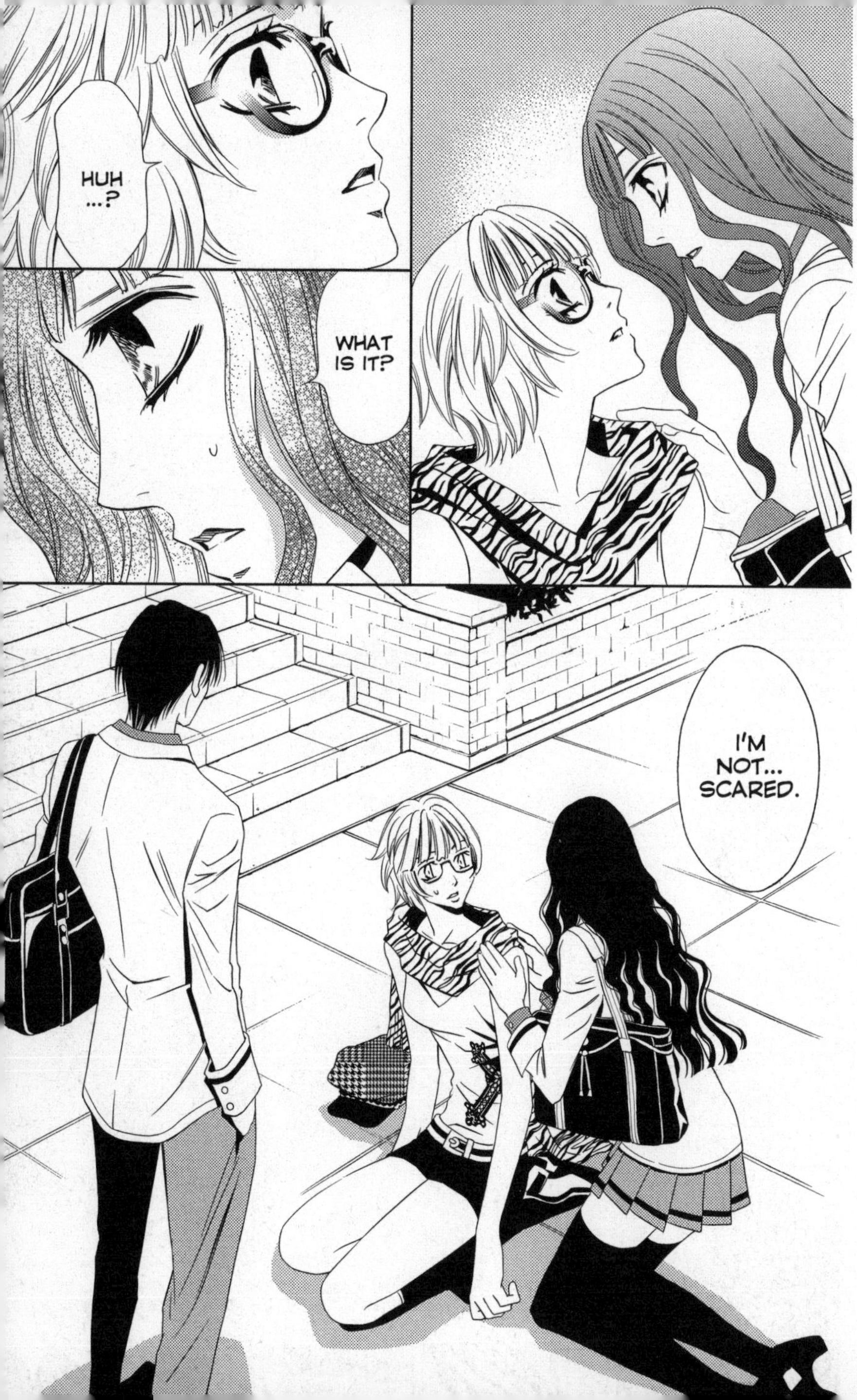
HUH ...?
WHAT IS IT?
I'M NOT... SCARED.

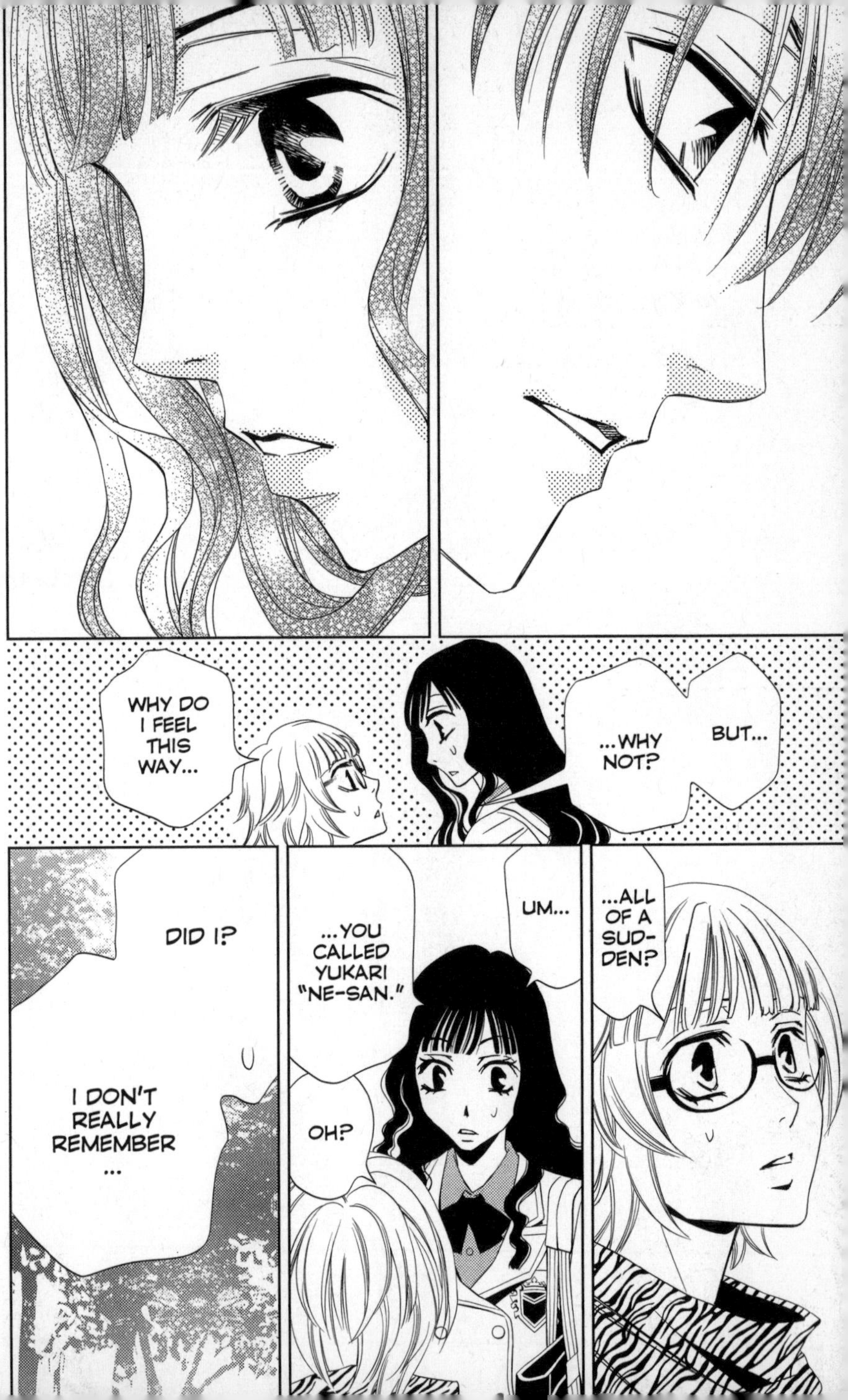
BUT...
...WHY NOT?
WHY DO I FEEL THIS WAY...
UM...
...YOU CALLED YUKARI "NE-SAN."
...ALL OF A SUD-DEN?
OH?
DID I?
I DON'T REALLY REMEMBER ...

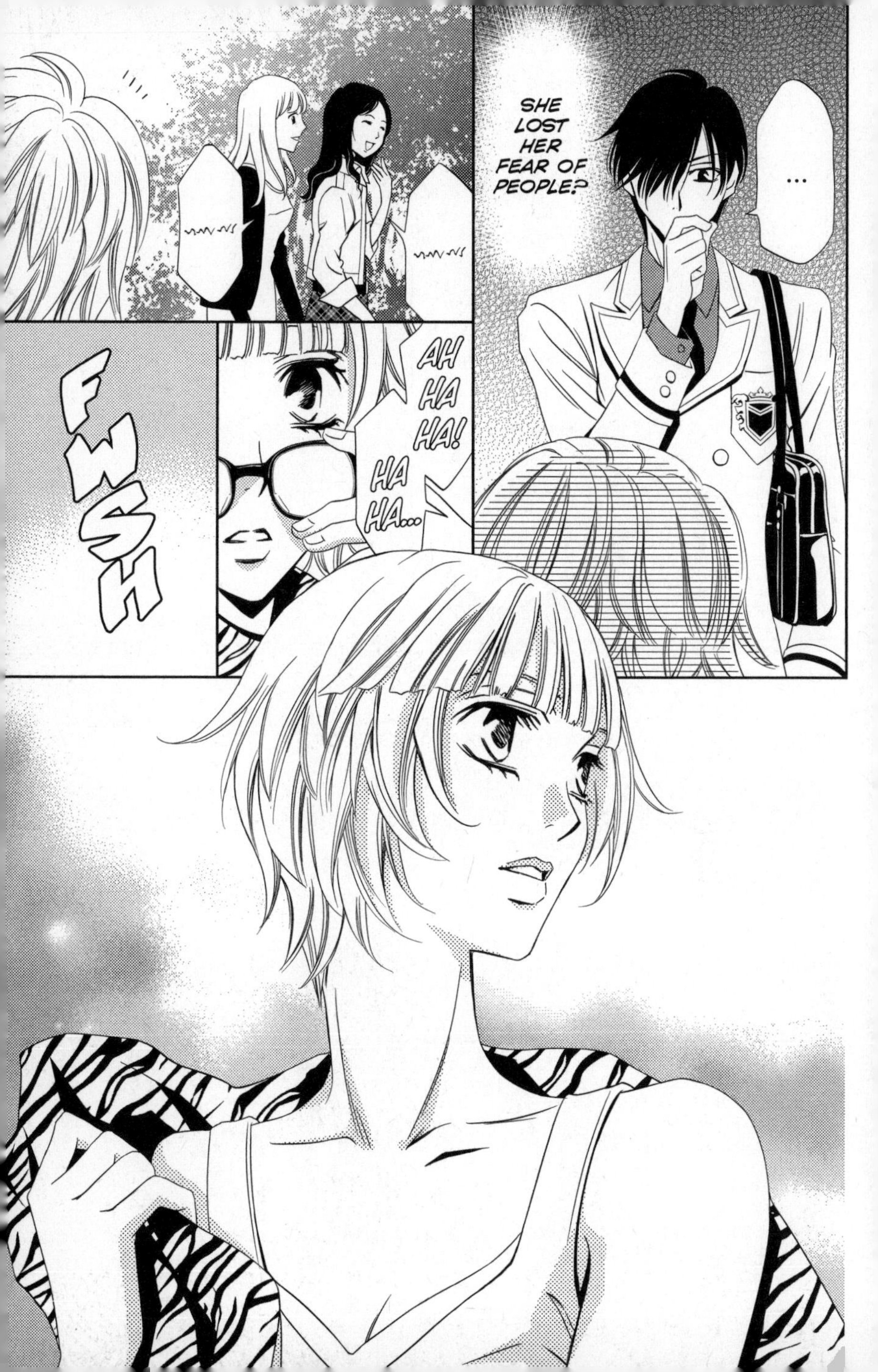
...
SHE LOST HER FEAR OF PEOPLE?
AH HA HA! HA HA...
FWSH

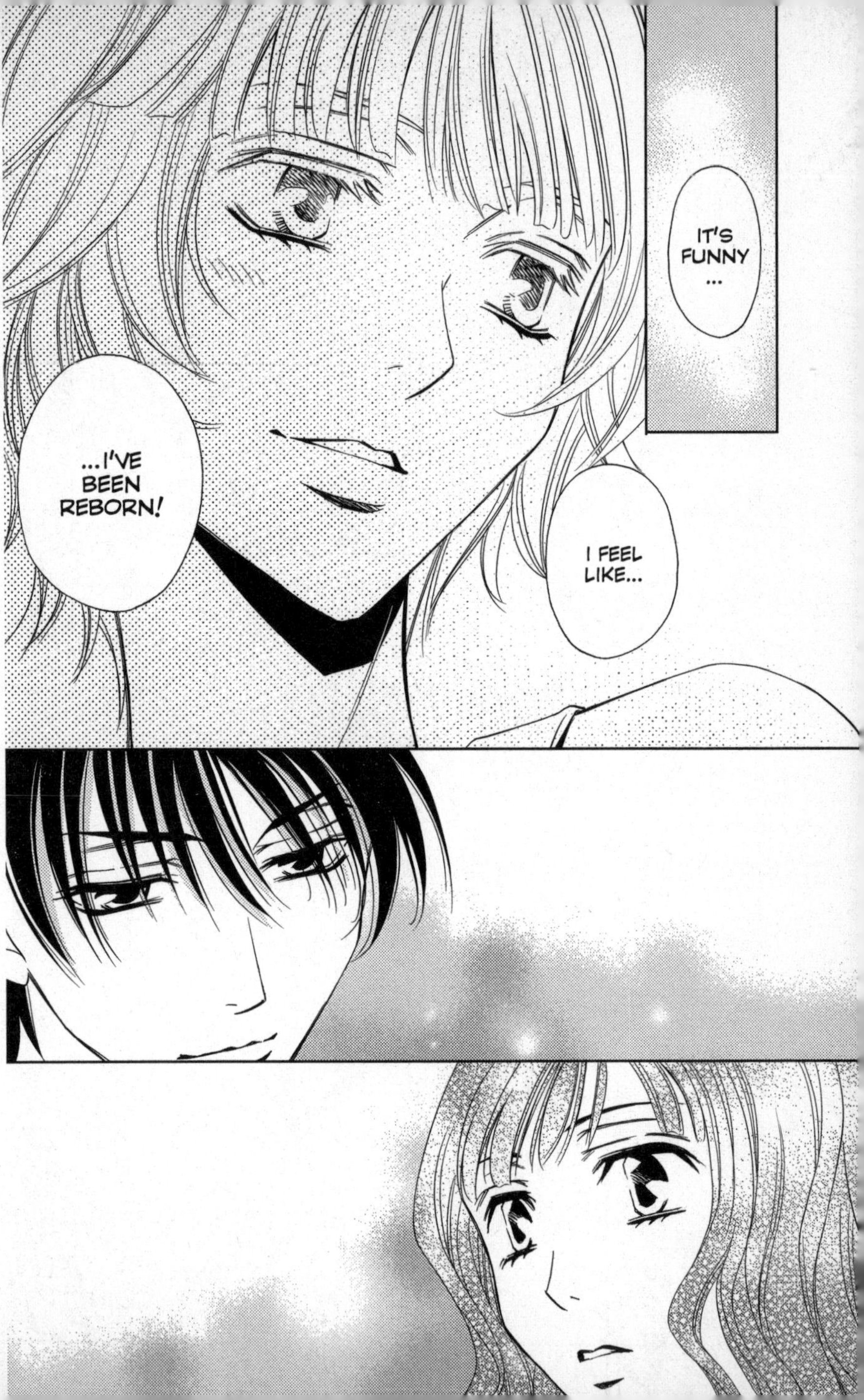
IT'S FUNNY ...
I FEEL LIKE...
...I'VE BEEN REBORN!

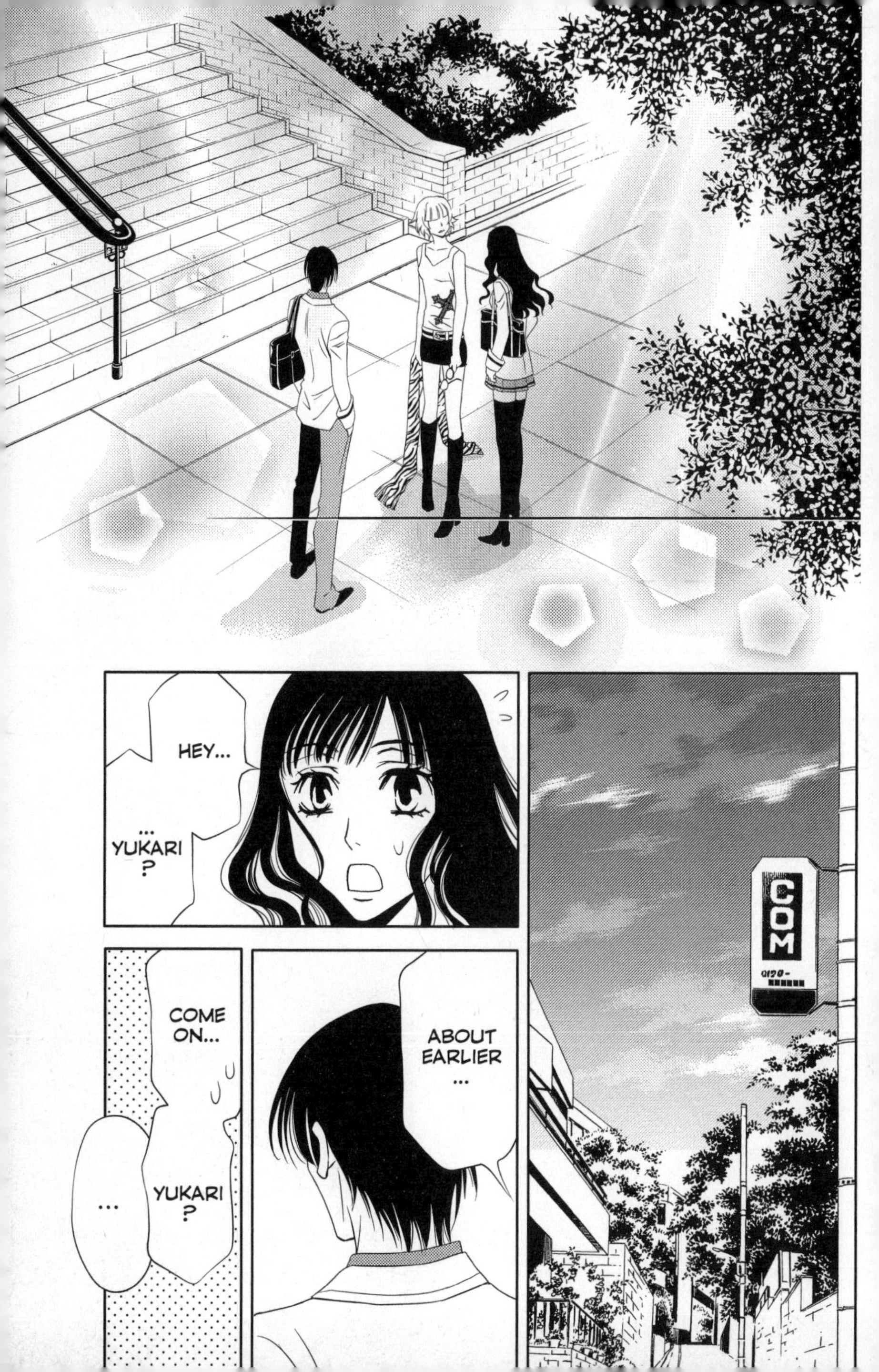
COM
HEY...
... YUKARI ?
ABOUT EARLIER ...
COME ON...
YUKARI ?
...

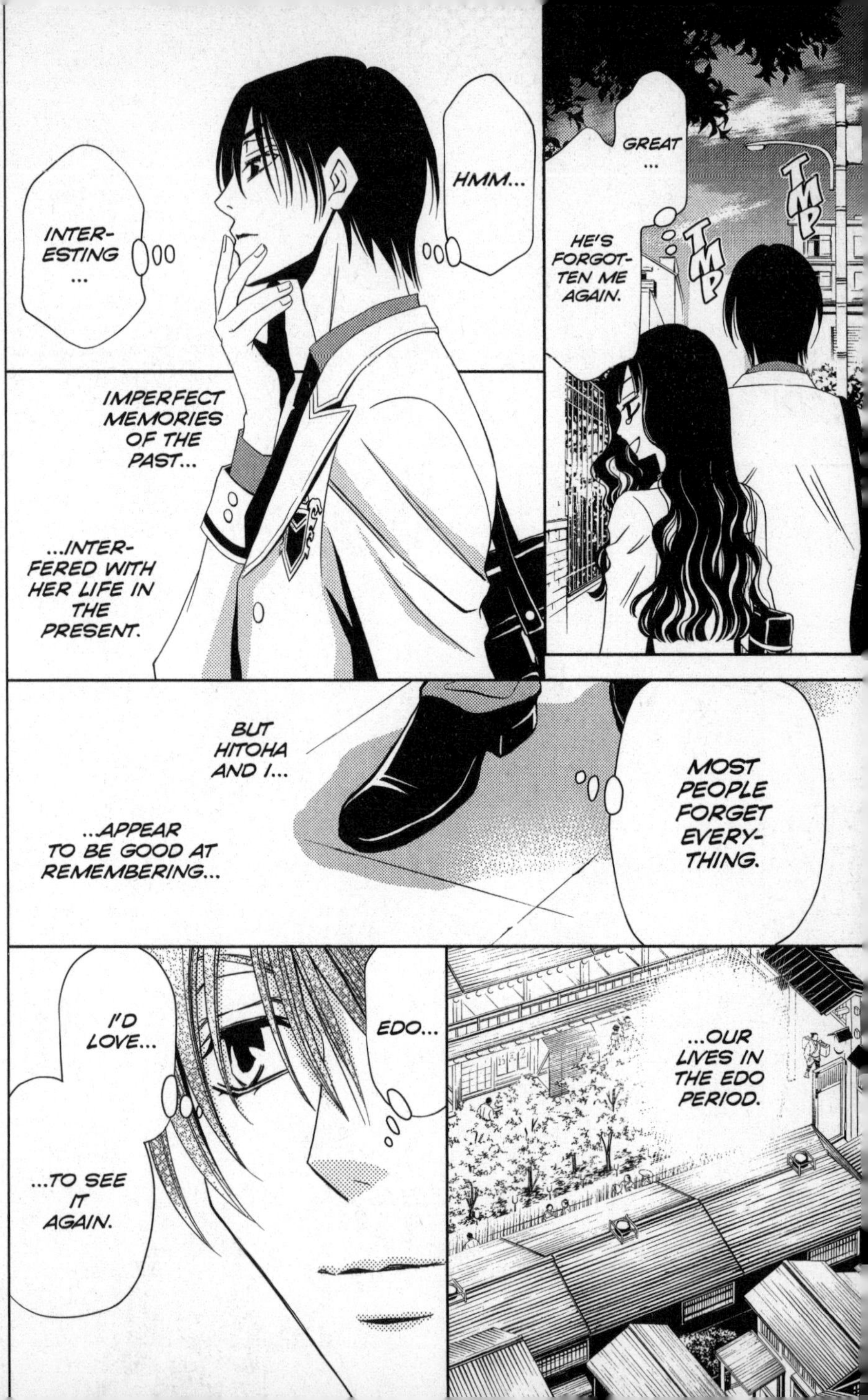
GREAT ...
HE'S FORGOT-TEN ME AGAIN.
TMP
TMP
HMM...
INTER-ESTING ...
IMPERFECT MEMORIES OF THE PAST...
...INTER-FERED WITH HER LIFE IN THE PRESENT.
MOST PEOPLE FORGET EVERY-THING.
BUT HITOHA AND I...
...APPEAR TO BE GOOD AT REMEMBERING...
...OUR LIVES IN THE EDO PERIOD.
EDO...
I'D LOVE...
...TO SEE IT AGAIN.

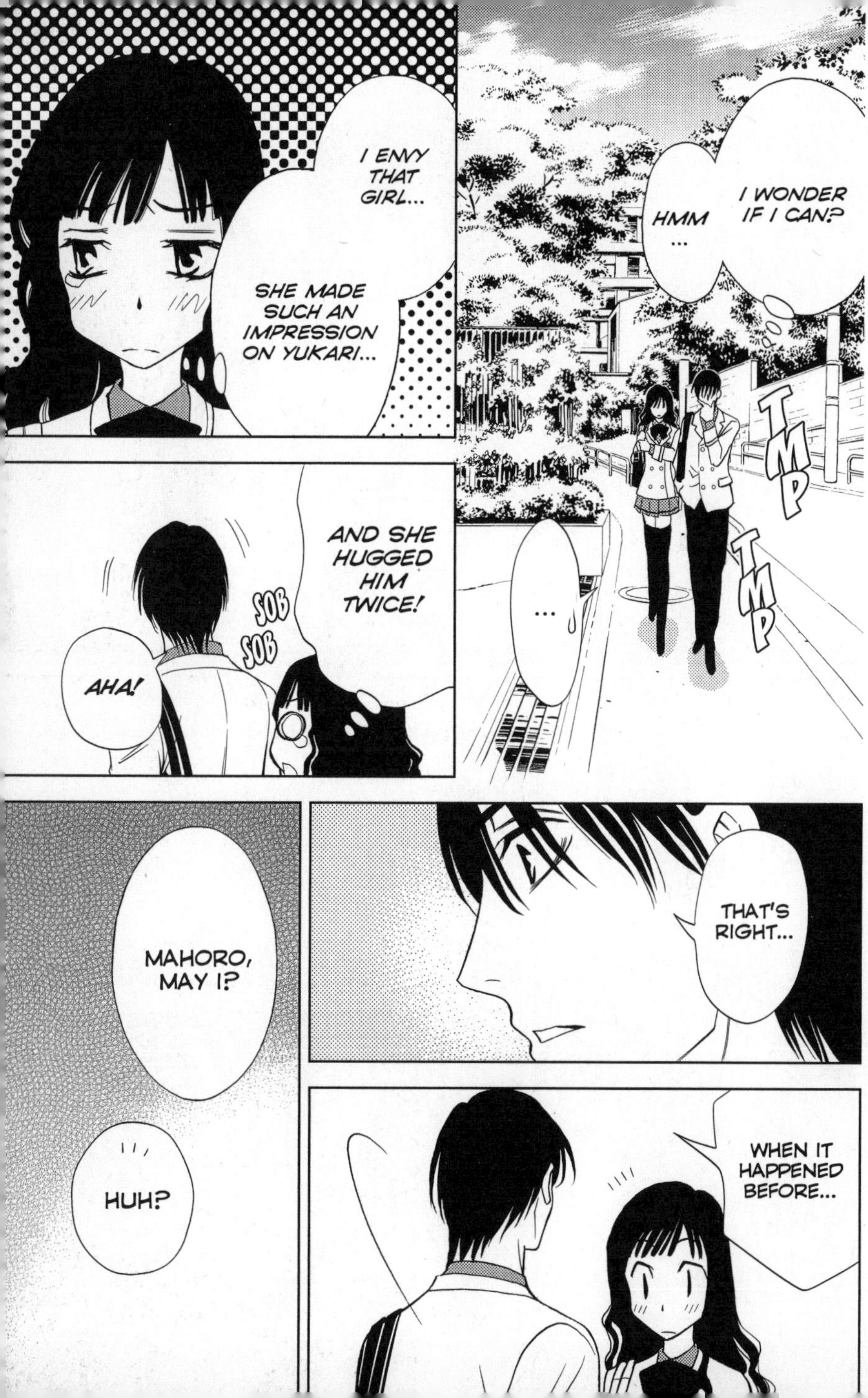
I WONDER IF I CAN?
HMM ...
TMP TMP
TMP TMP
...
I ENVY THAT GIRL...
SHE MADE SUCH AN IMPRESSION ON YUKARI...
AND SHE HUGGED HIM TWICE!
SOB SOB
AHA!
THAT'S RIGHT...
WHEN IT HAPPENED BEFORE...
MAHORO, MAY I?
HUH?

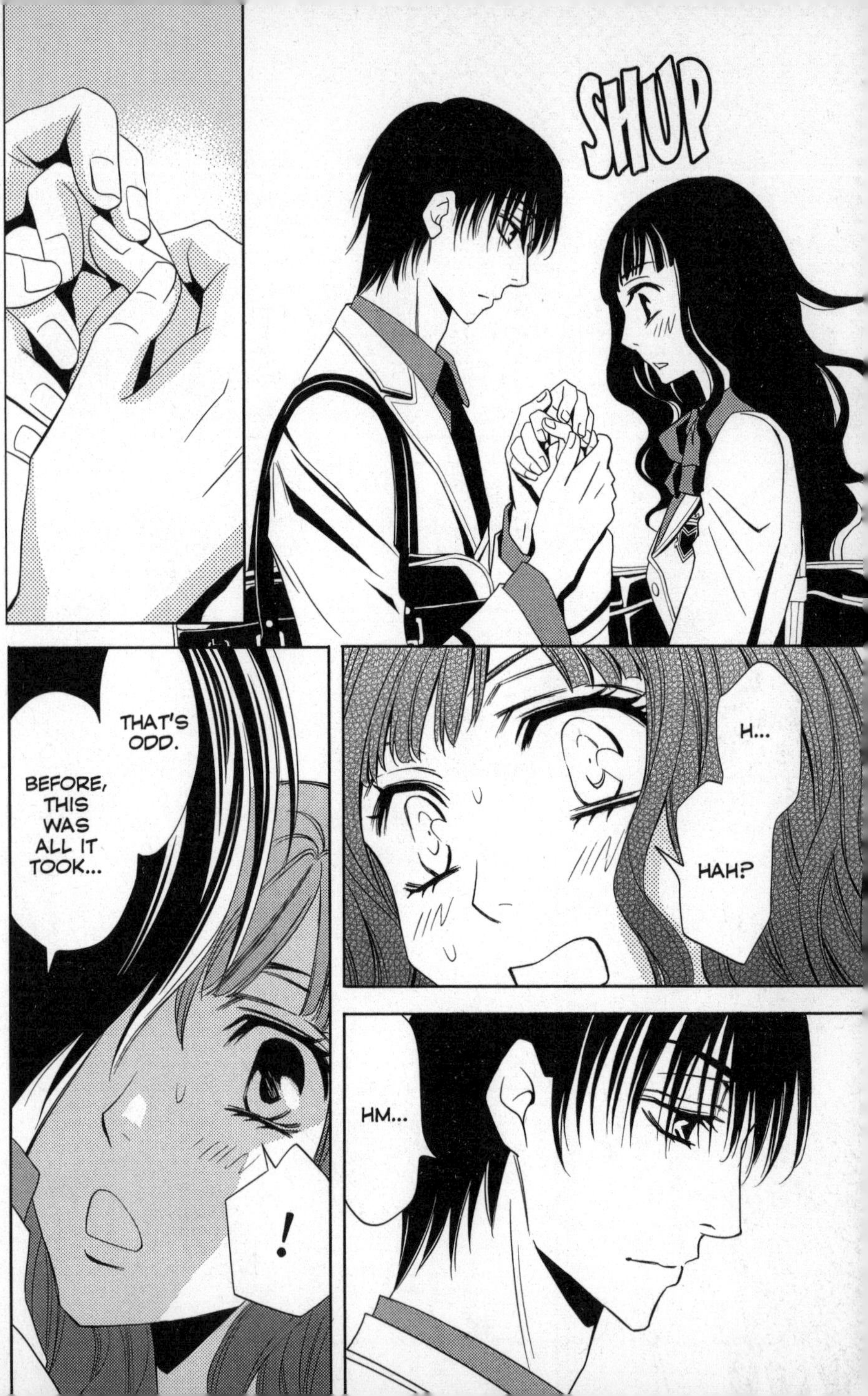
SHUP
H...
HAH?
HM...
THAT'S ODD.
BEFORE, THIS WAS ALL IT TOOK...
!

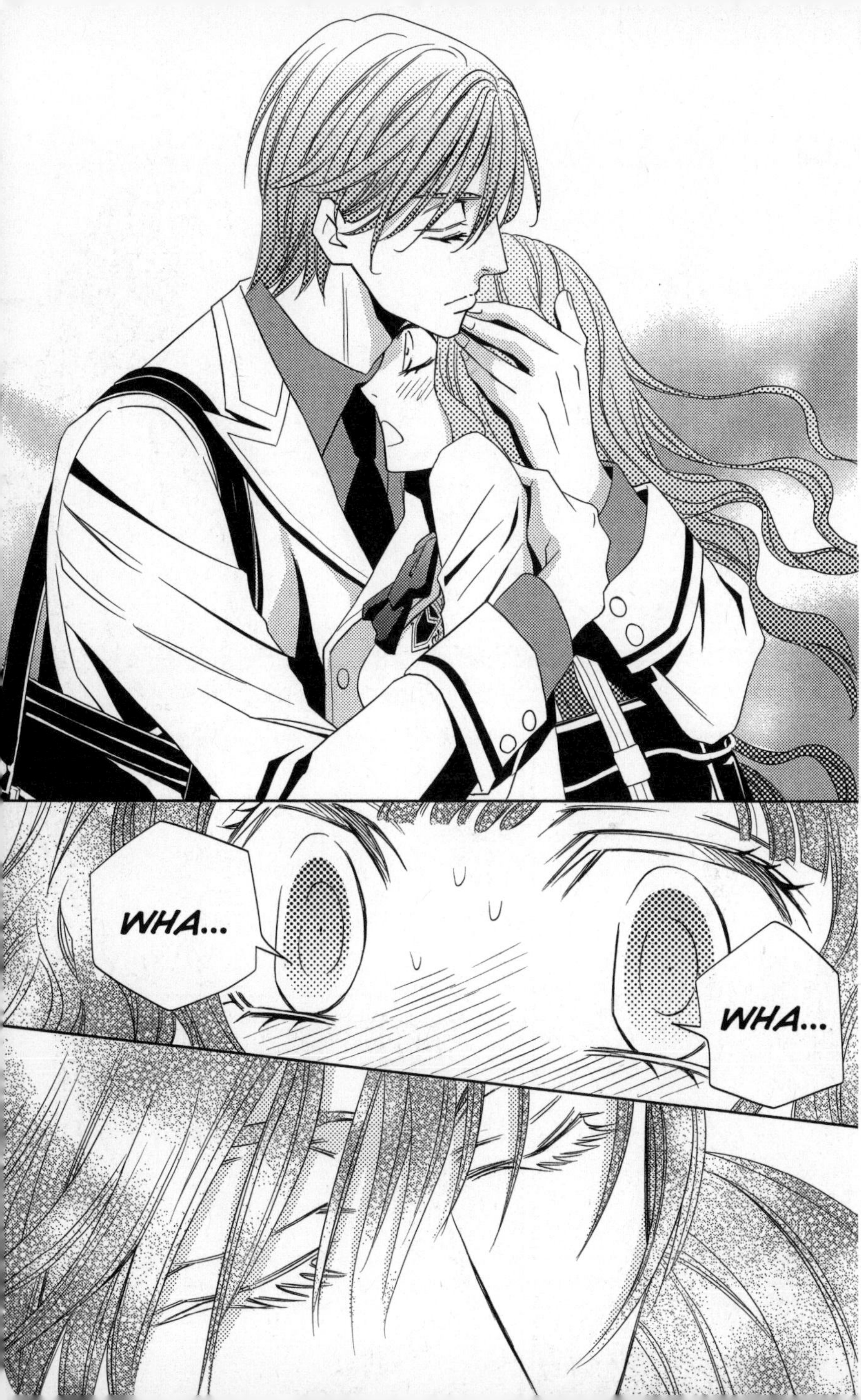
WHA...
WHA...

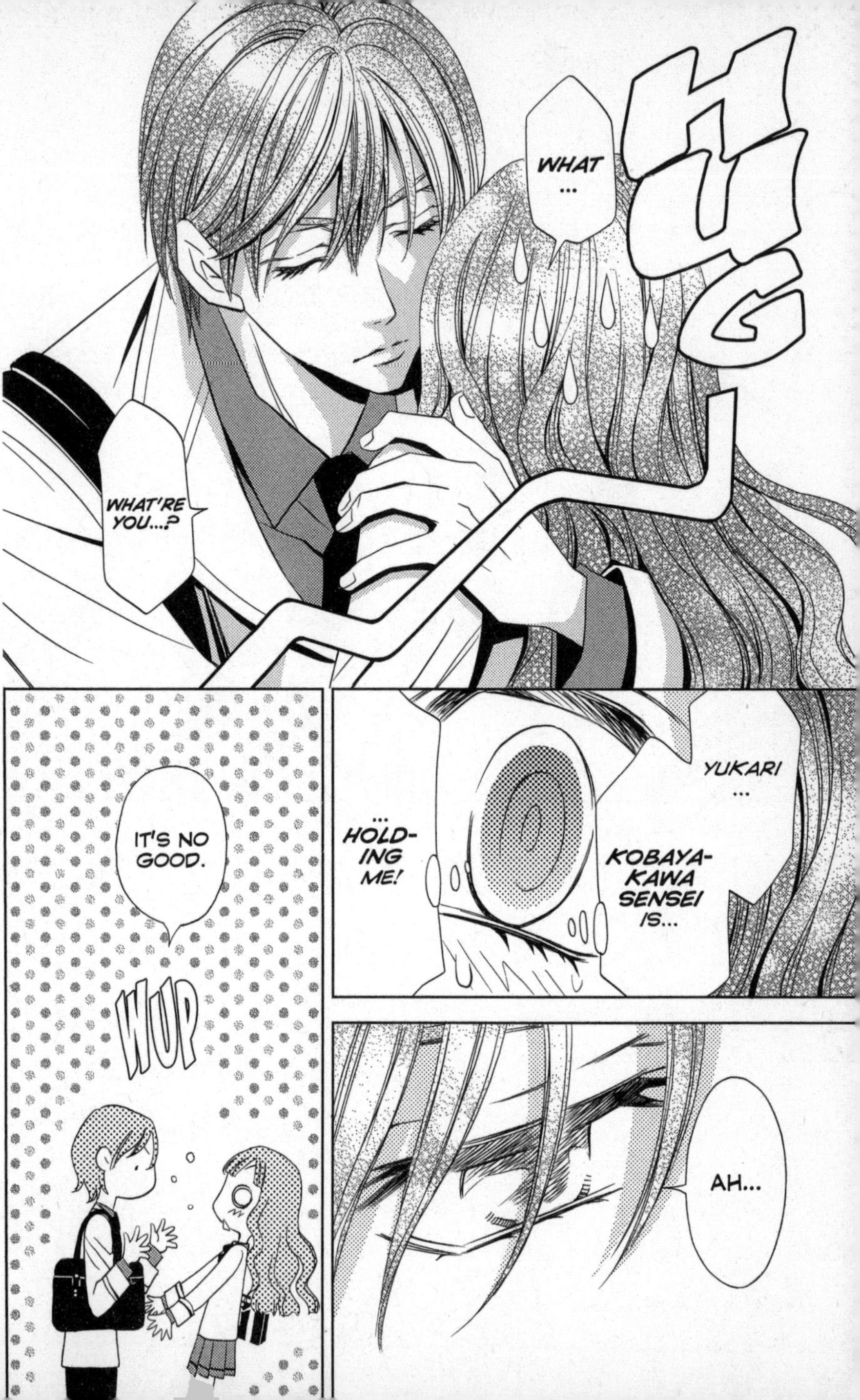
HUG
WHAT ...
WHAT'RE YOU...?
YUKARI ...
KOBAYA-KAWA SENSEI IS...
... HOLDING ME!
AH...
IT'S NO GOOD.
WUP

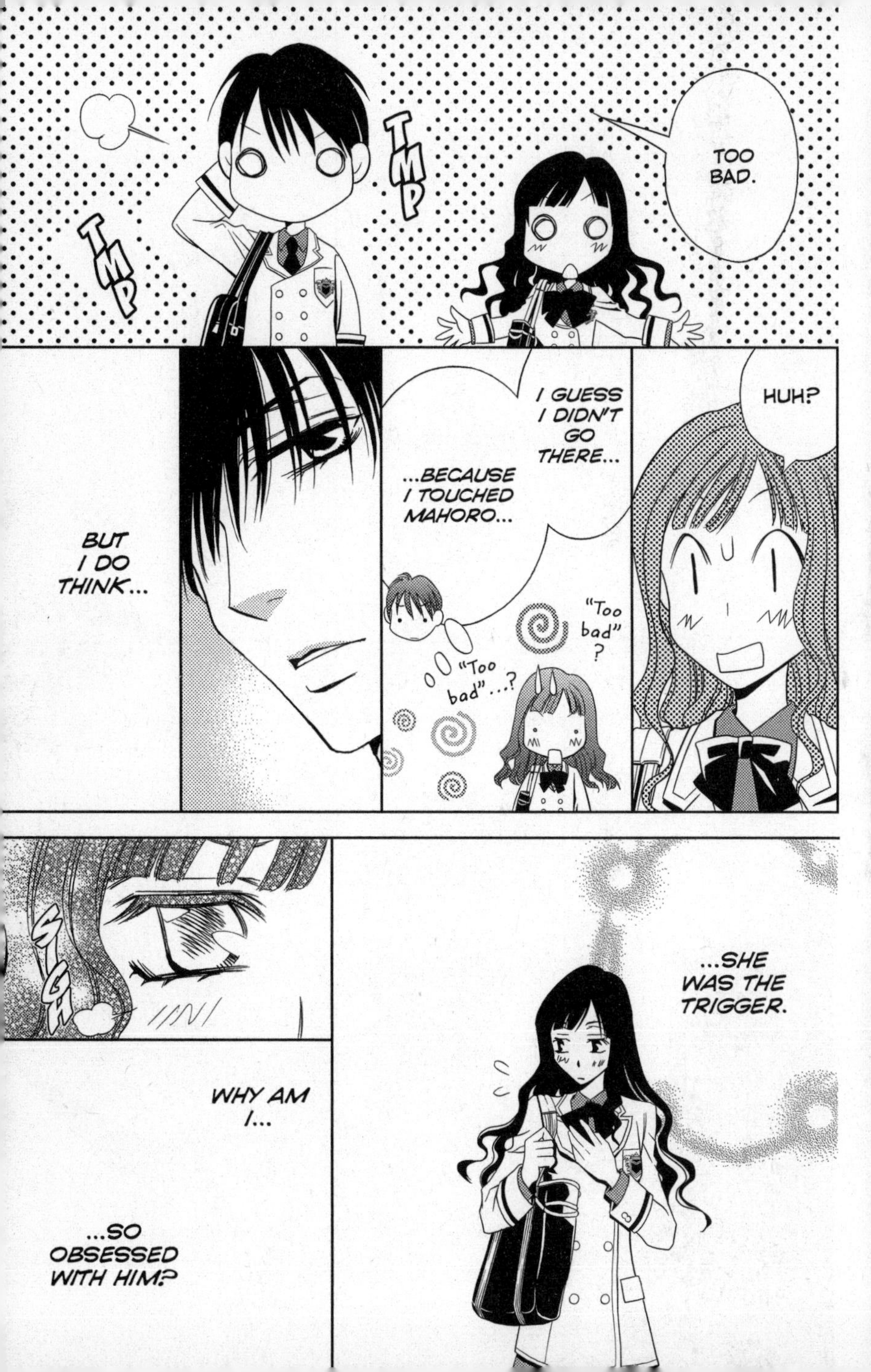
TOO BAD.
TMP
TMP
HUH?
I GUESS I DIDN'T GO THERE...
...BECAUSE I TOUCHED MAHORO...
"Too bad"?
"Too bad"...?
BUT I DO THINK...
...SHE WAS THE TRIGGER.
SIGH
WHY AM I...
...SO OBSESSED WITH HIM?

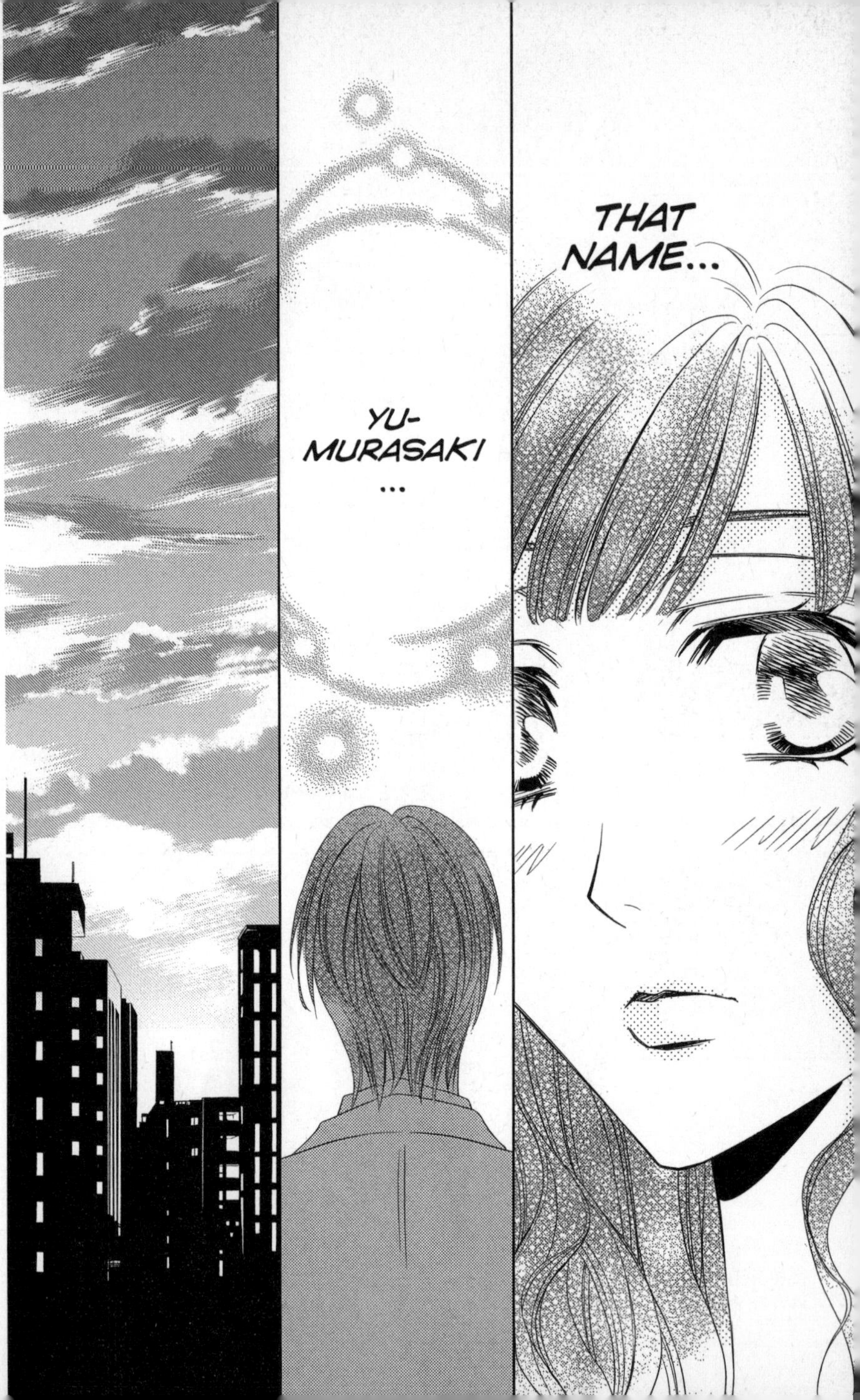
THAT NAME...
YU-MURASAKI ...

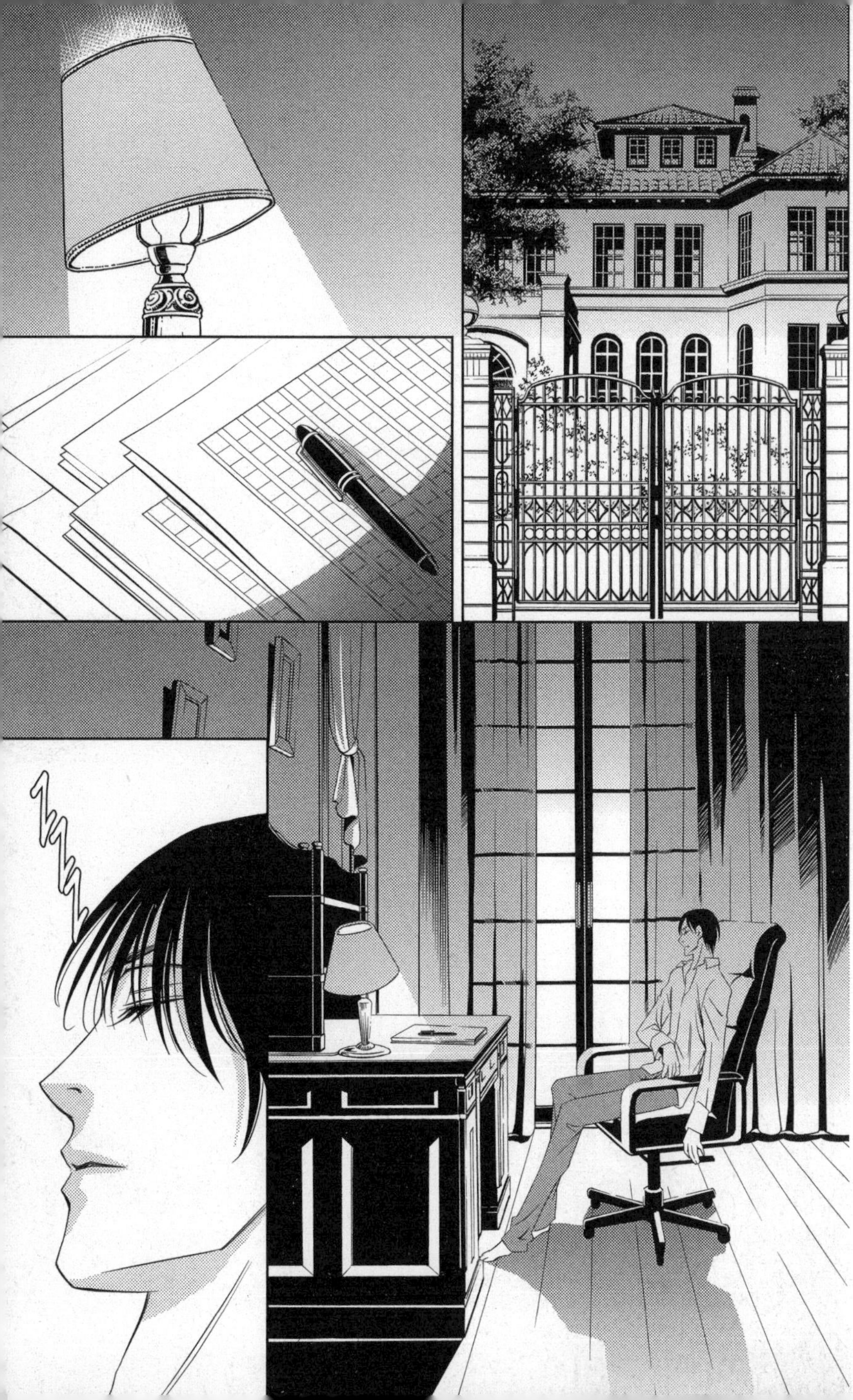

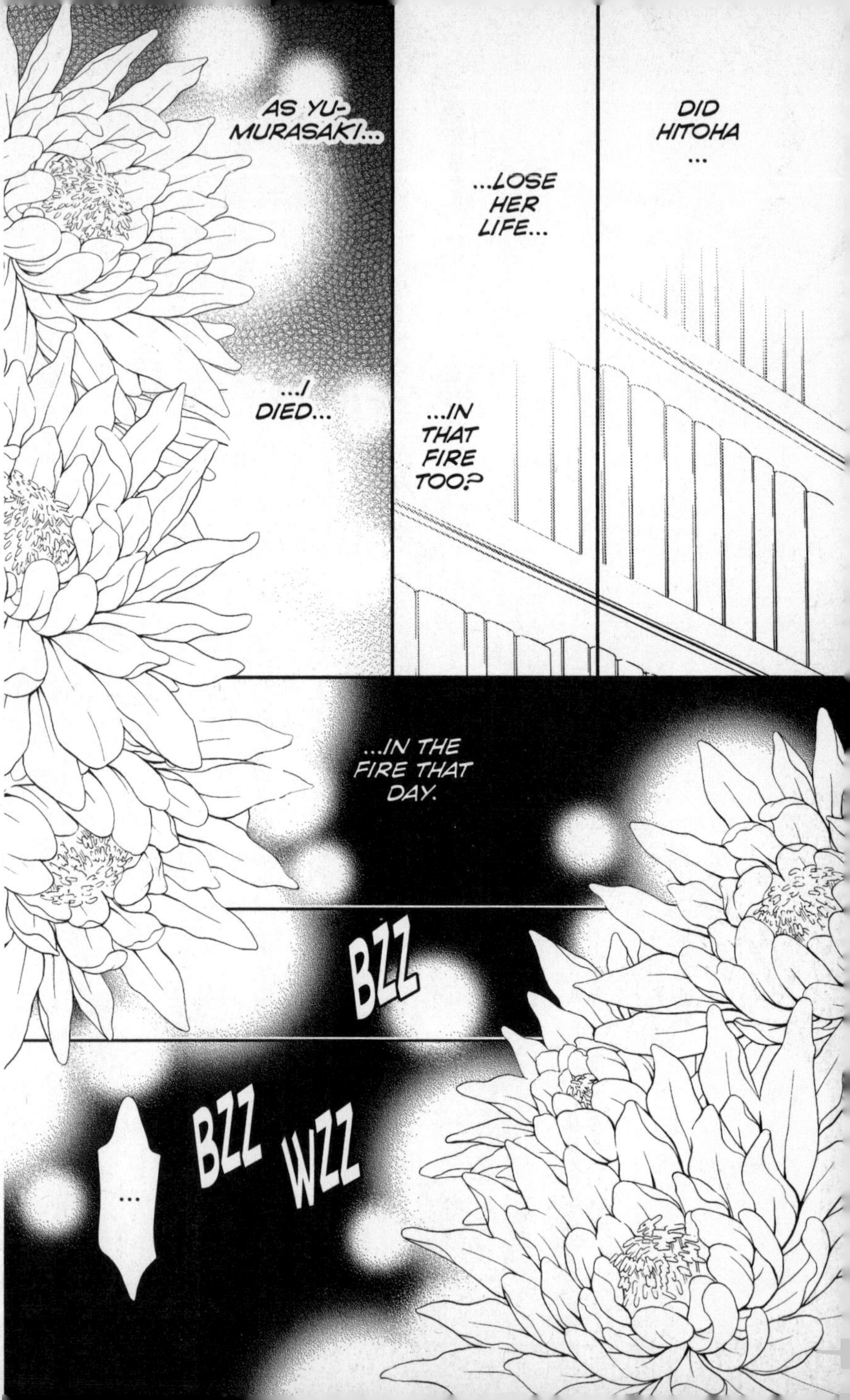
DID HITOHA ...
...LOSE HER LIFE...
...IN THAT FIRE TOO?
AS YU-MURASAKI...
...I DIED...
...IN THE FIRE THAT DAY.
BZZ
WZZ
BZZ
...

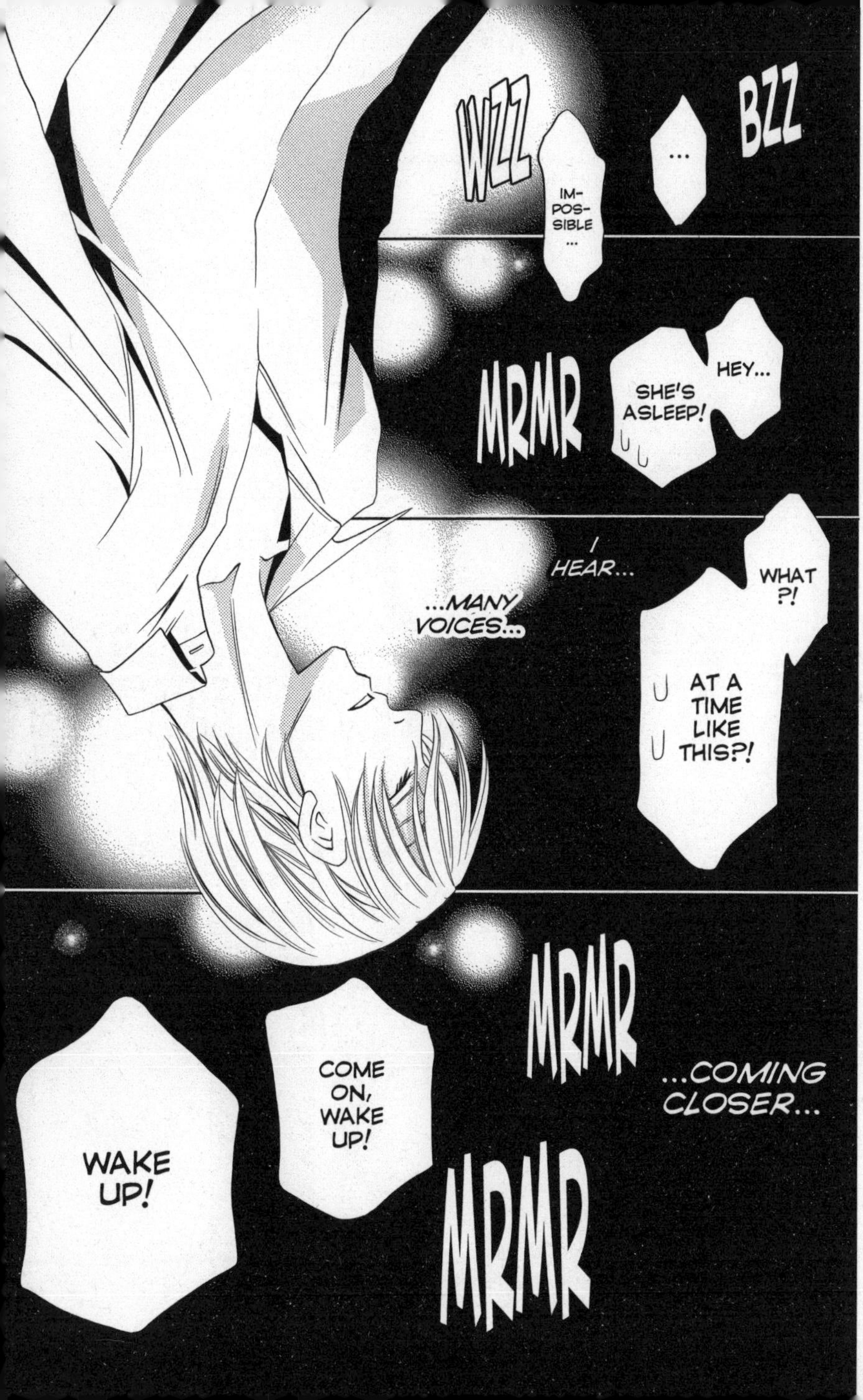
BZZ
...
IM-POSSIBLE...
WZZ
HEY... SHE'S ASLEEP!
MRMR
WHAT?! AT A TIME LIKE THIS?!
I HEAR...
...MANY VOICES...
...COMING CLOSER...
MRMR
MRMR
COME ON, WAKE UP!
WAKE UP!

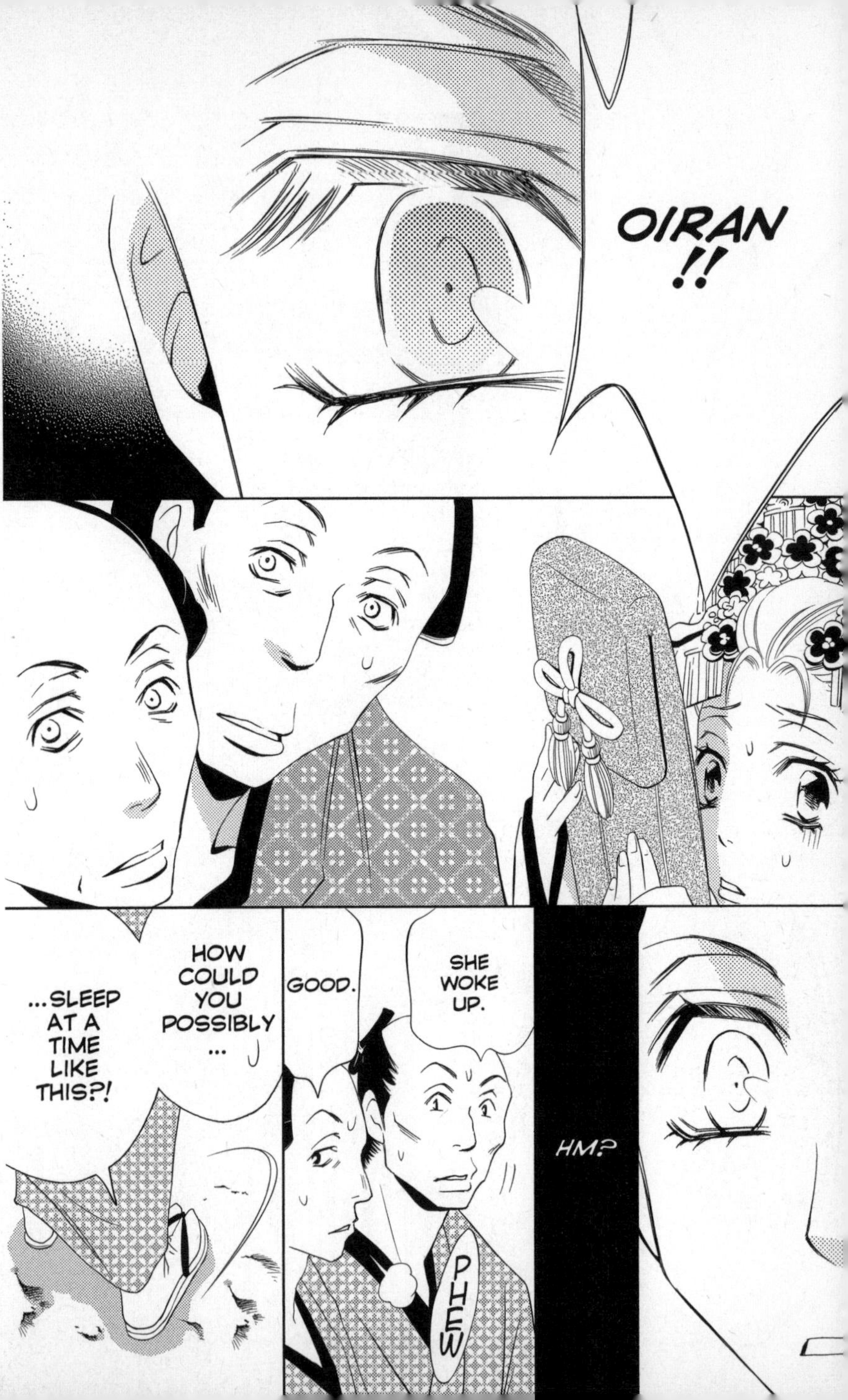
OIRAN !!
HM?
SHE WOKE UP.
GOOD.
PHEW
HOW COULD YOU POSSIBLY ...
...SLEEP AT A TIME LIKE THIS?!

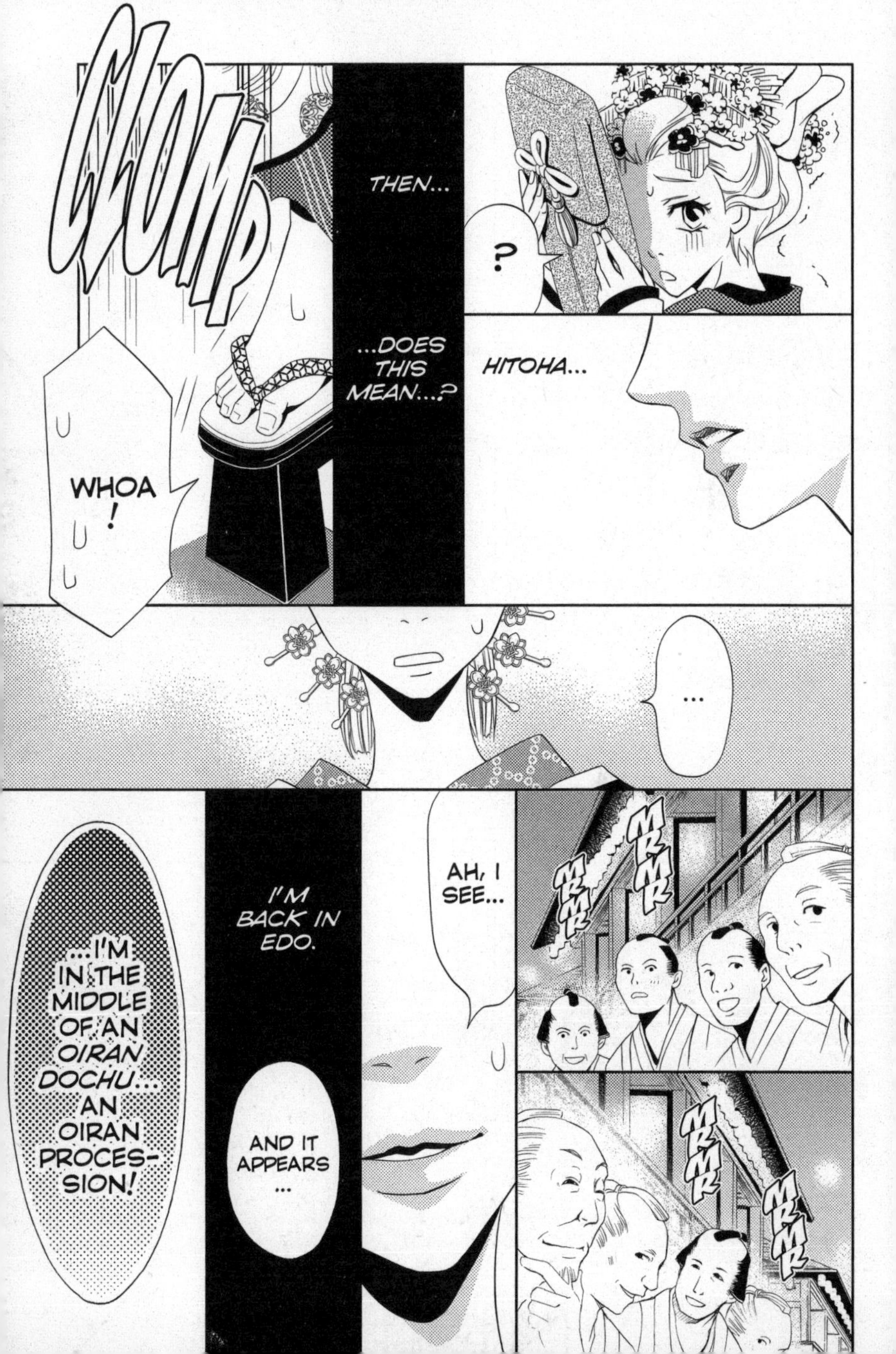
?
HITOHA...
THEN...
...DOES THIS MEAN...?
CLOMP
WHOA!
...
MRMR
MRMR
MRMR
MRMR
AH, I SEE...
AND IT APPEARS...
I'M BACK IN EDO.
...I'M IN THE MIDDLE OF AN OIRAN DOCHU... AN OIRAN PROCESSION!

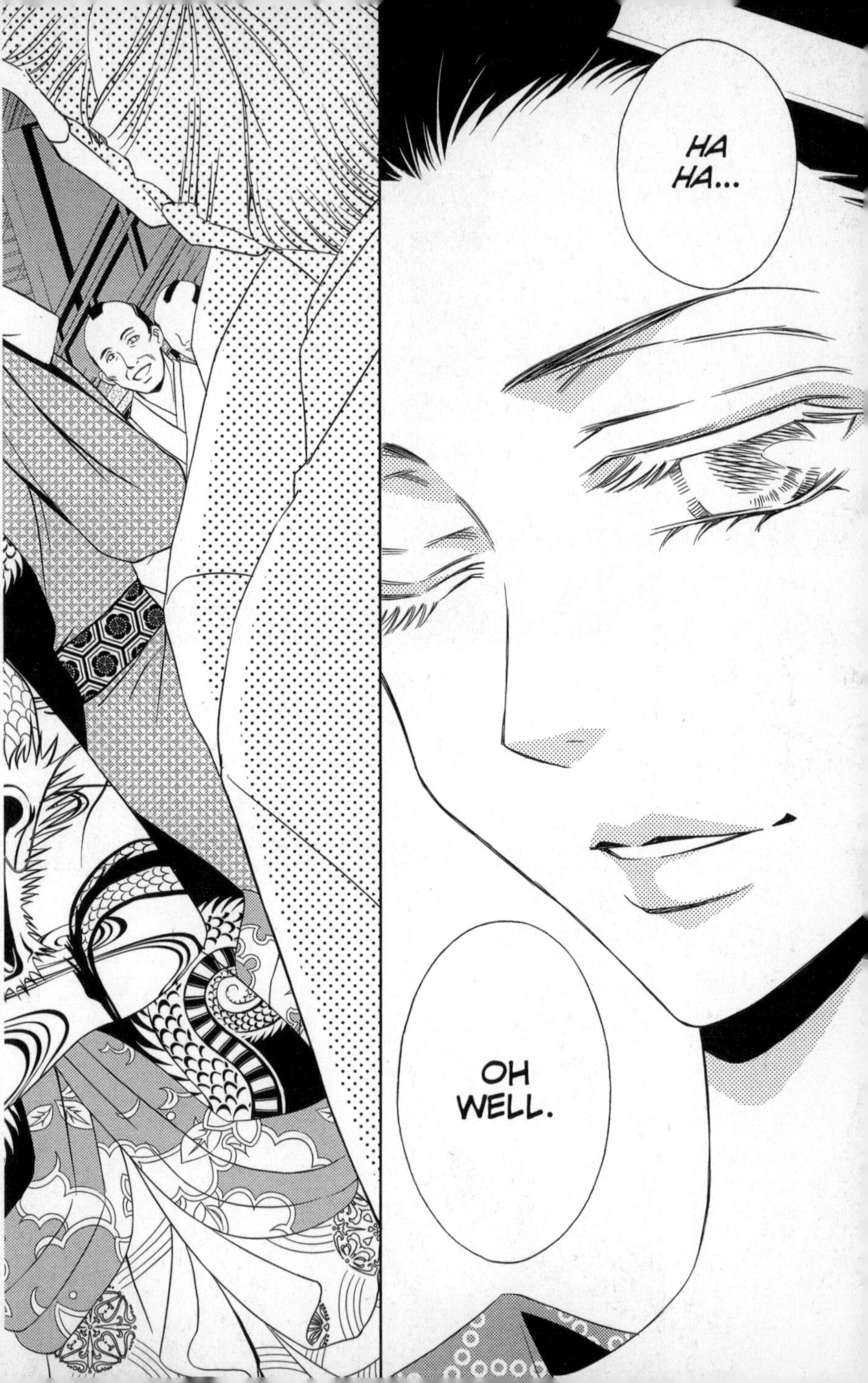
HA HA...
OH WELL.

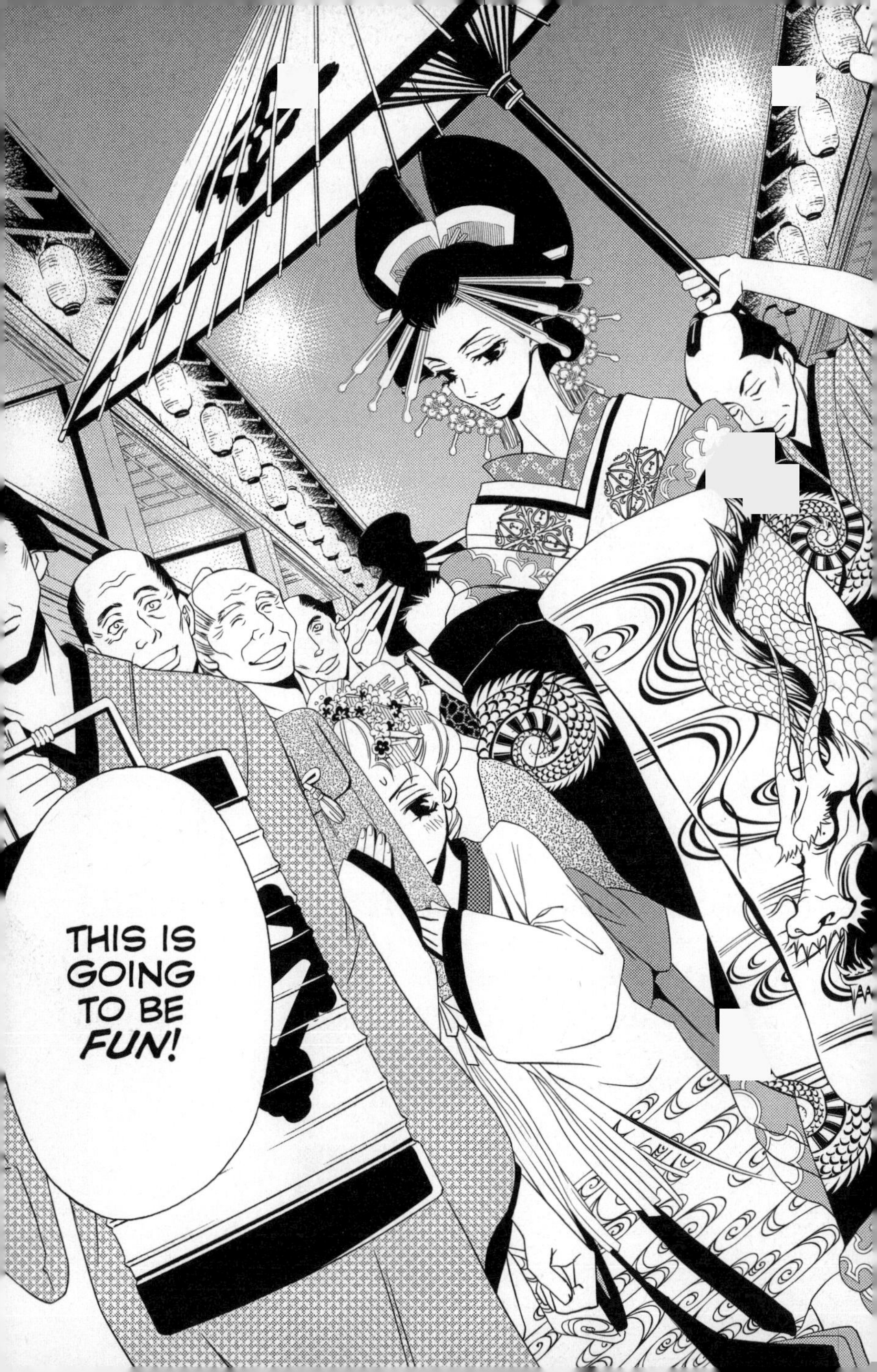
THIS IS GOING TO BE *FUN!*

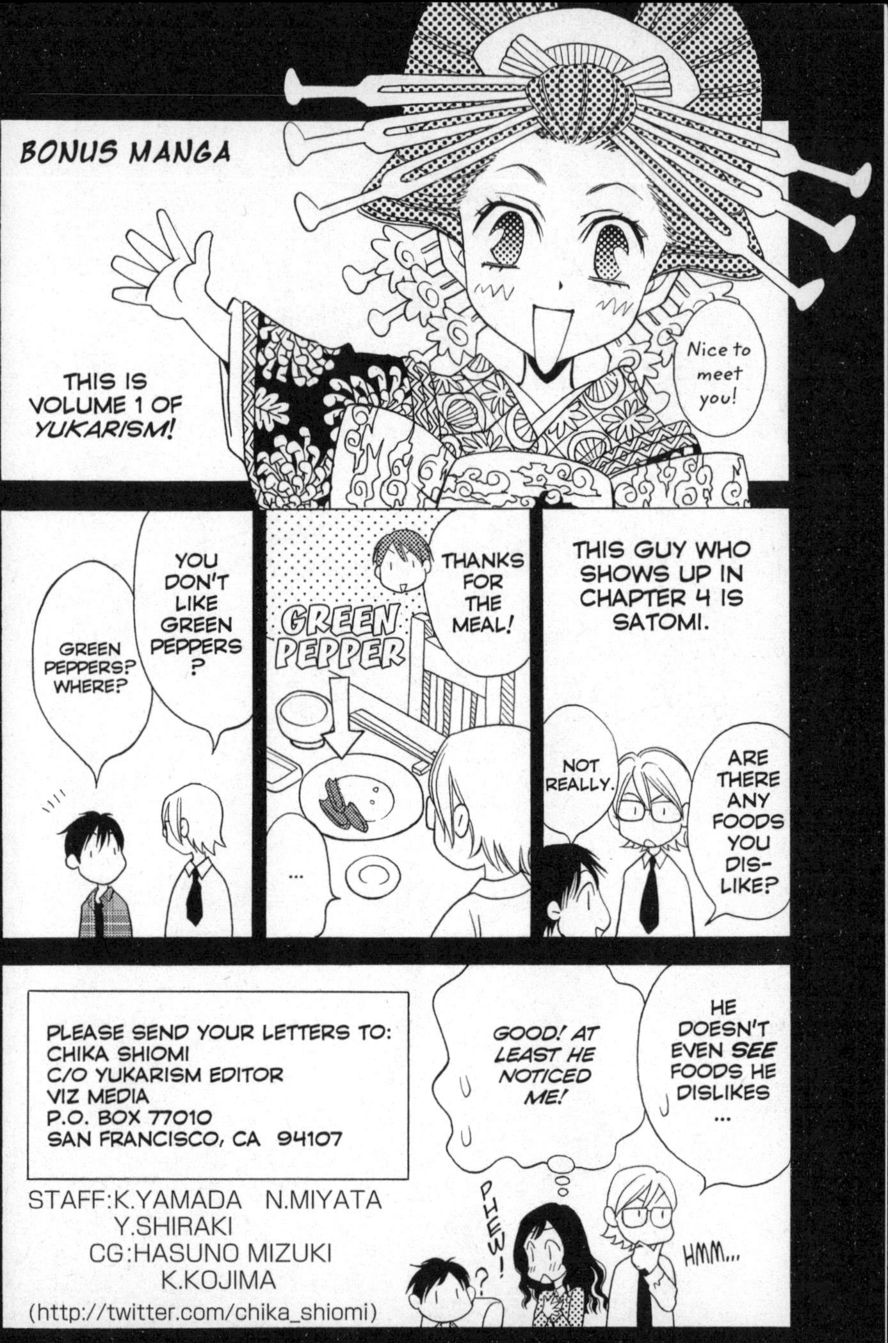
BONUS MANGA
THIS IS VOLUME 1 OF *YUKARISM!*
Nice to meet you!
THIS GUY WHO SHOWS UP IN CHAPTER 4 IS SATOMI.
ARE THERE ANY FOODS YOU DIS-LIKE?
NOT REALLY.
THANKS FOR THE MEAL!
GREEN PEPPER
...
YOU DON'T LIKE GREEN PEPPERS?
GREEN PEPPERS? WHERE?
HE DOESN'T EVEN *SEE* FOODS HE DISLIKES...
GOOD! AT LEAST HE NOTICED ME!
HMM...
PHEW!
?
PLEASE SEND YOUR LETTERS TO:
CHIKA SHIOMI
C/O YUKARISM EDITOR
VIZ MEDIA
P.O. BOX 77010
SAN FRANCISCO, CA 94107
STAFF:K.YAMADA N.MIYATA
Y.SHIRAKI
CG:HASUNO MIZUKI
K.KOJIMA
(http://twitter.com/chika_shiomi)

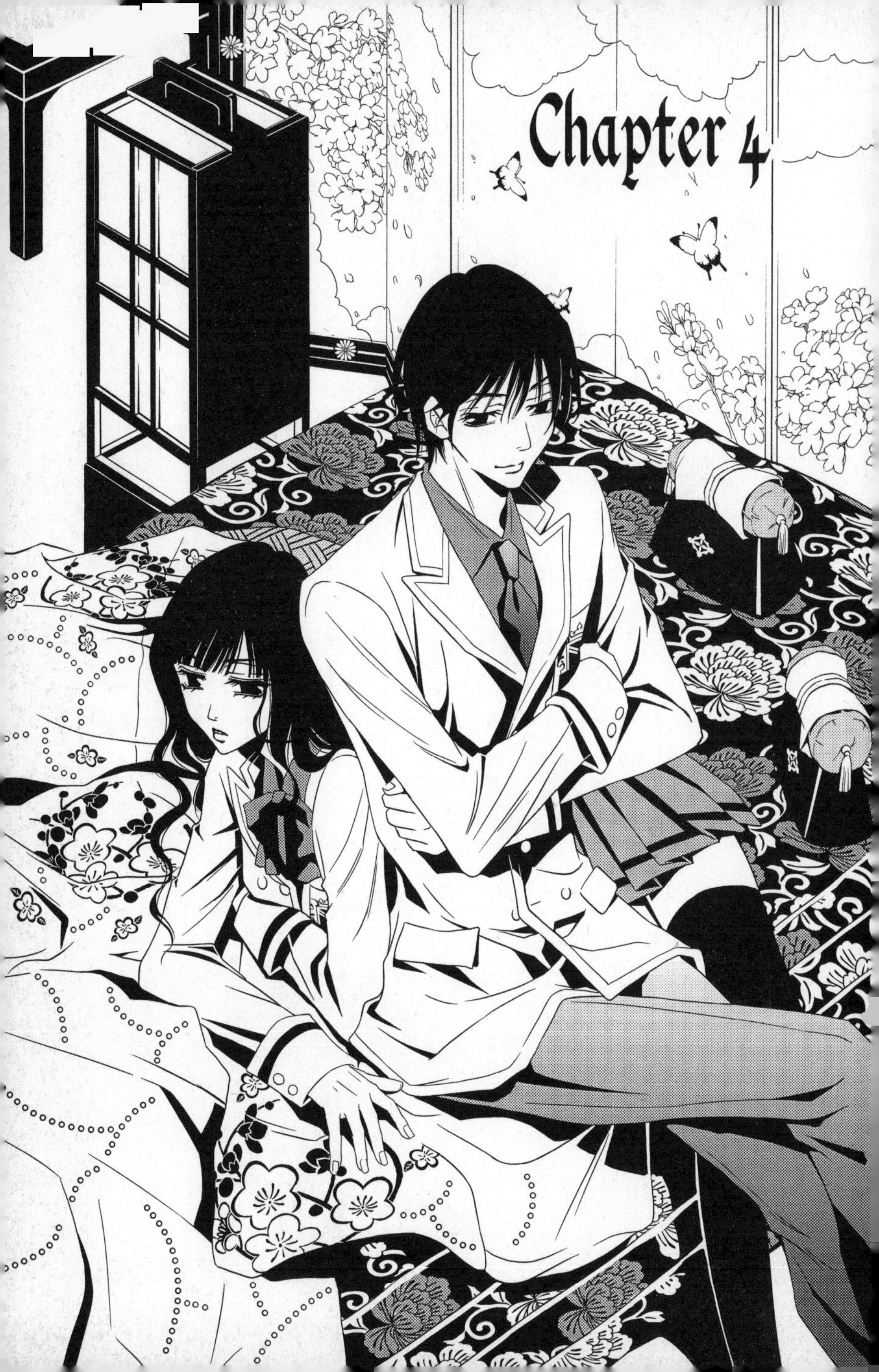
Chapter 4

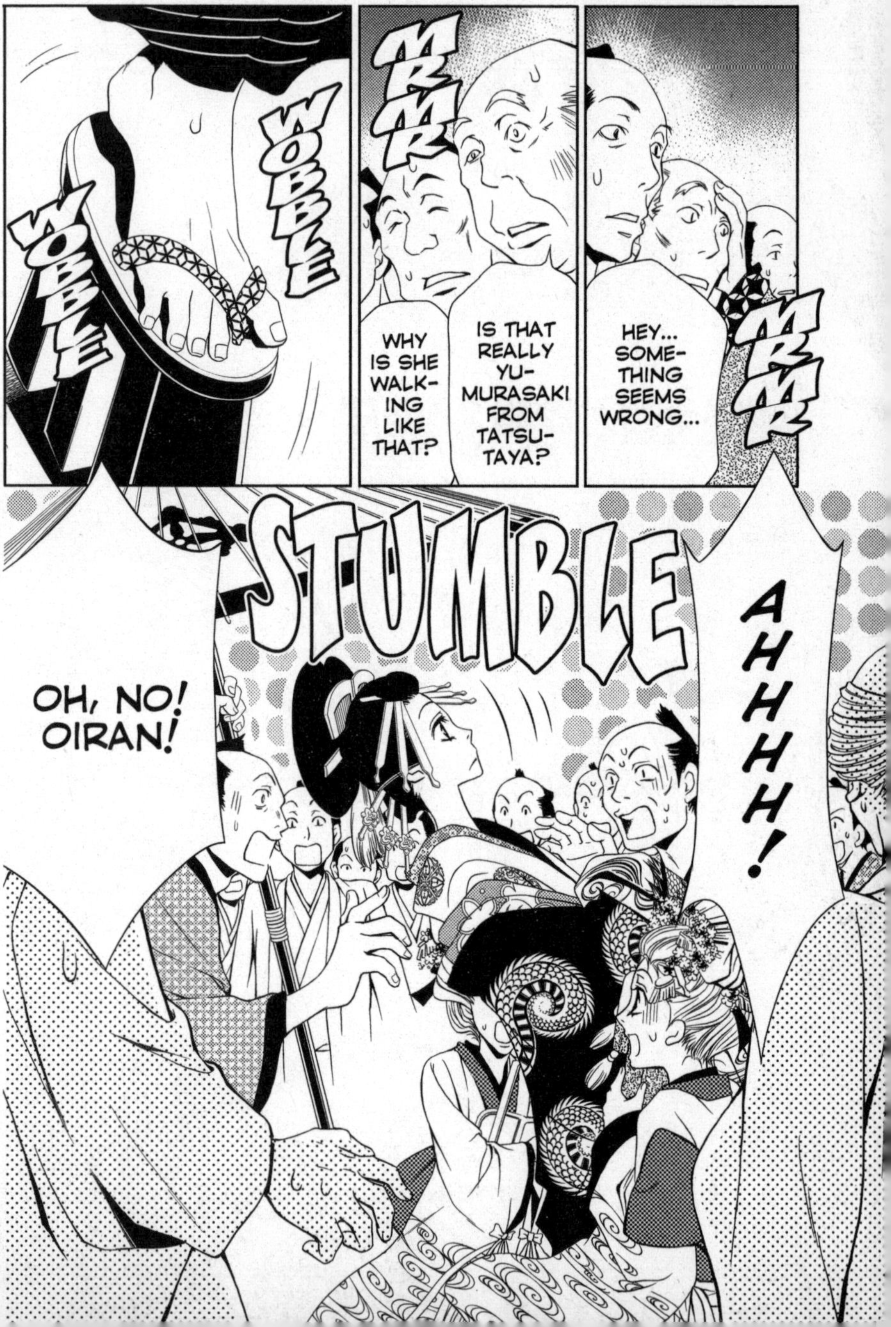
MRMR
HEY... SOMETHING SEEMS WRONG...
MRMR
IS THAT REALLY YU-MURASAKI FROM TATSU-TAYA?
WHY IS SHE WALKING LIKE THAT?
WOBBLE
WOBBLE
STUMBLE
AHHHH!
OH, NO! OIRAN!

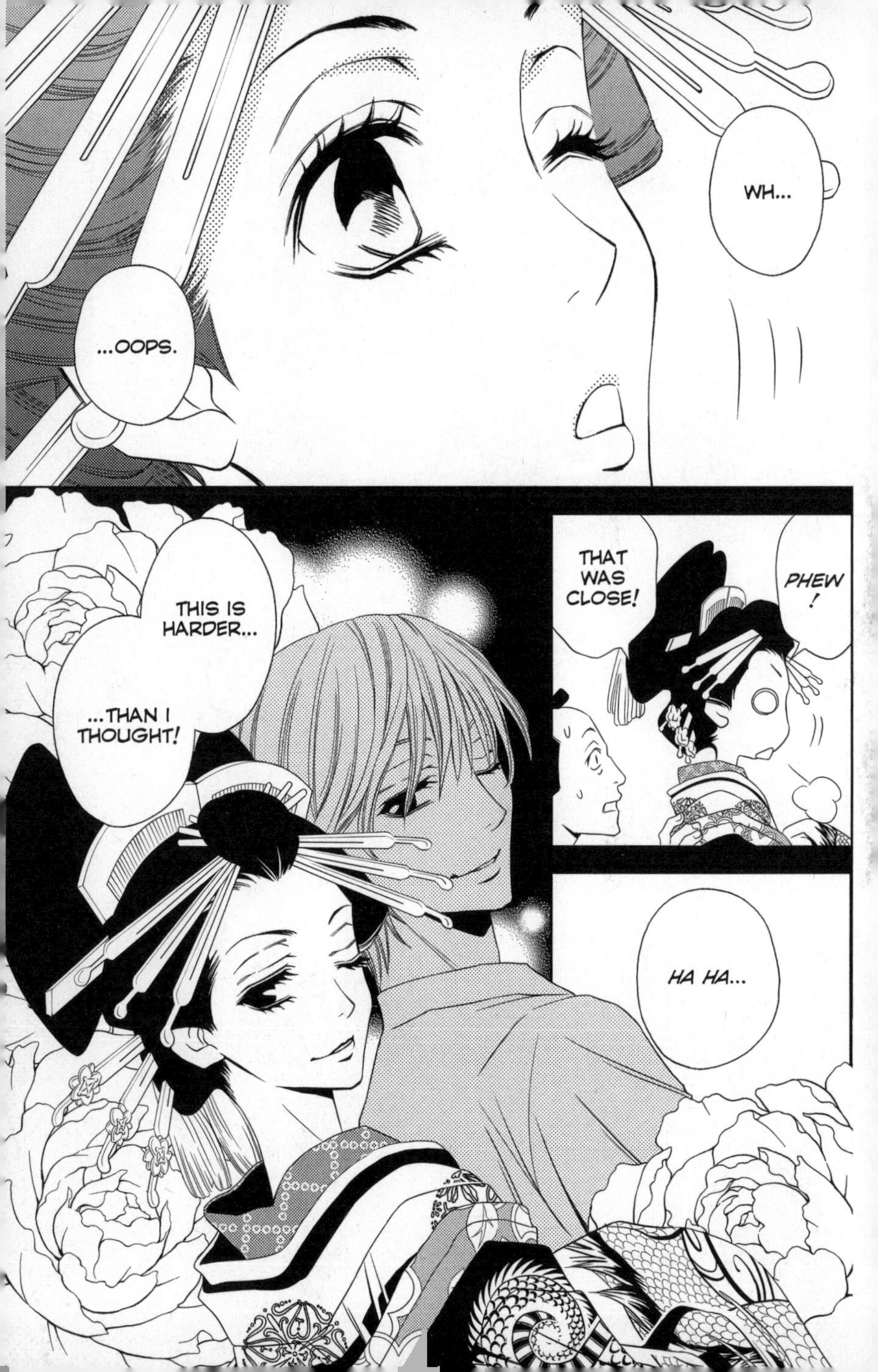
WH...
...OOPS.
PHEW!
THAT WAS CLOSE!
HA HA...
THIS IS HARDER...
...THAN I THOUGHT!

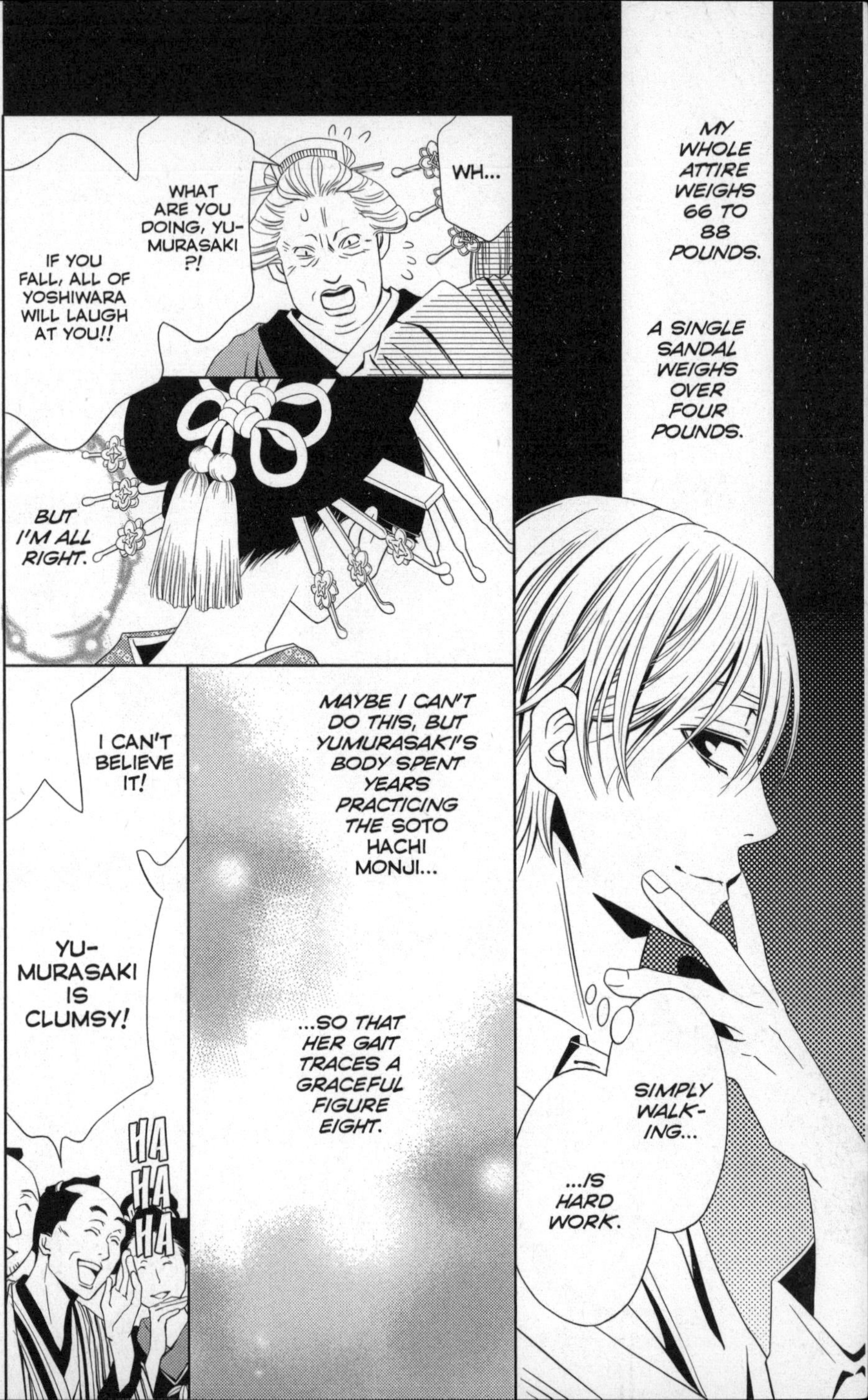
MY WHOLE ATTIRE WEIGHS 66 TO 88 POUNDS.
A SINGLE SANDAL WEIGHS OVER FOUR POUNDS.
SIMPLY WALKING...
...IS HARD WORK.
WH...
WHAT ARE YOU DOING, YU-MURASAKI ?!
IF YOU FALL, ALL OF YOSHIWARA WILL LAUGH AT YOU!!
BUT I'M ALL RIGHT.
MAYBE I CAN'T DO THIS, BUT YUMURASAKI'S BODY SPENT YEARS PRACTICING THE SOTO HACHI MONJI...
...SO THAT HER GAIT TRACES A GRACEFUL FIGURE EIGHT.
I CAN'T BELIEVE IT!
YU-MURASAKI IS CLUMSY!
HA HA HA HA

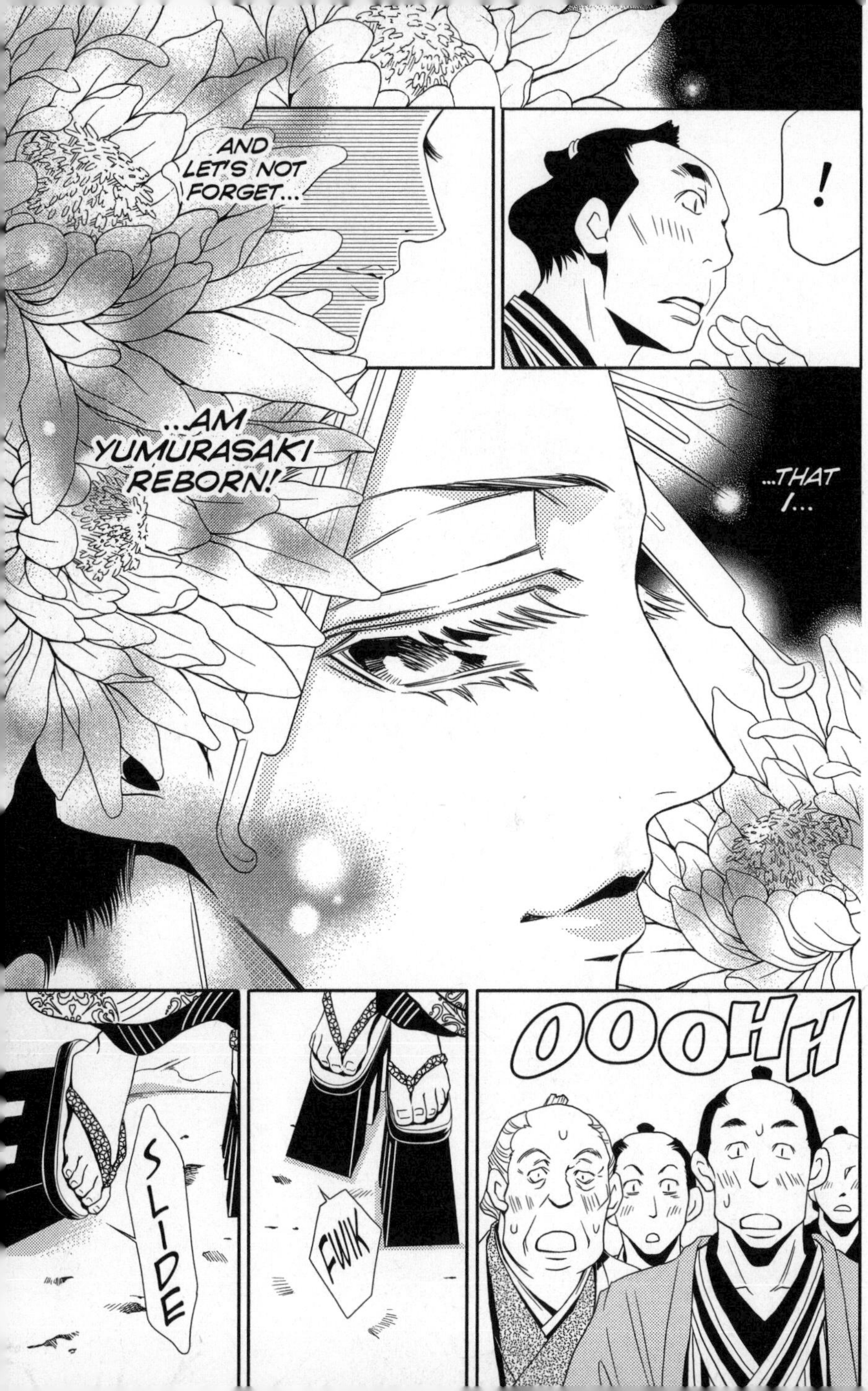
!
AND LET'S NOT FORGET...
...THAT I...
...AM YUMURASAKI REBORN!
OOOHH
FWIK
SLIDE

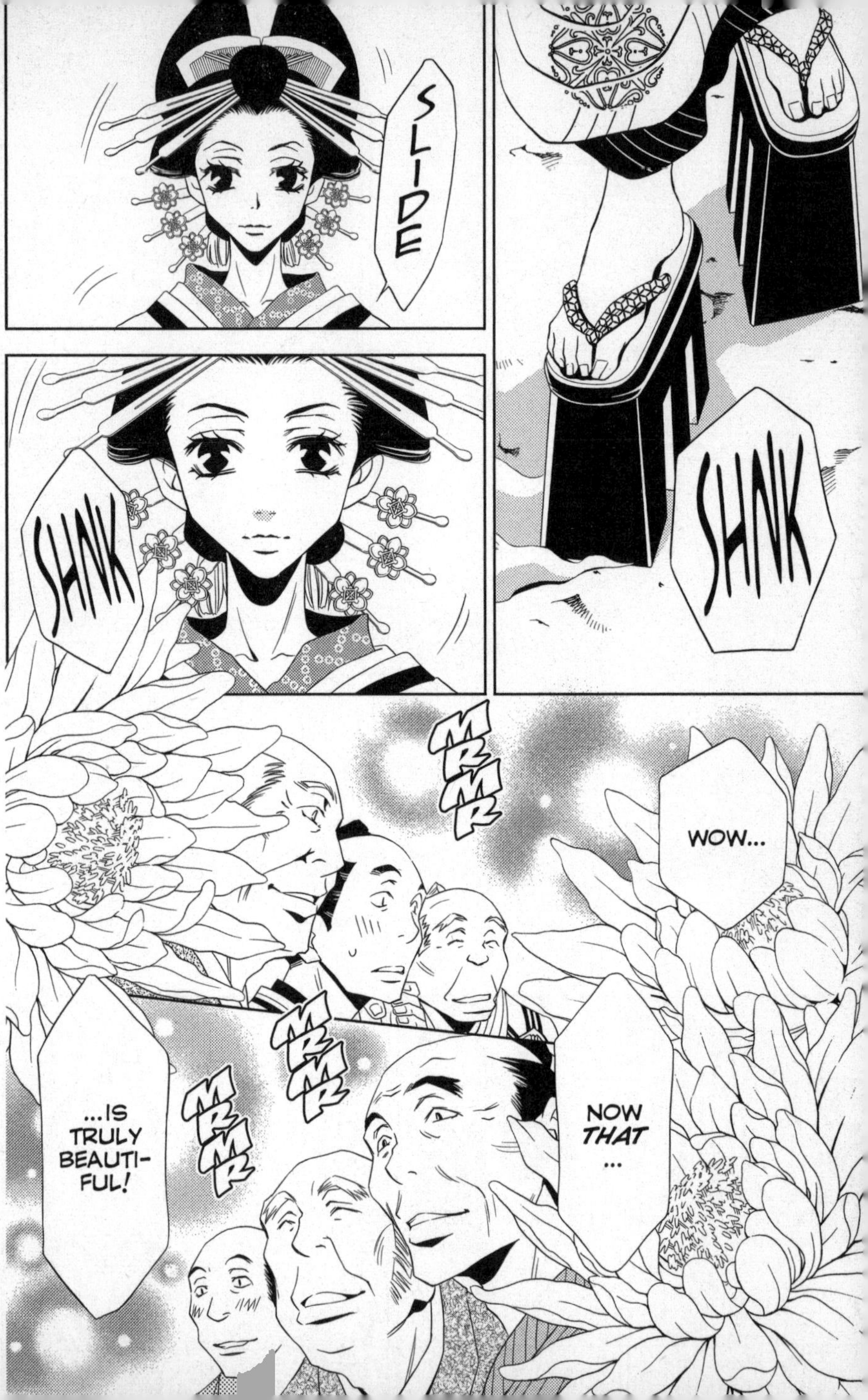
SHNK
SLIDE
SHNK
MRMR
WOW...
MRMR
NOW *THAT* ...
MRMR
...IS TRULY BEAUTIFUL!

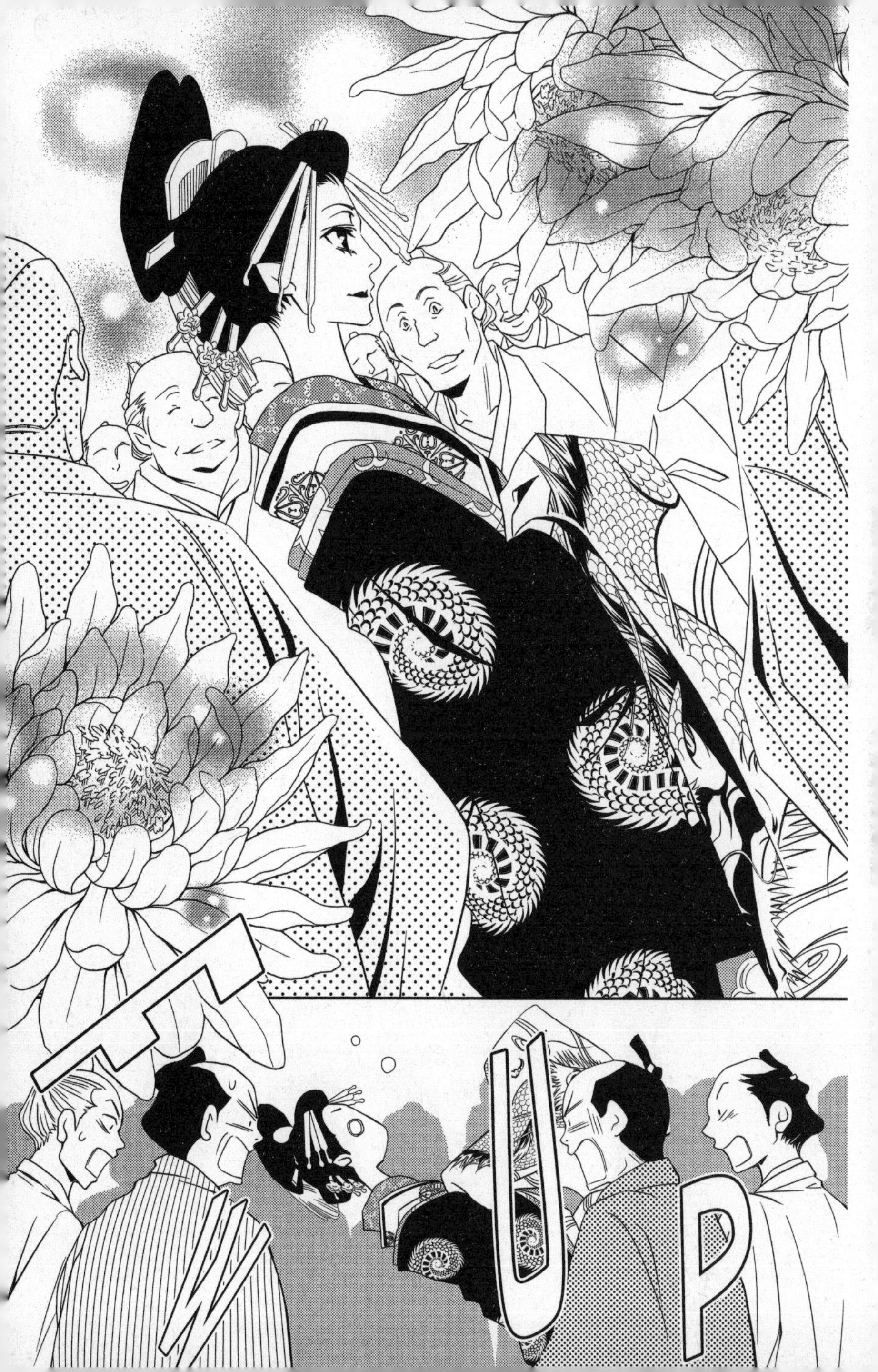
FWUP

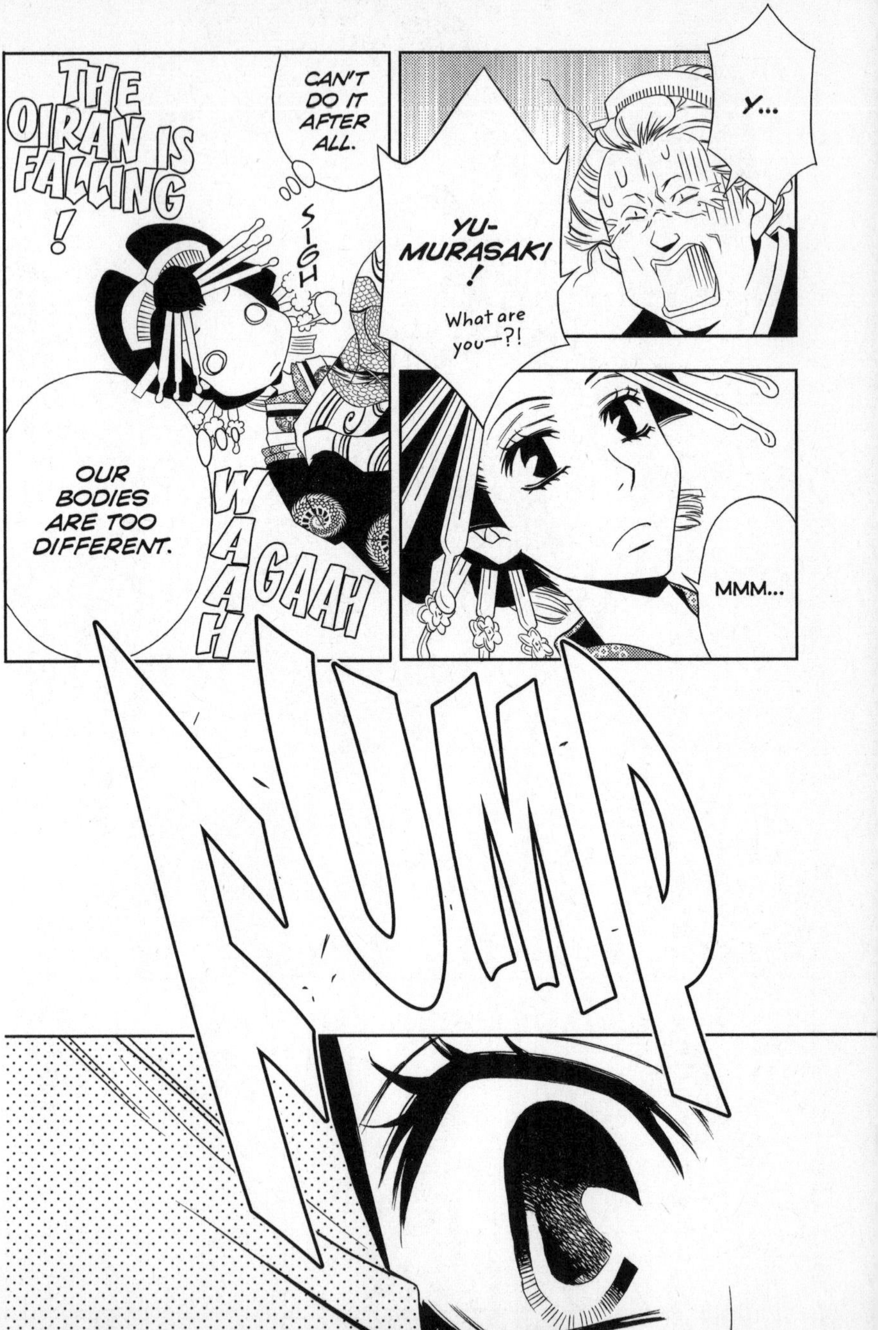
Y...
YU-MURASAKI!
What are you—?!
MMM...
CAN'T DO IT AFTER ALL.
SIGH
THE OIRAN IS FALLING!
OUR BODIES ARE TOO DIFFERENT.
WAAAH
GAAH
FUMP

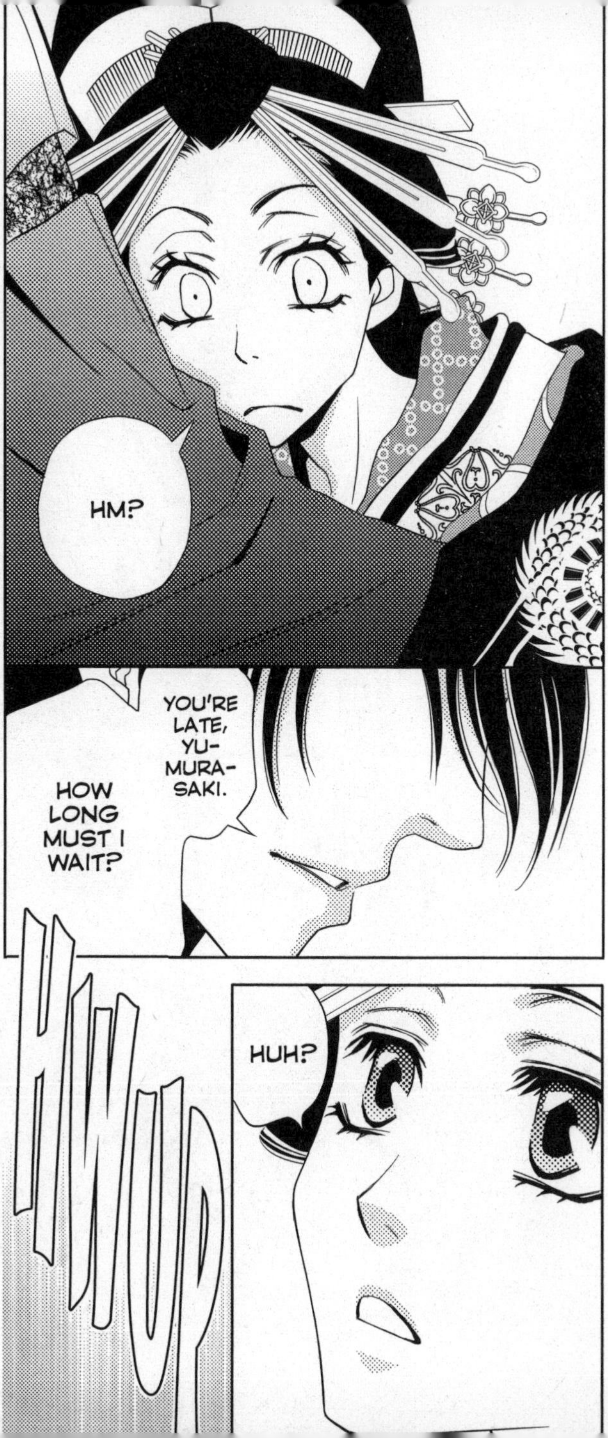
HM?
YOU'RE LATE, YU-MURA-SAKI.
HOW LONG MUST I WAIT?
HWUP
HUH?

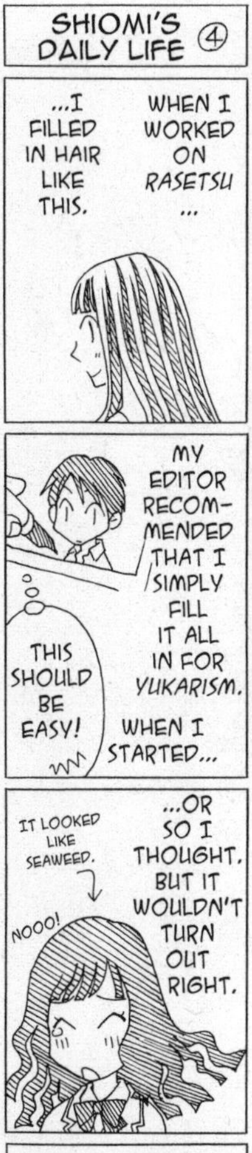
SHIOMI'S DAILY LIFE ④
WHEN I WORKED ON RASETSU...
...I FILLED IN HAIR LIKE THIS.
MY EDITOR RECOMMENDED THAT I SIMPLY FILL IT ALL IN FOR YUKARISM.
THIS SHOULD BE EASY!
WHEN I STARTED...
...OR SO I THOUGHT. BUT IT WOULDN'T TURN OUT RIGHT.
IT LOOKED LIKE SEAWEED.
NOOO!
IT TAKES LONGER THAN BEFORE.
IT LOOKS LIKE THEY'RE WEARING WEIRD HELMETS...
SOB SOB

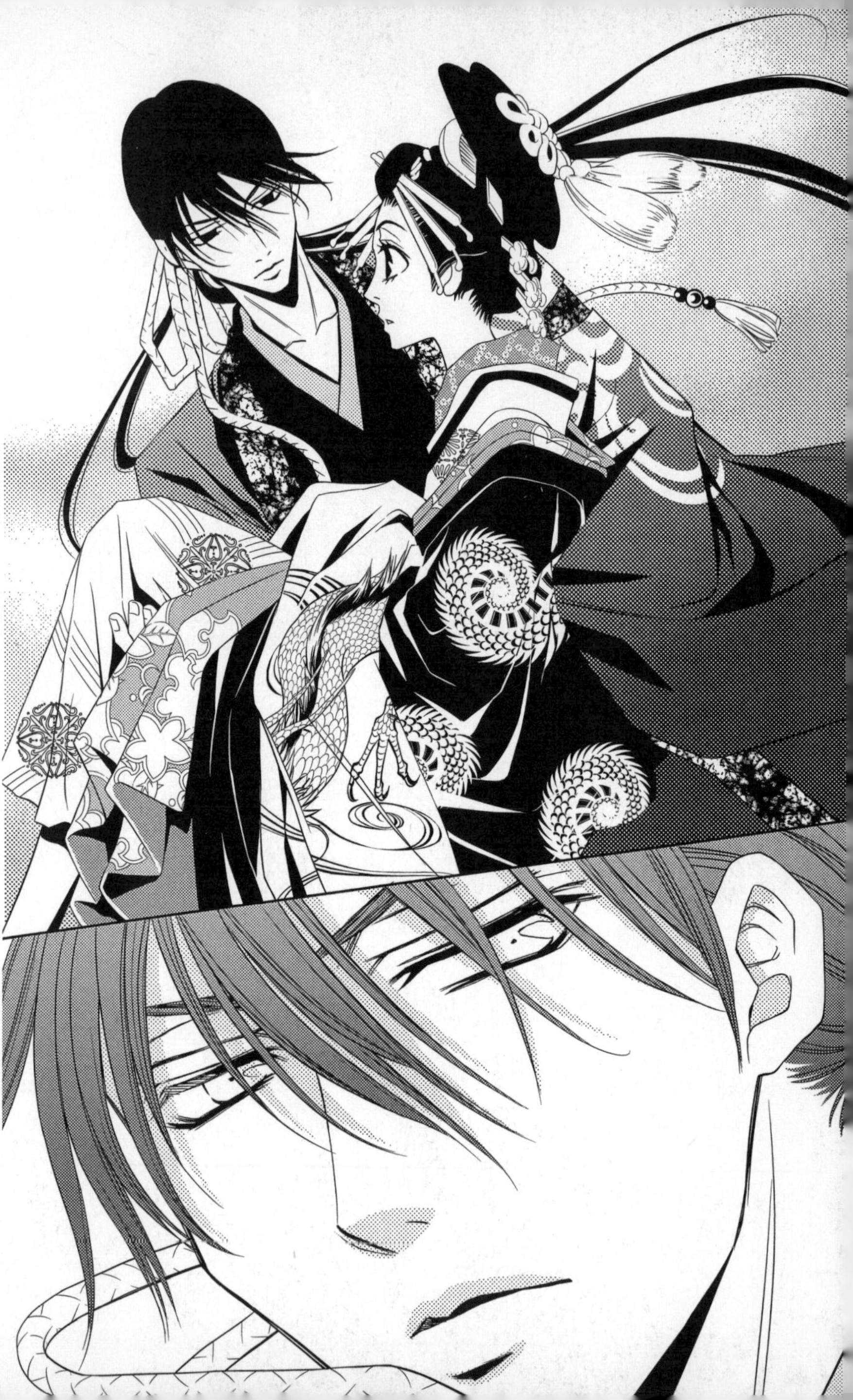

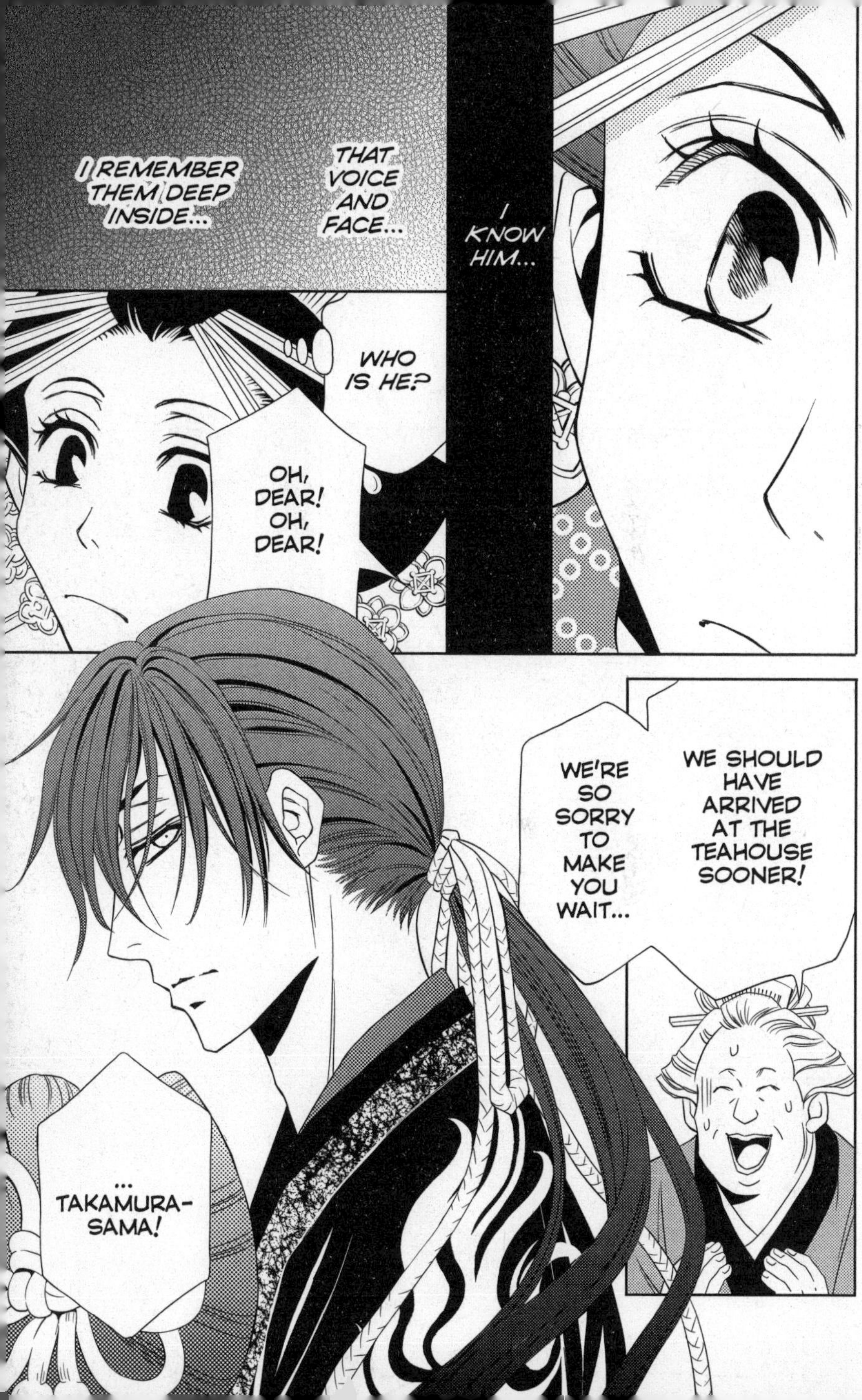
I KNOW HIM...
THAT VOICE AND FACE...
I REMEMBER THEM DEEP INSIDE...
WHO IS HE?
OH, DEAR! OH, DEAR!
WE SHOULD HAVE ARRIVED AT THE TEAHOUSE SOONER!
WE'RE SO SORRY TO MAKE YOU WAIT...
...TAKAMURA-SAMA!

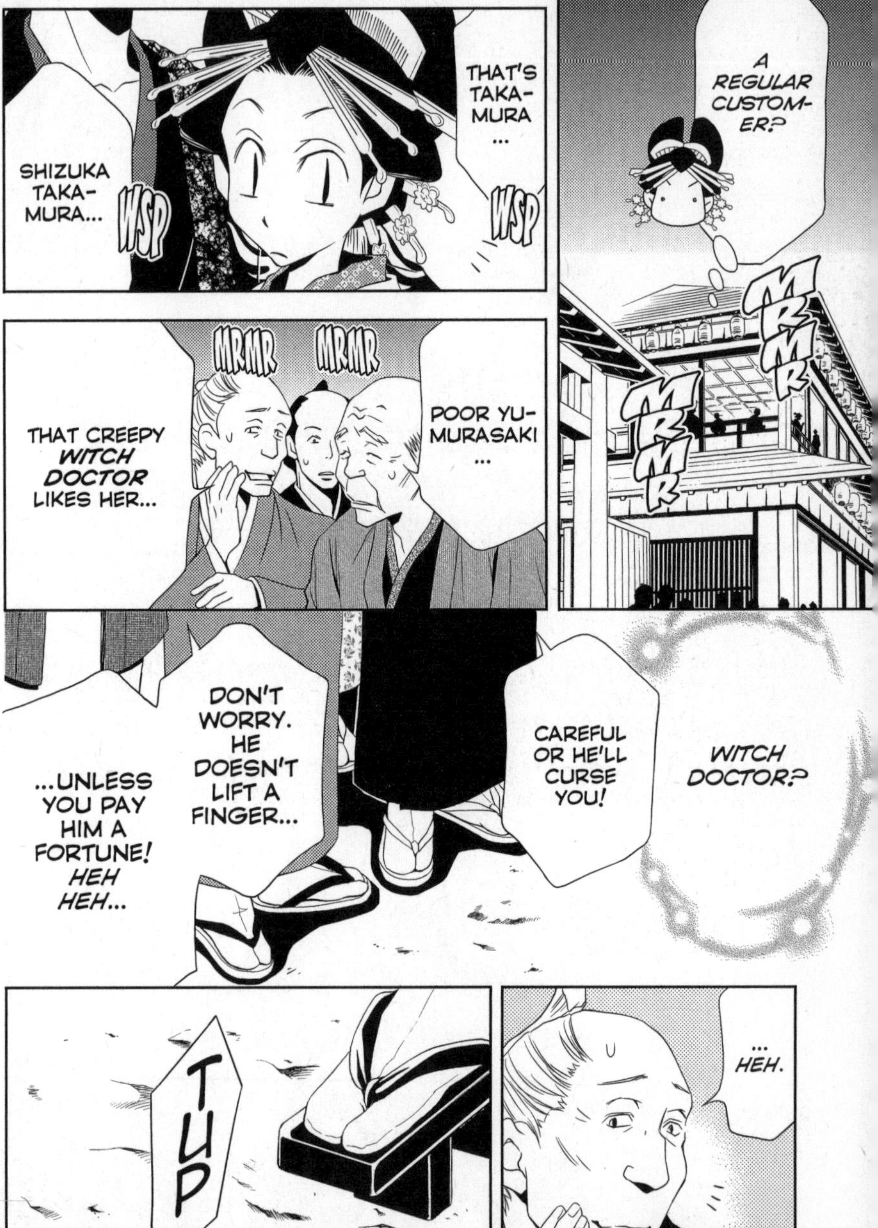
A REGULAR CUSTOMER?
MRMR
MRMR
THAT'S TAKAMURA...
WSP
SHIZUKA TAKAMURA...
WSP
MRMR
MRMR
POOR YUMURASAKI...
THAT CREEPY *WITCH DOCTOR* LIKES HER...
WITCH DOCTOR?
CAREFUL OR HE'LL CURSE YOU!
DON'T WORRY. HE DOESN'T LIFT A FINGER...
...UNLESS YOU PAY HIM A FORTUNE! *HEH HEH...*
...HEH.
TUP

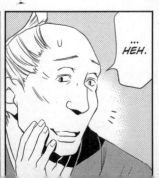

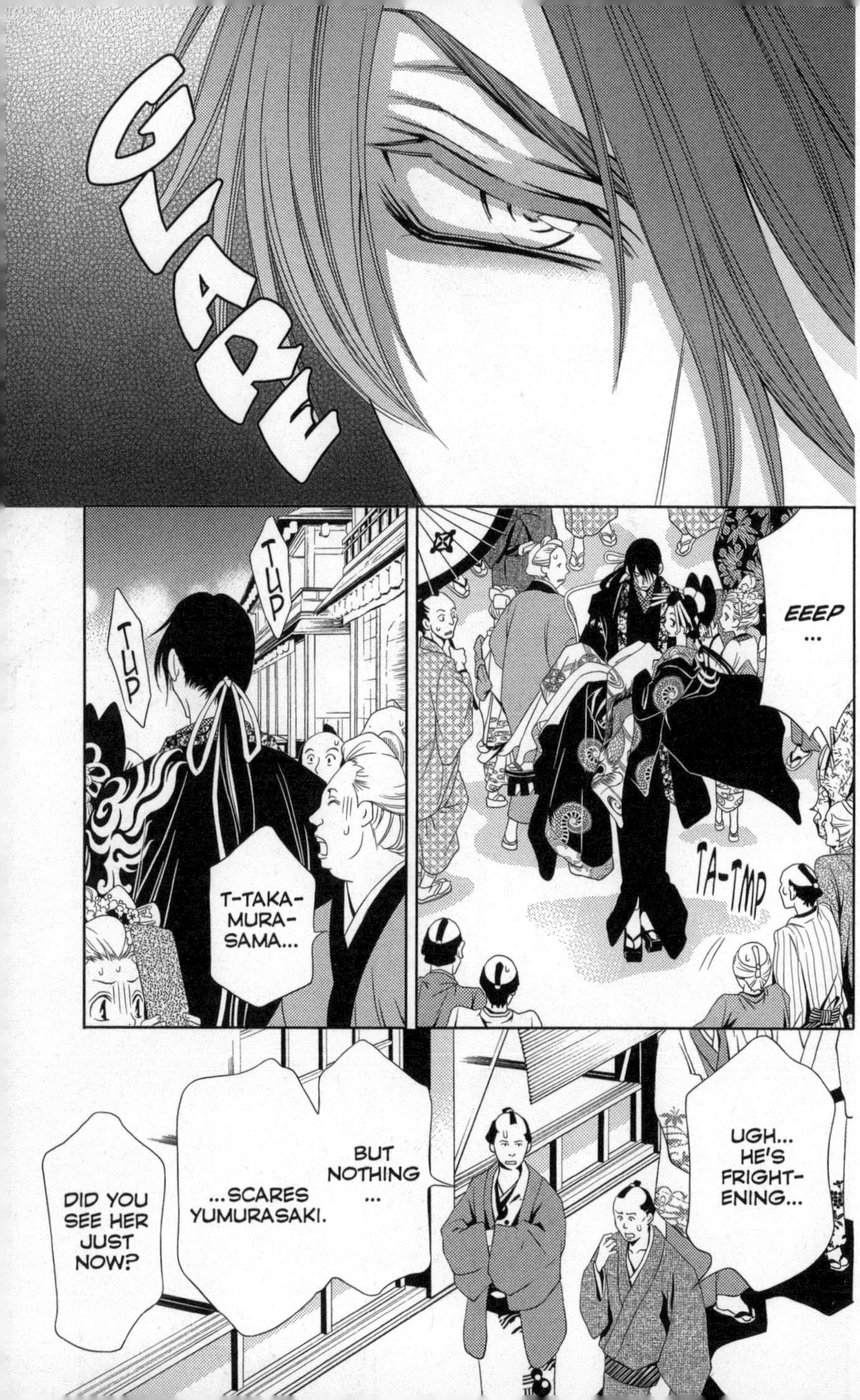
GLARE
EEEP...
TA-TMP
TUP
TUP
T-TAKAMURA-SAMA...
UGH... HE'S FRIGHTENING...
BUT NOTHING...
...SCARES YUMURASAKI.
DID YOU SEE HER JUST NOW?

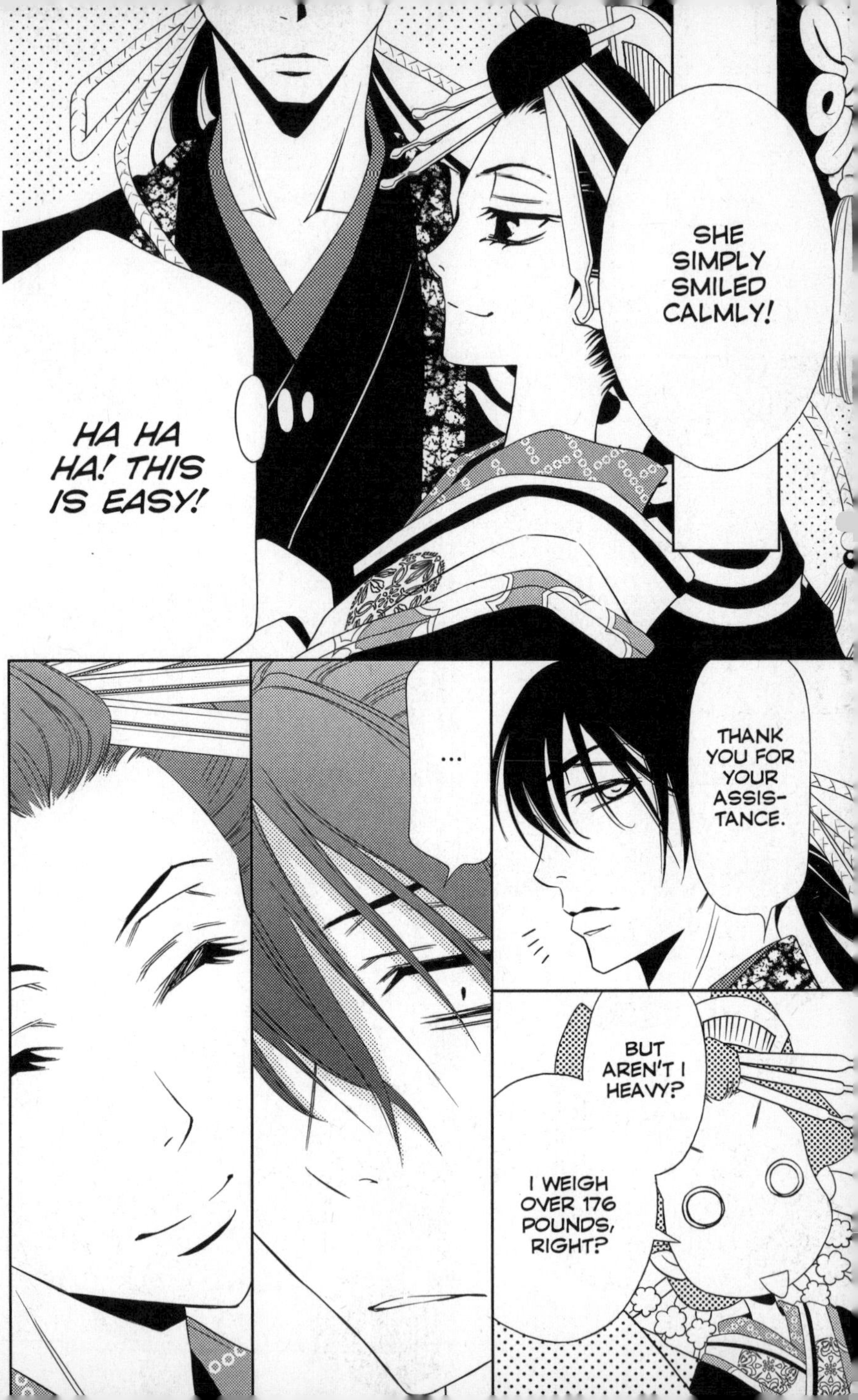
SHE SIMPLY SMILED CALMLY!
HA HA HA! THIS IS EASY!
THANK YOU FOR YOUR ASSIS-TANCE.
BUT AREN'T I HEAVY?
I WEIGH OVER 176 POUNDS, RIGHT?
...

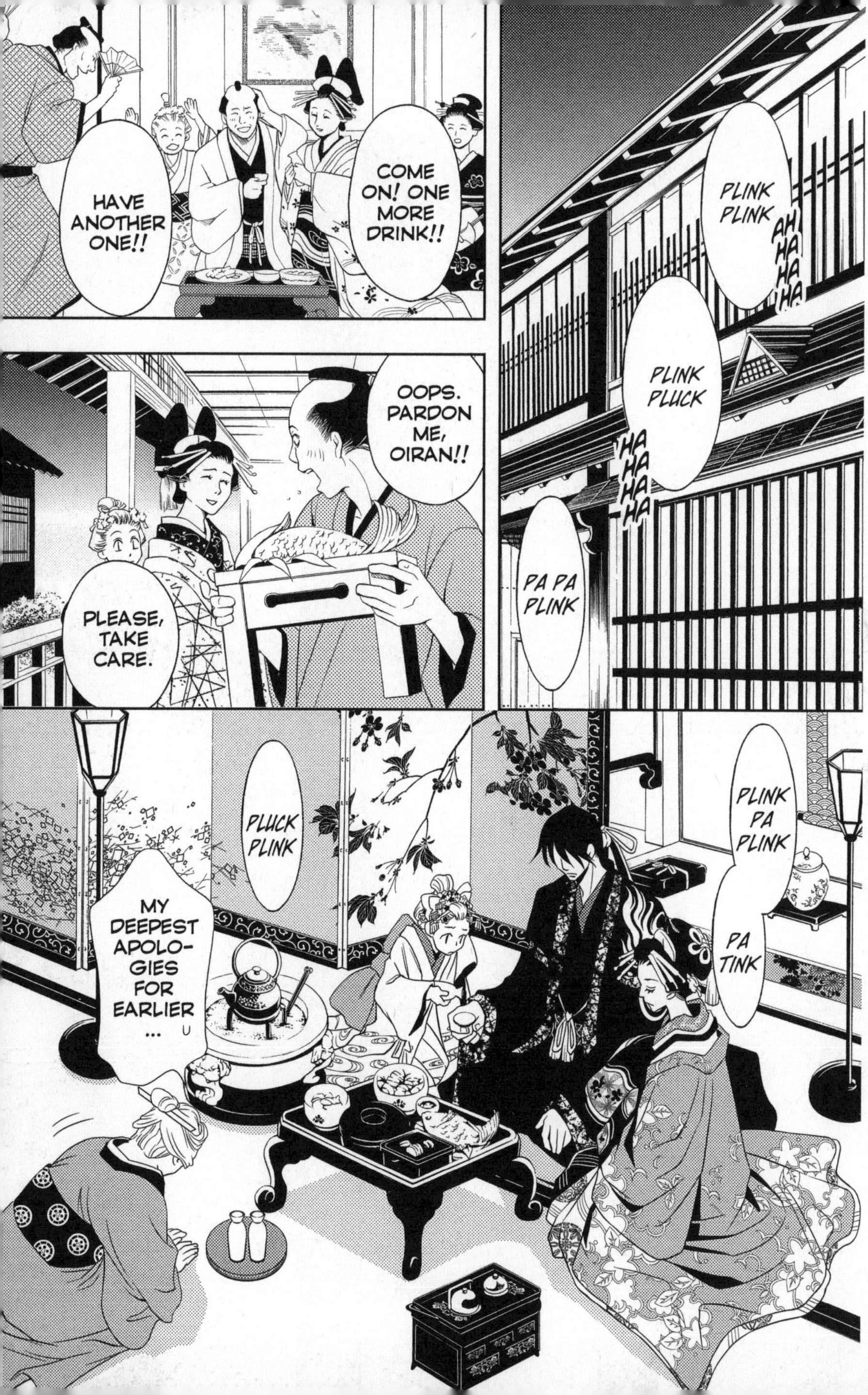
PLINK PLINK
AH HA HA HA HA
PLINK PLUCK
HA HA HA HA HA
PA PA PLINK
COME ON! ONE MORE DRINK!!
HAVE ANOTHER ONE!!
OOPS. PARDON ME, OIRAN!!
PLEASE, TAKE CARE.
PLINK PA PLINK
PA TINK
PLUCK PLINK
MY DEEPEST APOLO-GIES FOR EARLIER...

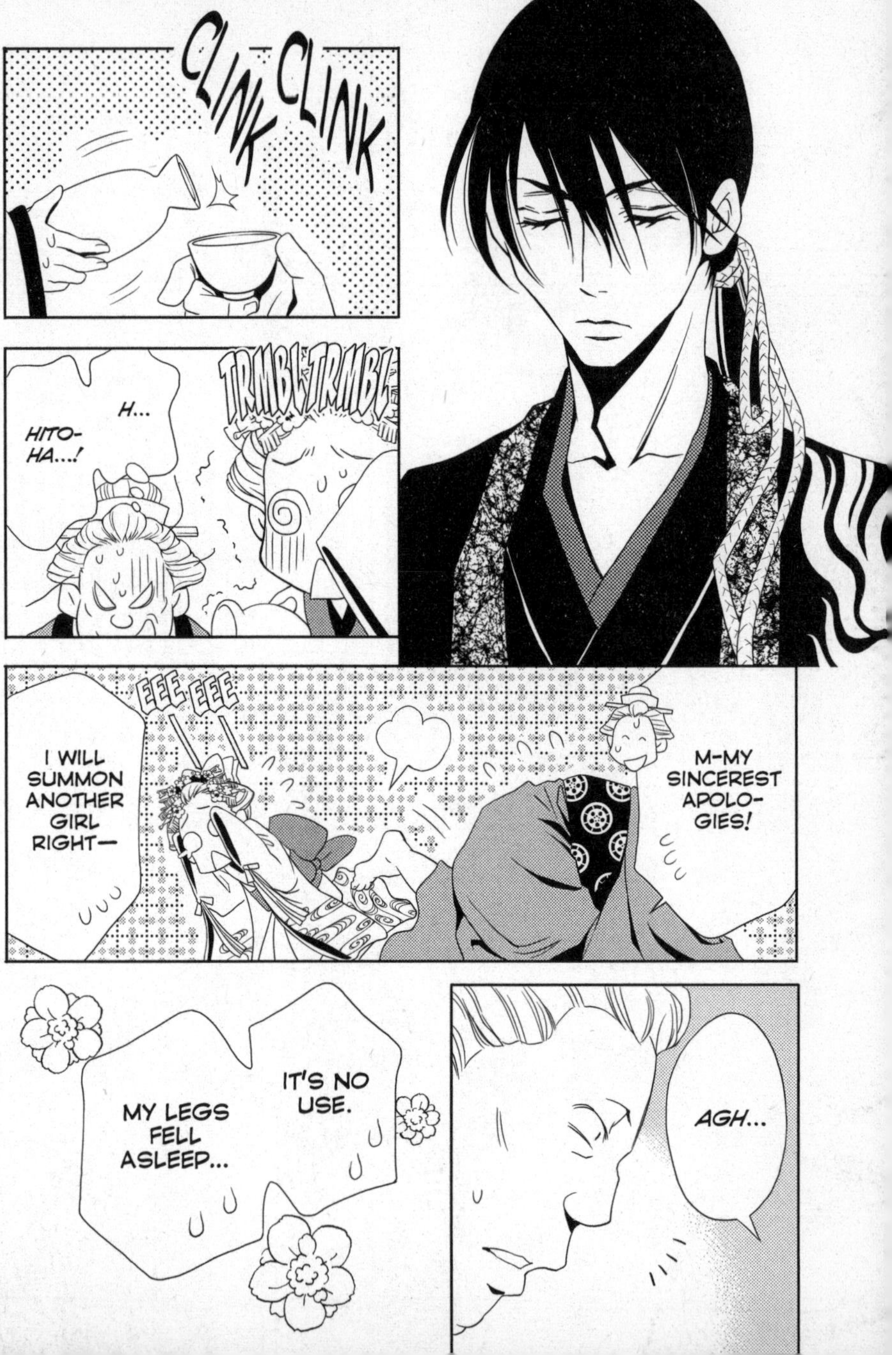
CLINK CLINK
TRMBL TRMBL
H...
HITO-HA...!
M-MY SINCEREST APOLOGIES!
EEE EEE
I WILL SUMMON ANOTHER GIRL RIGHT—
AGH...
IT'S NO USE.
MY LEGS FELL ASLEEP...

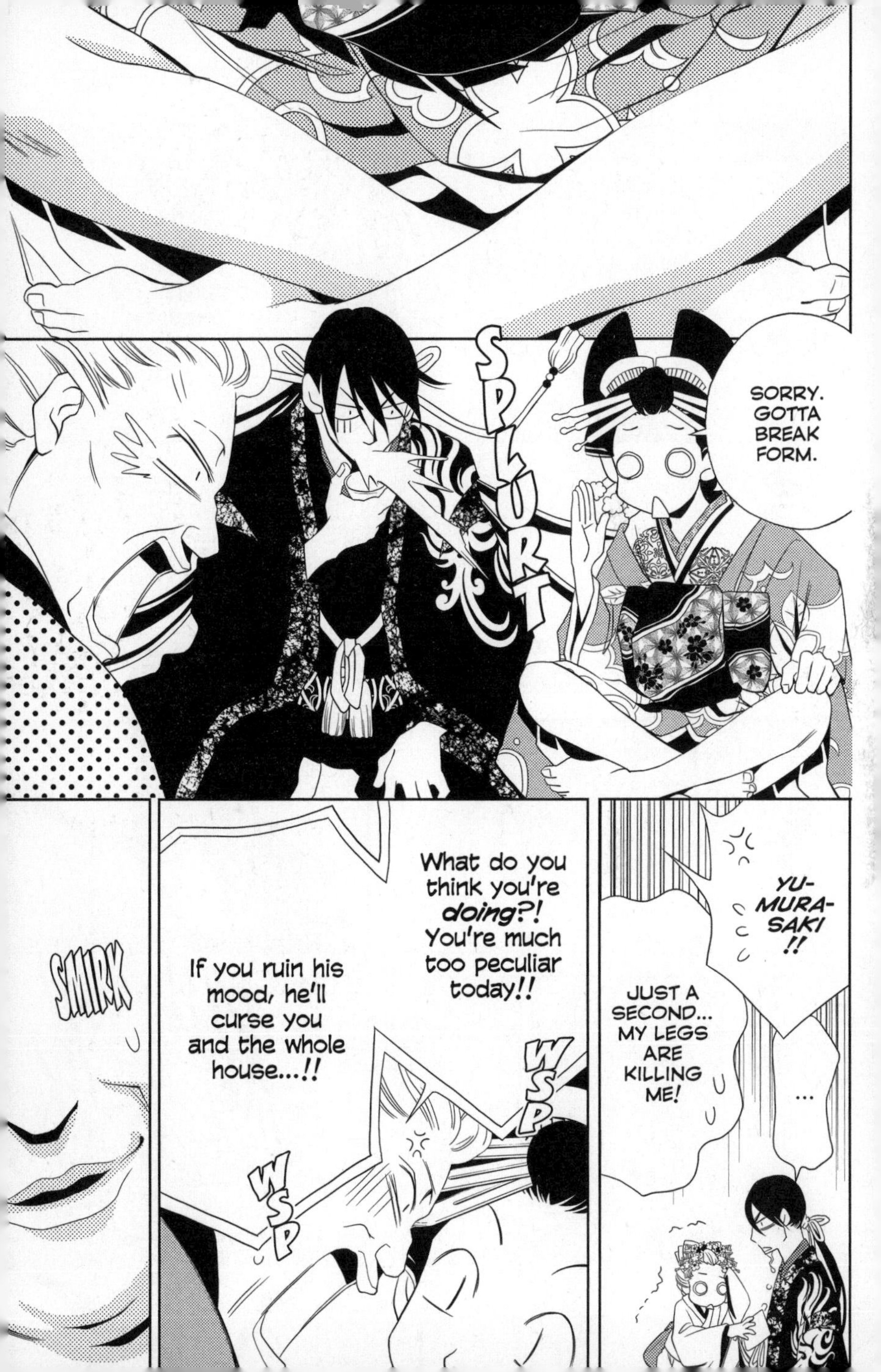
SORRY. GOTTA BREAK FORM.
SPLURT
YU-MURASAKI!!
JUST A SECOND... MY LEGS ARE KILLING ME!
...
What do you think you're *doing*?! You're much too peculiar today!!
WSP
If you ruin his mood, he'll curse you and the whole house...!!
WSP
SMIRK

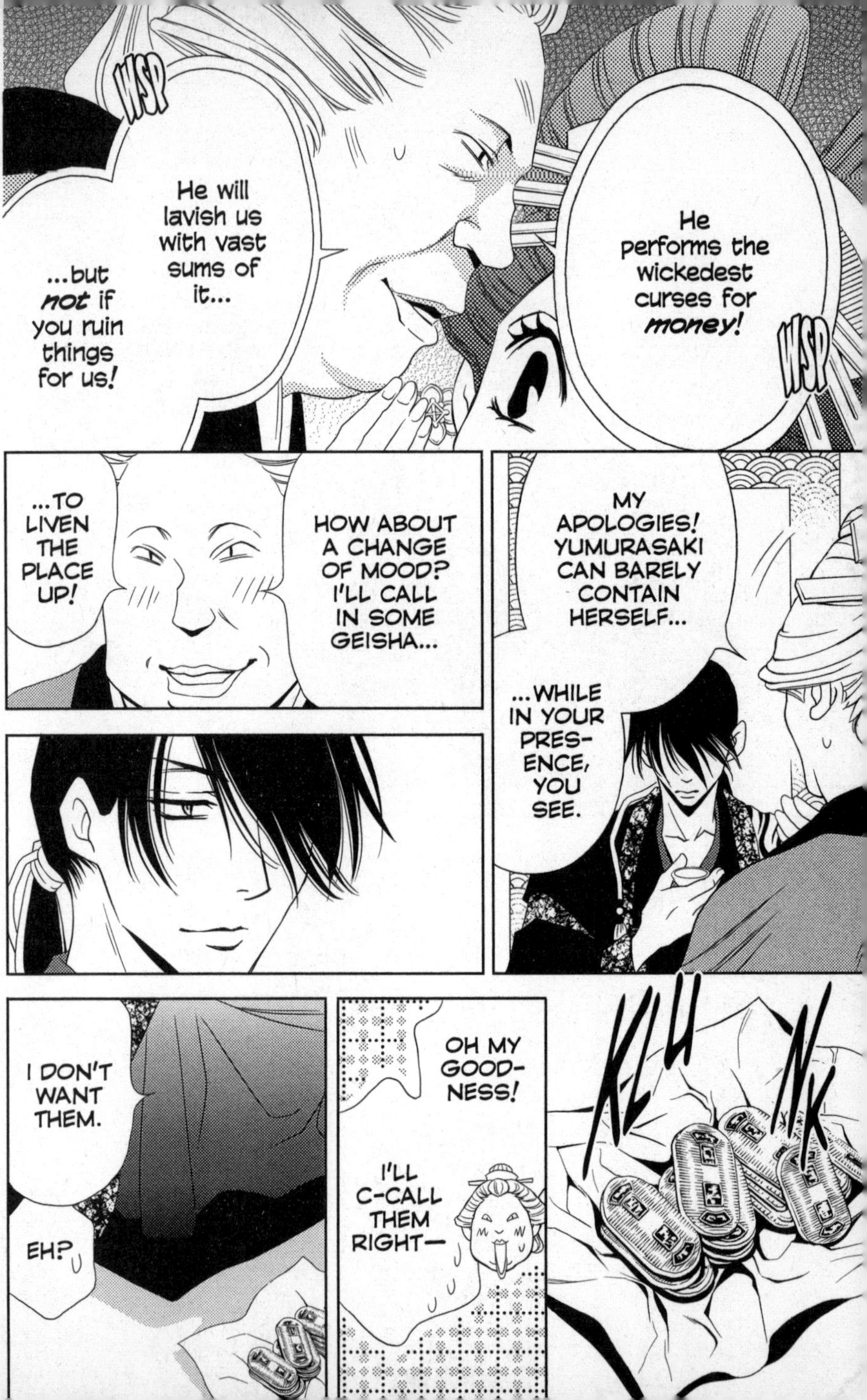
He performs the wickedest curses for *money*!
WSP
He will lavish us with vast sums of it...
...but *not* if you ruin things for us!
WSP
MY APOLOGIES! YUMURASAKI CAN BARELY CONTAIN HERSELF...
...WHILE IN YOUR PRES-ENCE, YOU SEE.
HOW ABOUT A CHANGE OF MOOD? I'LL CALL IN SOME GEISHA...
...TO LIVEN THE PLACE UP!
KLUNK
OH MY GOOD-NESS!
I'LL C-CALL THEM RIGHT—
I DON'T WANT THEM.
EH?

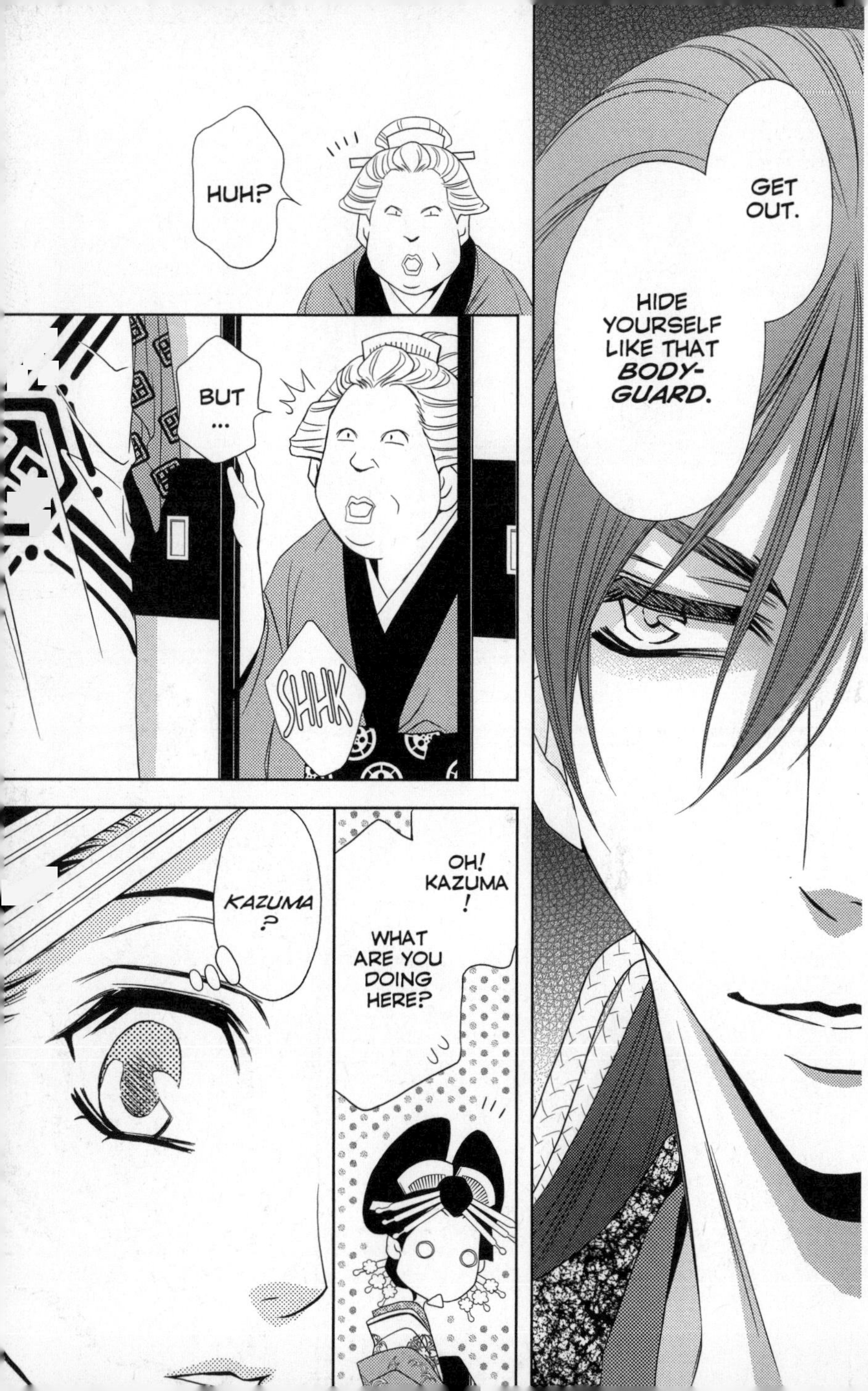
GET OUT.
HIDE YOURSELF LIKE THAT BODY-GUARD.
HUH?
BUT ...
SHHK
OH! KAZUMA!
WHAT ARE YOU DOING HERE?
KAZUMA?

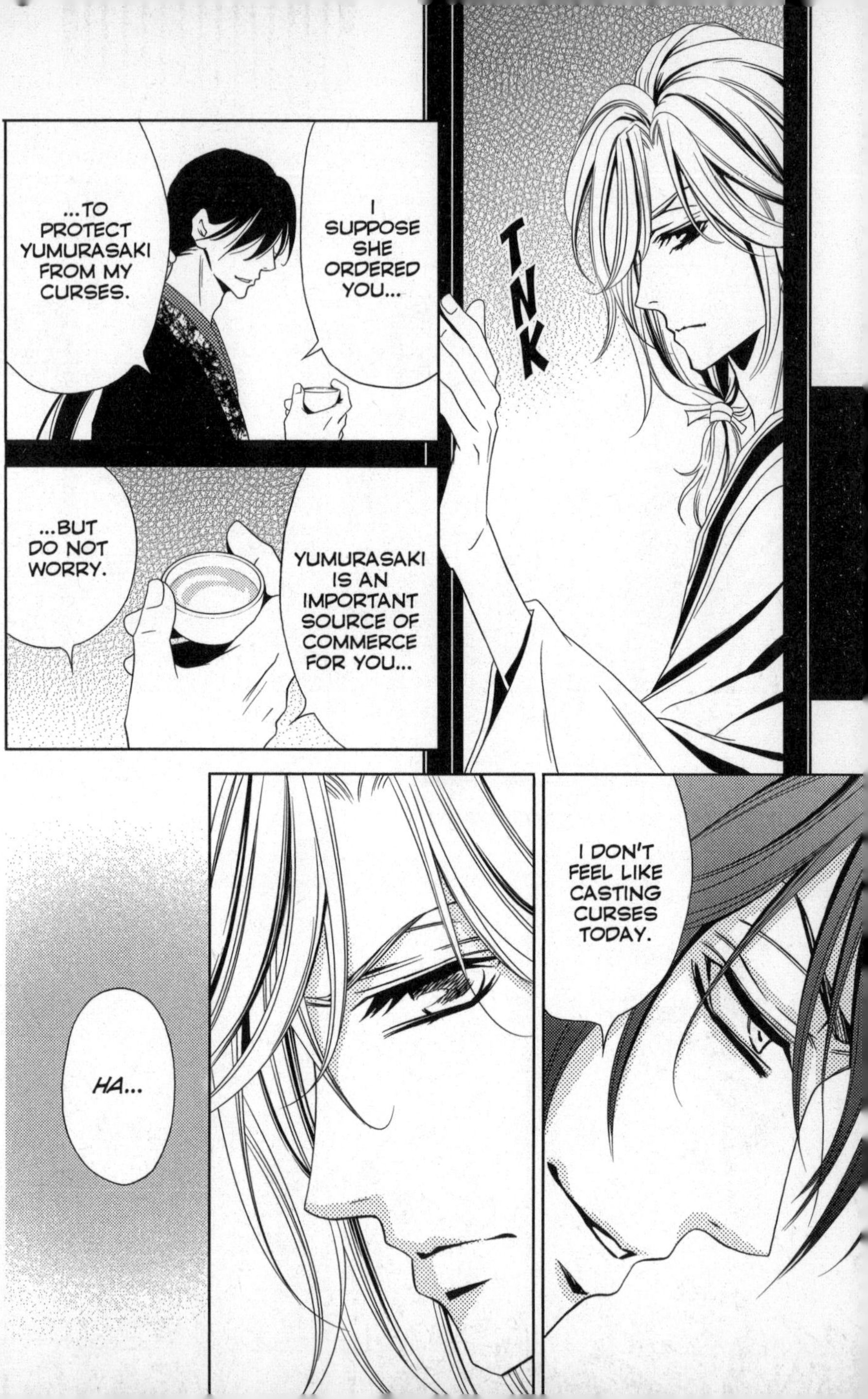
TNK
I SUPPOSE SHE ORDERED YOU...
...TO PROTECT YUMURASAKI FROM MY CURSES.
YUMURASAKI IS AN IMPORTANT SOURCE OF COMMERCE FOR YOU...
...BUT DO NOT WORRY.
I DON'T FEEL LIKE CASTING CURSES TODAY.
HA...

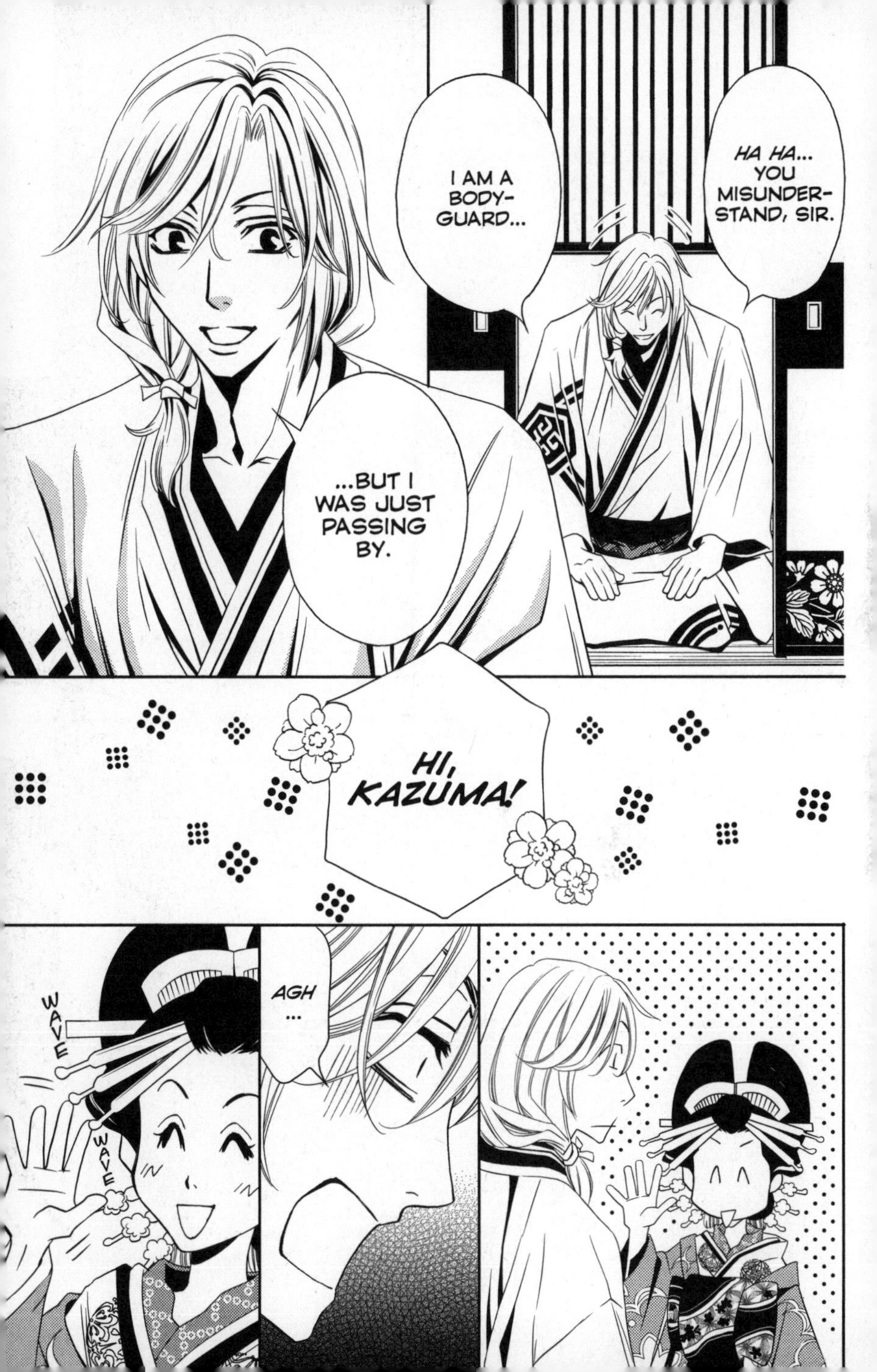
HA HA... YOU MISUNDER-STAND, SIR.
I AM A BODY-GUARD...
...BUT I WAS JUST PASSING BY.
HI, KAZUMA!
AGH ...
WAVE
WAVE

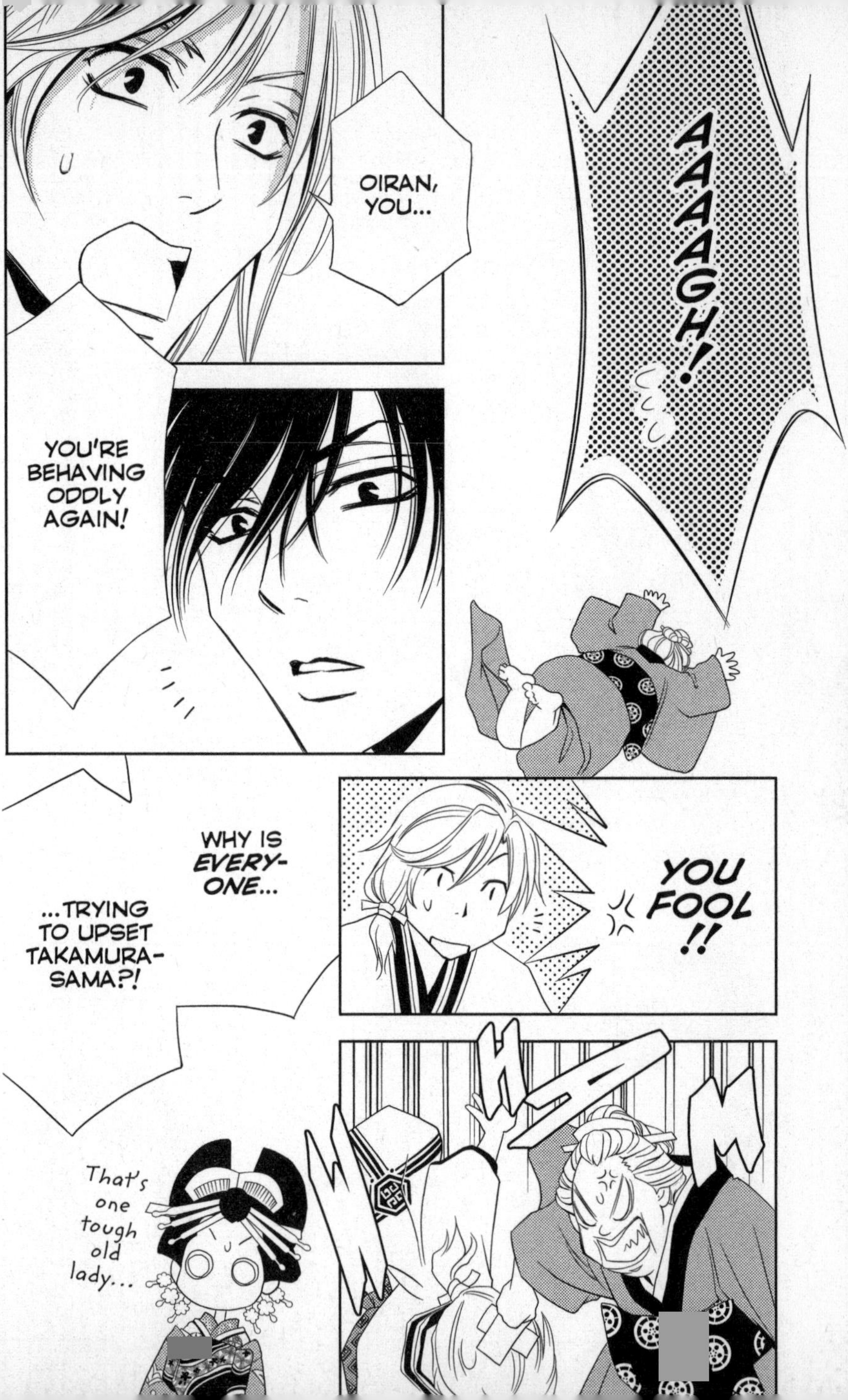
AAAAGH!
OIRAN, YOU...
YOU'RE BEHAVING ODDLY AGAIN!
YOU FOOL!!
WHY IS EVERYONE...
...TRYING TO UPSET TAKAMURA-SAMA?!
WHAM
That's one tough old lady...

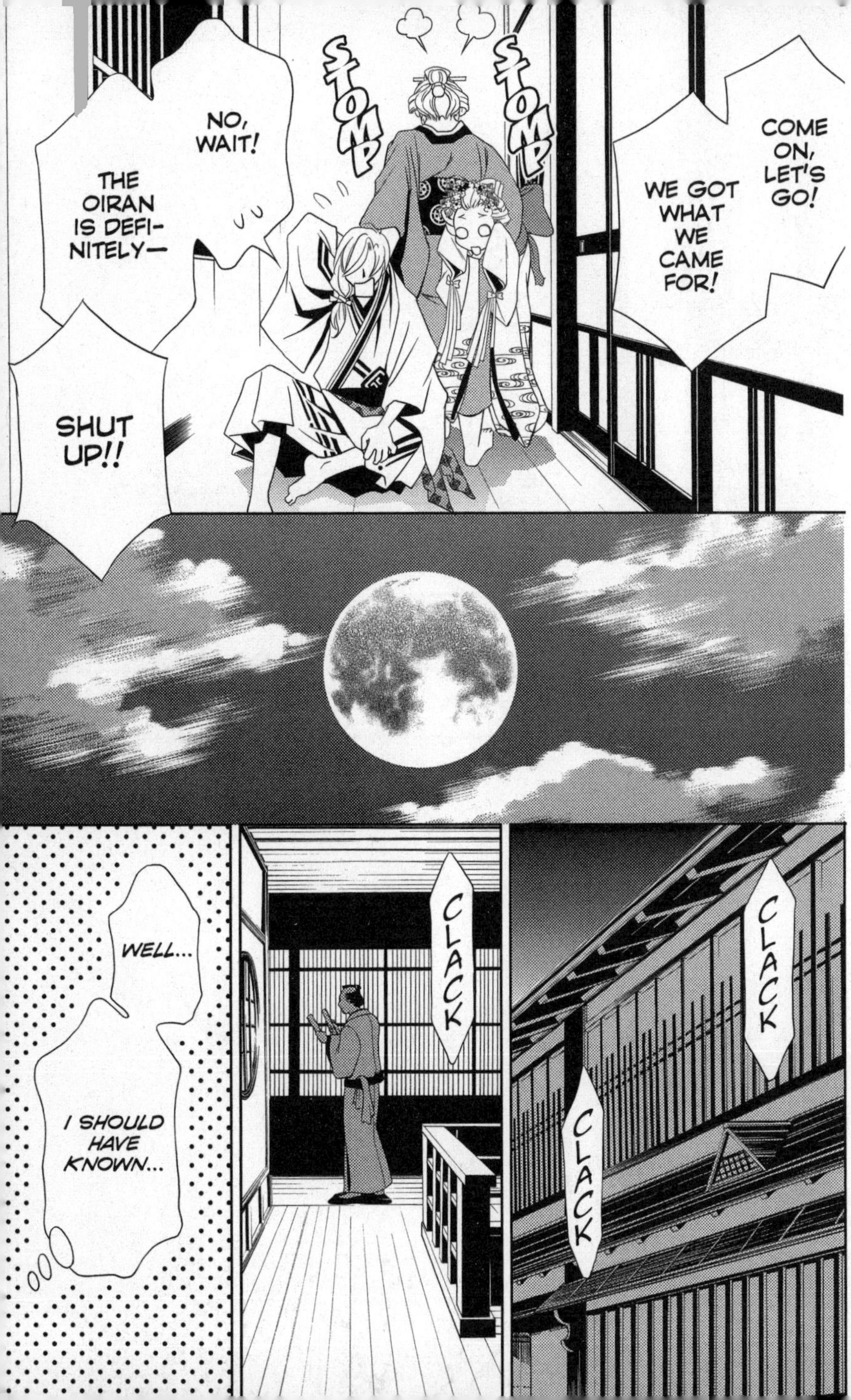
COME ON, LET'S GO!
WE GOT WHAT WE CAME FOR!
STOMP
STOMP
NO, WAIT!
THE OIRAN IS DEFI-NITELY—
SHUT UP!!
CLACK
CLACK
CLACK
WELL...
I SHOULD HAVE KNOWN...

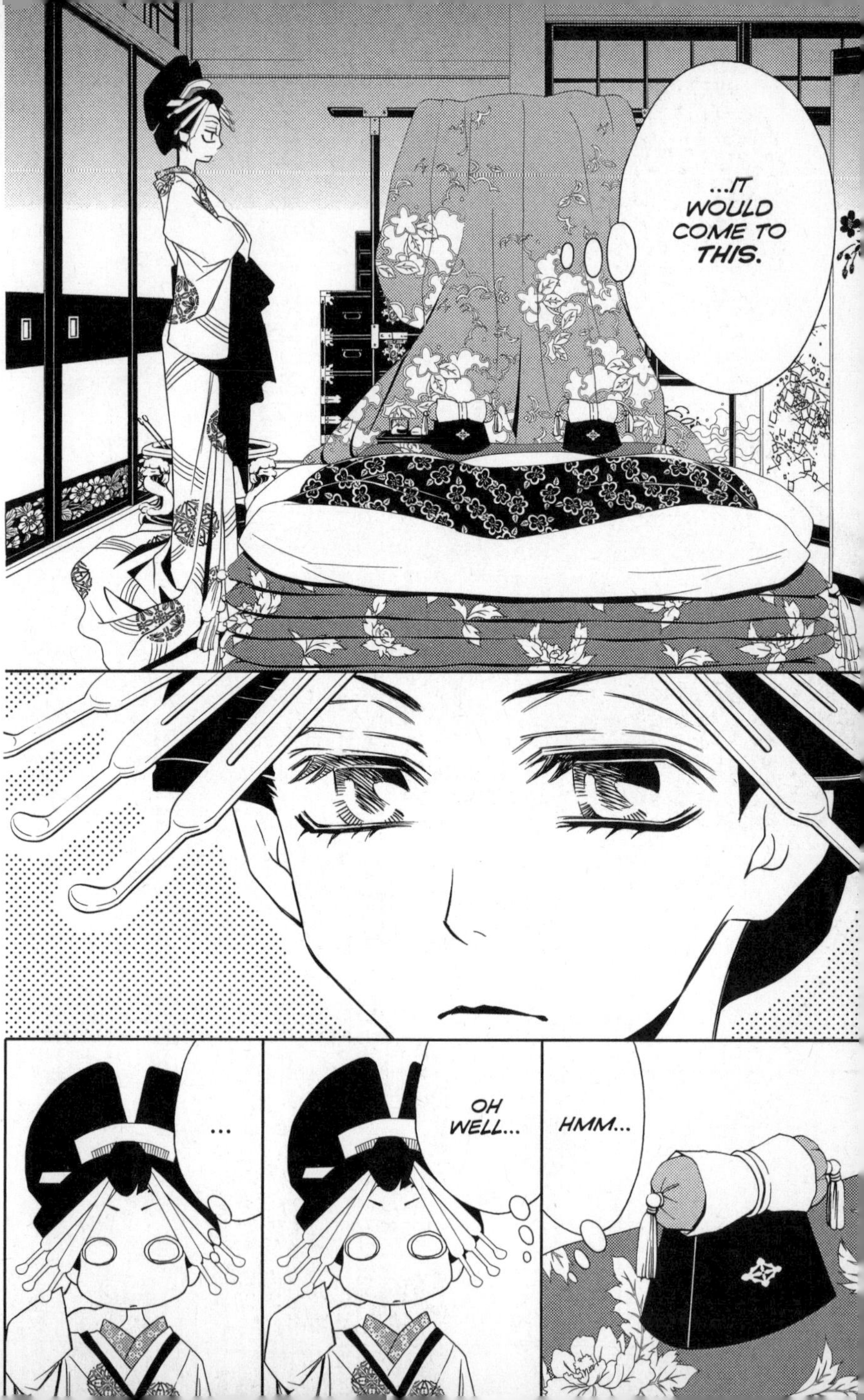
...IT WOULD COME TO THIS.
HMM...
OH WELL...
...

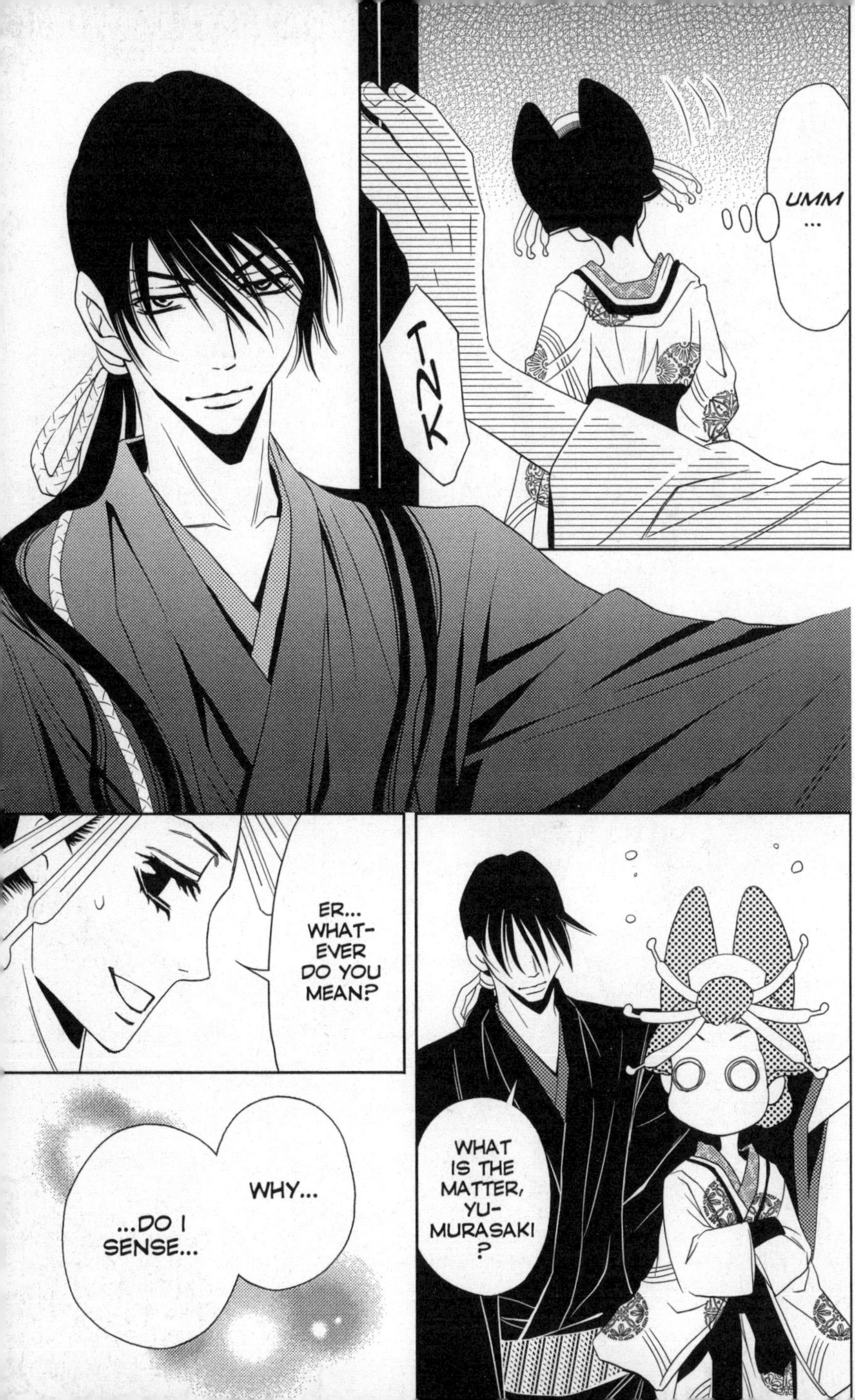
UMM ...
TNK
WHAT IS THE MATTER, YUMURASAKI?
ER... WHATEVER DO YOU MEAN?
WHY...
...DO I SENSE...

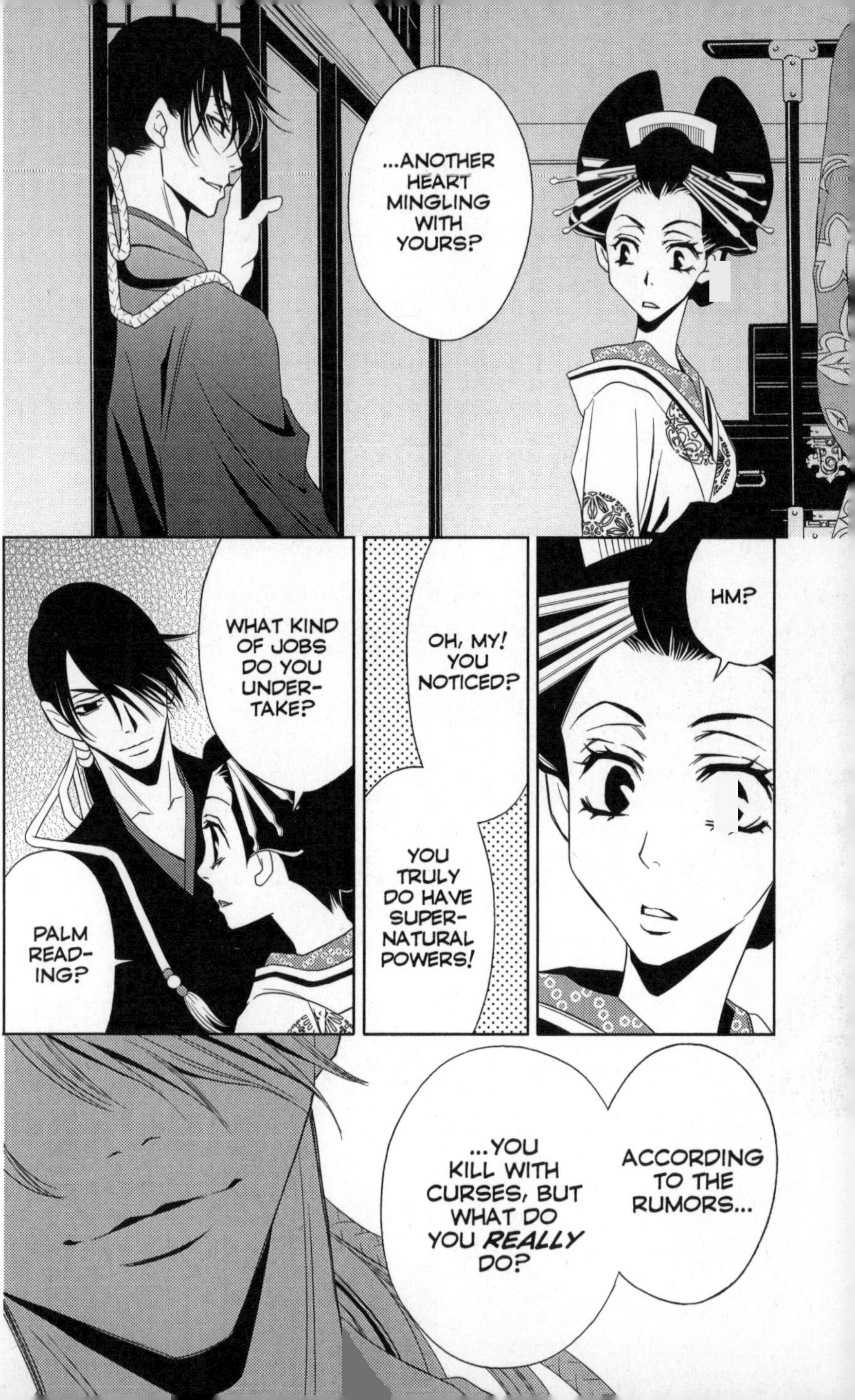
...ANOTHER HEART MINGLING WITH YOURS?
HM?
OH, MY! YOU NOTICED?
YOU TRULY DO HAVE SUPER-NATURAL POWERS!
WHAT KIND OF JOBS DO YOU UNDER-TAKE?
PALM READ-ING?
ACCORDING TO THE RUMORS...
...YOU KILL WITH CURSES, BUT WHAT DO YOU *REALLY* DO?

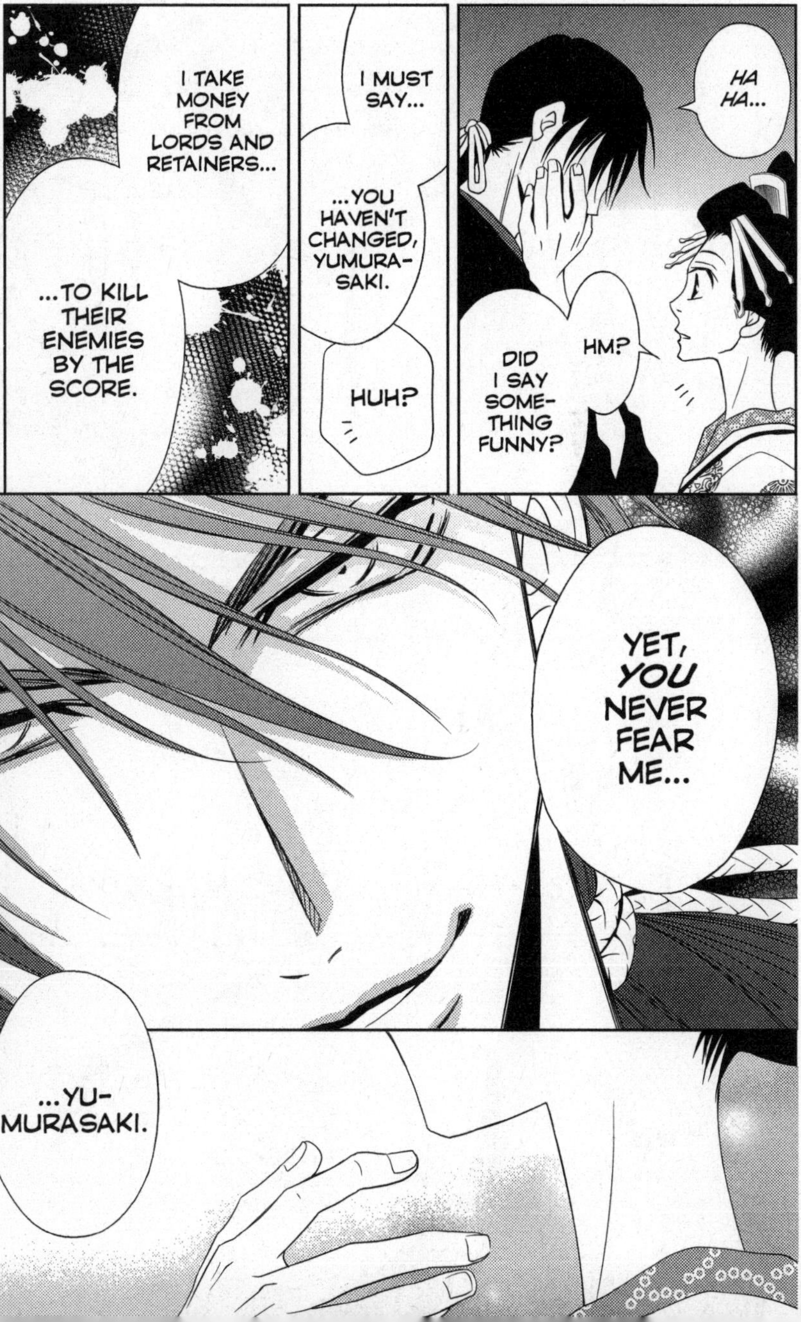
HA HA...
HM?
DID I SAY SOMETHING FUNNY?
I MUST SAY...
...YOU HAVEN'T CHANGED, YUMURASAKI.
HUH?
I TAKE MONEY FROM LORDS AND RETAINERS...
...TO KILL THEIR ENEMIES BY THE SCORE.
YET, *YOU* NEVER FEAR ME...
...YU-MURASAKI.

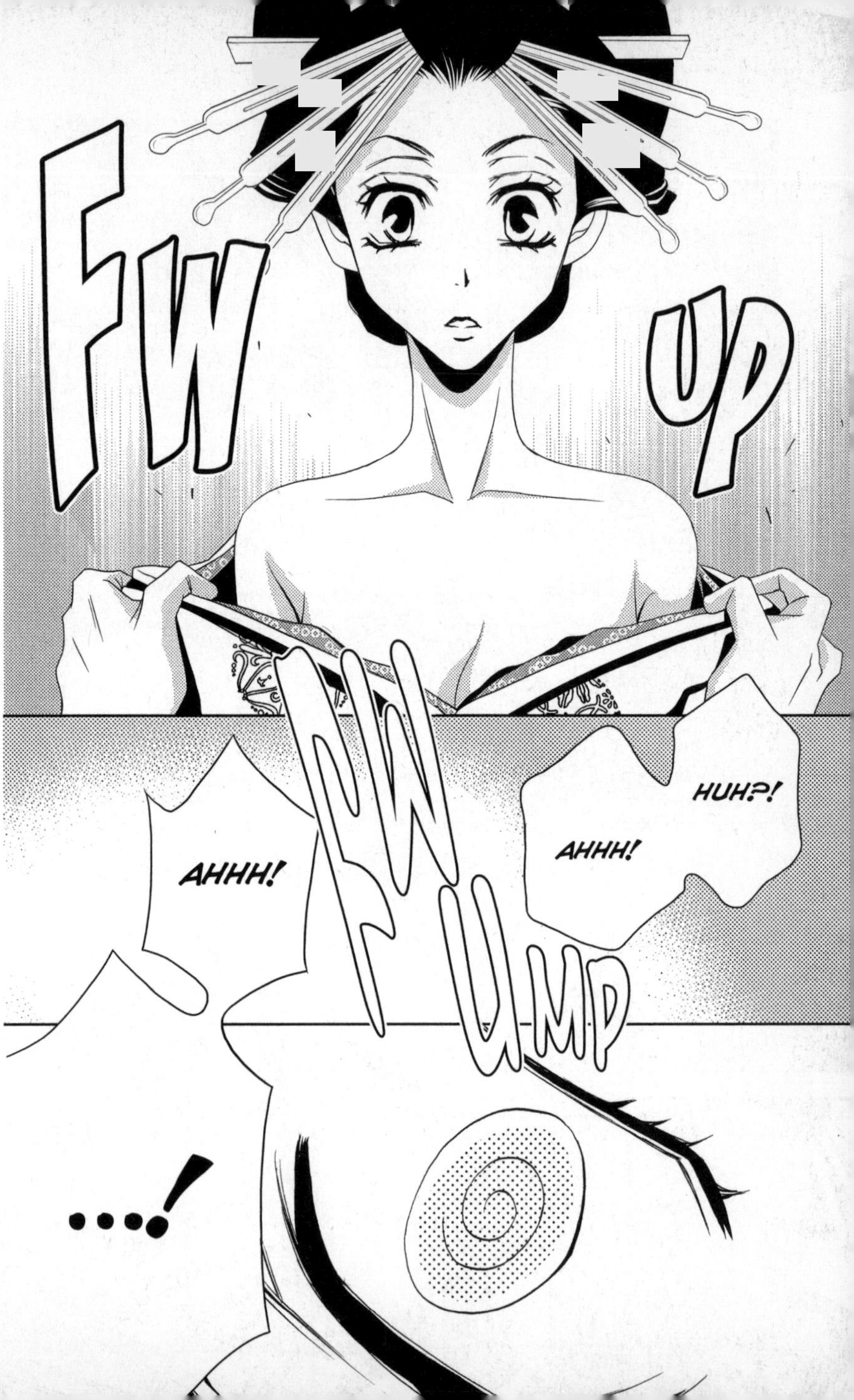
FW UP
HUH?!
AHHH!
AHHH!
FW UMP
...!

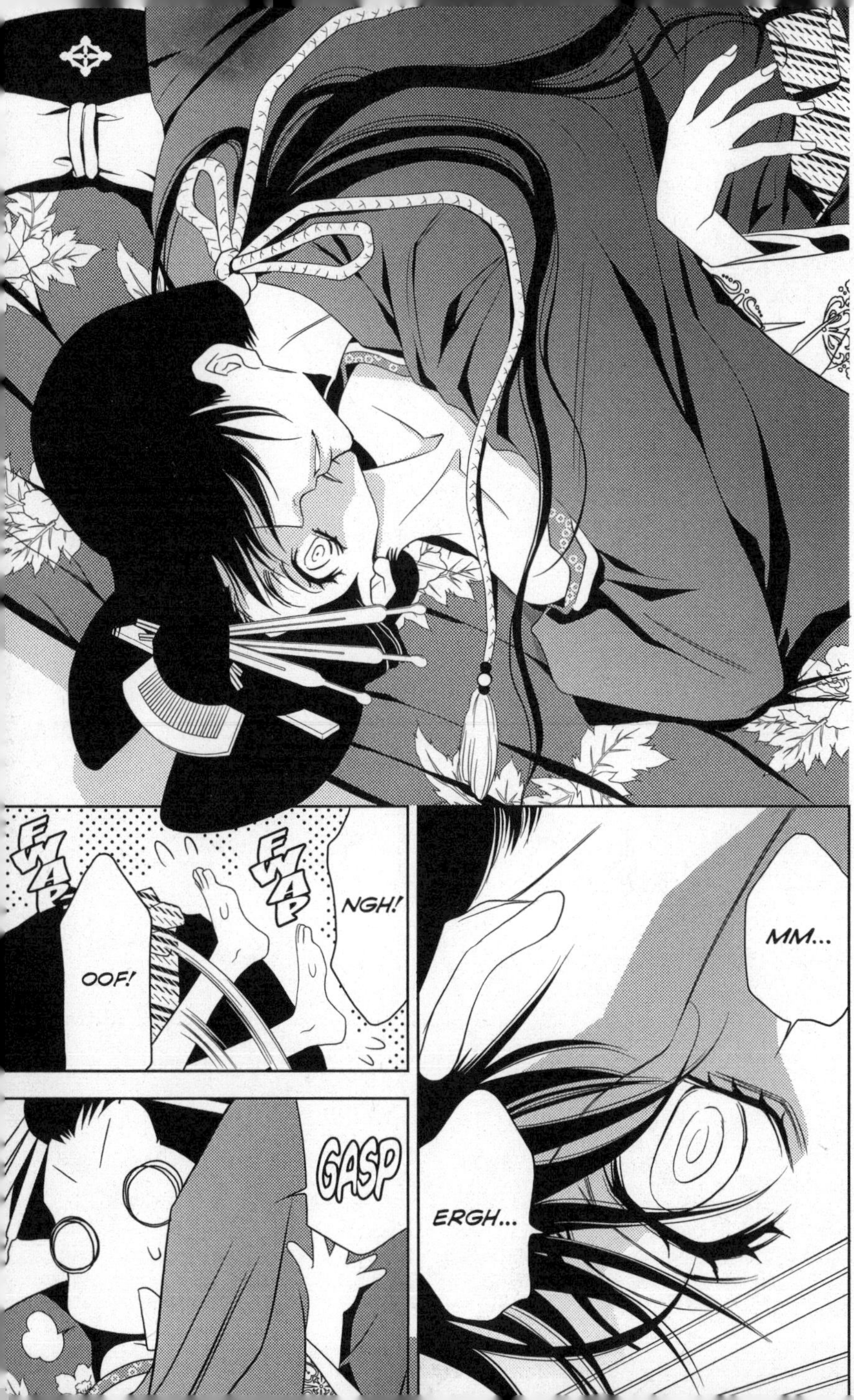
MM...
NGH!
FWAP
FWAP
OOF!
ERGH...
GASP

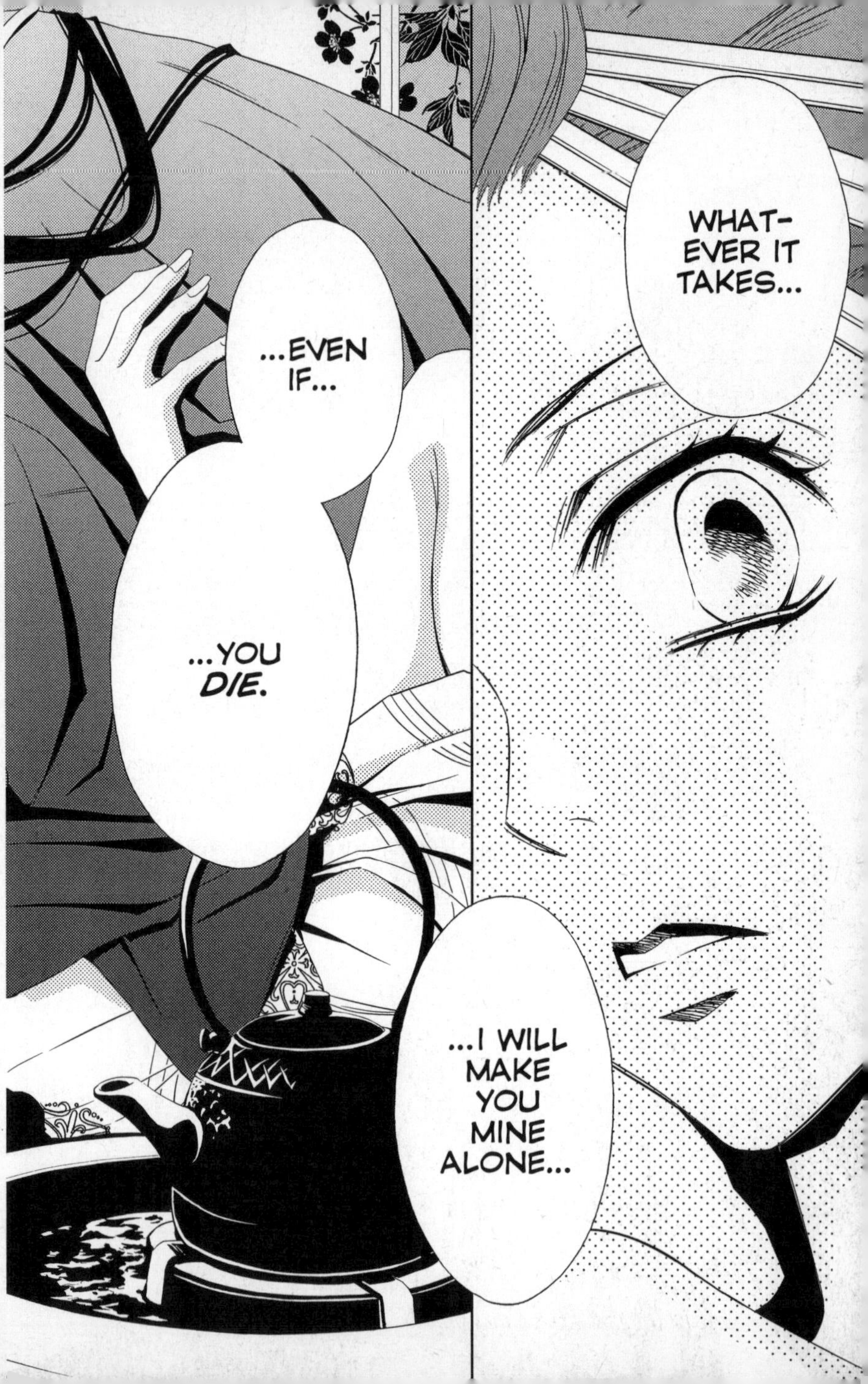
WHAT-EVER IT TAKES...
...I WILL MAKE YOU MINE ALONE...
...EVEN IF...
...YOU *DIE*.

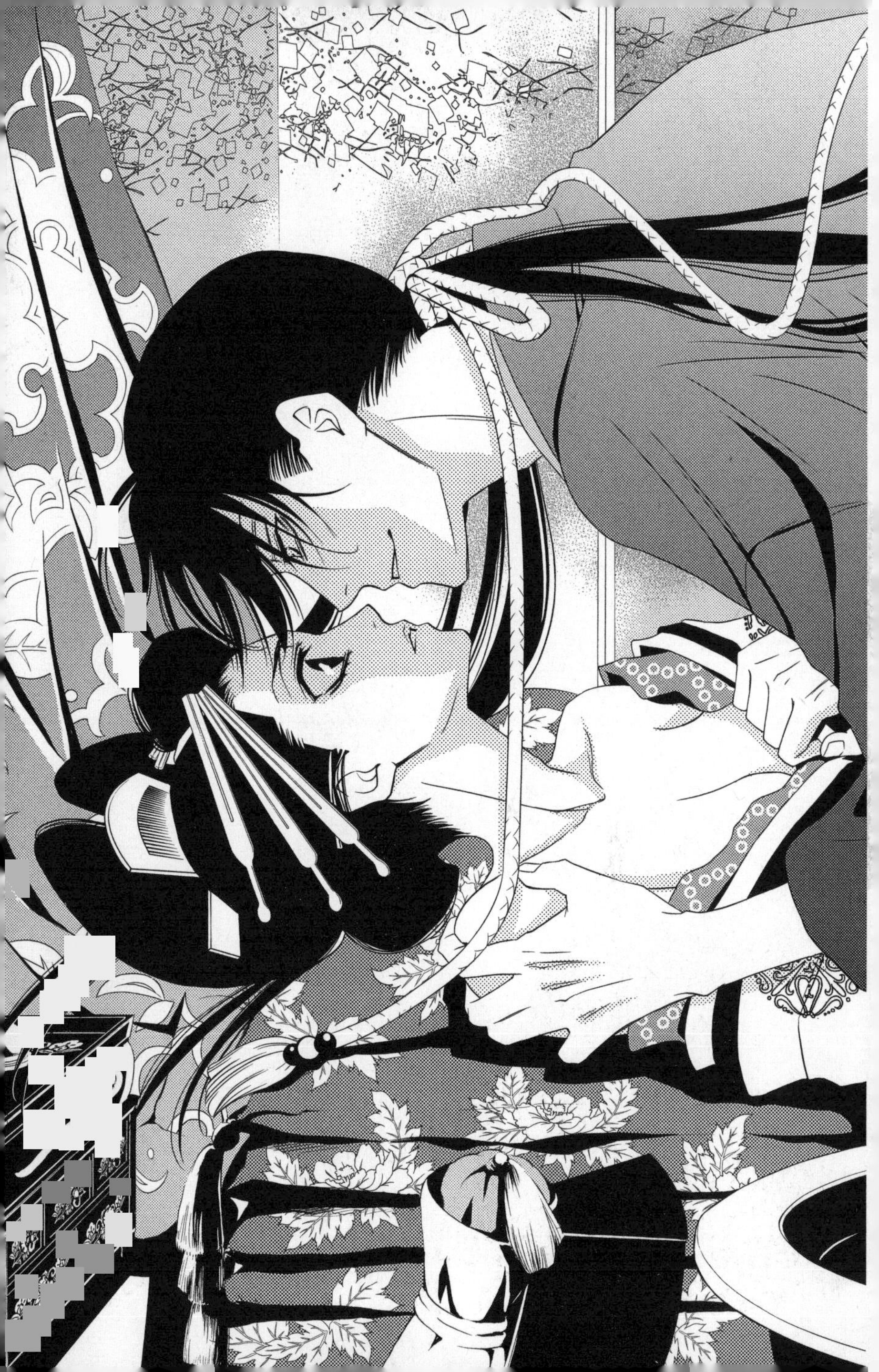

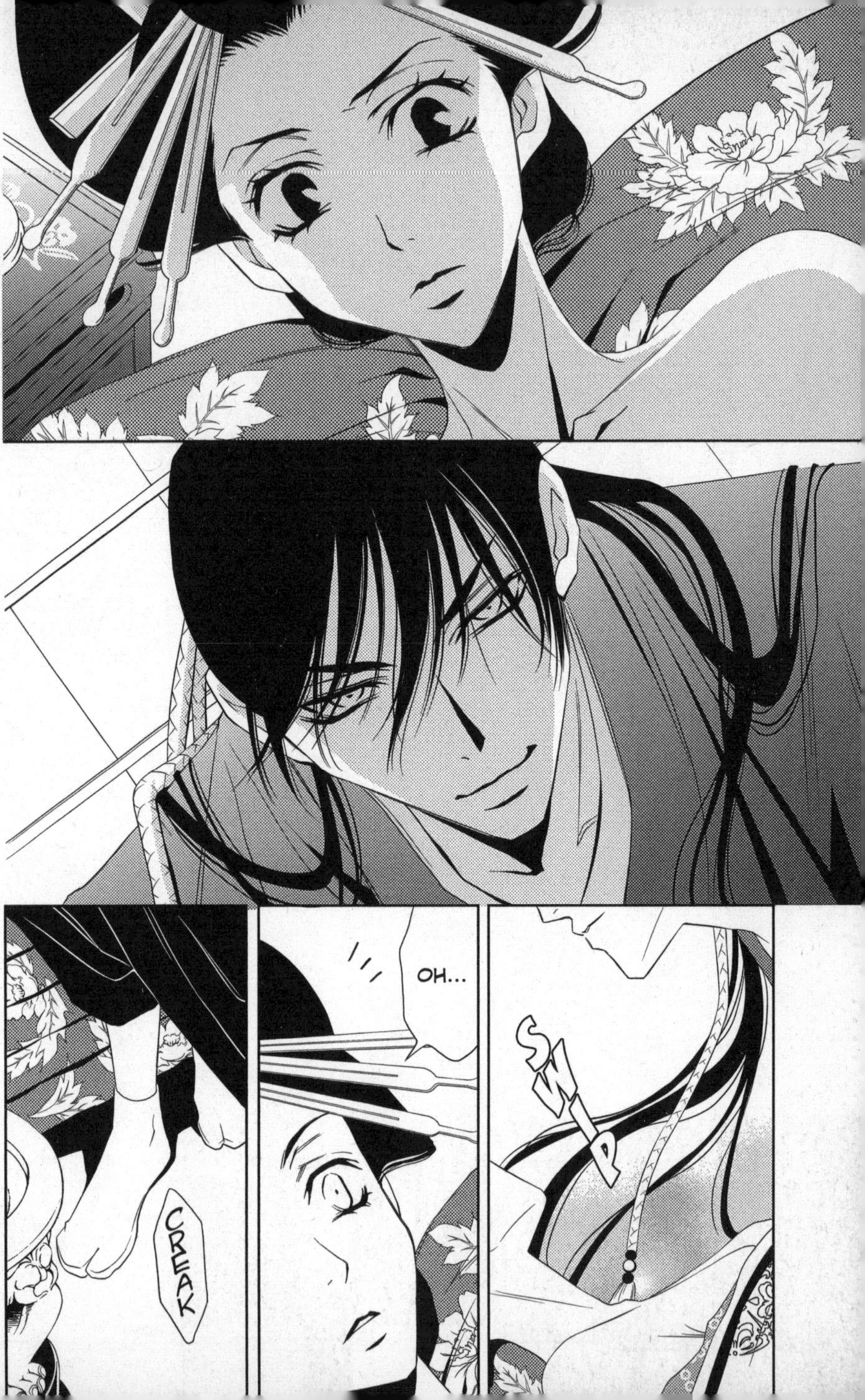
SNIP
OH...
CREAK

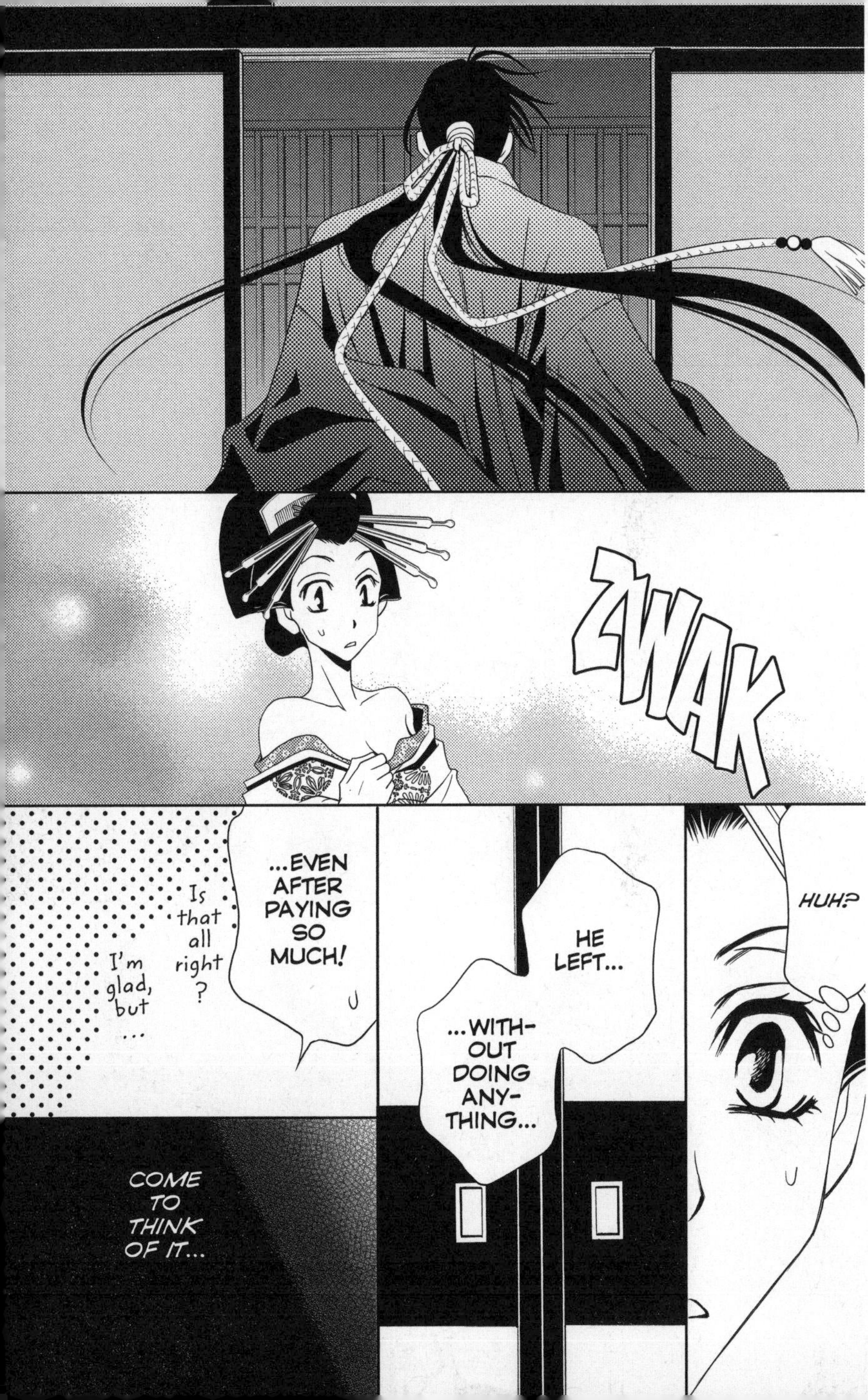
ZWAK
HUH?
HE LEFT...
...WITHOUT DOING ANYTHING...
...EVEN AFTER PAYING SO MUCH!
Is that all right?
I'm glad, but...
COME TO THINK OF IT...

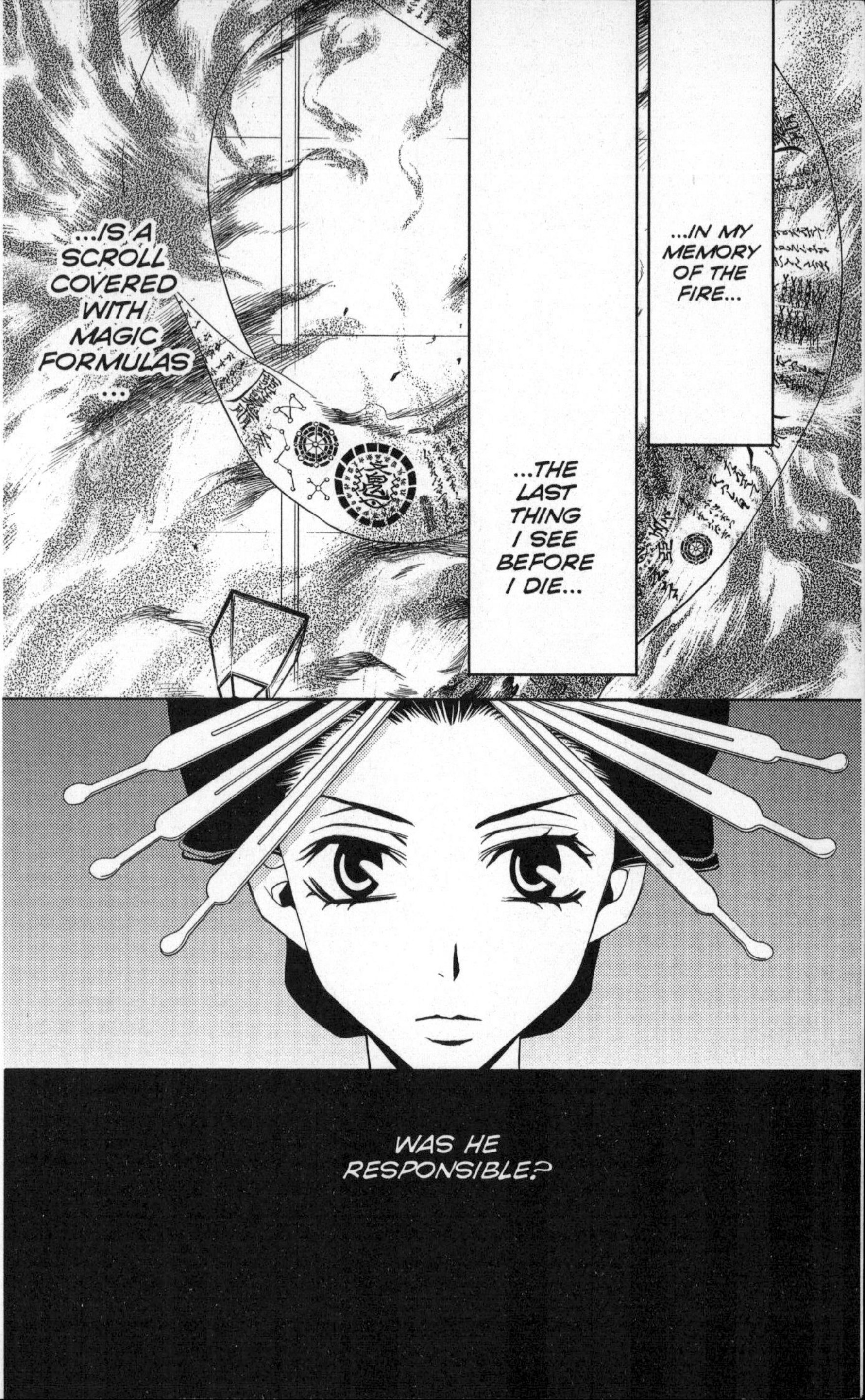
...IN MY MEMORY OF THE FIRE...
...THE LAST THING I SEE BEFORE I DIE...
...IS A SCROLL COVERED WITH MAGIC FORMULAS...
WAS HE RESPONSIBLE?

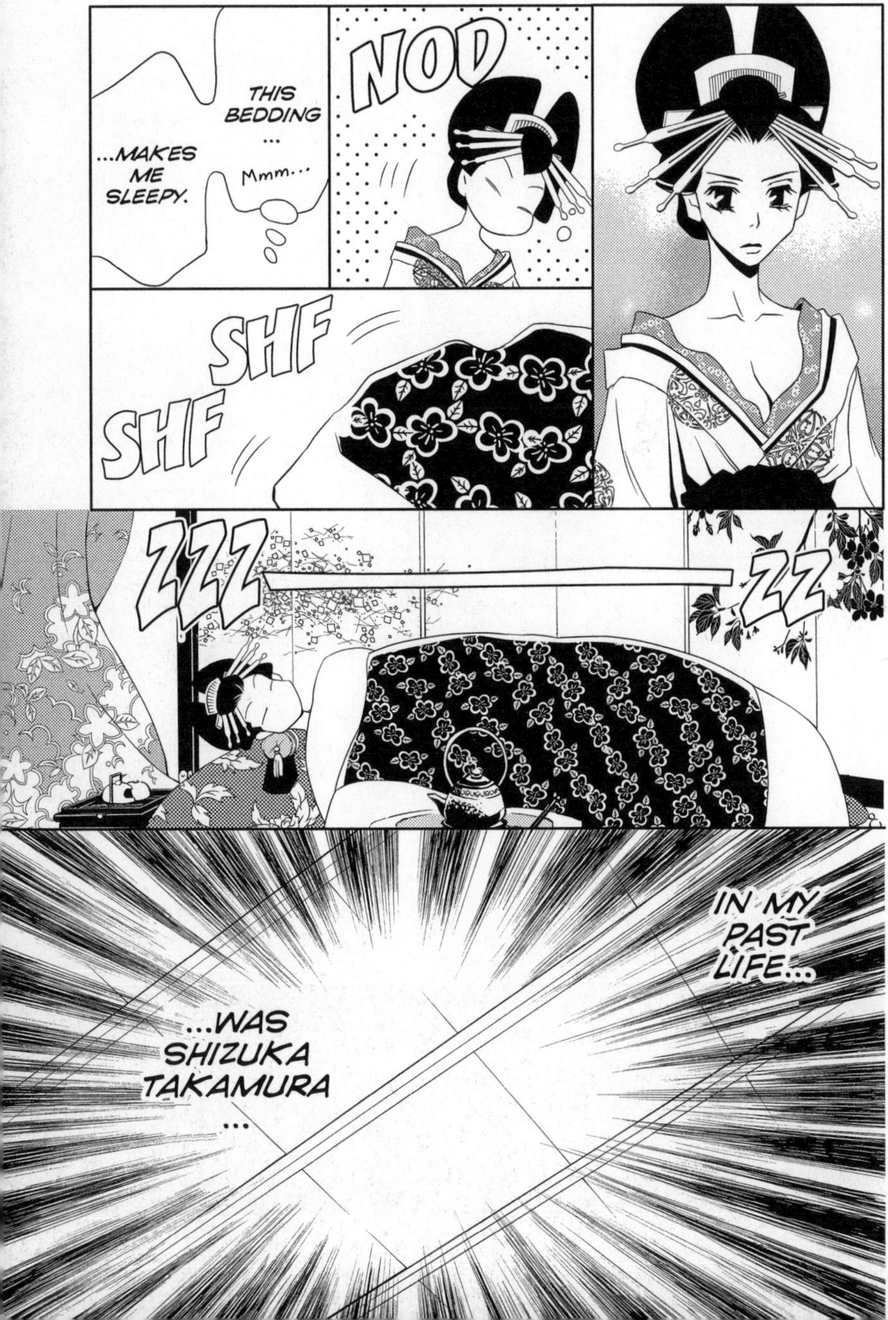
NOD
THIS BEDDING ...
Mmm...
...MAKES ME SLEEPY.
SHF
SHF
ZZZ
ZZ
IN MY PAST LIFE...
...WAS SHIZUKA TAKAMURA ...

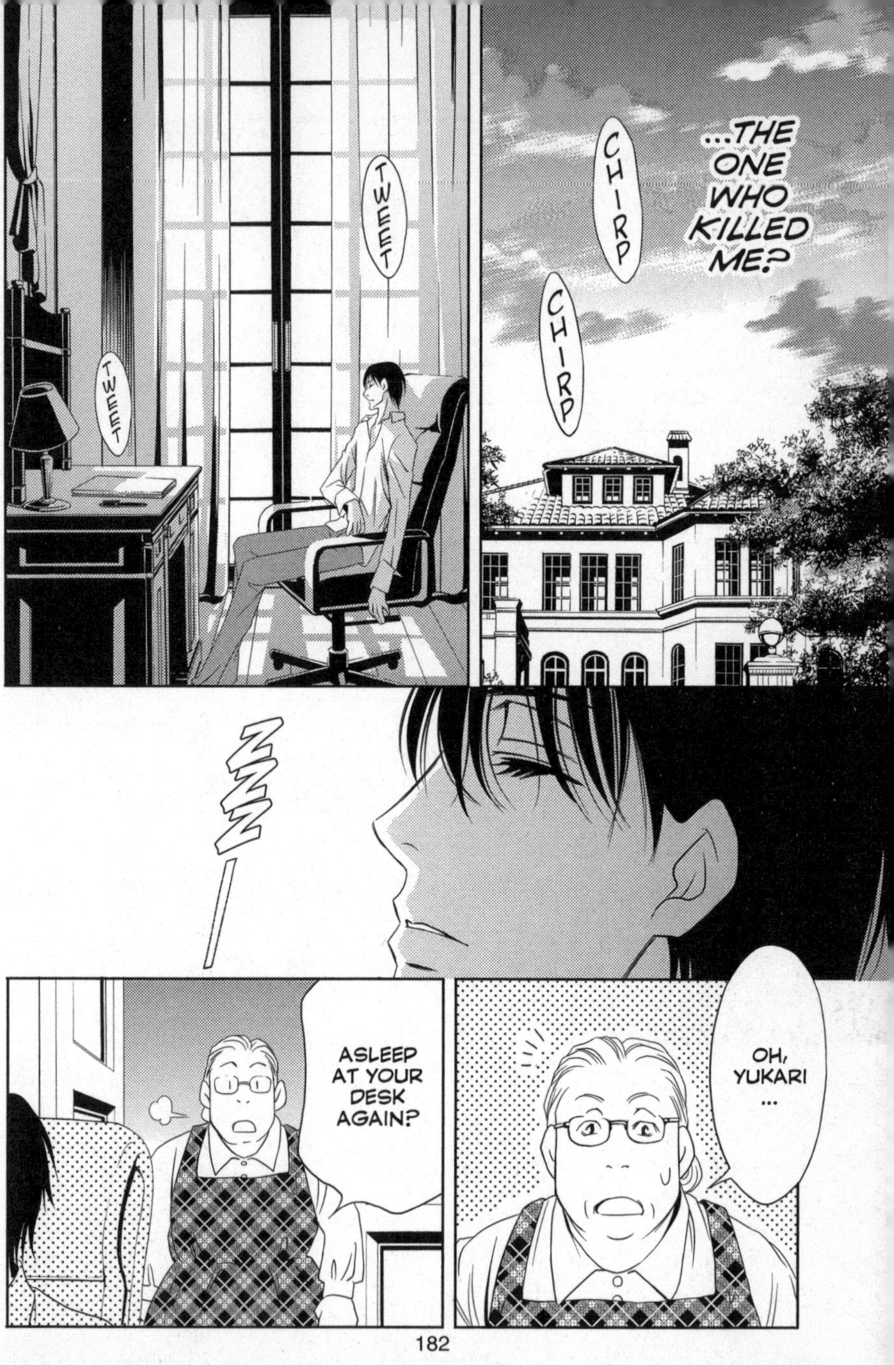
...THE ONE WHO KILLED ME?
CHIRP
CHIRP
TWEET
TWEET
ZZZ
OH, YUKARI ...
ASLEEP AT YOUR DESK AGAIN?

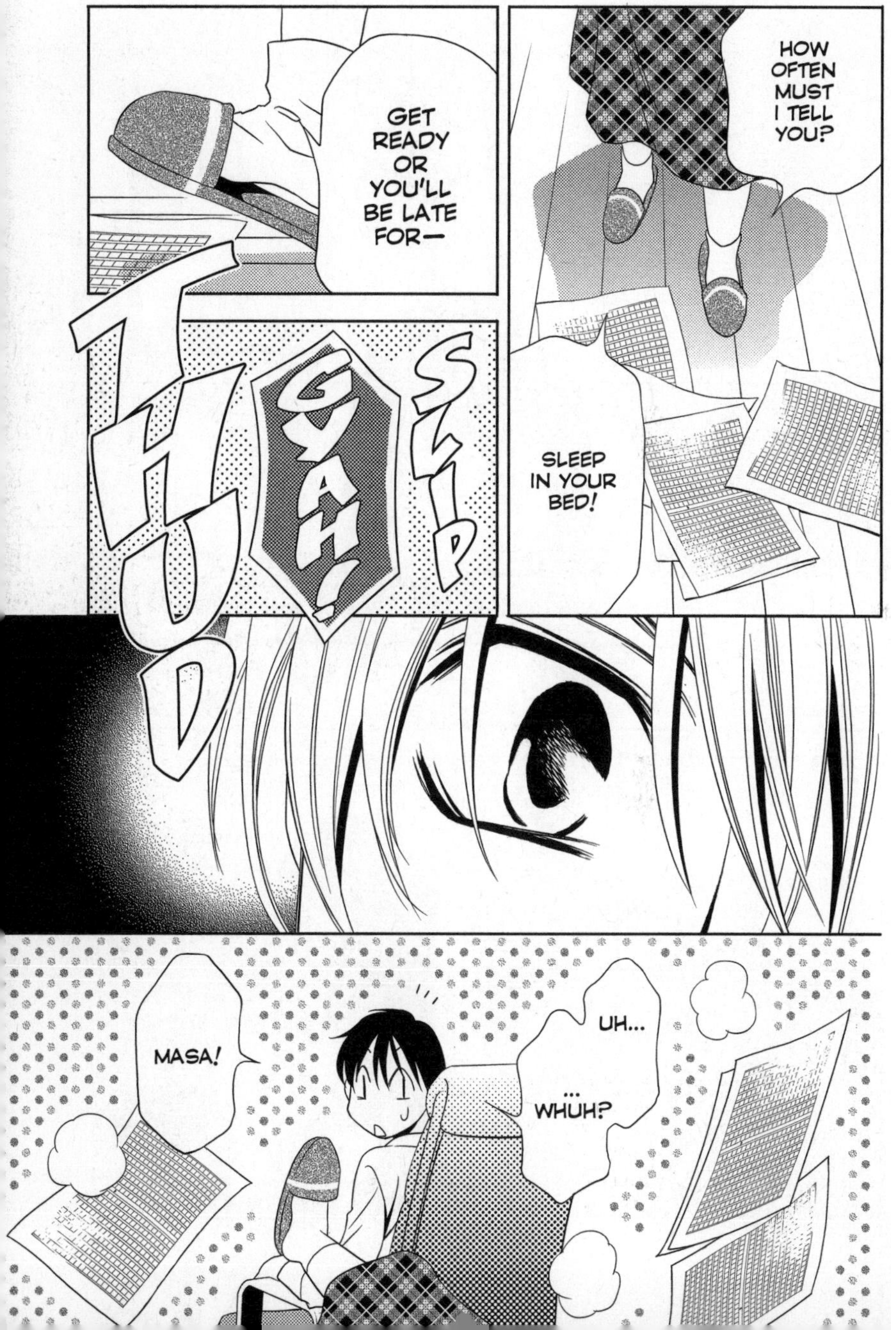
HOW OFTEN MUST I TELL YOU?
SLEEP IN YOUR BED!
GET READY OR YOU'LL BE LATE FOR—
SLIP
GYAH!
THUD
UH... ...WHUH?
MASA!

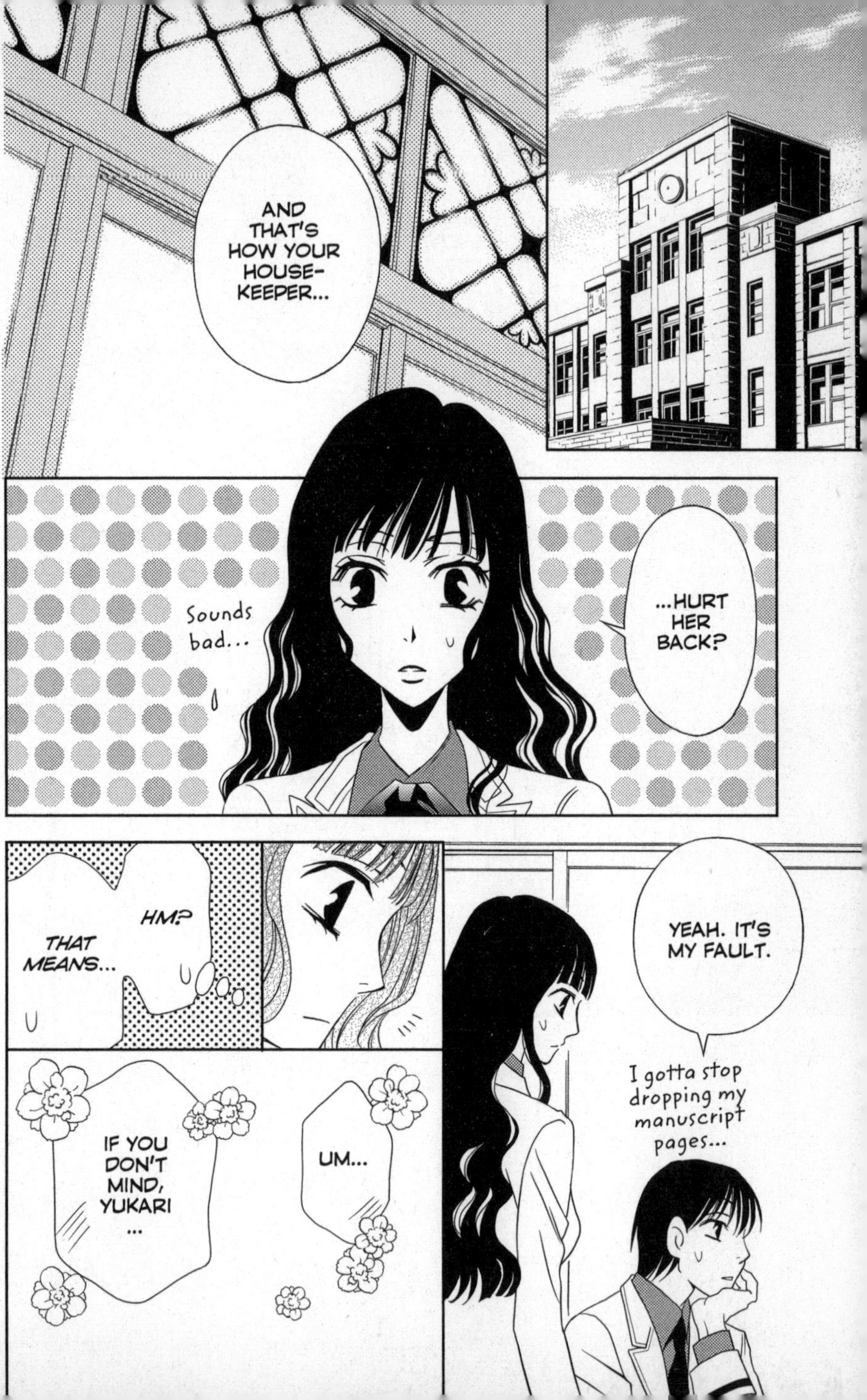
AND THAT'S HOW YOUR HOUSE-KEEPER...
...HURT HER BACK?
Sounds bad...
YEAH. IT'S MY FAULT.
I gotta stop dropping my manuscript pages...
HM?
THAT MEANS...
UM...
IF YOU DON'T MIND, YUKARI ...

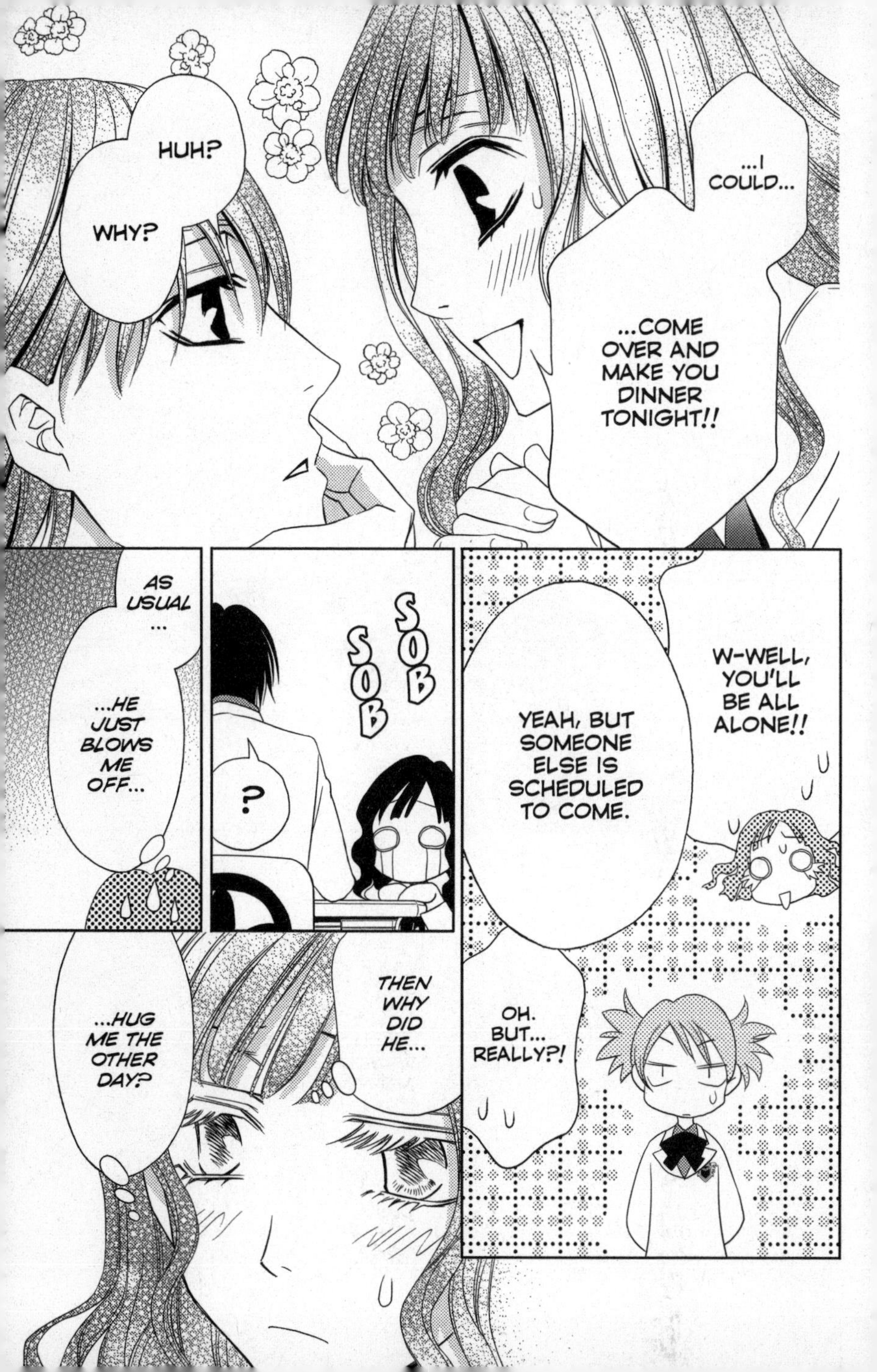
...I COULD...
...COME OVER AND MAKE YOU DINNER TONIGHT!!
HUH?
WHY?
W-WELL, YOU'LL BE ALL ALONE!!
YEAH, BUT SOMEONE ELSE IS SCHEDULED TO COME.
OH. BUT... REALLY?!
SOB SOB
?
AS USUAL...
...HE JUST BLOWS ME OFF...
THEN WHY DID HE...
...HUG ME THE OTHER DAY?

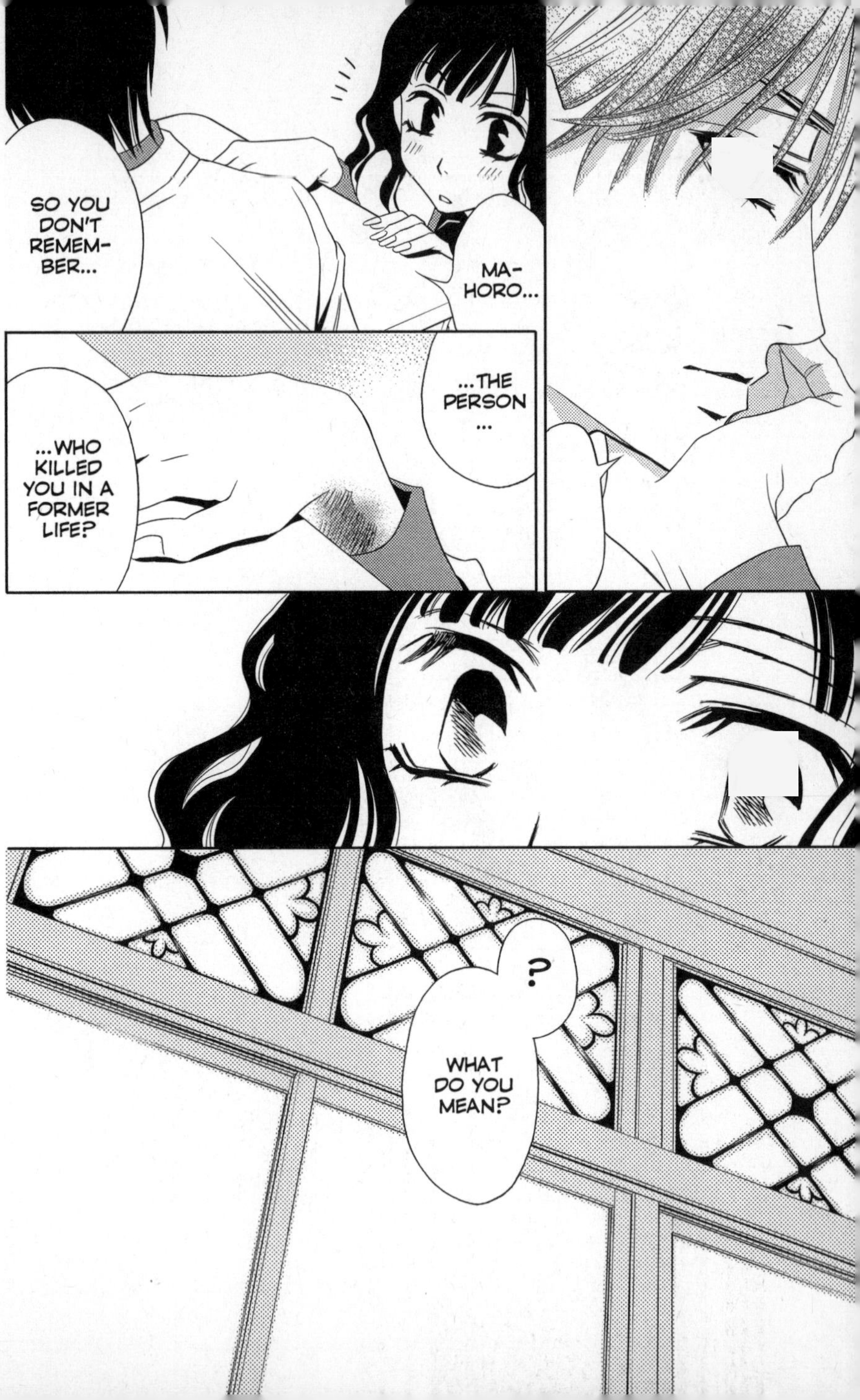
MA-HORO...
SO YOU DON'T REMEM-BER...
...THE PERSON...
...WHO KILLED YOU IN A FORMER LIFE?
?
WHAT DO YOU MEAN?

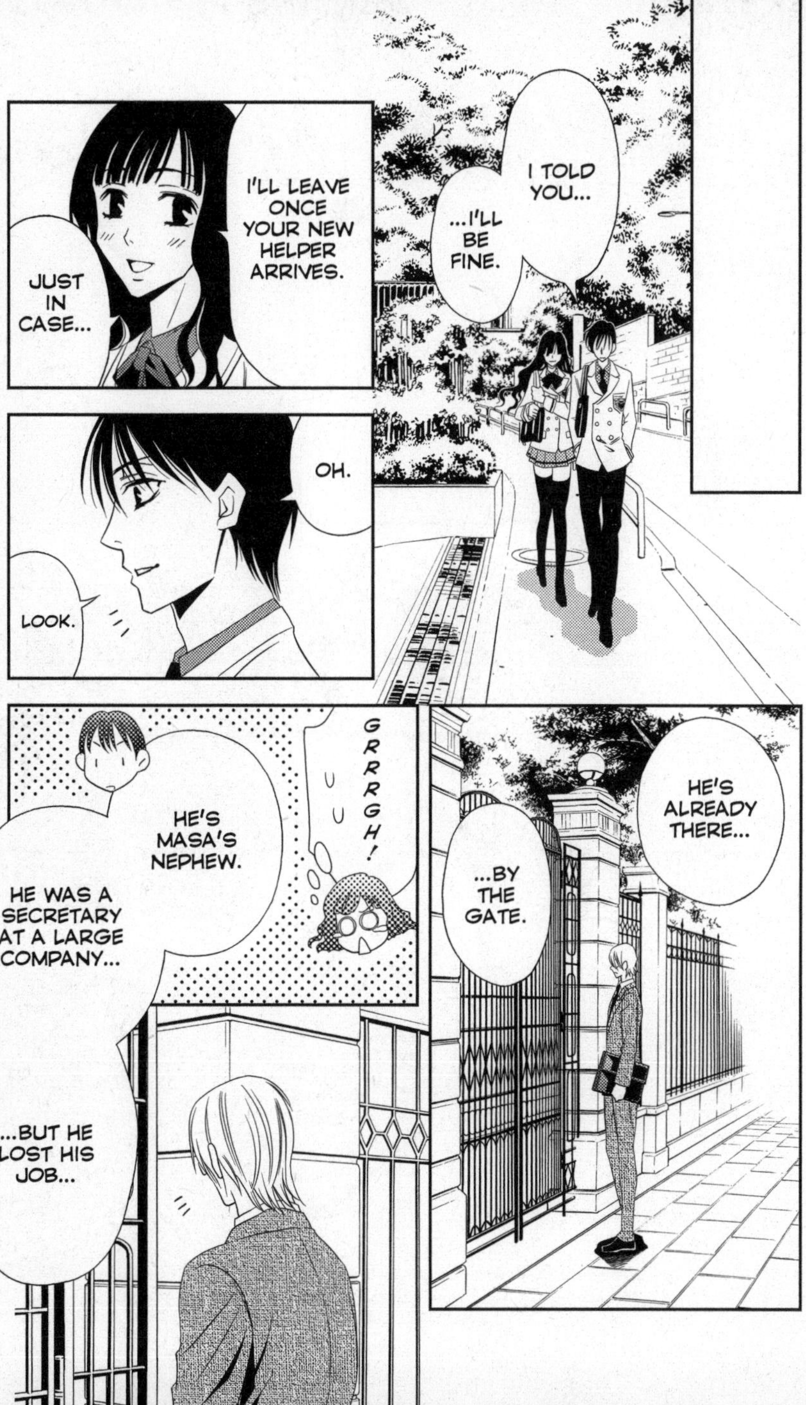
I TOLD YOU...
...I'LL BE FINE.
I'LL LEAVE ONCE YOUR NEW HELPER ARRIVES.
JUST IN CASE...
OH.
LOOK.
HE'S ALREADY THERE...
...BY THE GATE.
GRRRGH!
HE'S MASA'S NEPHEW.
HE WAS A SECRETARY AT A LARGE COMPANY...
...BUT HE LOST HIS JOB...

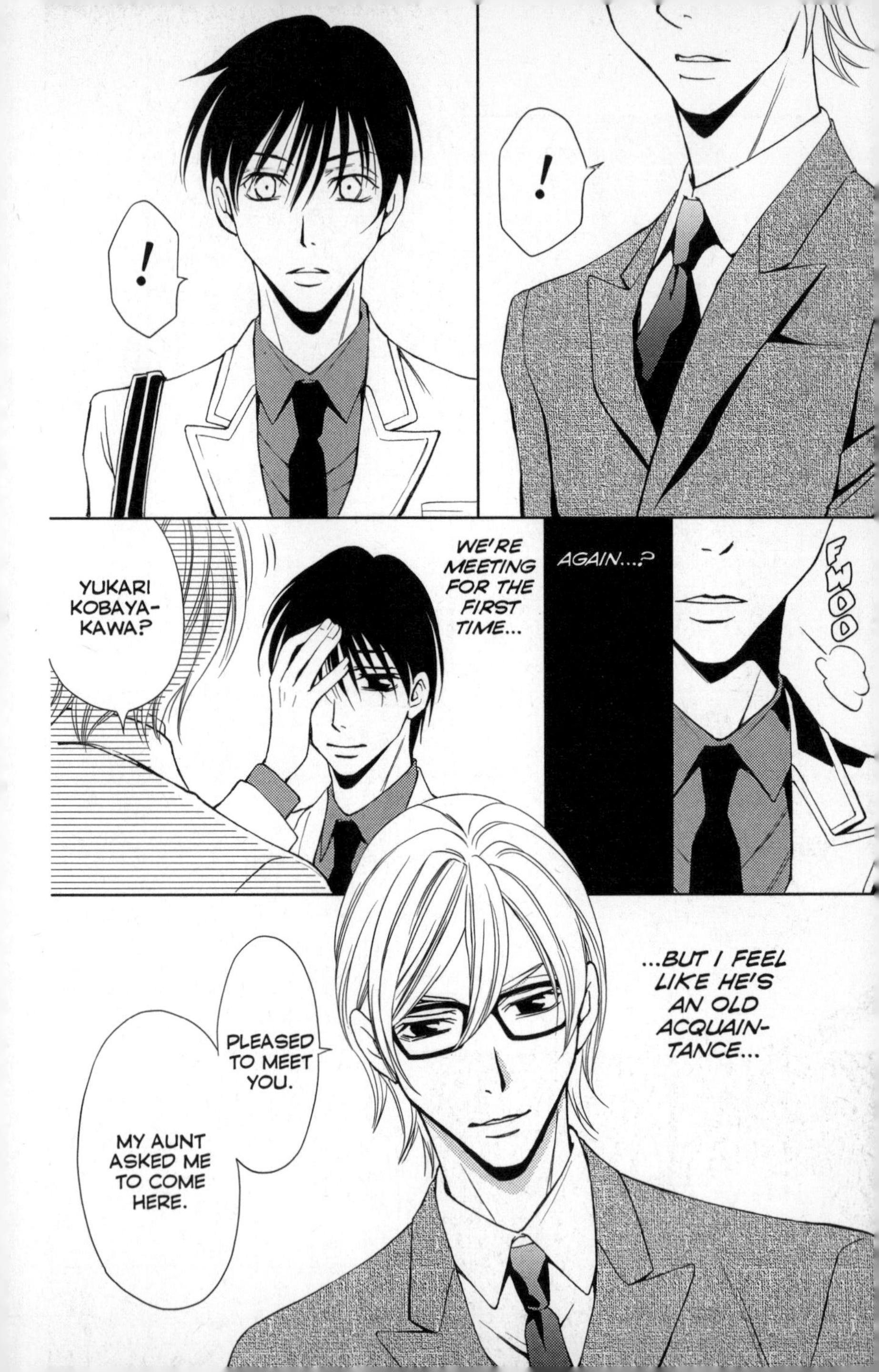
!
!
FWOO
WE'RE MEETING FOR THE FIRST TIME...
AGAIN...?
YUKARI KOBAYA-KAWA?
...BUT I FEEL LIKE HE'S AN OLD ACQUAIN-TANCE...
PLEASED TO MEET YOU.
MY AUNT ASKED ME TO COME HERE.

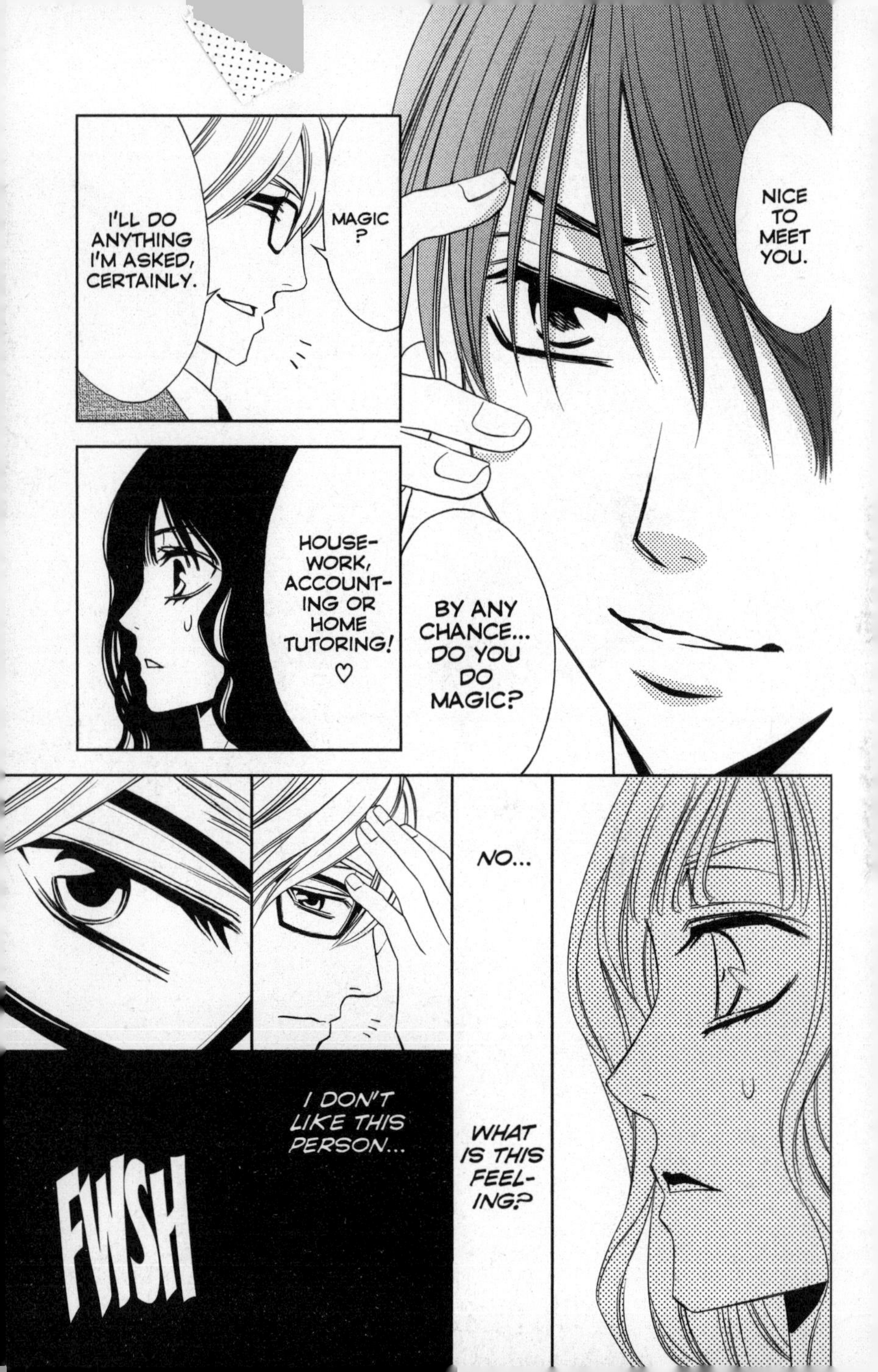

NICE TO MEET YOU.
BY ANY CHANCE... DO YOU DO MAGIC?
MAGIC?
I'LL DO ANYTHING I'M ASKED, CERTAINLY.
HOUSE-WORK, ACCOUNT-ING OR HOME TUTORING! ♡
WHAT IS THIS FEEL-ING?
NO...
I DON'T LIKE THIS PERSON...
FWSH

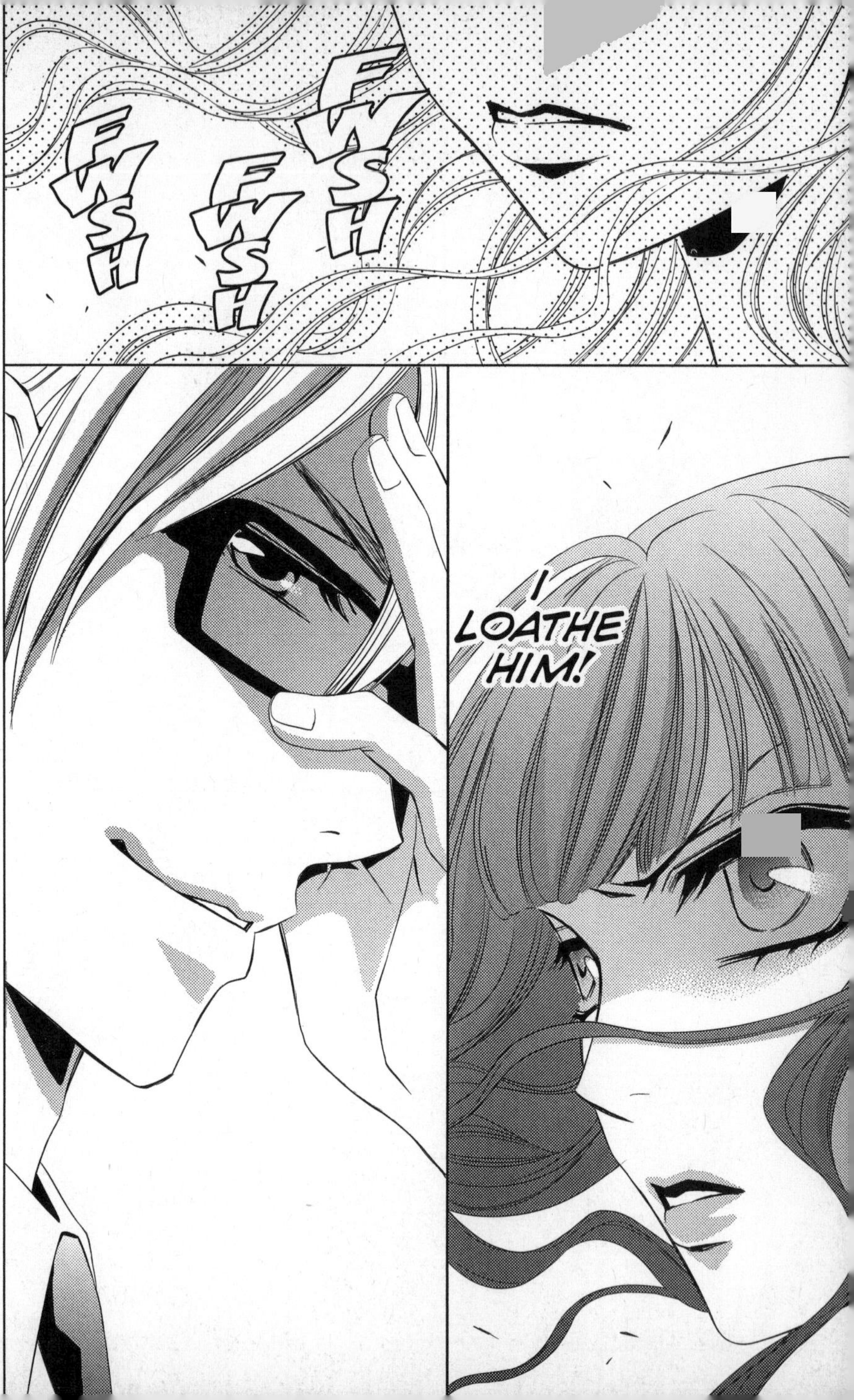
FWSH
FWSH
FWSH
I LOATHE HIM!

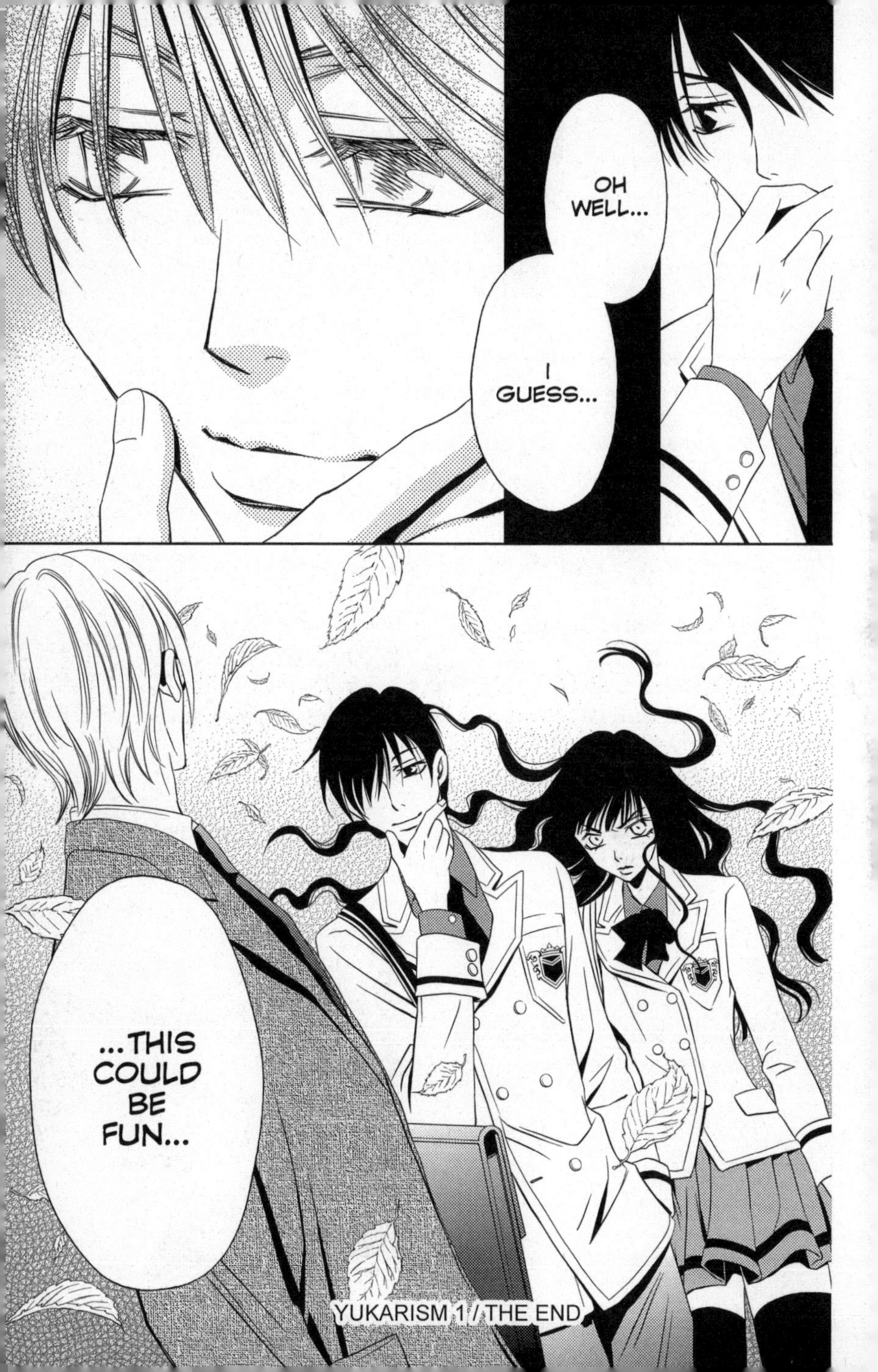
OH WELL...
I GUESS...
...THIS COULD BE FUN...
YUKARISM 1 / THE END

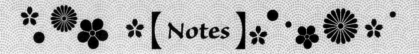

[Notes]

Yukari's past life occurs during the Edo period of Japan. Check out the notes below to help enrich your understanding of *Yukarism*.

Page 7, panel 3: Yukari

The kanji character 縁 (pronounced "yukari") means "connection" or "bond." The actual kanji for Yukari's name (紫), however, means "purple."

Page 7, panel 4: Katana

A traditional Japanese sword used in feudal Japan that has a moderately curved, slender, single-edged blade.

Page 31, panel 6: Sensei

An honorific used for teachers as well as professionals like doctors, lawyers and artists. Since Yukari is a writer, Mahoro is being respectful in addressing him as "Kobayakawa Sensei."

Page 36: Yoshiwara

A famous pleasure district in Edo (present-day Tokyo, Japan).

Page 38, panel 3: Edo Period

Also known as the Tokugawa period, the Edo period lasted from 1603 to 1868.

Page 56, panel 1: Oiran

A class of courtesan, especially during the Edo period. The kanji characters for *oiran* (花魁) mean "flower" and "harbinger," respectively.

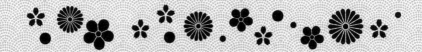

Page 59, panel 5: Yumurasaki
The kanji characters for Yumurasaki's name (夕紫) mean "evening" and "purple."

Page 65, panel 4: Ne-san
An honorific that means means "older sister," *ne-san* is used to address an older sister figure (similar to calling someone "Miss").

Page 92, panel 6: Chan
An honorific used among close friends.

Page 143, panel 10: Oiran Dochu
When an oiran walked through the streets on the way to or from an engagement, it was known as *oiran dochu* (花魁道中), which literally means the oiran is "in the middle of the road." These processions often caused quite a flurry amongst spectators watching her.

Page 150, panel 4: Soto Hachi Monji
There is a specific way that oiran walk called *soto hachi monji* (外八文字) where she slides each foot out, forward, then back in (as if emulating a figure eight).

Page 159, panel 3: Sama
An honorific used to address a person much higher in rank than oneself.

Page 164, panel 3: Geisha
A skilled entertainer who has been formally trained in song, dance and other types of entertainment in the traditional Japanese fashion.

Author Bio

Chika Shiomi debuted with the manga *Todokeru Toki o Sugitemo* (Even if the Time for Deliverance Passes), and her previous works include *Yurara* and *Rasetsu*. She loves reading manga, traveling and listening to music by Aerosmith and Guns N' Roses. Her favorite artists include Michelangelo, Hokusai, Bernini and Gustav Klimt.

YUKARISM

Volume 1
Shojo Beat Edition

STORY AND ART BY
CHIKA SHIOMI

Translation & Adaptation/John Werry
Touch-up Art & Lettering/Rina Mapa
Design/Izumi Evers
Editor/Amy Yu

Yukarism by Chika Shiomi
© Chika Shiomi 2011
All rights reserved.
First published in Japan in 2011 by
HAKUSENSHA, Inc., Tokyo.
English language translation rights arranged with
HAKUSENSHA, Inc., Tokyo.

Printed in the U.S.A.

Published by VIZ Media, LLC
P.O. Box 77010
San Francisco, CA 94107

10 9 8 7 6 5 4 3 2 1
First printing, December 2014

www.viz.com

www.shojobeat.com